PENGUIN BOOKS

THE PENGUIN BOOK OF
TWENTIETH-CENTURY SPEECHES

Brian MacArthur is associate editor of *The Times*. He was founder editor of *Today* and *The Times Higher Education Supplement*, editor of the *Western Morning News*, and former deputy editor of the *Sunday Times*. He has written *Eddy Shah, Today and the Fleet Street Revolution* and *Deadline Sunday* and edited *Gulf War Dispatches*. He has been interested in the power of oratory since first hearing Aneurin Bevan on the hustings in 1956. He has edited a companion anthology, *The Penguin Book of Historic Speeches*.

Brian MacArthur lives in London and has two daughters.

Council which wanted a statement about the Soviets. Noonan held her ground, reasoning that if she held off the bureaucrats they would have to scribble in their insert about the Soviets on the plane and they wouldn't have time to take something out. That was what happened.

The main question posed by the moving Pointe du Hoc speech is whether it was a speech by Ronald Reagan or by Peggy Noonan. It was, obviously, written by Noonan. But it was delivered by Reagan and it was his characteristic delivery of the words she wrote that worked the alchemy on the speech and made people weep. However brilliant the words, it is also the manner of delivery, the sincerity of the speaker, that makes a speech great.

Although many of the speeches in this anthology – for instance, Sir Roger Casement and Churchill – read as well as great literature, one objection to an anthology of speeches is that it inevitably presents oratory as literature, when in fact speeches are made to be heard. Speeches succeed, according to Lloyd George, by a combination of word, voice and gesture in moving their audiences to the action the orator desires. The nobler the action, the more exalted the orator. Yet many of the most effective speeches are quite unreadable in cold print and certainly unsuitable for an anthology. What Lord Morley said, in a discussion of Gladstone's Midlothian speeches, still rings true today: 'The statesman who makes or dominates a crisis, who has to rouse and mould the mind of senate or nation, has something else to think about than the production of literary masterpieces.'

That is particularly true of the British House of Commons, where the outstanding speakers rarely use notes except for their perorations, and explains why several brilliant oratorical triumphs – the maiden speech of F. E. Smith, Enoch Powell on the Hola Camp massacre, Iain Macleod demolishing Aneurin Bevan, Michael Foot defending the Callaghan government against a no-confidence motion, John Biffen on monetary policy or Margaret Thatcher on her resignation – make no appearance in this anthology. Many British MPs remember the speeches by Michael Foot, at bay before the barracking Tories, or Enoch Powell, denouncing his own government, as the best they ever heard in the Commons. Yet the interruptions to Commons speeches destroy their flow. They do not read as well as they were heard. Most speeches in translation suffer from the same defect, which is why both Chairman Mao and Mikhail Gorbachev are absent from this anthology.

Nor can an anthology capture the spell cast at the moment of delivery by the greatest speakers. That must be left to the imagination, though we can still capture some of their magic from contemporary accounts of their varying styles.

There is Patrick Pearse, speaking for Ireland: 'Calm and deliberate, in soft yet thrilling accents, his oration was almost sublime. Here was no rhetoric, no mathematical oratory: it was the soul of a patriot breathing words of love and devotion, of hope and truth and courage, no threnody but a paean of triumph such as might have come from out the tomb by which we were.'

There is Lloyd George, as described by A. J. P. Taylor: 'Lloyd George spoke with his audience, not to them, and snapped up phrases as they were thrown at him. "Ninepence for fourpence" was the result of one such interruption; making Germany pay to the last farthing, the less happy result of another. Lloyd George gave a music hall turn, worthy of Harry Lauder or George Robey, the prime minister of mirth.'

There is Stalin: 'When Stalin speaks with his knowing, comfortable smile, pointing with his forefinger, he does not, like other orators, make a breach between himself and his audience; he does not stand command-ingly on the platform while they sit below him, but very soon an alliance, an intimacy is established between him and his listeners. They, being made of the same stuff, are susceptible to the arguments, and both laugh merrily at the same simple stories.'

There is Hitler: 'He would lash himself to a pitch of near hysteria in which he would scream and spit out his resentment – men groaned or hissed, women sobbed involuntarily, caught up in the spell of powerful emotions of hatred and exaltation, from which all restraint had been removed.'

There is Bevan, as described by Michael Foot: 'Bevan wrought an alchemy before our eyes. He could mix fire with ice. He could evoke dreams and the boldest aspirations, yet the purpose always was to use the motive force thus generated to help forward the business in hand. He unleashed the imagination yet still wanted it tethered to the earth where the immediate enemy must be fought. "Oh! the brave music of a

THE PENGUIN BOOK OF
TWENTIETH-CENTURY
SPEECHES

EDITED BY BRIAN MacARTHUR

PENGUIN BOOKS

PENGUIN BOOKS

Published by the Penguin Group
Penguin Books Ltd, 27 Wrights Lane, London W8 5TZ, England
Penguin Putnam Inc., 375 Hudson Street, New York, New York 10014, USA
Penguin Books Australia Ltd, Ringwood, Victoria, Australia
Penguin Books Canada Ltd, 10 Alcorn Avenue, Toronto, Ontario, Canada M4V 3B2
Penguin Books (NZ) Ltd, 182–190 Wairau Road, Auckland 10, New Zealand

Penguin Books Ltd, Registered Offices: Harmondsworth, Middlesex, England

First published by Viking 1992
Published with revisions in Penguin Books 1993
7 9 10 8

Printed in England by Clays Ltd, St Ives plc

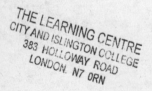

Each time a man stands up for an ideal,
or acts to improve the lot of others,
or strikes out against injustice,
he sends forth a tiny ripple of hope
and crossing each other from a million
different centres of energy and daring,
those ripples build a current that can
sweep down the mightiest walls of
oppression and resistance.

Robert Kennedy, 1966

CONTENTS

Contents

Contents

temperament. He set out his creed in *Mein Kampf*: 'The force which ever set in motion the great historical avalanches of religious and political movements is the magic power of the spoken word. The broad masses of a population are more amenable to the appeal of rhetoric than to any other force.' As for the orator: 'He will always follow the lead of the great mass in such a way that from the living emotion of his hearers the apt word that he needs will be suggested to him and in its turn this will go straight to the hearts of his hearers.'

That magic, hypnotic power is shown at its most effective in this anthology by Hitler's speech to the Düsseldorf Industry Club in 1932. When Hitler arrived, his reception from the West German industrialists was cool and reserved. Yet he spoke for two and a half hours without pause and made one of the best speeches of his life, setting out all his stock ideas brilliantly dressed up for his audience of businessmen. At the end they rose and cheered him wildly. Contributions from German industry started flowing into the Nazi treasury. Hitler by that one speech had won an important victory. That was the (relatively) emollient Hitler. The frightening and destructive power of his oratory, palpable even in translation, is shown in the extracts from the two other speeches in this collection.

Yet although the power of Hitler's speeches roused Germany to barbarity, and made Baldwin's case, most of the speeches in this anthology demonstrate the power of oratory for good rather than evil. They articulate dreams, offer hope, stir hearts and minds, and offer their audiences visions of a better world. The phrases by which they are remembered, whether the summons to the 'strenuous life' of Theodore Roosevelt or to the 'new frontier' of John F. Kennedy or the 'I have a dream' of Martin Luther King, sounded the trumpet for constructive action; and the defining principle of this anthology, beyond significance or eloquence, is that it selects speeches that sent forth the 'ripples of hope' that Robert Kennedy so memorably offered to South African students in 1966.

Those ripples of hope were sent forth by Emmeline Pankhurst and Betty Friedan for women's freedom; by Patrick Pearse, Roger Casement, Mahatma Gandhi, Fidel Castro and Nelson Mandela to nations and races that were oppressed; by John F. Kennedy and Harold Wilson and Margaret Thatcher and Ronald Reagan – in their different causes – to dispossessed constituencies that yearned for power. Few speeches sent forth more ripples of hope than those of Franklin D. Roosevelt – or of Winston Churchill when he mobilized the English language for war.

There are also destructive speeches. Leo Amery and Lloyd George destroyed Neville Chamberlain by their speeches in the Norway debate in the House of Commons in 1940. By his speech on race (the most elegantly constructed and most difficult to edit in this anthology), Enoch Powell barred his path to the highest office of state which, if that speech had not been made, would sooner or later have been his to command. On paper, Sir Geoffrey Howe made a rather plodding speech when he resigned as foreign secretary, but its very restraint, only barely concealing the inner fury and frustration of a man who had been so often slighted, initiated the downfall of Margaret Thatcher.

So much care is still given to speeches by contemporary politicians, moreover, that it is obvious that they still think oratory matters. An individual politician like Roy Jenkins will spend as much time in solitary preparation of a speech as Lloyd George. That care was put into Jenkins's Dimbleby Lecture and that lecture led to the creation of a new British political party, the Social Democrats. As Peggy Noonan explains, hours and often weeks were spent preparing major speeches by Ronald Reagan. Draft after draft of a speech would be submitted to Mrs Thatcher into the early hours of the morning until she was satisfied that every nuance of what she wanted to say was covered.

If any vindication of the power of modern oratory is required, there is a splendid account by Noonan of the making of Reagan's Pointe du Hoc speech in Normandy in 1984. The speech was important for Reagan. Not only was he addressing the citizens of Europe, but the speech was being broadcast live by all the American networks and an extract was wanted for the Reagan film at the Republican convention. Make it like the Gettysburg Address, she was told. Make people cry.

Noonan describes how she constructed the speech – first the big, emotional words and images, then the placing of Pointe du Hoc in time and space, then what happened in 1944 (mostly to stop the children chewing their Rice Krispies and make them reflect on the greatness of their grandfathers) and so on. As the speech was prepared, there was a White House battle between literature (Noonan) and the National Security

As Franklin D. Roosevelt and Winston Churchill were to show by their mastery of the wireless, Lloyd George was right. Since his forecast was made, orators have adapted not only to radio but also to the different demands of television, which has magnified the power of oratory and enabled speeches to be broadcast simultaneously round the world. Yet still the complaint is made that oratory is a declining art. According to Peggy Noonan, author of some of Ronald Reagan's most memorable oratory, the irony of modern speeches is that as our ability to disseminate them has exploded their quality has declined.

'Why? Lots of reasons, including that we as a nation no longer learn the rhythms of public utterance from Shakespeare and the Bible. When young Lincoln was sprawled in front of the fireplace reading *Julius Caesar* – "The abuse of greatness is, when it disjoins remorse from power" – he was, unconsciously, learning to be a poet. You say, "That was Lincoln, not the common man." But the common man was flocking to the docks to get the latest instalment of Dickens off the ship from England.

'The modern egalitarian impulse has made politicians leery of flaunting high rhetoric; attempts to reach, to find the right if esoteric quote or allusion seem pretentious. They don't really know what "the common man" thinks any more; they forget that we've all had at least some education and a number of us read on our own and read certain classics in junior high and high school. The guy at the gas station read *Call of the Wild* when he was fourteen, and sometimes thinks about it. Moreover, he has imagination. Politicians forget. They go in for the lowest common denominator – like a newscaster.'

Any contemporary observer who relishes great oratory and who observes the British general election or the American presidential election of 1992 cannot but agree with Noonan's thesis. Where are the visions and where the words that inspire men and women to greater things and make them vote with enthusiasm, even passion? Now we watch television, much of it banal beyond belief, for up to thirty hours a week, rarely go to church, and at school our children no longer get the deep grounding in our literary heritage that was once taken for granted. The springs of oratory are drying up.

Or are they? Perhaps Noonan despairs too soon – and also ignores the evidence of her own work, shown in this anthology by her speeches for

INTRODUCTION

Oratory is always a declining art. Every generation judges contemporary speakers unfavourably against the giants of the past. One of the most lyrical orators of the twentieth century was Lloyd George. Yet an Everyman collection of oratory published in the 1920s, which concluded with Lloyd George's speech of September 1914 as Britain went to war, lamented that oratory had given way to 'talk'. The change, according to the editor, could be seen in the natural colloquial style of Lloyd George compared with the oratorical styles of Lord Rosebery or Winston Churchill. Eighty years on that colloquial style, with which Lloyd George summoned the nation to 'the great pinnacle of sacrifice pointing like a rugged finger to heaven', strikes us not as talk but as magnificent oratory and we complain about the dull, colloquial style of George Bush or John Major.

Lloyd George himself made the same complaint when he wrote a short introduction to a collection of his speeches in 1929, arguing that the conditions of modern speaking were not conducive to the preparation of speeches that survived the controversy to which they were addressed. He was, nevertheless, an optimist. Acknowledging that first the school boards and the popular press and then the cheap entertainment offered by film, gramophone and broadcasting had been accused of destroying oratory, he pointed out that the Labour Party, the most powerful party in the state, had been created by spoken appeals from myriads of platforms.

'Broadcasting will give new life and sway to speech-making. Controversy may be ruled out yet awhile by timid counsels. In the end it will force its way to the disc. A sporting nation, which is also a political people, will insist on seeing the ball kicked in one of its favourite games. When that time comes, the style of oratory may be altered to the exigencies of the machine; but the true orator will adapt his art to the occasion, and the spoken word will be more potent than ever.'

become a thing of the past.' That change was an undoubted advantage for audiences, Lloyd George thought. In ninety-nine cases out of a hundred, lengthy prepared orations were 'boring, dreary, and wholly ineffective'. A perfectly phrased but badly delivered speech might be a dazzling essay, but it was not oratory.

So what is oratory? Quoting approvingly the maxim that oratory was the harlot of the arts, the British prime minister Stanley Baldwin pointed out that to tell the truth needed no art at all. God help the man who tries to think on it, he said. The gift of rhetoric had been responsible for more bloodshed than all the guns and explosives ever invented:

'If we look back only over the last century, was there anything more responsible for the French Revolution than the literary rhetoric of Rousseau, fanned by the verbal rhetoric of Robespierre and others, just as the Russian Revolution was due to the rhetoric of Kerensky – flatulent rhetoric which filled the bellies of his people with the east wind? That appalling twopenny-ha'penny gift of fluency, with the addition of a certain amount of training and of imagination in word-spinning, is the kind of rhetoric which stirs the emotions of the ignorant mob and sets it moving. It is because such forces can be set in motion by rhetoric that I have no regard for it but a positive horror.'

When circumstances required, Baldwin was himself capable of the telling, destructive phrase, as he showed when he condemned Britain's two main press proprietors for 'seeking power without responsibility, the prerogative of the harlot throughout the ages'. That positive horror nevertheless inspired Baldwin's own prosaic speaking style (which was unequally matched to the oratorical power of his German adversary Adolf Hitler). As seen by their opponents (if not by their followers, who were obviously uplifted by their speeches), the Baldwin thesis of the orator's destructive power is notably demonstrated within this anthology by Lenin, Stalin, Fidel Castro and Joseph McCarthy. Yet no orator of the twentieth century better illustrates that destructive power of oratory against which Baldwin warned than Hitler, undoubtedly the greatest speaker of the century. Churchill, the other main contender, roused a willing nation to war. Hitler changed a nation by his oratory.

As his biographer Alan Bullock explains, speech was the essential medium of Hitler's power not only over his audiences but his own

Reagan after the *Challenger* disaster and at Pointe du Hoc in Normandy. She herself, moreover, supplies the answer to the complaint that speeches today are prepared only for the 'sound bites' demanded by television. Speeches have always had sound bites or memorable phrases. 'With malice towards none. With charity towards all' (Lincoln); 'You shall not crucify mankind upon a cross of gold' (Bryan); 'He has not a single redeeming defect' (Disraeli on Gladstone) – all were nineteenth-century sound bites as surely as 'The only thing we have to fear is fear itself' or 'Ask not what your country can do for you' were memorable sound bites from our own century.

Even as Noonan was writing her book, moreover, Vaclav Havel, the playwright-president of Czechoslovakia, was eloquently celebrating the joy of a nation freed from Soviet tyranny – and without the help of a speech-writer. Whether it is the Pope in Poland, Nelson Mandela in South Africa, Ronald Reagan or Margaret Thatcher, Mario Cuomo, Edward Kennedy or Neil Kinnock, the Prince of Wales or Sir Geoffrey Howe or Salman Rushdie, the speeches from the past ten years that are collected in this anthology demonstrate that oratory can still help to overcome tyranny, defy despair, articulate the hopes and dreams of millions and change the world. Global television meanwhile ensures that speeches are heard by millions rather than the hundreds or thousands of the early twentieth century.

Oratory still flourishes but the style of oratory is always changing. Nineteenth-century orators might speak on only three great occasions a year. They would think about a speech for a fortnight and then spend several days polishing its phrases and committing the speech to memory (as Churchill often did a century later). Gladstone was the first British speaker to break with that tradition. During the Midlothian campaign he addressed several audiences at great length in less than a fortnight – and was attacked for departing from the dignity and decorum appropriate to a former prime minister.

When Lloyd George was at his peak, and speakers made at least a score of speeches a year outside parliament, he noted that addresses had become as a matter of course largely improvisations: 'The meticulous care with which words were chosen and sentences were framed and adorned and afterwards rooted in the memory has thus necessarily distant drum!" was a quotation he scornfully applied to those who wanted to escape from awkward present conflicts altogether ... Few speakers who have been called orators have indulged less in rhetoric and rodomontade. At his best he was never strident ... He hated grandiloquence; instead the bulk of his speeches was an intricate, intellectual elaboration, interspersed with paradox and irony ... He presented arguments emotionally and emotions argumentatively.'

More recently there is Neil Kinnock, who not long ago was described as daring to believe that oratory still had a part to play in British politics. 'Mr Kinnock does not just deliver a speech with his voice: he dances it with his feet and choreographs it with his body ... His timing is as good as that of any stand-up comic; he uses gesture as well as any serious actor; and, seldom still for a moment, his whole mobile demeanour suggests someone whose natural allegiance is just as much to the sports field as to the public platform.'

The sense of drama that still attends a major speech is captured well by Peggy Noonan. 'A speech is a soliloquy,' she says, 'one man on a bare stage with a big spotlight. He will tell us who he is and what he wants and how he will get it and what it means that he wants it and what it will mean when he does or does not get it, and ...

'He looks up at us in the balconies and clears his throat. "Ladies and gentlemen ..." We lean forward, hungry to hear. Now it will be said, now we will hear the thing we long for. A speech is part theatre and part political declaration; it is personal communication between a leader and his people; it is art, and all art is a paradox, being at once a thing of great power and great delicacy. A speech is poetry: cadence, rhythm, imagery, sweep! A speech reminds us that words, like children, have the power to make dance the dullest beanbag of a heart ... Speeches are important because they are one of the great constants of our political history. They have been not only the way we measure public men, they have been how we tell each other who we are ... They count. They more than count, they shape what happens.'

The drama that Noonan describes still attends the great political set-piece speeches and shows that oratory is not a declining art, even though some of the political leaders of the West, such as George Bush and John Major, are not natural orators, even though television places more emphasis on moving images than moving words.

Amidst the lazy illiteracy of so much modern speech, eloquent words still have power to pierce through all the banal platitudes and make audiences stop and think and sometimes even wonder. Our political leaders still search for the writers who can gild their prosaic visions (as was shown in 1992 again when Bush summoned Noonan back to add to his speeches the eloquence he so signally lacks himself). Political leaders still achieve power by the quality of their speeches; and we still need heroes who can articulate our hopes and dreams and who can say what in our hearts we want to hear.

My own introduction to great oratory occurred when Aneurin Bevan addressed a by-election meeting in Chester Corn Exchange after the Suez crisis. He wielded wit, invective and sarcasm against hecklers, as did Quintin Hogg (now Lord Hailsham) the following night. I was hooked. That style may seem to have passed in an era when audiences prefer their politics on television rather than the hustings, but it was kept alive in the sixties by Harold Wilson and John F. Kennedy and has flourished since then in the speeches of Ronald Reagan and Mario Cuomo, or Margaret Thatcher and Neil Kinnock, all of whom bring a sense of drama to political occasions – a drama that television covets and therefore nourishes.

My hope is that this anthology will be an inspiration to those in politics who seek to change the world and who wish to speak with the eloquence displayed throughout this book.

ACKNOWLEDGEMENTS

An anthology requires detailed reading and research and I gratefully acknowledge my debt to the following who helped with advice: Juliet Annan, Charles Anson, Roberto de Armas of the Cuban Embassy, Timothy Garton Ash, Jonathan Bastable, Tony Benn, Alan Bennett, Hugh Brogan, Stephen Brooks, Sir Alan Bullock, Lord Callaghan of Cardiff, Professor Colin Campbell, Charles Clarke, Brian Collett, the Czechoslovakian Embassy, Lord Dainton, Beryl Drinkwater, Margarette Driscoll, Alan Evans, Harold Evans, Lord Fitt, Gillian Fryer, Martyn Goff, Alan Golding, Roy Greenslade, John Grigg, A. H. Halsey, Nigel Hamilton, Denis Healey, Sir Edward Heath, Peter Hennessy, Louis Heren, Michael Heseltine, Anthony Howard, the Indian High Commission, Martin Jacques, Lord Jenkins of Putney, Canon Graham James, Monty Johnstone, Frank Keating, Maurice Kogan, Magnus Linklater, Tom McNally, Brenda and John Maddox, David Marquand, T. W. Roberts of Merthyr Tydfil Trades Council, Rosalind Miles, Peter Millar, Bryan Moynahan, Novosti Press Agency, David Owen, Edward Pearce, Richard Peel, Penny Perrick, Ben Pimlott, Ben Pogrund, Enoch Powell, Nigel Rees, Peter Riddell, David Rogers, Lord Runcie, Ruth Salazar, Mike Smith, Lord Soper, the South African Embassy, Hugh Skillen, Sir David Steel, Andrew J. Taylor, James Taylor, Andrew Thomas, Barry Turner, Charles Webster, John Whittingdale and Lord Wilson of Rievaulx.

Many speeches would be lost for ever unless they were kept in libraries and I acknowledge a profound debt to the London Library, the *Times* library, the Library of Congress, and the librarians of the National Museum of Labour History, the Imperial War Museum, the Institute of Jewish Affairs, the Weizmann Institute, the Campaign for Nuclear Disarmament, the Institute of Commonwealth Studies, the European Economic Commission and the German Historical Institute.

John Biffen, Michael Foot and Lord Jenkins of Hillhead were especially helpful.

My greatest debts are to Jackson Boggs, Daria Antonucci, Peter Rose and Toby Bourne for research in America and Britain: to Lynn Moorlen, Tony Lacey, Ellen Levine and Hilary Rubinstein; and, for their tolerance, Bridget, Tessa and Georgie MacArthur.

Sources

Several books have been particularly helpful and I acknowledge a sincere debt to their authors: Robert Blake (*The Conservative Party from Peel to Thatcher*), Hugh Brogan (*The Penguin History of the United States of America*), Roy Foster (*Modern Ireland 1600–1972*), Roy Jenkins (*Baldwin* and *A Life at the Centre*), Kenneth O. Morgan (*The People's Peace: British History 1945–1989* and *Labour People*), Peggy Noonan (*What I Saw at the Revolution*), Alan Palmer (*The Penguin Dictionary of Twentieth-century History*), and A. J. P. Taylor (*English History, 1914–1945*). Grateful thanks are also due to the following for permission to reprint copyright material: Aneurin Bevan: to Labour Party Library; Sir Winston S. Churchill: to Curtis Brown Ltd, London, on behalf of the Estate of Sir Winston S. Churchill; copyright the Estate of Sir Winston S. Churchill; Mario Cuomo: to New York State Chief Press Officer; Éamon de Valera: to Radio Telefis Eireann; William Faulkner: to Random House UK Ltd and Random House Inc. (reprinted from *Essays, Speeches and Public Letters*, ed. James Meriwether; copyright © 1965 by Random House Inc.); Betty Friedan: to Curtis Brown Ltd, New York (reprinted from *It Changed My Life* (Dell, 1991)); Hugh Gaitskell: to Labour Party Library; David Lloyd George: to Express Newspapers plc and Macmillan Publishing Company (reprinted from *Slings and Arrows* (Cassell, 1929)); Gideon Hausner: to Longman Group UK (reprinted from *Keesings*); Martin Luther King: to Joan Daves Literary Agency; Douglas MacArthur: to Time Warner Inc./Katz (reprinted from *Reminiscences* (De Capo, 1985; copyright © Time Warner Inc./Katz); Iain MacLeod: to Rt. Hon. Baroness MacLeod of Borve; Nelson Mandela: to Penguin Books Ltd and Anthony Sheil Associates (reprinted from *Higher Than Hope: The Authorised Biography* by Fatima Meer); General Bernard Montgomery: to Public Record Office and Controller of Her Majesty's Stationery Office; Oswald Mosley: to Lady Mosley (reprinted from *My Life* (Nelson, 1968)); Richard Nixon: to the Office of Richard M. Nixon; Kwame Nkrumah: to Zed Books (Panaf Books division, 1973; reprinted from *I Speak of Freedom*); J. Robert Oppenheimer: to Harvard University Press (reprinted from *Robert Oppenheimer: Letters and Recollections*, eds. Alice Kimball Smith and Charles Weiner; copyright © Alice Kimball Smith and Charles Weiner); Pope John Paul: to Incorporated Catholic Truth Society; Ronald Reagan: to Random House UK Ltd and Simon & Schuster Inc. (reprinted from *Speaking My Mind*; copyright © 1989 by Ronald Reagan; Chaim Rumkowski: to Penguin Books Ltd and Ellen Levine Literary Agency Inc. (reprinted from *Lodz Ghetto*, compiled and edited by Alan Adelson and Robert Lapides (Penguin Books, 1991; copyright © The Jewish Heritage Writing Project Inc., 1989); Salman Rushdie: to Aitken & Stone Ltd and Wylie, Aitken & Stone Inc. on behalf of the author; Bertrand Russell: to British

Broadcasting Corporation and The Bertrand Russell Peace Foundation Ltd; Alexander Solzhenitsyn: to Random House UK Ltd and Hanover Trust Company on behalf of the author. Report of the House of Lords and House of Commons Debates (Hansard): to Controller of Her Majesty's Stationery Office.

Every effort has been made to contact copyright holders. The publishers will be glad to rectify, in future editions, any errors or omissions brought to their notice.

THEODORE ROOSEVELT
Chicago, 10 April 1899

'The doctrine of the strenuous life'

Theodore Roosevelt (1856–1919) was still a child growing up in a philistine society when he decided to turn himself into a man of action. He built up his skinny body by dogged exercise and sought continually to prove his manliness. After Harvard he spent two tough years on a cattle ranch in Dakota. He boxed, wrestled and swam, and always carried a revolver.

At the turn of the century he was an influential Republican in New York and he became assistant secretary to the navy in 1897. He first won national fame as a colonel of the 'Rough Riders' in Cuba during the Spanish–American war of 1898. A year later, when this speech was given at the Appomattox Day celebration of the Hamilton Club, he became governor of New York.

This speech, made (as he put it) as 'the twentieth century looms before us big with the fate of many nations' and preaching the virtues of the 'strenuous life' of action, swelled the reputation that swept him into the vice-presidency in the election of 1900 and then, after the assassination of President McKinley, into the presidency.

I wish to preach not the doctrine of ignoble ease but the doctrine of the strenuous life; the life of toil and effort; of labour and strife; to preach that highest form of success which comes not to the man who desires mere easy peace but to the man who does not shrink from danger, from hardship, or from bitter toil, and who out of these wins the splendid ultimate triumph.

A life of ignoble ease, a life of that peace which springs merely from lack either of desire or of power to strive after great things, is as little worthy of a nation as of an individual . . .

We do not admire the man of timid peace. We admire the man who embodies victorious effort; the man who never wrongs his neighbour; who is prompt to help a friend; but who has those virile qualities necessary to win in the stern strife of actual life. It is hard to fail; but it is worse never to have tried to succeed. In this life we get nothing save by effort. Freedom from effort in the present, merely means that there has been stored up effort in the past. A man can be freed from the necessity of work only by the fact that he or his fathers before him have worked to good purpose. If the freedom thus purchased is used aright, and the man still does actual work, though of a different kind, whether as a writer or a General, whether in the field of politics or in the field of exploration and adventure, he shows he deserves his good fortune. But if he treats this period of freedom from the need of actual labour as a period not of preparation but of mere enjoyment, he shows that he is simply a cumberer on the earth's surface; and he surely unfits himself to hold his own with his fellows if the need to do so should again arise. A mere life of ease is not in the end a satisfactory life, and above all it is a life which ultimately unfits those who follow it for serious work in the world.

As it is with the individual so it is with the nation. It is a base untruth to say that happy is the nation that has no history. Thrice happy is the nation that has a glorious history. Far better it is to dare mighty things, to win glorious triumphs, even though checkered by failure, than to take rank with those poor spirits who neither enjoy much nor suffer much because they live in the grey twilight that knows neither victory nor defeat. If in 1861 the men who loved the Union had believed that peace was the end of all things and war and strife a worst of all things, and had acted up to their belief, we would have saved hundreds of thousands of lives, we would have saved hundreds of millions of dollars. Moreover, besides saving all the blood and treasure we then lavished, we would have prevented the heart-break of many women, the dissolution of many homes; and we would have spared the country those months of gloom and shame when it seemed as if our armies marched only to defeat. We could have avoided all this suffering, simply by shrinking from strife. And if we had thus avoided it we would have shown that we were weaklings and that we were unfit to stand among the great nations of the earth. Thank God for the iron in the blood of our fathers, the men who upheld the wisdom of Lincoln and bore sword or rifle in the armies of Grant! Let us, the children of the men who proved themselves equal to the mighty days – let us, the children of the men who carried the great Civil War to a triumphant conclusion, praise the God of our fathers that the ignoble counsels of peace were rejected, that the suffering and loss, the blackness of sorrow and despair, were unflinchingly faced, and the years of strife endured; for in the end the slave was freed, the Union restored, and the mighty American Republic placed once more as a helmeted queen among nations . . .

The timid man, the lazy man, the man who distrusts his country, the overcivilized man, who has lost the great fighting, masterful virtues, the ignorant man and the man of dull mind, whose soul is incapable of feeling the mighty lift that thrills 'stern men with empires in their brains' – all these, of course, shrink from seeing the nation undertake its new duties; shrink from seeing us build a navy and army adequate to our needs; shrink from seeing us do our share of the world's work by bringing order out of chaos in the great, fair tropic islands from which the valour of our soldiers and sailors has driven the Spanish flag. These are the men who fear the strenuous life, who fear the only national life which is really worth leading. They believe in that cloistered life which saps the hardy virtues in a nation, as it saps them in the individual; or else they are wedded to that base spirit of gain and greed which recognizes in commercialism the be-all and end-all of national life, instead of realizing that, though an indispensable element, it is after all but one of the many elements that go to make up true national greatness. No country can long endure if its foundations are not laid deep in the material prosperity which comes from thrift, from business energy and enterprise, from hard, unsparing effort in the fields of industrial activity; but neither was any nation ever yet truly great if it relied upon material prosperity alone.

I preach to you, then, my countrymen, that our country calls not for the life of ease, but for the life of strenuous endeavour.

The twentieth century looms before us big with the fate of many nations. If we stand idly by, if we seek merely swollen, slothful ease, and ignoble peace, if we shrink from the hard contests where men must win at hazard of their lives and at the risk of all they hold dear, then the bolder and stronger peoples will pass us by and will win for themselves the domination of the world. Let us therefore boldly face the life of strife, resolute to do our duty well and manfully; resolute to uphold righteousness by deed and by word; resolute to be both honest and brave, to serve high ideals, yet to use practical methods. Above all, let us shrink from no strife, moral or physical, within or without the nation, provided we are certain that the strife is justified; for it is only through strife, through hard and dangerous endeavour, that we shall ultimately win the goal of true national greatness.

•

JOSEPH CHAMBERLAIN
Birmingham, 15 May 1903

'I believe in a British Empire and I do not believe in a Little England'

The campaign for tariff reform, memorably advocated by Joseph Chamberlain (1836–1914) in this speech at Birmingham, split the Conservative Party, convulsed the country and eventually handed power for nearly two decades to the Liberals, led by Asquith and Lloyd George.

Chamberlain, at first a radical Liberal whose opposition to Irish Home Rule in 1886 had split the party and brought down the government, had joined the Tories and now proposed protection, renamed tariff reform, in order to unite the Dominions (such as Canada and South Africa) to the Empire by preferential tariffs.

He provoked a great sensation. 'The Birmingham speech', wrote Leo Amery, the Tory politician, was 'a challenge to free trade as direct and provocative as the theses which Luther nailed to the church door at Wittenberg. To many of the younger generation, passionately imperialist by conviction, beginning to be intellectually sceptical about free trade, the speech was a sudden crystallization of all their ideals in an imperious call to action.'

I cannot look forward without dread to handing over the security and existence of this great Empire to the hands of those who have made common cause with its enemies, who have charged their own countrymen with methods of barbarism, and who apparently have been untouched by that pervading sentiment which I found everywhere where the British flag floats, and which has done so much in recent years to draw us together. I should not require to go to South Africa in order to be convinced that this feeling has obtained deep hold on the minds and hearts of our children beyond the seas. It has had a hard life of it, this feeling of Imperial patriotism. It was checked for a generation by the apathy and the indifference which were the characteristics of our former relations with our Colonies, but it was never extinguished. The embers were still alight, and when in the late war this old country of ours showed that it was still possessed by the spirit of our ancestors, and that it was still prepared to count no sacrifice that was necessary in order to maintain the honour and the interests of the Empire, then you found a response from your children across the seas that astonished the whole world by a proof, an undeniable proof, of affection and regard.

Is it to end there? Are we to sink back into the old policy of selfish isolation which went very far to dry and even to sap the loyalty of our colonial brethren? I do not think so. I think these larger issues touch the people of this country. I think they have awakened to the enormous importance of a creative time like the present, and of taking advantage of the opportunities offered in order to make permanent what has begun so well. Remember, we are a kingdom, an old country. We proceed here on settled lines. We have our quarrels and our disputes, and we pass legislation which may be good or bad; but we know that, whatever changes there may be, at all events the main stream will ultimately reach its appointed destination. That is the result of centuries of constitutional progress and freedom.

But the Empire is not old. The Empire is new – the Empire is in its infancy. Now is the time when we can mould that Empire and when we and those who live with us can decide its future destinies. Just let us consider what that Empire is. I am not going tonight to speak of those hundreds of millions of our Indian and native fellow subjects for whom we have become responsible. I consider for the moment only our relations to that white British population that constitutes the majority in the great self-governing colonies of the Empire. Here in the United Kingdom there are some forty millions of us. Outside there are ten millions of men either directly descended from ancestors who left this country or more probably men who themselves in their youth left this country in order to find their fortunes in our possessions abroad. How long do you suppose that this proportion of population is going to endure? The development of those colonies has been delayed by many reasons – but mainly probably by a more material reason – by the fact that the United States of America has offered a greater attraction to British emigration.

But that has changed. The United States, with all their vast territory, are filling up; and even now we hear of tens of thousands of emigrants leaving the United States in order to take up the fresh and rich lands of our colony in Canada. It seems to me not at all an impossible assumption that before the end of this present century we may find our fellow subjects beyond the seas as numerous as we are at home. I want you to look forward. I want you to consider the infinite importance of this not only to yourselves but to your descendants. Now is the time when you can exert influence. Do you wish that if these ten millions become forty millions they shall still be closely, intimately, affectionately united to you, or do you contemplate the possibility of their being separated, going off each in his own direction, under a separate flag? Think what it means to your power and influence as a country; think what it means to your position among the nations of the world; think what it means to your trade and commerce – I put that last.

What is the meaning of an Empire? What does it mean to us? We have had a little experience. We have had a war, a war in which the majority of our children abroad had no apparent direct interest. We had no hold over them of any kind, and yet at one time during this war, by the voluntary decision of these people, at least 50,000 Colonial soldiers were standing shoulder to shoulder with British troops, displaying a gallantry equal to their own and the keenest intelligence. It is something for a beginning, and if this country were in danger, I mean if we were, as our forefathers were, face to face some day – Heaven forfend – with some great coalition of hostile nations, when we had with our backs to the wall to struggle for our very lives, it is my firm conviction there is nothing within the power of these self-governing colonies they would not do to come to our aid. I believe their whole resources in men and in money would be at the disposal of the Mother Country in such an event. That is something – something which it is wonderful to have achieved, and which it is worth almost any sacrifice to maintain . . .

I believe in a British Empire, in an Empire which, though it should be its first duty to cultivate friendship with all the nations of the world, should yet, even if alone, be self-sustaining and self-sufficient, able to maintain itself against the competition of all its rivals. And I do not believe in a Little England which shall be separated from all those to whom it would in the natural course look for support and affection, a Little England which would then be dependent absolutely on the mercy of those who envy its present prosperity, and who have shown they are ready to do all in their power to prevent its future union with the British races throughout the world.

The tariff-reform campaign was a disaster for the Conservative Party. It united the Liberals, lost the Tories the general election of 1906, put the Liberals into power for nearly twenty years, and was a major factor in pushing the Tories into rejecting Lloyd George's 1909 'People's Budget'.

Chamberlain was struck down by paralysis in 1906 and played no further part in politics.

•

THEODORE ROOSEVELT
Washington, DC, 14 April 1906

'*The men with the muck-rakes*'

The strenuous life. Ignoble ease. Theodore Roosevelt had a gift for the striking oratorical phrase. One of his maxims was speak softly and carry a big stick. He also gave a new word to the language when he compared investigative journalists to Bunyan's man with a muck-rake, in this speech at the laying of the cornerstone of the office building of the House of Representatives.

We now administer the affairs of a nation in which the extraordinary growth of population has been outstripped by the growth of wealth and the growth in complex interests. The material problems that face us today are not such as they were in Washington's time, but the underlying facts of human nature are the same now as they were then. Under altered external form we war with the same tendencies towards evil that were evident in Washington's time, and are helped by the same tendencies for good.

In Bunyan's *Pilgrim's Progress* you may recall the description of the Man with the Muck-rake, the man who could look no way but downward, with the muck-rake in his hand; who was offered a celestial crown for his muck-rake, but who would neither look up nor regard the crown he was offered, but continued to rake to himself the filth of the floor.

In *Pilgrim's Progress* the Man with the Muck-rake is set forth as the example of him whose vision is fixed on carnal instead of on spiritual things. Yet he also typifies the man who in this life consistently refuses to see aught that is lofty, and fixes his eyes with solemn intentness only on that which is vile and debasing. Now, it is very necessary that we should not flinch from seeing what is vile and debasing. There is filth on the floor, and it must be scraped up with the muck-rake; and there are times and places where this service is the most needed of all the services that can be performed. But the man who never does anything else, who never thinks or speaks or writes save of his feats with the muck-rake, speedily becomes, not a help to society, not an incitement to good, but one of the most potent forces for evil.

There are, in the body politic, economic and social, many and grave evils, and there is urgent necessity for the sternest war upon them. There should be relentless exposure of and attack upon every evil man whether politician or business man, every evil practice, whether in politics, in business, or in social life. I hail as a benefactor every writer or speaker, every man who, on the platform, or in book, magazine, or newspaper, with merciless severity makes such attack, provided always that he in his turn remembers that the attack is of use only if it is absolutely truthful. The liar is no whit better than the thief, and if his mendacity takes the form of slander, he may be worse than most thieves. It puts a premium upon knavery untruthfully to attack an honest man, or even with hysterical exaggeration to assail a bad man with untruth. An epidemic of indiscriminate assault upon character does not good, but very great harm. The soul of every scoundrel is gladdened whenever an honest man is assailed, or even when a scoundrel is untruthfully assailed . . .

My plea is, not for immunity to but for the most unsparing exposure of the politician who betrays his trust, of the big business man who makes or spends his fortune in illegitimate or corrupt ways. There should be a resolute effort to hunt every such man out of the position he has disgraced. Expose the crime, and hunt down the criminal; but remember that even in the case of crime, if it is attacked in sensational, lurid, and untruthful fashion, the attack may do more damage to the public mind than the crime itself. It is because I feel that there should be no rest in the endless war against the forces of evil that I ask that the war be conducted with sanity as well as with resolution. The men with the muck-rakes are often indispensable to the well-being of society; but only if they know when to stop raking the muck, and to look upward to the celestial crown above them, to the crown of worthy endeavor. There are beautiful things above and round about them; and if they gradually grow to feel that the whole world is nothing but muck, their power of usefulness is gone. If the whole picture is painted black there remains no hue whereby to single out the rascals for distinction from their fellows. Such painting finally induces a kind of moral colour-blindness; and people affected by it come to the conclusion that no man is really black, and no man really white, but they are all gray. In other words, they neither believe in the truth of the attack, nor in the honesty of the man who is attacked; they grow as suspicious of the accusation as of the offence; it becomes well-nigh hopeless to stir them either to wrath against wrong-doing or to enthusiasm for what is right; and such a mental attitude in the public gives hope to every knave, and is the despair of honest men.

•

DAVID LLOYD GEORGE
London, 30 July 1909

'The People's Budget'

The historic budget introduced in 1909 by David Lloyd George (1863–1945) proposed a modest supertax on the very rich and new taxes on land. Its aim, he said, was to wage implacable warfare against poverty and squalor. After the first national pension scheme of 1908, he had to provide for old-age pensions and to meet a heavy demand for naval construction. The budget was thrown out by the House of Lords after a momentous national controversy – an action which provoked the conflict between Lords and Commons that eventually led to the Parliament Act of 1911 and curbed the power of the hereditary lords.

Lloyd George's first full-scale defence of his budget was at Limehouse in London where he addressed an audience of 4,000 at the Edinburgh Castle. The speech provoked tumultuous applause from the audience of cockneys. It also provoked King Edward VII, who dispatched a message to Lloyd George from the royal yacht saying his speech was 'calculated to set class against class and to inflame the passions of the working and lower orders against people who happened to be owners of property'.

A master of improvised speech, Lloyd George, with his seductive, vibrant voice, was the greatest natural orator in an age of great orators. He spoke with his audiences and not to them. 'My platform is the country,' he said, and he gave his audiences a music-hall turn.

He mobilized the forces of change outside parliament as only a very few, such as Cobden, Gladstone and Joseph Chamberlain, had done before — but his driving passion was to action more than speech, to put far-reaching measures on the Statute Book and to root out the palpable injustices he saw all around him. He was the true founder of the Welfare State.

A few months ago a meeting was held not far from this hall, in the heart of the city of London, demanding that the government should launch out and run into enormous expenditure on the navy. That meeting ended up with a resolution promising that those who passed that resolution would give financial support to the government in their undertaking. There have been two or three meetings held in the City of London since, attended by the same class of people, but not ending up with a resolution promising to pay. On the contrary, we are spending the money, but they don't pay. What has happened since to alter their tone? Simply that we have sent in the bill. We started our four Dreadnoughts. They cost eight millions of money. We promised them four more; they cost another eight millions. Somebody has got to pay, and these gentlemen say, 'Perfectly true; somebody has got to pay, but we would rather that somebody were somebody else.' We started building; we wanted money to pay for the building; so we sent the hat round. We sent it round amongst the workmen and the miners of Derbyshire and Yorkshire, the weavers of Dumfries, who, like all their countrymen, know the value of money. They all brought in their coppers. We went round Belgravia, but there has been such a howl ever since that it has completely deafened us.

But they say, 'It is not so much the Dreadnoughts we object to, it is the pensions.' If they object to pensions, why did they promise them? They won elections on the strength of their promises. It is true they never carried them out. Deception is always a pretty contemptible vice, but to deceive the poor is the meanest of all crimes. But they say, 'When we promised pensions we meant pensions at the expense of the people for whom they were provided. We simply meant to bring in a bill to compel workmen to contribute to their own pensions.' If that is what they meant, why did they not say so? The budget is introduced not merely for the purpose of raising barren taxes, but taxes that are fertile taxes, taxes that will bring forth fruit – the security of the country which is paramount in the midst of all. The provision for the aged and deserving poor – it was time it was done. It is rather a shame for a rich country like ours – probably the richest country in the world, if not the richest the world has ever seen – that it should allow those who have toiled all their days to end in penury and possibly starvation. It is rather hard that an old workman should have to find his way to the gates of the tomb, bleeding and footsore, through the brambles and thorns of poverty. We cut a new path through it, an easier one, a pleasanter one, through fields of waving corn. We are raising money to pay for the new road, aye, and to widen it, so that 200,000 paupers shall be able to join in the march. There are many in the country blessed by Providence with great wealth, and if there are amongst them men who grudge out of their riches a fair contribution toward the less fortunate of their fellow countrymen, they are shabby rich men. We propose to do more by means of the budget. We are raising money to provide against the evils and the sufferings that follow from unemployment. We are raising money for the purpose of assisting our great friendly societies to provide for the sick and the widows and orphans. We are providing money to enable us to develop the resources of our own land. I do not believe any fair-minded man would challenge the justice and the fairness of the objects which we have in view in raising this money . . .

Have you been down a coal-mine? I was telling you I went down one the other day. We sank down into a pit half a mile deep. We then walked underneath the mountain, and we did about three-quarters of a mile with rock and shale above us. The earth seemed to be straining – around us and above us – to crush us in. You could see the pit-props bent and twisted and sundered until you saw their fibres split. Sometimes they give way, and then there is mutilation and death. Often a spark ignites, the whole pit is deluged in fire, and the breath of life is scorched out of hundreds of breasts by the consuming fire.

In the very next colliery to the one I descended, just three years ago, three hundred people lost their lives in that way; and yet when the Prime Minister and I knock at the door of these great landlords and say to them, 'Here, you know these poor fellows who have been digging up royalties at the risk of their lives, some of them are old, they have survived the perils of their trade, they are broken, they can earn no more. Won't you give something towards keeping them out of the workhouse?' – they scowl at you. And we say, 'Only a ha'penny, just a copper!' They say, 'You thieves!' And they turn their dogs on to us, and every day you can hear their bark. If this is an indication of the view taken by these great landlords of their responsibility to the people who, at the risk of life, create their wealth, then I say their day of reckoning is at hand.

The other day, at the great Tory meeting held at the Cannon Street Hotel, they had blazoned on the walls, 'We protest against the budget in the name of democracy, liberty, and justice.' Where does the democracy come in this landed system? Where is the justice in all these transactions? We claim that the tax we impose on land is fair, just, and moderate. They go on threatening that if we proceed they will cut down their benefactions and discharge labour. What kind of labour? What is the labour they are going to choose for dismissal? Are they going to threaten to devastate rural England, while feeding themselves and dressing themselves? Are they going to reduce their gamekeepers? That would be sad! The agricultural labourer and the farmer might then have some part of the game which they fatten with their labour. But what would happen to you in the season? No weekend shooting with the Duke of Norfolk for any of us! But that is not the kind of labour that they are going to cut down. They are going to cut down productive labour – builders and gardeners – and they are going to ruin their property so that it shall not be taxed. All I can say is this – the ownership of land is not merely an enjoyment, it is a stewardship. It has been reckoned as such in the past, and if they cease to discharge their functions, the security and defence of the country, looking after the broken in their villages and neighbourhoods – then those functions which are part of the traditional duties attached to the ownership of land and which have given to it its title – if they cease to discharge those functions, the time will come to reconsider the conditions under which land is held in this country. No country, however rich, can permanently afford to have quartered upon its revenue a class which declines to do the duty which it was called upon to perform. And, therefore, it is one of the prime duties of statesmanship to investigate those conditions.

But I do not believe it. They have threatened and menaced like that before. They have seen it is not to their interest to carry out these futile menaces. They are now protesting against paying their fair share of the taxation of the land, and they are doing so by saying: 'You are burdening the community; you are putting burdens upon the people which they cannot bear.' Ah! they are not thinking of themselves. Noble souls! It is not the great dukes they are feeling for; it is the market gardener, it is the builder, and it was, until recently, the small holder. In every debate in the House of Commons they said: 'We are not worrying for ourselves. We can afford it with our broad acres; but just think of the little man who has got a few acres,' and we were so very impressed with this tearful appeal that at last we said, 'We will leave him out.' And I almost expected to see Mr Prettyman jump over the table and say, 'Fall on my neck and embrace me.' Instead of that, he stiffened up, his face wreathed with anger, and he said, 'The budget is more unjust than ever.'

Oh! no. We are placing the burdens on the broad shoulders. Why should I put burdens on the people? I am one of the children of the people. I was brought up amongst them. I know their trials; and God forbid that I should add one grain of trouble to the anxiety which they bear with such patience and fortitude. When the Prime Minister did me the honour of inviting me to take charge of the national exchequer at a time of great difficulty, I made up my mind in framing the budget which was in front of me that at any rate no cupboard should be bared, no lot would be harder to bear. By that test, I challenge them to judge the budget.

•

DAVID LLOYD GEORGE
Caernarvon, 9 December 1909

'We are in for rough weather'

Lloyd George made many speeches on his People's Budget. After Limehouse, where he attacked dukes with their leaseholds of ever-increasing value, he spoke in Newcastle, where he said that fully equipped dukes, who cost as much to keep up as two Dreadnoughts, were just as great a terror and lasted longer. 'The question will be asked: "Should 500 men, ordinary men, chosen accidentally from among the unemployed, override the judgement, the deliberate judgement, of millions of people who are engaged in the industry which makes the wealth of the country?"' At Wolverhampton, he again attacked the hereditary principle.

At Caernarvon in Wales at the end of the year, there was a superb peroration to his speech, in which he set out his case for the betterment of the people.

These are the taxes, these are our proposals. What do our opponents object to? Where is the Socialism, injustice and wrong? Where is the oppression; where is the unfairness of it? Do they object to what we are spending the money for? They do not complain about our building Dreadnoughts; they want more, except that they want someone else to pay for them. Do they object to pensions? What do they object to? Is it unfair to raise money for these purposes? We are imposing no burdens upon the earnings of any working man. The vast majority – I am sure the whole – of the middle class of this country escape additional burdens. We put no burden upon the necessities of life of anyone. We are taxing the surplus. We are taxing the luxuries. If a man has enough after maintaining his wife and family, and can spare something upon whisky and tobacco, why should he not afterwards contribute towards the pensions and defences of the country? No; we are raising money by means that make it no more difficult for men to live, we are raising it for making provision for hundreds of thousands of workmen in the country who have nothing between them and starvation in old age except the charity of the parish. We propose a great scheme in order to set up a fund in this country that will see that no man suffers hunger in the dark days of sickness, breakdown in health, and unemployment which visit so many of us. That is what we are going to do. These schemes for the betterment of the people, we shall get them some day. We cannot get them without effort, and they will not be worth getting without effort. Freedom does not descend like manna from Heaven. It has been won step by step, by tramping the wilderness, fighting enemies, crossing Jordan, and clearing Jebusites out of the land. I do not regret that we cannot obtain these blessings except by fighting. The common people have taken no step that was worth taking without effort, sacrifice and suffering.

I cannot pretend to regret this conflict with which we are now confronted. It is well that democracies should now and again engage in these great struggles for a wider freedom and a higher life. They represent stages in the advance of the people from the bondage of the past to the blessings of the future. Those who dread these political convulsions, who apprehend from them nothing but destruction and danger, have read their history in vain. The race has nothing to fear except from stagnation. Against our will we have been precipitated into this tumult. For all that, we mean to win our way through it to a better time. The people may not secure all they seek, but if they bear themselves manfully they will achieve other ends they dare not even hope for now. Yesterday I visited the old village where I was brought up. I wandered through the woods familiar to my boyhood. There I saw a child gathering sticks for firewood, and I thought of the hours which I spent in the same pleasant and profitable occupation, for I also have been something of a 'backwoodsman'. And there is one experience taught me then which is of use to me today. I learnt as a child that it was little use going into the woods after a period of calm and fine weather, for I generally returned empty-handed; but after a great storm I always came back with an armful. We are in for rough weather. We may be even in for a winter of storms which will rock the forest, break many a withered branch, and leave many a rotten tree torn up by the roots. But when the weather clears, you may depend upon it that there will be something brought within the reach of the people that will give warmth and glow to their grey lives, something that will help to dispel the hunger, the despair, the oppression, and the wrong which now chill so many of their hearts.

•

WOODROW WILSON
Trenton, New Jersey, 5 September 1910

'With the new age, we shall show a new spirit'

Woodrow Wilson (1856–1924) was a reforming president of the University of Princeton when he abandoned teaching for politics in 1910 and campaigned as a democrat for the governorship of New Jersey. Two years earlier he had written a book on constitutional government in the United States in which he wrote that a president whom the nation trusted could not only lead it but form it to his own views. 'Let him once win the admiration and confidence of the country and no other single force can withstand him, no combination of forces will easily overpower him.'

A man of high ideals and high intellect, he was fifty-four when he made his first political address at the Taylor Opera House in Trenton, where he had just been nominated over three other candidates even though most of the delegates had never seen him.

It is first of all necessary that we should act in the right spirit. And the right spirit is not a spirit of hostility. We shall not act either justly or wisely if we attack established interests as public enemies. There has been too much indictment and too little successful prosecution for wrongs done; too much talk and too few practicable suggestions as to what is to be done. It is easy to condemn wrong and to fulminate against wrongdoers in effective rhetorical phrases; but that does not bring either reform or ease of mind. Reform will come only when we have done some careful thinking as to exactly what the things are that are being done in contravention of the public interest and as to the most simple, direct, and effective way of getting at the men who do them. In a self-governed country there is one rule for everybody, and that is the common interest. Everything must be squared by that. We can square it only by knowing its exact shape and movement. Government is not a warfare of interests. We shall not gain our ends by heat and bitterness, which make it impossible to think either calmly or fairly. Government is a matter of common counsel, and everyone must come into the consultation with the purpose to yield to the general view, the view which seems most nearly to correspond with the common interest. If any decline frank conference, keep out, hold off, they must take the consequences and blame only themselves if they are in the end badly served. There must be implacable determination to see the right done, but strong purpose, which does not flinch because some must suffer, is perfectly compatible with fairness and justice and a clear view of the actual facts.

This should be our spirit in the matter of reform, and this our method. And in this spirit we should do very definite things.

The future is not for parties 'playing politics', but for measures conceived in the largest spirit, pushed by parties whose leaders are statesmen, not demagogues, who love, not their offices, but their duty and their opportunity for service. We are witnessing a renaissance of public spirit, a reawakening of sober public opinion, a revival of the power of the people, the beginning of an age of thoughtful reconstruction that makes our thought hark back to the great age in which Democracy was set up in America. With the new age, we shall show a new spirit. We shall serve justice and candor, and all things that make for the right. Is not our own ancient party the party disciplined and made ready for this great task? Shall we not forget ourselves in making it the instrument of righteousness for the state and for the nation?

When I think of the flag which our ships carry, the only touch of color about them, the only thing that moves as if it had a settled spirit in it – in their solid structure, it seems to me I see alternate strips of parchment upon which are written the rights of liberty and justice and strips of blood spilled to vindicate those rights, and then – in the corner – a prediction of the blue serene into which every nation may swim that stands for these great things.

One man in the audience that afternoon was Joseph P. Tumulty, who subsequently became Wilson's personal secretary. 'The speech is over,' he wrote. 'Around me there is a swirling mass of men whose hearts have been touched by the great speech which is just at an end. Men stood about me with tears streaming from their eyes. Realizing that they had just stood in the presence of greatness, it seemed as if they had been lifted out of their selfish miasma of politics and, in the spirit of the Crusaders, were ready to dedicate themselves to the cause of liberating their state from the bondage of special interests.'

Wilson won the election and became a strong reforming leader who broke with the bosses who had nominated him. There was an eloquence, an elevation in Wilson's speeches that stirred men's hearts, according to the historian Hugh Brogan. The progressive programme that Wilson pushed through the state legislature brought him nationwide attention. Two years later, he beat Theodore Roosevelt, William Taft and Eugene V. Debs for the presidency.

•

THEODORE ROOSEVELT
Osawatomie, Kansas, 1910

'The new nationalism'

After becoming president of the United States on the assassination of President McKinley in 1901, Theodore Roosevelt won the election of 1904 with an overwhelming majority, but withdrew from politics in 1908 for a two-year world tour and went big-game hunting in Africa.

On his return he tried to re-enter politics. The 'New Nationalism' he now preached not only embraced most of the political and social reforms of the moment but also accepted as both 'inevitable and necessary' the concentration of economic power in big corporations. Roosevelt would regulate rather than dissolve them, maintaining instead of destroying their contributions to America's wealth. Big business would be matched by big government.

This was the programme that he presented in his speech at Osawatomie, Kansas, in August 1910.

We come here today to commemorate one of the epoch-making events of the long struggle for the rights of man, the long struggle for the uplift of humanity. Our country – this great republic – means nothing unless it means the triumph of a real democracy, the triumph of popular government, and, in the long run, of an economic system under which each man shall be guaranteed the opportunity to show the best that there is in him. That is why the history of America is now the central feature of the history of the world; for the world has set its face hopefully towards our democracy; and, O my fellow citizens, each one of you carries on your shoulders not only the burden of doing well for the sake of your own country, but the burden of doing well and seeing that this nation does well for the sake of mankind . . .

At many stages in the advance of humanity, conflict between the men who possess more than they have earned and the men who have earned more than they possess is the central condition of progress. In our day it appears as the struggle of free men to gain and hold the right of self-government as against the special interests, who twist the methods of free government into machinery for defeating the popular will. At every stage, and under all circumstances, the essence of the struggle is to equalize opportunity, destroy privilege, and give to the life and citizenship of every individual the highest possible value both to himself and to the commonwealth . . .

Practical equality of opportunity for all citizens, when we achieve it, will have two great results. First, every man will have a fair chance to make of himself all that in him lies; to reach the highest point to which his capacities, unassisted by special privilege of his own and unhampered by the special privilege of others, can carry him, and to get for himself and his family substantially what he has earned. Second, equality of opportunity means that the commonwealth will get from every citizen the highest service of which he is capable. No man who carries the burden of the special privileges of another can give to the commonwealth that service to which it is fairly entitled . . .

National efficiency has many factors. It is a necessary result of the principle of conservation widely applied. In the end it will determine our failure or success as a Natiôn. National efficiency has to do, not only with natural resources and with men, but it is equally concerned with institutions. The State must be made efficient for the work which concerns only the people of the State; and the Nation for that which concerns all the people. There must remain no neutral ground to serve as a refuge for lawbreakers, and especially for lawbreakers of great wealth, who can hire the vulpine legal cunning which will teach them how to avoid both jurisdictions. It is a misfortune when the national legislature fails to do its duty in providing a national remedy, so that the only national activity is the purely negative activity of the judiciary in forbidding the state to exercise power in the premises . . .

The American people are right in demanding that New Nationalism, without which we cannot hope to deal with new problems.

The New Nationalism puts the national need before sectional or personal advantage. It is impatient of the utter confusion that results from local legislatures attempting to treat national issues as local issues. It is still more impatient of the impotence which springs from overdivision of governmental powers, the impotence which makes it possible for local selfishness or for legal cunning, hired by wealthy special interests, to bring national activities to a deadlock. This New Nationalism regards the executive power as the steward of the public welfare. It demands of the judiciary that it shall be interested primarily in human welfare rather than in property, just as it demands that the representative body shall represent all the people rather than any one class or section of the people . . .

The object of government is the welfare of the people. The material progress and prosperity of a nation are desirable chiefly so far as they lead to the moral and material welfare of all citizens. Just in proportion as the average man and woman are honest, capable of sound judgment and high ideals, active in public affairs – but, first of all, sound in their home life, and the father and mother of healthy children whom they bring up well – just so far, and no further, we may count our civilization a success. We must have – I believe we have already – a genuine and permanent moral awakening, without which no wisdom of legislation or administration really means anything; and, on the other hand, we must try to secure the social and economic legislation without which any improvement due to purely moral agitation is necessarily evanescent . . . No matter how honest and decent we are in our private lives, if we do not have the right kind of law and the right kind of administration of the law, we cannot go forward as a nation. That is imperative; but it must be an addition to, and not a substitution for, the qualities that make up good citizens. In the last analysis, the most important elements in any man's career must be the sum of those qualities which, in the aggregate, we speak of as character. If he has not got it, then no law that the wit of man can devise, no administration of the law by the boldest and strongest executive, will avail to help him. We must have the right kind of character – character that makes a man, first of all, a good man in the home, a good father, a good husband – that makes a man a good neighbor. You must have that, and, then, in addition, you must have the kind of law and the kind of administration of the law which will give to those qualities in the private citizen the best possible chance for development. The prime problem of our nation, is to get the right type of good citizenship, and, to get it, we must have progress, and our public men must be genuinely progressive.

After failing to win the Republican nomination against William Taft, the incumbent president, in 1912, Roosevelt stood as an independent progressive candidate. He polled more votes than Taft but split the vote and allowed Woodrow Wilson to win.

•

EMMELINE PANKHURST
Canada, 14 January 1912

'This last fight for human freedom'

Emmeline Pankhurst (1858–1928), leader of the British suffragettes, formed the Women's Franchise League in 1889 but it was not until 1903 that she was persuaded by her daughter Christabel (1880–1958) to found the more militant Women's Social and Political Union. After a meeting in 1906 with Herbert Asquith, the Liberal prime minister, she despaired of winning the vote from a Liberal government and began to resort to militant tactics.

She was first arrested in 1908 after suffragettes tried to 'rush' the House of Commons, and was sent to prison for three months. She was arrested again the next year (when forcible feeding was introduced to deal with the hunger strikes of the suffragettes) at the door of the House of Commons.

This speech was given on a tour of Canada. She spoke for two hours and was greeted by loud and prolonged cheers.

Women never took a single step forward without being pushed

back first of all by their opponents. We did not mind being laughed at as long as by laughter we could get our way to the vote. But the laughter was also turned against the statesman who refused to answer us. The statesman is a sort of serious individual not to be mocked or jeered at, but it was somewhat undignified for the first minister of the crown to make his way out by the rear entrance with a horse cloth over his head or to pass by an underground passage to the post office and then be shot down the parcel tube. People began to take us seriously then. A leading paper, when Mr Asquith went to Birmingham, sent a wire to its local correspondent. 'Never mind the prime minister. What are the suffragettes doing?'

Our next move was the canvass, and with a distinct woman's platform we took the field. We said, 'Vote against the government till it gives women the vote.' Candidates then began to complain that we took their audiences from them, but our reply was that the country was free, and if they wished to have a bigger house they should give better speeches.

Particularly in the working class districts we gained ground and we found that as we went into the social problems that were within the province of women we found the support of men who were not skilled in party lore, but had human hearts. We then became a real power in the election and government candidates where we worked against them were often defeated . . .

There has been a great deal of talk lately of new legislation for those who are about to enter into marriage. Woman should have a say as one of the contracting parties. There are the questions of divorce and of the training of children. Who knows better of these matters than do women? There are also the trades and professions which are at the present time open to women. It is only right that we should have some say in the legislation concerning us. We have heard much of the English divorce law. It is a disgrace to any civilized country. The only redeeming feature of the matter is that the bulk of men are better than the law allows. But there is the minority, and the law should be severe for them. They are as bad as the law allows them to be. If woman only had weight in politics this would be rectified soon. She will serve to call more attention to such questions of national welfare. If we are to have any divorce law at all, and that is a much-debated question, it should be a law that is equal both for man and woman. Unless women get the vote we have no guarantee that it will be so. There is again the legal status of married persons. Nature has given the child two parents, the law gives but one, and it is the father when the child is born in wedlock, but if the child is born out of wedlock, it is the mother. Men have made these laws, but what we want is to have Nature's law as man's law . . .

If we look around in the world, where do we see women happy, well treated and satisfied unless where the world has been made what women wish it to be? Men are responsible if they allow the present condition of things to continue. Women have the power to work out their own salvation. But as it is, if a woman is ruined, if a child is injured, man is responsible for it all. It is a responsibility I would not care to have, and, as things are, I would not be a man for all the world. If women fail as men have failed, then they will bear the burden with them. But since men cannot protect and shield us, let us share the duty with them, let us use our power so that woman may be a participant, not to tyrannize over man but to take a share in the responsibilities of ruling, without which there is no real representative government. What we really are interested in in this fight is the uplifting of the sex and better conditions of humanity than men can secure. In the legal home there is but the man. What we want is the combined intelligence of man and woman working for the salvation of the children of the race. This will make for the world a better time than ever before in its history. It will raise mankind to heights of which now it has little conception. We must only make this last fight for human freedom that as the class distinction disappeared so that sex distinction may pass, and then you will get better things than men can by themselves secure.

•

EDWARD CARSON
London, 11 February 1914

'Ulster is asking to be let alone'

Edward Carson, born and educated in Dublin, was Unionist MP for Dublin for twenty-six years before becoming MP for a Belfast seat, 1918–21. He was Solicitor-General in the administrations of Salisbury and Balfour. In 1910 he organized British resistance to Irish Home Rule and set up an Ulster Unionist Council in 1911. A year later he established the Ulster Volunteers, a private army of 80,000 men pledged to resist Home Rule.

He was the most powerful defender of the interests of Ulster in the British House of Commons. As Asquith wrestled with the issue of Home Rule in 1914, he had come to accept in some form the temporary exclusion of Ulster. He used the King's speech and the debate on the address to create a conciliatory atmosphere.

'The event of the afternoon', Asquith wrote on 11 February, 'was Carson's speech. He followed a somewhat arid display by the Impeccable and was really very impressive. I wrote him a line of congratulation.'

Ulster is not asking for concessions. Ulster is asking to be let alone. When you talk of concessions, what you really mean is, 'We want to lay down what is the minimum of wrong we can do to Ulster.' Let me tell you that the results of two years' delay and the treatment we have received during these two years have made your task and made our task far more difficult. You have driven these men to enter into a covenant for their mutual protection. No doubt you have laughed at their covenant. Have a good laugh at it now. Well, so far as I am concerned, I am not the kind of man who will go over to Ulster one day and say, 'Enter into a covenant', and go over next day and say, 'Break it.' But there is something more. You have insulted them. I do not say the Prime Minister has done so. I would be wrong if I were to say that he has done so. He has treated them seriously, but the large body of his colleagues in the rank and file of his party have taken every opportunity of jeering at these men, of branding them as braggarts and bluffers and cowards, and all the rest of it. Well, do not you see that having done that, these men can never go back, and never will go back, and allow these gibes and insults and sneers to prove true.

The Speech from the Throne talks of the fears of these men. Yes, they have, I think, genuine fears for their civil and religious liberty under the Bill, but do not imagine that that is all that these men are fighting for. They are fighting for a great principle, and a great ideal. They are fighting to stay under the Government which they were invited to come under, under which they have flourished, and under which they are content, and to refuse to come under a Government which they loathe and detest. Men do not make sacrifices or take up the attitude these men in Ulster have taken up on a question of detail or paper safeguards. I am not going to argue whether they are right or wrong in resisting. It would be useless to argue it, because they have thoroughly made up their minds, but I say this: If these men are not morally justified when they are attempted to be driven out of one Government with which they are satisfied, and put under another which they loathe, I do not see how resistance ever can be justified in history at all . . .

Believe me, whatever way you settle the Irish question, there are only two ways to deal with Ulster. It is for statesmen to say which is the best and right one. She is not a part of the community which can be bought. She will not allow herself to be sold. You must therefore either coerce her if you go on, or you must, in the long run, by showing that good government can come under the Home Rule Bill, try and win her over to the case of the rest of Ireland. You probably can coerce her – though I doubt it. If you do, what will be the disastrous consequences not only to Ulster, but to this country and the Empire? Will my fellow countryman, the Leader of the Nationalist party, have gained anything? I will agree with him – I do not believe he wants to triumph any more than I do. But will he have gained anything if he takes over these

people and then applies for what he used to call – at all events his
party used to call – the enemies of the people to come in and
coerce them into obedience? No, Sir, one false step taken in relation
to Ulster will, in my opinion, render for ever impossible a solution
of the Irish question. I say this to my Nationalist fellow countrymen, and, indeed, also to the Government: you have never tried to
win over Ulster. You have never tried to understand her position.
You have never alleged, and can never allege, that this Bill gives
her one atom of advantage. Nay, you cannot deny that it takes
away many advantages that she has as a constituent part of the
United Kingdom. You cannot deny that in the past she had
produced the most loyal and law-abiding part of the citizens of
Ireland. After all that, for these two years, every time we came
before you your only answer to us – the majority of you, at all
events – was to insult us, and to make little of us. I say to the
leader of the Nationalist party, if you want Ulster, go and take her,
or go and win her. You have never wanted her affections; you
have wanted her taxes . . .

•

KEIR HARDIE
Bradford, 11 April 1914

'The sunshine of Socialism'

*Keir Hardie (1856–1915), who left school at seven, was one of the founding
fathers of the British Labour Party and shaped the political history of the
Labour movement. He was a legend even in his lifetime, a fierce spokesman for
the working classes who was variously described as a latter-day Jesus or as
Moses leading the children of Labour towards the promised land.*

*He was the main founder of the Independent Labour Party, set up at a
meeting in Bradford in 1893; a Labour MP from 1892, when he shocked the
House of Commons by driving to Westminster in a cloth cap and tweed jacket
escorted by a trumpeter; a principal negotiator when the Labour Representative*

Committee (the forerunner of the Labour Party) was born in 1900; and became the first chairman of the parliamentary Labour Party in 1906.

The twenty-first anniversary of the ILP was an emotional occasion, again held in Bradford. This was Hardie's address.

I shall not weary you by repeating the tale of how public opinion has changed during those twenty-one years. But, as an example, I may recall the fact that in those days, and for many years thereafter, it was tenaciously upheld by the public authorities, here and elsewhere, that it was an offence against laws of nature and ruinous to the State for public authorities to provide food for starving children, or independent aid for the aged poor. Even safety regulations in mines and factories were taboo. They interfered with the 'freedom of the individual'. As for such proposals as an eight-hour day, a minimum wage, the right to work, and municipal houses, any serious mention of such classed a man as a fool.

These cruel, heartless dogmas, backed up by quotations from Jeremy Bentham, Malthus, and Herbert Spencer, and by a bogus interpretation of Darwin's theory of evolution, were accepted as part of the unalterable laws of nature, sacred and inviolable, and were maintained by statesmen, town councillors, ministers of the Gospel, and, strangest of all, by the bulk of the Trade Union leaders. That was the political, social, and religious element in which our Party saw the light. There was much bitter fighting in those days. Even municipal contests evoked the wildest passions.

And if today there is a kindlier social atmosphere it is mainly because of the twenty-one years' work of the ILP.

Scientists are constantly revealing the hidden powers of nature. By the aid of the X-rays we can now see through rocks and stones; the discovery of radium has revealed a great force which is already healing disease and will one day drive machinery; Marconi, with his wireless system of telegraphy and now of telephony, enables us to speak and send messages for thousands of miles through space.

Another discoverer, by means of the same invisible medium, can blow up ships, arsenals, and forts at a distance of eight miles.

But though these powers and forces are only now being revealed, they have existed since before the foundation of the world. The scientists, by sympathetic study and laborious toil, have brought them within our ken. And so, in like manner, our Socialist propaganda is revealing hidden and hitherto undreamed of powers and forces in human nature.

Think of the thousands of men and women who, during the past twenty-one years, have toiled unceasingly for the good of the race. The results are already being seen on every hand, alike in legislation and administration. And who shall estimate or put a limit to the forces and powers which yet lie concealed in human nature?

Frozen and hemmed in by a cold, callous greed, the warming influence of Socialism is beginning to liberate them. We see it in the growing altruism of Trade Unionism. We see it, perhaps, most of all in the awakening of women. Who that has ever known woman as mother or wife has not felt the dormant powers which, under the emotions of life, or at the stern call of duty, are even now momentarily revealed? And who is there who can even dimly forecast the powers that lie latent in the patient drudging woman, which a freer life would bring forth? Woman, even more than the working class, is the great unknown quantity of the race.

Already we see how their emergence into politics is affecting the prospects of men. Their agitation has produced a state of affairs in which even Radicals are afraid to give more votes to men, since they cannot do so without also enfranchising women. Our interests are theirs, and theirs ours. Henceforward we must march forward as comrades in the great struggle for human freedom.

The Independent Labour Party has pioneered progress in this country, is breaking down sex barriers and class barriers, is giving a lead to the great women's movement as well as to the great working-class movement. We are here beginning the twenty-second year of our existence. The past twenty-one years have been years of continuous progress, but we are only at the beginning. The emancipation of the worker has still to be achieved and just as the ILP in the past has given a good, straight lead, so shall the ILP in the future, through good report and through ill, pursue the even tenor of its way, until the sunshine of Socialism and human freedom break forth upon our land.

The Labour Party formed a minority government in 1924 under Ramsay MacDonald and won full power in 1929.

•

DAVID LLOYD GEORGE
London, 21 September 1914

'*The great pinnacle of sacrifice*'

Many speeches were made in the autumn of 1914 rallying the British for the war with Germany – but none matched in sheer poetic eloquence this address by Lloyd George, whose war speeches were described as standing like 'superannuated spells'.

Although there was a broad consensus about the justice of the war, the one element required to make it acceptable to a liberal society was some kind of broad, humane justification to explain what the war was really about.

'Lloyd George remained suspiciously silent during the early weeks,' says the British historian Kenneth O. Morgan. 'But in an eloquent address to a massed audience of his Welsh fellow-countrymen at the Queen's Hall, London, he committed himself without reserve to a fight to the finish. He occupied, or claimed to occupy, the highest moral ground. It was, he declared, a war on behalf of liberal principles, a crusade on behalf of the "little five-foot-five nations" . . .

'It was not surprising that a claim that the war was a holy cause, backed up not only by the leaders of all the Christian churches but by all the Liberal pantheon of heroes from Fox to Gladstone, met with an instant response, not least in the smaller nations of Scotland and Wales within Britain itself.'

This is the story of two little nations. The world owes much to little nations ... The greatest art in the world was the work of little nations; the most enduring literature of the world came from little nations; the greatest literature of England came when she was a nation of the size of Belgium fighting a great Empire. The heroic deeds that thrill humanity through generations were the deeds of little nations fighting for their freedom. Yes, and the salvation of mankind came through a little nation. God has chosen little nations as the vessels by which He carries His choicest wines to the lips of humanity, to rejoice their hearts, to exalt their vision, to stimulate and strengthen their faith; and if we had stood by when two little nations were being crushed and broken by the brutal hands of barbarism, our shame would have rung down the everlasting ages.

But Germany insists that this is an attack by a lower civilization upon a higher one. As a matter of fact, the attack was begun by the civilization which calls itself the higher one. I am no apologist for Russia; she has perpetrated deeds of which I have no doubt her best sons are ashamed. What Empire has not? But Germany is the last Empire to point the finger of reproach at Russia. Russia has made sacrifices for freedom – great sacrifices. Do you remember the cry of Bulgaria when she was torn by the most insensate tyranny that Europe has ever seen? Who listened to that cry? The only answer of the 'higher civilization' was that the liberty of the Bulgarian peasants was not worth the life of a single Pomeranian soldier. But the 'rude barbarians' of the North sent their sons by the thousand to die for Bulgarian freedom. What about England? Go to Greece, the Netherlands, Italy, Germany, France – in all those lands I could point out places where the sons of Britain have died for the freedom of those peoples. France has made sacrifices for the freedom of other lands than her own. Can you name a single country in the world for the freedom of which modern Prussia has ever sacrificed a single life? By the test of our faith the highest standard of civilization is the readiness to sacrifice for others.

Have you read the Kaiser's speeches? They are full of the glitter and bluster of German militarism – 'mailed fist' and 'shining armour'. Poor old mailed fist! Its knuckles are getting a little bruised. Poor shining armour! The shine is being knocked out of it. There is the same swagger and boastfulness running through the whole of the speeches. The extract which was given in the *British Weekly* this week is a very remarkable product as an illustration of the spirit we have to fight. It is the Kaiser's speech to his soldiers on the way to the front:

> Remember that the German people are the chosen of God. On me, the German Emperor, the Spirit of God has descended. I am His sword, His weapon and His Vicegerent. Woe to the disobedient, and death to cowards and unbelievers.

Lunacy is always distressing, but sometimes it is dangerous; and when you get it manifested in the head of the State, and it has become the policy of a great Empire, it is about time that it should be ruthlessly put away. I do not believe he meant all these speeches; it was simply the martial straddle he had acquired. But there were men around him who meant every word of them. This was their religion. Treaties? They tangle the feet of Germany in her advance. Cut them with the sword! Little nations? They hinder the advance of Germany. Trample them in the mire under the German heel. The Russian Slav? He challenges the supremacy of Germany in Europe. Hurl your legions at him and massacre him! Britain? She is a constant menace to the predominance of Germany in the world. Wrest the trident out of her hand. Christianity? Sickly sentimentalism about sacrifice for others! Poor pap for German digestion! We will have a new diet. We will force it upon the world. It will be made in Germany – the diet of blood and iron. What remains? Treaties have gone. The honour of nations has gone. Liberty has gone. What is left? Germany. Germany is left! '*Deutschland über Alles!*'

That is what we are fighting – that claim to predominance of a material, hard civilization which, if it once rules and sways the world, liberty goes, democracy vanishes. And unless Britain and her sons come to the rescue it will be a dark day for humanity.

Have you followed the Prussian Junker and his doings? We are not fighting the German people. The German people are under the heel of this military caste, and it will be a day of rejoicing for the German peasant, artisan and trader when the military caste is broken. You know its pretensions. They give themselves the air of demigods. They walk the pavements, and civilians and their wives are swept into the gutter; they have no right to stand in the way of a great Prussian soldier. Men, women, nations – they all have to go. He thinks all he has to say is, 'We are in a hurry.' That is the answer he gave to Belgium – 'Rapidity of action is Germany's greatest asset,' which means, 'I am in a hurry; clear out of my way.' You know the type of motorist, the terror of the roads, with a sixty-horse-power car, who thinks the roads are made for him, and knocks down anybody who impedes the action of his car by a single mile an hour. The Prussian Junker is the road-hog of Europe. Small nationalities in his way are hurled to the roadside, bleeding and broken. Women and children are crushed under the wheels of his cruel car, and Britain is ordered out of his road. All I can say is this: if the old British spirit is alive in British hearts, that bully will be torn from his seat. Were he to win, it would be the greatest catastrophe that has befallen democracy since the day of the Holy Alliance and its ascendancy.

They think we cannot beat them. It will not be easy. It will be a long job; it will be a terrible war; but in the end we shall march through terror to triumph. We shall need all our qualities – every quality that Britain and its people possess – prudence in counsel, daring in action, tenacity in purpose, courage in defeat, moderation in victory; in all things faith.

It has pleased them to believe and to preach the belief that we are a decadent and degenerate people. They proclaim to the world through their professors that we are a non-heroic nation skulking behind our mahogany counters, whilst we egg on more gallant races to their destruction. This is a description given of us in Germany – 'a timorous, craven nation, trusting to its Fleet'. I think they are beginning to find their mistake out already – and there are half a million young men of Britain who have already registered a vow to their King that they will cross the seas and hurl that insult to British courage against its perpetrators on the battlefields of France and Germany. We want half a million more; and we shall get them.

I envy you young people your opportunity. They have put up the age limit for the Army, but I am sorry to say I have marched a good many years even beyond that. It is a great opportunity, an opportunity that only comes once in many centuries to the children of men. For most generations sacrifice comes in drab and weariness of spirit. It comes to you today, and it comes today to us all, in the form of the glow and thrill of a great movement for liberty, that impels millions throughout Europe to the same noble end. It is a great war for the emancipation of Europe from the thraldom of a military caste which has thrown its shadows upon two generations of men, and is now plunging the world into a welter of bloodshed and death. Some have already given their lives. There are some who have given more than their own lives; they have given the lives of those who are dear to them. I honour their courage, and may God be their comfort and their strength. But their reward is at hand; those who have fallen have died consecrated deaths. They have taken their part in the making of a new Europe – a new world. I can see signs of its coming in the glare of the battlefield.

The people will gain more by this struggle in all lands than they comprehend at the present moment. It is true they will be free of the greatest menace to their freedom. That is not all. There is something infinitely greater and more enduring which is emerging already out of this great conflict – a new patriotism, richer, nobler, and more exalted than the old. I see amongst all classes, high and low, shedding themselves of selfishness, a new recognition that the honour of the country does not depend merely on the maintenance of its glory in the stricken field, but also in protecting its homes from distress. It is bringing a new outlook for all classes. The great flood of luxury and sloth which had submerged the land is receding, and a new Britain is appearing. We can see for the first time the fundamental things that matter in life, and that have been obscured from our vision by the tropical growth of prosperity.

May I tell you in a simple parable what I think this war is doing for us? I know a valley in North Wales, between the mountains and the sea. It is a beautiful valley, snug, comfortable, sheltered by the mountains from all the bitter blasts. But it is very enervating, and I remember how the boys were in the habit of climbing the hill above the village to have a glimpse of the great mountains in the distance, and to be stimulated and freshened by the breezes which came from the hilltops, and by the great spectacle of their grandeur. We have been living in a sheltered valley for generations. We have been too comfortable and too indulgent – many, perhaps, too selfish – and the stern hand of fate has scourged us to an elevation where we can see the great everlasting things that matter for a nation – the great peaks we had forgotten, of Honour, Duty, Patriotism, and, clad in glittering white, the great pinnacle of Sacrifice pointing like a rugged finger to Heaven. We shall descend into the valleys again; but as long as the men and women of this generation last, they will carry in their hearts the image of those great mountain peaks whose foundations are not shaken, though Europe rock and sway in the convulsions of a great war.

From the moment of his Queen's Hall speech, Lloyd George challenged Asquith, the prime minister. 'Unconsciously, perhaps even unwillingly, he was offering himself as the man who could run the war better,' says A. J. P. Taylor. Lloyd George became prime minister in 1916 and led Britain to victory.

•

BENITO MUSSOLINI
Milan, 25 November 1914

'You have not seen the last of me'

By 1914 Benito Mussolini (1883–1945) was the undisputed leader of the Italian Socialist Party. Now, however, he was under attack because he wanted Italy to join the fight against Germany. He argued that Italy could come into her own as a great European power only if she played a part in the war which would decide who was to rule the continent. As a result, Socialists in Milan had decreed his expulsion from the party.

According to an eyewitness, there was a furious crowd of at least three thousand in the Casa del Popolo and a 'diabolical tumult' and an atmosphere of deep hostility as Mussolini addressed his former comrades. The meeting closed with a resolution for the expulsion of the heretic.

Pale and visibly trembling, wearing a shabby black suit with trousers so short they scarcely reached his ankles, Mussolini stepped on to the platform. The jeering grew louder and coins and chairs were thrown on to the stage as he shouted back at the angry delegates.

You think to sign my death-warrant, but you are mistaken. Today you hate me, because in your heart of hearts you still love me.

But you have not seen the last of me! Twelve years of my party life are, or ought to be, a sufficient guarantee of my faith in Socialism. Socialism is something which takes root in the heart. What divides me from you now is not a small dispute, but a great question over which the whole of Socialism is divided . . .

Time will prove who is right and who is wrong in the formidable question which now confronts Socialism, and which it has never had to face before in the history of humanity, since never before has there been such a conflagration as exists today, in which millions of the proletariat are pitted one against the other. This war, which has much in common with those of the

Napoleonic period, is not an everyday event. Waterloo was fought in 1814; perhaps 1914 will see some other principles fall to the ground, will see the salvation of liberty, and the beginning of a new era in the world's history – and especially in the history of the proletariat, which at all critical moments has found me here with you in this same spot, just as it found me in the street.

But I tell you that from now onwards I shall never forgive nor have pity on anyone who in this momentous hour does not speak his mind for fear of being hissed or shouted down.

I shall neither forgive nor have pity on those who are purposely reticent, those who show themselves hypocrites and cowards. And you will find me still on your side. You must not think that the middle classes are enthusiastic about our intervention. They snarl and accuse us of temerity, and fear that the proletariat, once armed with bayonets, will use them for their own ends.

Do not think that in taking away my membership card you will be taking away my faith in the cause, or that you will prevent my still working for Socialism and revolution.

Mussolini served in the war, was invalided out of the army in 1917, and founded the Italian Fascist Party in Milan in 1919.

•

EMMELINE PANKHURST
London, 30 November 1914

'There are women who never thought to envy men their manhood'

When the First World War started, both Emmeline Pankhurst and her daughter Christabel (1880–1958) declared a truce and encouraged women to join the armed forces or to go into industry.

At a meeting organized by the Women's Social and Political Union at the Kingsway Hall, Emmeline appealed to men to fight for the right, arguing that women had shown an example of self-discipline by laying down their arms in the heat of the combat for enfranchisement.

One reason for the fall off in recruitment, she suggested, might be the many advertisements offering young men jobs that could well be given to women . . .

We women are the weaker sex. (*Laughter.*) We have been told that our hands are full with our domestic concerns and our maternal duties. In times of peace we have a good deal to say on that, but in times of war we are compelled to take men at their word. Men say to us, 'Leave the fighting to us. It does not become women to fight. We protect women. We fight for you. We shield you from the difficulties and ills of life.' Well, this is a testing time for men and women, too. We take you, gentlemen, at your word. We say it is the duty of men to do their best to redeem their pledges to women. We have not been allowed to prepare ourselves for self-defence because we are women. (*'Hear, hear'* . . .)

During the last few days I have been thanking God I was not a superior person (*laughter*), and that I had not a facile pen or a great sense of saturnine humour so that I must indulge in something parallel to Nero's fiddling while Rome burned. I cannot find words strong enough to condemn the people who at this moment are haggling with imperfect knowledge over diplomacy and what led to the war, and who is to blame for it. I will tell you who is to blame if things are not as they ought to be. It is you enfranchised men. It is the Bernard Shaws and all the rest of them. (*Cheers and laughter.*) They say the science of government is only suited to the male sex. Then when you face a great national peril and your very existence as a nation is at stake, they begin to argue in newspaper columns in order that our enemy may quote them on the walls of Belgium. If we have rulers who are wrongdoers, it is the fault of the people who made them rulers. When the war is over will be the time to settle these questions of diplomacy. Here we are in the war. Our honour, our reputation, our very existence are at stake. It is a time for people either to criticize helpfully or to hold their tongues. If we women, with our grievances against men, can hold our tongues, I think other people might do so. (*Cheers.*) If there are mistakes, the right and proper thing to do if you love your country is to try to get things put right quietly by influence . . .

The views I have always held I still hold. Nothing is more horrible than wars of aggression. But I believe that, whatever faults we have had in the past, now we are engaged in a righteous war. Much as I love peace, I believe there are times when it is right to fight. And I say to young men: There are women today who never thought to envy men their manhood, but who would, at least for this purpose, be glad to be men. (*Cheers.*)

Christabel Pankhurst staged her last demonstration in July 1915. Thirty thousand women marched through central London with the slogan: 'We demand the right to serve.' The demand was soon granted. Nearly 200,000 women entered government departments. A quarter of a million worked on the land. Half a million took over clerical work in offices. Women acted as conductors on buses.

Women eventually secured the vote in 1918. Emmeline lived in Canada from 1919 to 1926; Christabel spent most of her later life in Canada and America. She was made a Dame of the British Empire in 1936.

•

PATRICK PEARSE
Dublin, 1 August 1915

'*Ireland unfree shall never be at peace*'

Patrick Pearse (1879–1916) was a founder member of the Irish Volunteers and was inducted into the Irish Republican Brotherhood in 1913. His panegyric at the graveside of O'Donovan Rossa was the apogee of his oratorical career and part of a carefully prepared campaign in the year leading up to the Easter Rising. O'Rossa, one of the most bitter but also most courageous of the old Fenians, had died after a long illness in America and was to be buried at Glasnevin Cemetery in Dublin. The funeral was arranged as a propaganda exercise and there were hundreds of thousands at Glasnevin.

It was Pearse's greatest test and he rose to the occasion with a speech which was his masterpiece. In his idealization of Rossa, Pearse sketched himself and heralded the approaching revolution. His peroration was open defiance of the British in Dublin Castle.

The souvenir of the funeral said: 'Cold, lifeless print cannot convey even an idea of the depth and intensity of feeling in which his words were couched. Calm and deliberate, in soft yet thrilling accents, his oration was almost sublime. Here was no rhetoric, no mathematical oratory; it was the soul of a patriot breathing words of love and devotion, of hope and truth and courage, no threnody, but a paean of triumph such as might have come from out of the tomb by which we were . . .'

It has seemed right, before we turn away from this place in which we have laid the mortal remains of O'Donovan Rossa, that one among us should, in the name of all, speak the praise of that valiant man, and endeavour to formulate the thought and the hope that are in us as we stand around his grave. And if there is anything that makes it fitting that I, rather than some other, I rather than one of the grey-haired men who were young with him and shared in his labour and in his suffering, should speak here, it is perhaps that I may be taken as speaking on behalf of a new generation that has been rebaptized in the Fenian faith, and that has accepted the responsibility of carrying out the Fenian programme. I propose to you then that, here by the grave of this unrepentant Fenian, we renew our baptismal vows; that, here by the grave of this unconquered and unconquerable man, we ask of God, each one for himself, such unshakable purpose, such high and gallant courage, such unbreakable strength of soul as belonged to O'Donovan Rossa.

Deliberately here we avow ourselves, as he avowed himself in the dock, Irishmen of one allegiance only. We of the Irish Volunteers, and you others who are associated with us in today's task and duty, are bound together and must stand together henceforth in brotherly union for the achievement of the freedom of Ireland. And we know only one definition of freedom: it is Tone's definition, it is Mitchel's definition, it is Rossa's definition. Let no man blaspheme the cause that the dead generations of

Ireland served by giving it any other name and definition than their name and their definition.

We stand at Rossa's grave not in sadness but rather in exaltation of spirit that it has been given to us to come thus into so close a communion with that brave and splendid Gael. Splendid and holy causes are served by men who are themselves splendid and holy. O'Donovan Rossa was splendid in the proud manhood of him, splendid in the heroic grace of him, splendid in the Gaelic strength and clarity and truth of him. And all that splendour and pride and strength was compatible with a humility and a simplicity of devotion to Ireland, to all that was olden and beautiful and Gaelic in Ireland, the holiness and simplicity of patriotism of a Michael O'Clery or of an Eoghan O'Growney. The clear true eyes of this man almost alone in his day visioned Ireland as we of today would surely have her: not free merely, but Gaelic as well; not Gaelic merely, but free as well.

In a closer spiritual communion with him now than ever before or perhaps ever again, in a spiritual communion with those of his day, living and dead, who suffered with him in English prisons, in communion of spirit too with our own dear comrades who suffer in English prisons today, and speaking on their behalf as well as our own, we pledge to Ireland our love, and we pledge to English rule in Ireland our hate. This is a place of peace, sacred to the dead, where men should speak with all charity and with all restraint; but I hold it a Christian thing, as O'Donovan Rossa held it, to hate evil, to hate untruth, to hate oppression, and, hating them, to strive to overthrow them. Our foes are strong and wise and wary but, strong and wise and wary as they are, they cannot undo the miracles of God who ripens in the hearts of young men the seeds sown by the young men of a former generation. And the seeds sown by the young men of '65 and '67 are coming to their miraculous ripening today. Rulers and Defenders of Realms had need to be wary if they would guard against such processes. Life springs from death; and from the graves of patriot men and women spring living nations. The Defenders of this Realm have worked well in secret and in the open. They think that they have pacified

Ireland. They think that they have purchased half of us and intimidated the other half. They think that they have foreseen everything, think that they have provided against everything; but the fools, the fools, the fools! – they have left us our Fenian dead, and while Ireland holds these graves, Ireland unfree shall never be at peace.

•

MAHATMA GANDHI
Benares, 4 February 1916

'There is no salvation for India'

As a barrister in South Africa from 1907 to 1914, Mohandas Gandhi conducted passive-resistance campaigns of protest at the Transvaal Government's discrimination against its Indian minority settlers. He returned to India in 1915 and gradually emerged as leader of the Congress movement.

In September 1915, Mrs Annie Besant, a remarkable Englishwoman who had made India her home, announced the formation of a Home Rule League. Earlier, in 1892, she started a school in Benares which was expanded into the Hindu University Central College in 1916. An illustrious gathering of notables was there for the opening ceremonies, including the Viceroy and many bejewelled maharajas, maharanis, rajas and high officials in all their dazzling panoply.

Gandhi addressed the meeting on 4 February. As the audience grew unruly and arguments broke out, it broke up before he could finish. 'India had never heard such a forthright, unvarnished speech,' says Louis Fisher, Gandhi's biographer. 'Gandhi spared no one, least of all those present. In 1916 the ear [of India] began to catch the voice of a man who was courageous and indiscreet, a little man who lived like a poor man and defended the poor to the face of the rich, a holy man in an ashram.'

Our language is the reflection of ourselves, and if you tell me that our languages are too poor to express the best thought, then I say that the sooner we are wiped out of existence the better for us. Is there a man who dreams that English can ever become the national language of India? (*Cries of 'Never'.*) Why this handicap on the nation? Just consider for one moment what an unequal race our lads have to run with every English lad. I had the privilege of a close conversation with some Poona professors. They assured me that every Indian youth, because he reached his knowledge through the English language, lost at least six precious years of life. Multiply that by the number of students turned out by our schools and colleges, and find out for yourselves how many thousand years have been lost to the nation. The charge against us is that we have no initiative. How can we have any if we are to devote the precious years of our life to the mastery of a foreign tongue? . . .

The only education we receive is English education. Surely we must show something for it. But suppose that we had been receiving during the past fifty years education through our vernaculars, what should we have today? We should have today a free India, we should have our educated men, not as if they were foreigners in their own land but speaking to the heart of the nation; they would be working amongst the poorest of the poor, and whatever they would have gained during the past fifty years would be a heritage for the nation. (*Applause* . . .)

His Highness the Maharajah who presided yesterday over our deliberations spoke about the poverty of India . . . But what did we witness in the great pandal in which the foundation ceremony was performed by the Viceroy. Certainly a most gorgeous show, an exhibition of jewellery which made a splendid feast for the eyes of the greatest jeweller who chose to come from Paris. I compare with the richly bedecked noblemen the millions of the poor. And I feel like saying to these noblemen, 'There is no salvation for India unless you strip yourselves of this jewellery and hold it in trust for your countrymen in India.' ('*Hear, hear*' *and applause.*)

Sir, whenever I hear of a great palace rising in any great city of India, be it in British India or be it in India which is ruled by our great chiefs, I become jealous at once, and I say, 'Oh, it is the money that has come from the agriculturists.' Over seventy-five per cent of the population are agriculturists and Mr Higginbotham told us last night in his own felicitous language that they are the men who grow two blades of grass in the place of one. But there cannot be much spirit of self-government about us if we take away or allow others to take away from them almost the whole of the results of their labour. Our salvation can only come through the farmer. Neither the lawyers, nor the doctors, not the rich landlords are going to secure it . . .

I was talking the other day to a member of the much-abused civil service. I have not very much in common with the members of that service, but I could not help admiring the manner in which he was speaking to me. He said: 'Mr Gandhi, do you for one moment suppose that all we, civil servants, are a bad lot, that we want to oppress the people whom we have come to govern?' 'No,' I said. 'Then if you get an opportunity put in a word for the much-abused civil service?' And I am here to put in that word. Yes, many members of the Indian civil service are most decidedly overbearing; they are tyrannical, at times thoughtless . . .

But what does that signify? They were gentlemen before they came here, and if they have lost some of the moral fibre, it is a reflection upon ourselves. (*Cries of 'No'.*) Just think out for yourselves, if a man who was good yesterday has become bad after having come in contact with me, is he responsible that he has deteriorated or am I? The atmosphere of sycophancy and falsity that surrounds them on their coming to India demoralizes them, as it would many of us. It is well to take the blame sometimes. If we are to receive self-government, we shall have to take it. We shall never be granted self-government. Look at the history of the British Empire and the British nation; freedom-loving as it is, it will not be a party to give freedom to a people who will not take it themselves.

•

PROCLAMATION OF THE IRISH REPUBLIC
*The Provisional Government of the Irish Republic
to the People of Ireland*
Dublin, 24 April 1916

'Ireland summons her children to the flag'

*The Easter Rising, a rebellion in Dublin on 24–29 April 1916 seeking immedi-
ate independence for Ireland, was led by Patrick Pearse and James Connolly of
Sinn Féin. The proclamation was mainly the work of Pearse, who proclaimed
a provisional government of the Irish Republic, as its president, from the
General Post Office which served as the rebel headquarters.*

Irishmen and Irishwomen: In the name of God and of the dead
generations from which she receives her old tradition of nationhood, Ireland, through us, summons her children to her flag and
strikes for her freedom.

Having organized and trained her manhood through her secret
revolutionary organization, the Irish Republican Brotherhood, and
through her open military organizations, the Irish Volunteers, and
the Irish Citizen Army, having patiently perfected her discipline,
having resolutely waited for the right moment to reveal itself, she
now seizes that moment, and, supported by her exiled children in
America and by gallant allies in Europe, but relying in the first on
her own strength, she strikes in full confidence of victory.

We declare the right of the people of Ireland to the ownership
of Ireland, and to the unfettered control of Irish destinies, to be
sovereign and indefeasible. The long usurpation of that right by a
foreign people and government has not extinguished the right,
nor can it ever be extinguished except by the destruction of the
Irish people. In every generation the Irish people have asserted
their right to national freedom and sovereignty; six times during
the past three hundred years they have asserted it in arms. Standing
on that fundamental right and again asserting it in arms in the face

of the world, we hereby proclaim the Irish republic as a sovereign independent state, and we pledge our lives and the lives of our comrades-in-arms to the cause of its freedom, of its welfare, and of its exaltation among the nations.

The Irish republic is entitled to, and hereby claims, the allegiance of every Irishman and Irishwoman. The republic guarantees religious and civil liberty, equal rights and equal opportunities to all its citizens, and declares its resolve to pursue the happiness and prosperity of the whole nation and of all its parts, cherishing all the children of the nation equally, and oblivious of the differences carefully fostered by an alien government, which have divided a minority from the majority in the past.

Until our arms have brought the opportune moment for the establishment of a permanent national government, representative of the whole people of Ireland, and elected by the suffrages of all her men and women, the Provisional Government, hereby constituted, will administer the civil and military affairs of the republic in trust for the people. We place the cause of the Irish republic under the protection of the Most High God, whose blessing we invoke upon our arms, and we pray that no one who serves that cause will dishonour it by cowardice, inhumanity, or rapine. In this supreme hour the Irish nation must, by its valour and discipline, and by the readiness of its children to sacrifice themselves for the common good, prove itself worthy of the august destiny to which it is called.

Signed on behalf of the provisional government,

Thomas J. Clarke, Sean MacDiarmada, Thomas MacDonagh, P. H. Pearse, Eamonn Ceannt, James Connolly, Joseph Plunkett

Pearse, Connolly and twelve other rebel leaders were court-martialled and executed. Pearse was shot at 3.30 a.m. on 3 May. In his speech from the dock, eloquent even in the face of death, Pearse told his captors: 'We seem to have lost. We have not lost. To refuse to fight would have been to lose; to fight is to win. We have kept faith with the past and handed on a tradition to the future ... You cannot conquer Ireland. You cannot extinguish the Irish passion for freedom. If our deed has not been sufficient to win freedom, then our children will win it by a better deed.'

•

ROGER CASEMENT
London, 1916

'*In Ireland alone, in this twentieth century, is loyalty held to be a crime*'

On his retirement from the British consular service in 1911, Roger Casement became a fervent Irish nationalist. At the outbreak of the First World War, he sought to recruit Irish prisoners of war for the German army. He went to Berlin to secure German aid for Irish independence but the Germans preferred the British Empire to a free Ireland and considered Casement a nuisance.

On the eve of the Easter Rising, he travelled to Ireland in a German U-boat to warn that there would be no German aid and that a rising would not succeed. He landed near Tralee but was quickly arrested by the British. He was taken to London and tried for high treason at the Old Bailey by an English Lord Chief Justice and an English jury. He was refused permission to conduct his own case and was allowed to speak only after the jury found him guilty.

His defiance in the dock and the powerful oratory of his defence explains why, for the Irish, he remains a patriot martyr. The speech has been described (by William Blunt) as the finest document in patriotic literature, finer than anything in Plutarch or elsewhere in Pagan literature. Years later Jawaharlal Nehru, leader of the Indian movement for independence from the British, said it seemed to point out exactly how a subject nation should feel.

My Lord Chief Justice, as I wish my words to reach a much wider audience than I see before me here, I intend to read all that I propose to say. What I shall read now is something I wrote more than twenty days ago. I may say, my lord, at once, that I protest against the jurisdiction of this court in my case on this charge, and the argument, that I am now going to read, is addressed not to this court, but to my own countrymen.

There is an objection, possibly not good in law, but surely good on moral grounds, against the application to me here of this old English statute, 565 years old, that seeks to deprive an Irishman today of life and honour, not for 'adhering to the King's enemies', but for adhering to his own people.

When this statute was passed, in 1351, what was the state of men's minds on the question of a far higher allegiance – that of a man to God and His kingdom? The law of that day did not permit a man to forsake his Church, or deny his God, save with his life. The 'heretic', then, had the same doom as the 'traitor'.

Today a man may forswear God and His heavenly kingdom, without fear or penalty – all earlier statutes having gone the way of Nero's edicts against the Christians, but that constitutional phantom 'the king' can still dig up from the dungeons and torture-chambers of the Dark Ages a law that takes a man's life and limb for an exercise of conscience.

If true religion rests on love, it is equally true that loyalty rests on love. The law that I am charged under has no parentage in love, and claims the allegiance of today on the ignorance and blindness of the past.

I am being tried, in truth, not by my peers of the live present, but by the fears of the dead past; not by the civilization of the twentieth century, but by the brutality of the fourteenth; not even by a statute framed in the language of the land that tries me, but emitted in the language of an enemy land – so antiquated is the law that must be sought today to slay an Irishman, whose offence is that he puts Ireland first.

Loyalty is a sentiment, not a law. It rests on love, not on restraint. The government of Ireland by England rests on restraint, and not on law; and since it demands no love, it can evoke no loyalty . . .

Judicial assassination today is reserved only for one race of the king's subjects – for Irishmen, for those who cannot forget their allegiance to the realm of Ireland. The kings of England, as such, had no rights in Ireland up to the time of Henry VIII, save such as rested on compact and mutual obligation entered into between them and certain princes, chiefs, and lords of Ireland. This form of legal right, such as it was, gave no king of England lawful power to impeach an Irishman for high treason under this statute of King Edward III of England until an Irish Act, known as Poyning's Law, the tenth of Henry VII, was passed in 1494 at Drogheda, by the Parliament of the Pale in Ireland, and enacted as law in that part of Ireland. But, if by Poyning's Law an Irishman of the Pale could be indicted for high treason under this Act, he could be indicted in only one way, and before one tribunal – by the laws of the Realm of Ireland and in Ireland. The very law of Poyning, which, I believe, applies this statute of Edward III to Ireland, enacts also for the Irishman's defence 'all these laws by which England claims her liberty'.

And what is the fundamental charter of an Englishman's liberty? That he shall be tried by his peers. With all respect, I assert this court is to me, an Irishman, charged with this offence, a foreign court – this jury is for me, an Irishman, not a jury of my peers to try me on this vital issue, for it is patent to every man of conscience that I have a right, an indefeasible right, if tried at all, under this statute of high treason, to be tried in Ireland, before an Irish court and by an Irish jury. This court, this jury, the public opinion of this country, England, cannot but be prejudiced in varying degrees against me, most of all in time of war. I did not land in England. I landed in Ireland. It was to Ireland I came; to Ireland I wanted to come; and the last place I desired to land was in England.

But for the Attorney-General of England there is only 'England'; there is no Ireland; there is only the law of England, no right of Ireland; the liberty of Ireland and of an Irishman is to be judged by the power of England. Yet for me, the Irish outlaw, there is a land of Ireland, a right of Ireland, and a charter for all Irishmen to appeal to, in the last resort, a charter, that even the very statutes of England itself cannot deprive us of – nay more, a charter that Englishmen themselves assert as the fundamental bond of law that connects the two kingdoms. This charge of high treason involves a moral responsibility, as the very terms of the indictment against myself recite, inasmuch as I committed the acts

I am charged with to the 'evil example of others in like case'. What was the evil example I set to others in the like case, and who were these others? The 'evil example' charged is that I asserted the right of my own country and the 'others' I appealed to, to aid my endeavour, were my own countrymen. The example was given, not to Englishmen, but to Irishmen, and the 'like case' can never arise in England, but only in Ireland. To Englishmen I set no evil example, for I made no appeal to them. I asked no Englishman to help me. I asked Irishmen to fight for their rights. The 'evil example' was only to other Irishmen, who might come after me, and in 'like case' seek to do as I did. How, then, since neither my example, nor my appeal was addressed to Englishmen, can I be rightfully tried by them?

If I did wrong in making that appeal to Irishmen to join with me in an effort to fight for Ireland, it is by Irishmen, and by them alone, I can be rightfully judged. From this court and its jurisdiction I appeal to those I am alleged to have wronged, and to those I am alleged to have injured by my 'evil example' and claim that they alone are competent to decide my guilt or innocence. If they find me guilty, the statute may affix the penalty, but the statute does not override or annul my right to seek judgement at their hands.

This is so fundamental a right, so natural a right, so obvious a right, that it is clear that the Crown were aware of it when they brought me by force and by stealth from Ireland to this country. It was not I who landed in England, but the Crown who dragged me here, away from my own country to which I had returned with a price upon my head, away from my own countrymen whose loyalty is not in doubt, and safe from the judgement of my peers whose judgement I do not shrink from. I admit no other judgement but theirs. I accept no verdict save at their hands.

I assert from this dock that I am being tried here, not because it is just, but because it is unjust. Place me before a jury of my own countrymen, be it Protestant or Catholic, Unionist or Nationalist, Sinn Féineach or Orangemen, and I shall accept the verdict, and bow to the statute and all its penalties. But I shall accept no meaner finding against me, than that of those, whose loyalty I have endangered by my example, and to whom alone I made appeal. If they adjudge me guilty, then guilty I am. It is not I who am afraid of their verdict – it is the Crown. If this is not so, why fear the test? I fear it not. I demand it as my right.

This is the condemnation of English rule, of English-made law, of English government in Ireland, that it dare not rest on the will of the Irish people, but exists in defiance of their will: that it is a rule, derived not from right, but from conquest.

Conquest, my Lord, gives no title; and, if it exists over the body, it fails over the mind. It can exert no empire over men's reason and judgement and affections; and it is from this law of conquest without title to the reason, judgement, and affection of my own countrymen that I appeal.

I can answer for my own acts and speeches. While one English party was responsible for preaching a doctrine of hatred, designed to bring about civil war in Ireland, the other, and that the party in power, took no active steps to restrain a propaganda that found its advocates in the Army, Navy, and Privy Council – in the House of Parliament, and in the State Church – a propaganda the methods of whose expression were so 'grossly illegal and utterly unconstitutional' that even the Lord Chancellor of England could find only words and no repressive action to apply to them. Since lawlessness sat in high places in England, and laughed at the law as at the custodians of the law, what wonder was it that Irishmen should refuse to accept the verbal protestations of an English Lord Chancellor as a sufficient safeguard for their lives and liberties? I know not how all my colleagues on the Volunteer Committee in Dublin reviewed the growing menace, but those with whom I was in closest cooperation redoubled, in face of these threats from without, our efforts to unite all Irishmen from within. Our appeals were made to Protestant and Unionist as much almost as to Catholic and Nationalist Irishmen. We hoped that, by the exhibition of affection and goodwill on our part toward our political opponents in Ireland, we should yet succeed in winning them from the side of an English party whose sole interest in our country lay in its oppression in the past, and in the present in its degradation to the mean and narrow needs of their political animosities. It is true that they based their actions, so they averred, on 'ears for the empire', and on a very diffuse loyalty that took in all the peoples of the empire, save only the Irish. That blessed word *empire* that bears so paradoxical resemblance to charity! For if charity begins at home, *empire* begins in other men's homes, and both may cover a multitude of sins. I, for one, was determined that Ireland was much more to me than *empire*, and, if charity begins at home, so must loyalty. Since arms were so necessary to make our organization a reality, and to give to the minds of Irishmen, menaced with the most outrageous threats, a sense of security, it was our bounden duty to get arms before all else. I decided, with this end in view, to go to America, with surely a better right to appeal to Irishmen there for help in a hour of great national trial, than those envoys of *empire* could assert for their weekend descents on Ireland, or their appeals to Germany.

If, as the right honourable gentleman, the present Attorney-General, asserted in a speech at Manchester, Nationalists would neither fight for Home Rule nor pay for it, it was our duty to show him that we knew how to do both. Within a few weeks of my arrival in the United States, the fund that had been opened to secure arms for the Volunteers of Ireland amounted to many thousands of pounds. In every case the money subscribed, whether it came from the purse of the wealthy man, or from the still readier pocket of the poor man, was Irish gold.

We have been told, we have been asked to hope, that after this war Ireland will get Home Rule, as a reward for the lifeblood shed in a cause which, whomever else its success may benefit, can surely not benefit Ireland. And what will Home Rule be in return for what its vague promise has taken, and still hopes to take away from Ireland? It is not necessary to climb the painful stairs of Irish History – that treadmill of a nation, whose labours are as vain for her own uplifting as the convict's exertions are for his redemption, to review the long list of British promises made only to be broken – of Irish hopes, raised only to be dashed to the ground. Home Rule, when it comes, if come it does, will find an Ireland drained of all that is vital to its very existence unless it be that unquenchable hope we build on the graves of the dead. We are told that if Irishmen go by the thousand to die, not for Ireland, but for Flanders, for Belgium, for a patch of sand in the deserts of Mesopotamia, or a rocky trench on the heights of Gallipoli, they are winning self-government for Ireland. But if they dare to lay down their lives on their native soil, if they dare to dream even that freedom can be won only at home by men resolved to fight for it there, then they are traitors to their country, and their dream and their deaths are phases of a dishonourable phantasy.

But history is not so recorded in other lands. In Ireland alone, in this twentieth century, is loyalty held to be a crime. If loyalty be something less than love and more than law, then we have had enough of such loyalty for Ireland and Irishmen. If we are to be indicted as criminals, to be shot as murderers, to be imprisoned as convicts, because our offence is that we love Ireland more than we value our lives, then I do not know what virtue resides in any offer of self-government held out to brave men on such terms. Self-government is our right, a thing born in us at birth, a thing no more to be doled out to us, or withheld from us, by another people than the right to life itself – than the right to feel the sun, or smell the flowers, or to love our kind. It is only from the convict these things are withheld, for crime committed and proven – and Ireland, that has wronged no man, has injured no land, that has sought no dominion over others – Ireland is being treated today among the nations of the world as if she were a convicted criminal. If it be treason to fight against such an unnatural fate as this, then I am proud to be a rebel, and shall cling to my 'rebellion' with the last drop of my blood. If there be no right of rebellion against the state of things that no savage tribe would endure without resistance, then I am sure that it is better for men to fight and die without right than to live in such a state of right as this. Where all your rights have become only an accumulated wrong, where men must beg with bated breath for leave to subsist in their own land, to think their own thoughts, to sing their own songs, to gather the fruits of their own labours, and, even while they beg, to see things inexorably withdrawn from them – then, surely, it is a braver, a saner and truer thing to be a rebel, in act and in deed, against such circumstances as these, than to tamely accept it, as the natural lot of men.

Casement was condemned to death and hanged. His so-called Black Diaries containing homosexual passages were circulated by British agents to discredit him and discourage any movement for a reprieve. Thanks to Casement, Sinn Féin got the credit for the Easter Rising – and the independence of Ireland triumphed when he was hanged.

●

WOODROW WILSON
Washington, DC, 2 April 1917

'The world must be made safe for democracy'

When the First World War broke out, Woodrow Wilson immediately issued a proclamation of neutrality. Yet real neutrality was impossible for a nation so powerful as America, especially after the Lusitania *with her 1,198 passengers, including 128 Americans, was sunk by a German torpedo in 1915. American opinion was appalled.*

Wilson sent strong notes of protest to Berlin and made a memorable speech in which he proclaimed: 'There is no such thing as a man being too proud to fight. There is no such thing as a nation being so right that it does not need to convince others by force that it is right.'

In 1916 Wilson was re-elected president by a slender majority. He directed a note to the belligerent governments offering an honourable excuse to start negotiations. After this tactic failed, he delivered an address to Congress on 'Peace without victory'. The announcement that Germany was resorting to unrestricted submarine warfare – that all Allied or neutral vessels in the Atlantic would be torpedoed without warning – abruptly destroyed Wilson's dream.

One month after his second inaugural address, he went before a joint session of Congress to ask for a declaration that a state of war existed between Germany and the United States – and got what he wanted by a nearly unanimous vote on 6 April, Good Friday.

With a profound sense of the solemn and even tragical character of the step I am taking and of the grave responsibilities which it involves, but in unhesitating obedience to what I deem my constitutional duty, I advise that the Congress declare the recent course of the imperial German government to be in fact nothing less than war against the government and people of the United States; that it formally accept the status of belligerent which has thus been thrust upon it; and that it take immediate steps not only to put the country in a more thorough state of defence, but also to exert all its power and employ all its resources to bring the government of the German Empire to terms and end the war . . .

We are accepting this challenge of hostile purpose because we know that in such a government, following such methods, we can never have a friend; and that in the presence of its organized power, always lying in wait to accomplish we know not what purpose, there can be no assured security for the democratic governments of the world. We are now about to accept the gage of battle with this natural foe to liberty and shall, if necessary, spend the whole force of the nation to check and nullify its pretensions and its power. We are glad, now that we see the facts with no veil of false pretence about them, to fight thus for the ultimate peace of the world and for the liberation of its peoples, the German peoples included: for the rights of nations great and small and the privilege of men everywhere to choose their way of life and of obedience. The world must be made safe for democracy. Its peace must be planted upon the tested foundations of political liberty. We have no selfish ends to serve. We desire no conquest, no dominion. We seek no indemnities for ourselves, no material compensation for the sacrifices we shall freely make. We are but one of the champions of the rights of mankind. We shall be satisfied when those rights have been made as secure as the faith and the freedom of nations can make them.

Just because we fight without rancor and without selfish object, seeking nothing for ourselves but what we shall wish to share with all free peoples, we shall, I feel confident, conduct our operations as belligerents without passion and ourselves observe with proud punctilio the principles of right and of fair play we profess to be fighting for . . .

It will be all the easier for us to conduct ourselves as belligerents in a high spirit of right and fairness because we act without animus, not in enmity toward a people or with the desire to bring any injury or disadvantage upon them, but only in armed opposition to an irresponsible government which has thrown aside all considerations of humanity and of right and is running amuck. We are, let me say again, the sincere friends of the German people, and shall desire nothing so much as the early re-establishment of intimate relations of mutual advantage between us – however hard it may be for them, for the time being, to believe that this is spoken from our hearts. We have borne with their present government through all these bitter months because of that friendship – exercising a patience and forbearance which would otherwise have been impossible. We shall, happily, still have an opportunity to prove that friendship in our daily attitude and actions toward the millions of men and women of German birth and native sympathy who live amongst us and share our life, and we shall be proud to prove it toward all who are in fact loyal to their neighbors and to the government in the hour of test. They are, most of them, as true and loyal Americans as if they had never known any other fealty or allegiance. They will be prompt to stand with us in rebuking and restraining the few who may be of a different mind and purpose. If there should be disloyalty, it will be dealt with with a firm hand of stern repression; but, if it lifts its head at all, it will lift it only here and there and without countenance except from a lawless and malignant few.

It is a distressing and oppressive duty, gentlemen of the Congress, which I have performed in thus addressing you. There are, it may be, many months of fiery trial and sacrifice ahead of us. It is a fearful thing to lead this great peaceful people into war, into the most terrible and disastrous of all wars, civilization itself seeming to be in the balance. But the right is more precious than peace, and we shall fight for the things which we have always carried nearest our hearts – for democracy, for the right of those who submit to authority to have a voice in their own governments, for the dominion of right by such a concert of free peoples as shall bring peace and safety to all nations and make the world itself at last free. To such a task we can dedicate our lives and our fortunes, everything that we are and everything that we have, with the pride of those who know that the day has come when America is privileged to spend her blood and her might for the principles that gave her birth and happiness and the peace which she has treasured. God helping her, she can do no other.

Wilson's address set the United States on a new course; armed neutrality was impracticable and the world must be made safe for democracy. He was rewarded with tumultuous cheers. They were no comfort. 'My message today was a message of death for our young men,' he said afterwards. 'How strange it seems to applaud that.'

•

V. I. LENIN
Petrograd, 15 April 1917

'A new phase in the history of Russia begins'

After the Russian revolution of March 1917, Lenin travelled back to Petrograd from Switzerland, passing through Germany in a sealed train provided by the German general staff, who counted on the Bolsheviks spreading disaffection among the Russian soldiers.

An honour guard of Kronstadt sailors in striped jerseys and red pompon hats met Lenin at the Finland Station. A brass band played the 'Marseillaise'. Lenin was taken to the imperial waiting-room where he addressed a dense crowd and immediately snubbed any hope that the Bolsheviks would close democratic ranks with the Mensheviks. He appealed directly for civil war and international revolution.

Dear comrades, soldiers, sailors and workers! I am happy to greet in your persons the victorious Russian revolution, and greet you as the vanguard of the worldwide proletarian army ... The piratical imperialist war is the beginning of civil war throughout Europe ... The hour is not far distant when the peoples will turn their arms against their own capitalist exploiters ... The worldwide socialist revolution has already dawned ... Germany is seething ... Any day now the whole of European capitalism may crash. The Russian revolution accomplished by you has prepared the way and opened a new epoch. Long live the worldwide socialist revolution!

As Lenin left the room, an officer on the platform outside saluted him and a detachment of soldiers with bayonets stood to attention. A great roar of a cheer went up from the revolutionary workers and sailors of Petrograd who had come to greet him. The sailors presented arms and their commander reported to Lenin for duty. They wanted him to speak, it was whispered. Lenin walked a few paces and took off his bowler hat.

I don't know yet whether you agree with the Provisional Government. But I know very well that when they give you sweet speeches and make many promises they are deceiving you and the whole Russian people. The people need peace. The people need bread and land. And they give you war, hunger, no food, and the land remains with the landowners. Sailors, comrades, you must fight for the revolution, fight to the end.

Lenin remained in Petrograd until 18 July, when the failure of an abortive Soviet coup d'état forced him to escape again to Finland. He returned to Petrograd on 23 October and from his headquarters in the Smolny Institute led the rising which captured the government offices. The Bolshevik forces went into action on 25 October. The key points in the city were occupied. Members of the provisional *government were prisoners or fugitives. That afternoon, Lenin announced to a meeting of the Petrograd Soviet the triumph of 'the workers' and peasants' revolution'.*

Comrades, the workers' and peasants' revolution, about the necessity of which the Bolsheviks have always spoken, has been accomplished.

What is the significance of this workers' and peasants' revolution? Its significance is, first of all, that we shall have a Soviet government, our own organ of power, in which the bourgeoisie will have no share whatsoever. The oppressed masses will themselves create a power. The old state apparatus will be shattered to its foundations and a new administrative apparatus set up in the form of the Soviet organizations.

From now on, a new phase in the history of Russia begins, and this, the third Russian revolution, should in the end lead to the victory of socialism.

One of our urgent tasks is to put an immediate end to the war. It is clear to everybody that in order to end this war, which is closely bound up with the present capitalist system, capital itself must be fought.

We shall be helped in this by the world working-class movement, which is already beginning to develop in Italy, Britain and Germany.

The proposal we make to international democracy for a just and immediate peace will everywhere awaken an ardent response among the international proletarian masses. All the secret treaties must be immediately published in order to strengthen the confidence of the proletariat.

Within Russia a huge section of the peasantry have said that they have played long enough with the capitalists, and will now march with the workers. A single decree putting an end to landed proprietorship will win us the confidence of the peasants. The peasants will understand that the salvation of the peasantry lies only in an alliance with the workers. We shall institute genuine workers' control over production.

We have now learned to make a concerted effort. The revolution that has just been accomplished is evidence of this. We possess the strength of mass organization, which will overcome everything and lead the proletariat to the world revolution.

We must now set about building a proletarian socialist state in Russia.

Long live the world socialist revolution! (*Stormy applause.*)

That evening the second All-Russian Congress of Soviets proclaimed the transfer of all power throughout Russia to Soviets of Workers', Soldiers' and Peasants' Deputies. As Lenin stood at the reading-stand, he was greeted by a long-rolling ovation. When it finished, he said simply: 'We shall now proceed to construct the socialist order.' Again there was an overwhelming human roar. The congress adopted decrees on peace and on the land and approved the composition of the Council of People's Commissars – the first workers' and peasants' government.

Yet the Bolsheviks were massively defeated in the elections that followed. When the Constituent Assembly, the dream of Russia's revolutionaries and liberals for nearly a century, met in January 1918, it was dissolved by force.

The Bolsheviks seized power and went on, particularly under Lenin's successor Joseph Stalin, to construct one of the worst tyrannies of the twentieth century. 'Lenin and the party, the man and the instrument, were now indissolubly one,' says E. H. Carr. 'The foundations had been laid of the ascendancy in the party of the single leader.'

●

LEON TROTSKY
Moscow, 19 March 1918

'We need an army'

Trotsky was arrested as a revolutionary at the age of eighteen and sent to Siberia, where he escaped to join Lenin in London in 1902. He was back in St Petersburg in 1905, organizing the first Soviet. Again arrested and sent to Siberia, he escaped and spent several years as a revolutionary organizer in central Europe and beyond.

He returned to Petrograd (ex-St Petersburg) from America in May 1917 and was chairman of the Petrograd Soviet during the October revolution. At Brest-Litovsk his superb debating skills delayed the signing of the harsh treaty. On the outbreak of the civil war, he became Commissar for War and created the Red Army, even though he had no military experience.

Trotsky wrote in My Life: *'The problem was to make a clean sweep of the remains of the old army and in its place to build, under fire, a new army, whose plan was not to be discovered in any book.'*

Trotsky lived for almost two years in an armoured train which served as the mobile headquarters of the new army. By his ferocious energy, his insistence on military authority, his personal exposure in crucial battles and, above all, by stirring his followers to fight by the exaltation of his speeches and manifestos he created an army that finally defeated the Whites.

One of those speeches was given to the Moscow Soviet of Workers', Soldiers' and Peasants' Deputies.

Comrades! Our Soviet Socialist Republic needs a well-organized army.

In the world situation in which it has been the will of history to place us, amid the conditions of unprecedented difficulty that surround us, conditions that, again, are not of our making, we need to be strong ... We say, comrades, that Russia, exhausted and unarmed, will inevitably become the slave of international imperialism united against her if the international proletariat does not save her in time by its support, and if we ourselves do not organize our own defence ...

We must arm and fight, so as to ensure the mere possibility of carrying out our programme; and that, if the European proletariat fails to come to our aid in the fatal moment of our tragic lonely struggle, then, by remaining unarmed, we may perish altogether. We were the first to raise the flag of revolt amid this bloody and black night of imperialist war, and it is hard for us, sometimes almost beyond our strength, to fight against the iron ring of enemies that surrounds us. Is it surprising if we are not accomplishing all that we wanted to accomplish?

We need an army, which would give us powerful strength for the inevitable coming struggle with international imperialism. With the aid of this army we shall not only defend ourselves but shall be in a position to help the struggle of the international proletariat.

For there can be no doubt that, the more international imperialism grabs and strangles, the more passionate and terrible will be the wrath of the European worker-soldier who, emerging from the trenches, will find at home, as the result of his inhuman sufferings, his family reduced to poverty and hunger, and his country in a state of economic collapse.

Let those of little faith, yielding to weariness, no longer wish to hear of the revolutionary movement of the proletariat of other countries, of the victory of the world revolution: we declare that the moment of social explosion in all states is inevitably approaching, and we, to whom history has given victory sooner than the rest, with all the possibilities that follow from this, must be ready, at the first thunderclap of the world revolution, to bring armed help to our foreign brothers in revolt.

For proper organization of the army and, in particular for expedient utilization of the specialists, we need revolutionary discipline. We are introducing this with determination at the top, but we need with no less vigour to introduce it down below, arousing a sense of responsibility among the masses. When the people realize that discipline is being introduced now not in order to defend the moneybags of the bourgeoisie, not to restore the land to the landlords, but, on the contrary, in order to consolidate and defend all the conquests made by the revolution, they will approve even the strictest of measures aimed at the establishment of discipline. We must at all costs and at any price implant discipline in the Red Army – not the previous sort, the automatic discipline of the rod, but conscious, collective discipline, based on revolutionary enthusiasm and clear understanding by the workers and peasants of their duty to their own classes.

We shall not be halted by any difficulties. It may be that, in order to bring our cause to triumph and accomplish our great tasks, we shall have for a time to work not eight hours but ten and twelve hours a day. So what? We shall work twice as hard, we shall harness ourselves together, we shall go forward along the road of labour discipline and creative work. We did not say, and we do not say now, that everything will come by itself. No, the difficulties that face us are beyond counting. But we have proved to be richer in spirit, resources and forces than we ourselves had thought we were: and that is no small thing, that is the pledge of victory.

Let us work tirelessly, so that at the moment when the European proletariat rise up, we shall be able to go fully armed to their aid and, together with them, in a combined effort, overthrow for ever the power of capital! . . .

The Soviet Republic needs an army that will be able to fight and conquer.

It is the responsibility of the Soviet power to make sure that none of the separate institutions or units of the people's army are transformed into centres of counter-revolution, into instruments directed against the workers and peasants. Political control over the entire organization and life of the army will be entrusted to military commissars. The post of military commissar is one of the most responsible and most honourable in the Soviet Republic. The commissar will safeguard the closest internal bond between the Army and the Soviet regime as a whole. The commissar will incarnate the principle of revolutionary duty and indestructible discipline. The commissar will ensure, with the full force of his authority and power, immediate and unquestioning fulfilment of the operational and combat instructions issued by the military leaders.

These are the principles which the Government lays down as the basis for creating the Army: universal and obligatory military training in schools, factories and villages; immediate formation of firm cadres from the most self-sacrificing fighters; bringing in military commissars as guardians of the highest interests of the revolution and of socialism.

In the name of the Socialist Republic, the Council of People's Commissars calls upon all Soviets, all conscious workers and peasants, all honest citizens who are devoted to the people's cause, to redouble their efforts in the great work of safeguarding the independence and freedom of our country.

Liberated Russia will not be enslaved. It will arise and grow strong, it will cast out the beasts of prey, it will live in fraternal unity with the liberated peoples of all lands.

All that is needed is that, in these dark days of calamity affecting the whole people, all true sons of Revolutionary Russia shall have no thought, no desire, no commitment but the salvation of our blood-drained homeland.

Let there be no wavering, no doubts! Work, order, perseverance, discipline, self-sacrifice – and we shall triumph!

•

EUGENE V. DEBS
Cleveland, Ohio, 14 September 1918

'While there is a lower class, I am in it'

Eugene Victor Debs (1855–1926), founder of the American Railway Union, was one of the most attractive men thrown up by the American labour movement. When the ARU instituted a boycott of Pullman trains, the Attorney-General accused the union of acting in restraint of trade and sent troops against its strikers. The strike and boycott collapsed and Debs served six months in prison where he was converted to socialism.

He formed the Socialist Party of America in 1900 and stood as a candidate in the presidential elections of 1904, 1908 and 1912 when he polled 900,000 votes in the contest with Wilson, Roosevelt and Taft.

A bitter opponent of what he thought was a bloody war of the plutocracies in 1914–18, appalled by the campaign against freedom of speech which had shut down the German-language as well as the socialist press and determined to demonstrate what was happening to the constitutional guarantee of free speech, Debs made a speech in Canton denouncing the war.

At the federal court in Cleveland, he was found guilty of trying to obstruct the Conscription Act. The Wilson administration made sure that such wickedness would never go unpunished by pushing through Espionage and Sedition Acts. Debs remained in prison until Wilson left office, when he was pardoned by President Harding.

Before sentence was passed, Debs addressed the judge.

Your Honor, years ago I recognized my kinship with all living beings, and I made up my mind that I was not one bit better than the meanest on earth. I said then, and I say now, that while there is a lower class, I am in it, while there is a criminal element, I am of it, and while there is a soul in prison, I am not free . . .

Standing here this morning, I recall my boyhood. At fourteen I went to work in a railroad shop; at sixteen I was firing a freight engine on a railroad. I remember all the hardships and privations of that earlier day, and from that time until now my heart has been with the working class. I could have been in Congress long ago. I have preferred to go to prison . . .

I am thinking this morning of the men in the mills and factories; of the men in the mines and on the railroads. I am thinking of the women who for a paltry wage are compelled to work out their barren lives; of the little children who in this system are robbed of their childhood and in their tender years are seized in the remorseless grasp of Mammon and forced into the industrial dungeons, there to feed the monster machines while they themselves are being starved and stunted, body and soul. I see them dwarfed and diseased and their little lives broken and blasted because in this high noon of our twentieth-century Christian civilization money is still so much more important than the flesh and blood of childhood. In very truth gold is god today and rules with pitiless sway in the affairs of men.

In this country – the most favoured beneath the bending skies – we have vast areas of the richest and most fertile soil, material resources in inexhaustible abundance, the most marvelous productive machinery on earth, and millions of eager workers ready to apply their labour to that machinery to produce in abundance for every man, woman, and child – and if there are still vast numbers of our people who are the victims of poverty and whose lives are an unceasing struggle all the way from youth to old age, until at last death comes to their rescue and stills their aching hearts and lulls these hapless victims to dreamless sleep, it is not the fault of the Almighty: it cannot be charged to nature, but it is due entirely to the outgrown social system in which we live, that ought to be abolished not only in the interest of the toiling masses but in the higher interest of all humanity . . .

I believe, Your Honor, in common with all Socialists, that this nation ought to own and control its own industries. I believe, as all Socialists do, that all things that are jointly needed and used ought to be jointly owned – that industry, the basis of our social life, instead of being the private property of the few and operated for their enrichment, ought to be the common property of all, democratically administered in the interest of all . . .

I am opposing a social order in which it is possible for one man who does absolutely nothing that is useful to amass a fortune of hundreds of millions of dollars, while millions of men and women who work all the days of their lives secure barely enough for a wretched existence.

This order of things cannot always endure. I have registered my protest against it. I recognize the feebleness of my effort, but fortunately I am not alone. There are multiplied thousands of others who, like myself, have come to realize that before we may truly enjoy the blessings of civilized life, we must reorganize society upon a mutual and cooperative basis; and to this end we have organized a great economic and political movement that spreads over the face of all the earth.

There are today upwards of sixty millions of Socialists, loyal, devoted adherents to this cause, regardless of nationality, race, creed, colour, or sex. They are all making common cause. They are spreading with tireless energy the propaganda of the new social order. They are waiting, watching, and working hopefully through all the hours of the day and the night. They are still in a minority. But they have learned how to be patient and to bide their time. They feel – they know, indeed – that the time is coming, in spite of all opposition, all persecution, when this emancipating gospel will spread among all the peoples, and when this minority will become the triumphant majority and, sweeping into power, inaugurate the greatest social and economic change in history.

In that day we shall have the universal commonwealth – the harmonious cooperation of every nation with every other nation on earth . . .

Your Honour, I ask no mercy and I plead for no immunity. I realize that finally the right must prevail. I never so clearly comprehended as now the great struggle between the powers of greed and exploitation on the one hand and upon the other the rising hosts of industrial freedom and social justice.

I can see the dawn of the better day for humanity. The people are awakening. In due time they will and must come to their own . . .

I am now prepared to receive your sentence.

•

DAVID LLOYD GEORGE
Wolverhampton, 24 November 1918

'*A fit country for heroes to live in*'

When the war ended on 11 November 1918, Lloyd George assumed total command. Acclaimed as 'the man who won the war', he was the most dominant British political leader since Cromwell and won an overwhelming triumph at the general election in December 1918.

Britain had just emerged from a great peril, Lloyd George said in this speech at Wolverhampton within two weeks of the war's ending. But it was not an hour for boasting.

There is, as I never witnessed before, a new comradeship of classes, and I am glad, as an old political fighter – who has been hard hit and has been able to return the blows, always in a spirit of meekness – that we are approaching the new problems in a spirit of comradeship. Let us keep it as long as we can. I have no doubt human nature will prevail yet, but for the moment let us finish the task together, and when we have finished it, then let us play political football. You can afford to do it then. But the work is not over yet – the work of the nation, the work of the people, the work of those who have sacrificed. Let us work together first.

What is our task? To make Britain a fit country for heroes to live in. I am not using the word 'heroes' in any spirit of boastfulness, but in the spirit of humble recognition of the fact. I cannot think what these men have gone through. I have been there at the door of the furnace and witnessed it, but that is not being in it, and I saw them march into the furnace. There are millions of men who will come back. Let us make this a land fit for such men to live in. There is no time to lose. I want us to take advantage of this new spirit. Don't let us waste this victory merely in ringing joybells. Let us make victory the motive power to link the old land up in such measure that it will be nearer the sunshine than ever before, and that at any rate it will lift those who have been living in the dark places to a plateau where they will get the rays of the sun. We cannot undertake that without a new Parliament. Those of you who have been at the front have seen the star shells, how they light up the darkness and illuminate all the obscure places. The Great War has been like a gigantic star shell, flashing all over the land, illuminating the country and showing up the dark, deep places. We have seen places that we have never noticed before, and we mean to put these things right.

What is the first thing the Great War has shown us? The appalling waste of human material in the country. There is hardly any material placed by Providence in this country which is so much wasted as human life and human strength and human intellect – the most precious and irreplaceable material of all. I have previously said something about the figures of the recruiting officers. Those who were in charge of recruiting came to the conclusion that if the people of this country had lived under proper conditions, were properly fed and housed, had lived under healthy conditions – had lived their lives in their full vigour – you could have had a million more men available and fit to put into the army. It is not merely that. When life has not been lost, its vitality has been depressed. There are millions who are below par. You cannot keep even animals in their full vigour unless you give them good conditions. You cannot do it with men and women, and you cannot bring up children under bad conditions. There are millions of men's lives which have been lost as a result of the war, but there are millions more of maimed lives in the sense of undermined constitutions through atrocious social conditions in consequence of the terrors of this Great War. You must put that right. Put it at its lowest – trade, commerce and industry all suffer through it. A vigorous community of strong, healthy men and women is more valuable even from the commercial and industrial point of view than a community which is below par in consequence of bad conditions. Treat it if you like not as a human proposition, but as a business proposition. It is good business to see that the men, the women and the children of this country are brought up and sustained under conditions that will give strength and vigour to their frames, more penetration and endurance to their intelligence, and more spirit and heart than ever to face the problems of life which will always be problems that will require fighting right from the cradle to the tomb. That is the first problem. One of the ways of dealing with that is, of course, to deal with housing conditions. Slums are not fit homes for the men who have won this war or for their children. They are not fit nurseries for the children who are to make an Imperial race, and there must be no patching up. This problem has got to be undertaken in a way never undertaken before, as a great national charge and duty. The housing of the people must be a national concern.

•

HENRY CABOT LODGE
Washington, DC, 12 August 1919

'American I was born'

Senator Lodge, Senate majority leader and chairman of the Foreign Relations Committee, was the principal critic of Woodrow Wilson as he attempted to sell the League of Nations to Americans reared on George Washington's warning that the United States should stand aloof from permanent alliances.

He disliked Wilson, believed that America should play an important role in world affairs, and needed to shape a strategy that all Republicans – both isolationists and internationalists – could accept. He argued, therefore, that the League should be accepted with 'reservations' which, by limiting American obligations, would make it impossible for the League or any of its members to involve the nation in important international commitments without the consent of Congress.

Lodge's arguments in 1919, particularly about national sovereignty, were persuasive twenty-five years later when the United Nations was established. His influence can be especially detected in the veto granted to the great powers in the UN Security Council.

His speech on 12 August 1919 was Lodge's first statement of his position in the Senate. He prepared for the occasion with great care, delivered the speech devoid of emphasis or accentuation, rarely raised his eyes from his manuscript – but his words unleashed a storm of applause from the galleries and it was minutes before order was restored.

The independence of the United States is not only more precious to ourselves but to the world than any single possession. Look at the United States today. We have made mistakes in the past. We have had shortcomings. We shall make mistakes in the future and fall short of our own best hopes. But none the less is there any country today on the face of the earth which can compare with this in ordered liberty, in peace, and in the largest freedom? I feel that I can say this without being accused of undue boastfulness, for it is the simple fact, and in making this treaty and taking on these obligations all that we do is in a spirit of unselfishness and in a desire for the good of mankind. But it is well to remember that we are dealing with nations every one of which has a direct individual interest to serve, and there is grave danger in an unshared idealism. Contrast the United States with any country on the face of the earth today and ask yourself whether the situation of the United States is not the best to be found. I will go as far as anyone in world service, but the first step to world service is the maintenance of the United States.

You may call me selfish if you will, conservative or reactionary, or use any other harsh adjective you see fit to apply, but an American I was born, an American I have remained all my life. I can never be anything else but an American, and I must think of the United States first, and when I think of the United States first in an arrangement like this I am thinking of what is best for the world, for if the United States fails the best hopes of mankind fail with it. I have never had but one allegiance – I cannot divide it now. I have loved but one flag and I cannot share that devotion and give affection to the mongrel banner invented for a league. Internationalism, illustrated by the Bolshevik and by the men to whom all countries are alike provided they can make money out of them, is to me repulsive. National I must remain, and in that way I like all other Americans can render the amplest service to the world. The United States is the world's best hope, but if you fetter her in the interests and quarrels of other nations, if you tangle her in the intrigues of Europe, you will destroy her power for good and endanger her very existence. Leave her to march freely through the centuries to come as in the years that have gone. Strong, generous, and confident, she has nobly served mankind. Beware how you trifle with your marvelous inheritance, this great land of ordered liberty, for if we stumble and fall freedom and civilization everywhere will go down in ruin.

We are told that we shall 'break the heart of the world' if we do not take this league just as it stands. I fear that the hearts of the vast majority of mankind would beat on strongly and steadily and without any quickening if the league were to perish altogether. If it should be effectively and beneficiently changed the people who would lie awake in sorrow for a single night could be easily gathered in one not very large room but those who would draw a long breath of relief would reach to millions.

We hear much of visions and I trust we shall continue to have visions and dream dreams of a fairer future for the race. But visions are one thing and visionaries are another, and the mechanical appliances of the rhetorician designed to give a picture of a present which does not exist and of a future which no man can predict are as unreal and shortlived as the steam or canvas clouds, the angels suspended on wires and the artificial lights of the stage. They pass with the moment of effect and are shabby and tawdry in the daylight. Let us at least be real. Washington's entire honesty of mind and his fearless look into the face of all facts are qualities which can never go out of fashion and which we should all do well to imitate.

Ideals have been thrust upon us as an argument for the league until the healthy mind which rejects cant revolts from them. Are ideals confined to this deformed experiment upon a noble purpose, tainted, as it is, with bargains and tied to a peace treaty which might have been disposed of long ago to the great benefit of the world if it had not been compelled to carry this rider on its back? 'Post equitem sedet atra cura,' Horace tells us, but no blacker care ever sat behind any rider than we shall find in this covenant of doubtful and disputed interpretation as it now perches upon the treaty of peace.

No doubt many excellent and patriotic people see a coming fulfillment of noble ideals in the words 'league for peace.' We all respect and share these aspirations and desires, but some of us see no hope, but rather defeat, for them in this murky covenant. For we, too, have our ideals, even if we differ from those who have tried to establish a monopoly of idealism. Our first ideal is our country, and we see her in the future, as in the past, giving service to all her people and to the world. Our ideal of the future is that she should continue to render that service of her own free will.

She has great problems of her own to solve, very grim and perilous problems, and a right solution, if we can attain to it, would largely benefit mankind. We would have our country strong to resist a peril from the West, as she has flung back the German menace from the East. We would not have our politics distracted and embittered by the dissensions of other lands. We would not have our country's vigor exhausted or her moral force abated, by everlasting meddling and muddling in every quarrel, great and small, which afflicts the world. Our ideal is to make her ever stronger and better and finer, because in that way alone, as we believe, can she be of the greatest service to the world's peace and to the welfare of mankind.

•

WOODROW WILSON
Pueblo, Colorado, 25 September 1919

'Man will see the truth'

When the Senate baulked at the League of Nations covenant, which he had negotiated with the Allied leaders in Paris, Wilson, aged sixty-three, set out on a great speaking tour through the West to rally the people to him and overcome Senator Lodge. Thirty speeches were planned in twenty days.

'Worn out by his labours; appalled at what might flow from the repudiation of his handiwork; filled with a prophet's vision and also, unfortunately, with the vanity of Jonah, he refused all compromise,' says Hugh Brogan. 'His eloquence was never greater. He defended the treaty with a passion worthy of a better cause ... The choice, he assured them again and again, trying to press home the lessons of his own education, lay between peace with the treaty, faults and all, or war without it.'

At Pueblo, Colorado, where this speech was made, he suffered complete nervous exhaustion and collapsed. The tour was cancelled and Wilson returned to the White House, where he suffered a massive stroke. The treaty was defeated in the Senate by a small margin. For the fifteen remaining months of his presidency, Wilson lay inert in the White House, doing nothing, saying nothing.

Again and again, my fellow citizens, mothers who lost their sons in France have come to me and, taking my hand, have shed tears upon it not only, but they had added, 'God bless you, Mr President!' Why, my fellow citizens, should they pray God to bless me? I advised the Congress of the United States to create the situation that led to the death of their sons. I ordered their sons oversea. I consented to their sons being put in the most difficult parts of the battle line, where death was certain, as in the impenetrable difficulties of the forest of Argonne. Why should they weep upon my hand and call down the blessings of God upon me? Because they believe that their boys died for something that vastly transcends any of the immediate and palpable objects of the war. They believe, and they rightly believe, that their sons saved the liberty of the world. They believe that wrapped up with the liberty of the world is the continuous protection of that liberty by the concerted powers of all civilized people. They believe that this sacrifice was made in order that other sons should not be called upon for a similar gift – the gift of life, the gift of all that died – and if we did not see this thing through, if we fulfilled the dearest present wish of Germany and now dissociated ourselves from those alongside whom we fought in the war, would not something of the halo go away from the gun over the mantelpiece, or the sword? Would not the old uniform lose something of its significance? These men were crusaders. They were not going forth to prove the might of the United States. They were going forth to prove the might of justice and right, and all the world accepted them as crusaders, and their transcendent achievement has made all the world believe in America as it believes in no other nation organized in the modern world. There seems to me to stand between us and the rejection or qualification of this treaty the serried ranks of those boys in khaki, not only these boys who came home, but those dear ghosts that still deploy upon the fields of France.

My friends, on last Decoration Day I went to a beautiful hillside near Paris, where was located the cemetery of Suresnes, a cemetery given over to the burial of the American dead. Behind me on the slopes was rank upon rank of living American soldiers, and lying before me upon the levels of the plain was rank upon rank of departed American soldiers. Right by the side of the stand where I spoke there was a little group of French women who had adopted those graves, had made themselves mothers of those dear ghosts by putting flowers every day upon those graves, taking them as their own sons, their own beloved, because they had died in the same cause – France was free and the world was free because America had come! I wish some men in public life who are now opposing the settlement for which these men died could visit such a spot as that. I wish that the thought that comes out of those graves could penetrate their consciousness. I wish that they could feel the moral obligation that rests upon us not to go back on those boys, but to see the thing through, to see it through to the end and make good their redemption of the world. For nothing less depends upon this decision, nothing less than the liberation and salvation of the world . . .

You will say, 'Is the League an absolute guarantee against war?' No; I do not know any absolute guarantee against the errors of human judgment or the violence of human passion, but I ask you this: if it is not an absolute insurance against war, do you want no insurance at all? Do you want nothing? Do you want not only no probability that war will not recur, but the probability that it will recur? The arrangements of justice do not stand of themselves, my fellow citizens. The arrangements of this treaty are just, but they need the support of the combined power of the great nations of the world. And they will have that support. Now that the mists of this great question have cleared away, I believe that men will see the truth, eye to eye and face to face. There is one thing that the American people always rise to and extend their hand to, and that is the truth of justice and of liberty and of peace. We have accepted that truth and we are going to be led by it, and it is going to lead us, and through us the world, out into pastures of quietness and peace such as the world never dreamed of before.

•

ALFRED E. SMITH
New York, 29 October 1919

'*A man as low and mean as I can picture*'

Al Smith, a Roman Catholic who left school at fourteen, was a New York Democrat politician who became governor in 1919. At Tammany Hall he gathered round him a generation of equally remarkable younger men and women, including Harry Hopkins, Frances Perkins, Robert Moses and Franklin Delano Roosevelt, and instituted honest government.

At the mass meeting in Carnegie Hall at which this speech was made, Smith (1873–1944) made an irreparable break with William Randolph Hearst, the powerful owner of a newspaper chain extending from New York to California and the newspaper baron on whom Citizen Kane *was based. Hearst had combined with Tammany Hall to elect the local administration but had been scurrilously attacking the governor for 'starving' children because he refused to reduce the price of milk.*

Smith had expected to debate with Hearst at the meeting called by a citizens' committee but Hearst refused to meet him. Smith's speech therefore meant that he had decided to fight the influence of one of the richest of men, who used his newspapers to wield power.

He asked for absolute silence and attention. 'I feel that I am here tonight upon a mission as important not only to myself but to this city, to this state and to this country as I could possibly perform.' As he reached his peroration, he declared that nearly every paper had commended his administration except the paper that belonged to the man who wanted to tell him what he ought to do. Then he launched his assault on America's most powerful newspaper mogul.

I cannot think of a more contemptible man – my power of imagination fails me to bring into my mind's eye a more despicable man than the man that exploits the poor. Any man that leads you to believe that your lot in life is not all right, any man that conjures up for you a fancied grievance against your government or against the man at the head of it, to help himself, is breeding the seeds of an anarchy and a dissatisfaction more disastrous to the welfare of the community than any other teaching that I can think of, because, at least, the wildest anarchist, the most extreme Socialist, the wildest radical that you can think of, may at least be sincere in his own heart. He may think that it is right when he preaches it. But the man that preaches to the poor of this or of any other community discontent and dissatisfaction to help himself and to make good his side of the argument, and to destroy, as he said himself he would, the Governor of the State, is a man as low and as mean as I can picture ... Follow back the history of this man's newspapers since he came to this part of the country, and you will have to read out of his newspapers this remarkable fact: That in this great democracy, in this land of the free and in this home of the brave, there has never been a man elected to office yet that has not been tainted in some way. If the Hearst newspapers were the text books for the children of our schools, they would have to spell out of its every line that no man can be trusted in this country after he is put into public office; that no man thinks enough about it; no man has enough of regard for it; no man has enough of real Christian charity to do the thing right; no man that ever held great public office had enough of respect and regard for his mother and his wife and his children and his friends to be right in office. About that there can be no question, because no public man in this State, from Grover Cleveland right down to today, has ever escaped this fellow. We all know that. The children on the street know it.

Nobody that ever went to the Governor's office went there with a graver sense of the responsibility of that office than I did. What could there possibly be about me that I should be assailed in this reckless manner by this man? I have more reason probably than any man I will meet tonight to have a strong love and a strong devotion for this country, for this State, and for this city. Look at what I have received at its hands: I left school and went to work before I was fifteen years of age. I worked hard, night and day; I worked honestly and conscientiously at every job that I was ever put at, until I went to the Governor's chair in Albany. What can it be? It has got to be jealousy, it has got to be envy, it has got to be hatred, or it has to be something that nobody understands, that makes me come down here, into the city of New York, before this audience, and urge them to organize in this city to stay the danger that comes from these papers, to the end that the health, and welfare, and the comfort of this people, of the people of this State, may be promoted, and we may get rid of this pestilence that walks in the darkness.

Smith was governor of New York for a second term from 1923 to 1929. At the 1924 Democratic convention he was beaten for the presidential nomination after 103 ballots. He gained the nomination in 1928 but was beaten by Herbert Hoover.

•

GEORGE V
Belfast, 22 June 1921

'*The eyes of the whole Empire are on Ireland today*'

Under the 1920 Government of Ireland Act there were to be two Home Rule parliaments: one for most of Ireland at Dublin (which Sinn Féin refused to recognize), the other for the six counties of Ulster at Belfast. The act secured the Ulster Unionists from Dublin rule and they grudgingly accepted their own parliament and their own government.

King George V resolved to open the first North of Ireland parliament himself, in spite of the risk of assassination. Jan Smuts, the South African statesman, drafted a warm plea for civil peace which was accepted by Lloyd George, who was looking for a way out of the Irish imbroglio.

According to A. J. P. Taylor, George V's initiative 'was perhaps the greatest service performed by a British monarch in modern times'. That view is considered 'sentimental' by the Irish historian R. F. Foster, who argues that Lloyd George's hand was forced by the unpalatable alternative of governing the sixteen counties as a Crown colony under martial law.

Members of the Senate and of the House of Commons – for all who love Ireland, as I do with all my heart, this is a profoundly moving occasion in Irish history. My memories of the Irish people date back to the time when I spent many happy days in Ireland as a midshipman. My affection for the Irish people has been deepened by successive visits since that time, and I have watched with constant sympathy the course of their affairs. I could not have allowed myself to give Ireland by deputy alone my earnest prayers and good wishes in the new era which opens with this ceremony, and I have therefore come in person, as the Head of the Empire, to inaugurate this Parliament on Irish soil. I inaugurate it with deep-felt hope, and I feel assured that you will do your utmost to make it an instrument of happiness and good government for all parts of the community which you represent.

This is a great and critical occasion in the history of the six counties, but not for the six counties alone, for everything which interests them touches Ireland, and everything which touches Ireland finds an echo in the remotest parts of the Empire. Few things are more earnestly desired throughout the English-speaking world than a satisfactory solution of the age-long Irish problems which for generations embarrassed our forefathers, as they now weigh heavily upon us. Most certainly there is no wish nearer my own heart than that every man of Irish birth, whatever be his creed and wherever be his home, should work in loyal cooperation with the free communities on which the British Empire is based.

I am confident that the important matters entrusted to the control and guidance of the Northern Parliament will be managed with wisdom and with moderation, with fairness and due regard to every faith and interest, and with no abatement of that patriotic devotion to the Empire which you proved so gallantly in the Great War. Full partnership in the United Kingdom and religious freedom Ireland has long enjoyed. She now has conferred upon her the duty of dealing with all the essential tasks of domestic legislation and government; and I feel no misgiving as to the spirit in which you who stand here today will carry out the all-important functions entrusted to your care.

My hope is broader still. The eyes of the whole Empire are on Ireland today – that Empire in which so many nations and races have come together in spite of ancient feuds, and in which new nations have come to birth within the lifetime of the youngest in this hall. I am emboldened by that thought to look beyond the sorrow and the anxiety which have clouded of late my vision of Irish affairs. I speak from a full heart when I pray that my coming to Ireland today may prove to be the first step towards an end of strife amongst her people, whatever their race or creed. In that hope I appeal to all Irishmen to pause, to stretch out the hand of forbearance and conciliation, to forgive and to forget, and to join in making for the land which they love a new era of peace, contentment and good will. It is my earnest desire that in Southern Ireland too there may ere long take place a parallel to what is now passing in this hall; that there a similar occasion may present itself and a similar ceremony be performed.

For this the Parliament of the United Kingdom has in the fullest measure provided the powers; for this the Parliament of Ulster is pointing the way. The future lies in the hands of my Irish people themselves. May this historic gathering be the prelude of a day in which the Irish people, North and South, under one Parliament or two, as those Parliaments may themselves decide, shall work together in common love for Ireland upon the sure foundation of mutual justice and respect.

The response to the king's speech was immediate. Éamon de Valera, president of the Irish republic, agreed to negotiate and a truce followed on 8 July. Fighting ended three days later. Civil war followed in Ireland but the Irish Free State was approved by the British parliament on 5 December 1922.

•

MAHATMA GANDHI
Ahmadabad, 23 March 1922

'Non-violence is the first article of my faith'

Gandhi became leader of the Indian National Congress in 1920 and the congress adopted his programme of Satyagraha, non-violent non-cooperation, which he had earlier practised in South Africa. 'I discovered that pursuit of truth did not admit of violence being inflicted on one's opponent,' Gandhi wrote, 'but that he must be weaned from error by patience and sympathy. For what appears to be truth to one may appear to be error to the other. And patience means self-suffering. So the doctrine came to mean vindication of truth, not by the infliction of suffering on the opponent but on one's self.'

Supporting the Satyagraha campaign, Gandhi travelled throughout India, often speaking to meetings of more than 100,000 Indians. He was constantly shadowed by the police but it was not until 1922 that he was arrested and charged with sedition for three articles in his magazine Young India. *The great trial at Ahmadabad, at which Gandhi pleaded guilty, followed.*

'Men's minds involuntarily turned to another great trial 1,900 years ago when Jesus stood before Pontius Pilate,' said a contemporary Indian account. 'Mr Gandhi's statement was in his best form, terse and lucid, courageous and uncompromising, with just that touch of greatness which elevates it to the level of a masterpiece. Never before was such a prisoner arraigned before a British Court of Justice. Never before were the laws of an all-powerful government so defiantly, yet with such humility, challenged.'

Non-violence is the first article of my faith. It is the last article of my faith. But I had to make my choice. I had either to submit to a system which I considered has done an irreparable harm to my country or incur the risk of the mad fury of my people bursting forth when they understood the truth from my lips. I know that my people have sometimes gone mad. I am deeply sorry for it; and I am therefore, here, to submit not to a light penalty but to the highest penalty. I do not ask for mercy. I do not plead any extenuating act. I am here, therefore, to invite and submit to the highest penalty that can be inflicted upon me for what in law is a deliberate crime and what appears to me to be the highest duty of a citizen. The only course open to you, Mr Judge, is, as I am just going to say in my statement, either to resign your post or inflict on me the severest penalty if you believe that the system and law you are assisting to administer are good for the people. I do not expect that kind of conversion. But by the time I have finished with my statement you will, perhaps, have a glimpse of what is raging within my breast to run this maddest risk which a sane man can run.

Gandhi then read his statement to the court.

I owe it perhaps to the Indian public and to the public in England, to placate which this prosecution is mainly taken up, that I should explain why from a staunch loyalist and cooperator I have become an uncompromising disaffectionist and Non-Cooperator. To the court too I should say why I plead guilty to the charge of promoting disaffection towards the Government established by law in India.

My public life began in 1893 in South Africa in troubled weather. My first contact with British authority in that country was not of a happy character. I discovered that as a man and an Indian I had no rights. On the contrary I discovered that I had no rights as a man because I was an Indian.

But I was not baffled. I thought that this treatment of Indians was an excrescence upon a system that was intrinsically and mainly good. I gave the Government my voluntary and hearty cooperation, criticizing it fully where I felt it was faulty but never wishing its destruction.

Consequently when the existence of the Empire was threatened in 1899 by the Boer challenge, I offered my services to it, raised a volunteer ambulance corps and served at several actions that took place for the relief of Ladysmith. Similarly in 1906 at the time of the Zulu revolt I raised a stretcher-bearer party and served till the end of the 'rebellion'. On both these occasions I received medals and was even mentioned in despatches. For my work in South Africa I was given by Lord Hardinge a Kaiser-i-Hind Gold Medal. When the war broke out in 1914 between England and Germany I raised a volunteer ambulance corps in London consisting of the then resident Indians in London, chiefly students. Its work was acknowledged by the authorities to be valuable. Lastly in India when a special appeal was made at the War Conference in Delhi in 1917 by Lord Chelmsford for recruits, I struggled at the cost of my health to raise a corps in Kheda and the response was being made when the hostilities ceased and orders were received that no more recruits were wanted. In all these efforts at service I was actuated by the belief that it was possible by such services to gain a status of full equality in the Empire for my countrymen.

The first shock came in the shape of the Rowlatt Act, a law designed to rob the people of all real freedom. I felt called upon to lead an intensive agitation against it. Then followed the Punjab horrors beginning with the massacre at Jallianwala Bagh and culminating in crawling orders, public floggings and other indescribable humiliations. The Punjab crime was white-washed and most culprits went not only unpunished but remained in service and some continued to draw pensions from the Indian revenue, and in some cases were even rewarded. I saw too that not only did the reforms not mark a change of heart, but they were only a method of further draining India of her wealth and of prolonging her servitude.

I came reluctantly to the conclusion that the British connection had made India more helpless than she ever was before, politically and economically. A disarmed India has no power of resistance against any aggressor if she wanted to engage in an armed conflict with him. So much is this the case that some of our best men consider that India must take generations before she can achieve the Dominion status. She has become so poor that she has little power of resisting famines. Before the British advent, India spun and wove in her millions of cottages just the supplement she needed for adding to her meagre agricultural resources. The cottage industry, so vital for India's existence, has been ruined by incredibly heartless and inhuman processes as described by English witnesses.

Little do town-dwellers know how the semi-starved masses of Indians are slowly sinking to lifelessness. Little do they know that their miserable comfort represents the brokerage they get for the work they do for the foreign exploiter, that the profits and the brokerage are sucked from the masses. Little do they realize that the Government established by law in British India is carried on for this exploitation of the masses. No sophistry, no jugglery in figures can explain away the evidence the skeletons in many villages present to the naked eye. I have no doubt whatsoever that both England and the town-dwellers of India will have to answer, if there is a God above, for this crime against humanity which is perhaps unequalled in history. The law itself in this country has been used to serve the foreign exploiter. My unbiased examination of the Punjab Martial Law cases has led me to believe that at least ninety-five per cent of convictions were wholly bad. My experience of political cases in India leads me to the conclusion that in nine out of every ten the condemned men were totally innocent. Their crime consisted in love of their country. In ninety-nine cases out of a hundred, justice has been denied to Indians as against Europeans in the Courts of India. This is not an exaggerated picture. It is the experience of almost every Indian who has had anything to do with such cases. In my opinion the administration of the law is thus prostituted consciously or unconsciously for the benefit of the exploiter.

The greatest misfortune is that Englishmen and their Indian associates in the administration of the country do not know that they are engaged in the crime I have attempted to describe. I am satisfied that many English and Indian officials honestly believe that they are administering one of the best systems devised in the world and that India is making steady though slow progress. They do not know that a subtle but effective system of terrorism and an organized display of force on the one hand and the deprivation of all powers of retaliation or self-defence on the other have emasculated the people and induced in them the habit of simulation. This awful habit has added to the ignorance and the self-deception of the administrators. Section 124-A under which I am happily charged is perhaps the prince among the political sections of the Indian Penal Code designed to suppress the liberty of the citizen. Affection cannot be manufactured or regulated by law. If one has no affection for a person or thing one should be free to give the fullest expression to his disaffection so long as he does not contemplate, promote or incite to violence. But the section under which Mr Banker and I are charged is one under which mere promotion of disaffection is a crime. I have studied some of the cases tried under it, and I know that some of the most loved of India's patriots have been convicted under it. I consider it a privilege, therefore, to be charged under it. I have endeavoured to give in their briefest outline the reasons for my disaffection. I have no personal ill-will against any single administrator, much less can I have any disaffection towards the King's person. But I hold it to be a virtue to be disaffected towards a Government which in its totality has done more harm to India than any previous system. India is less manly under the British rule than she ever was before. Holding such a belief, I consider it to be a sin to have affection for the system. And it has been a precious privilege for me to be able to write what I have in the various articles tendered in evidence against me.

In fact I believe that I have rendered a service to India and England by showing in Non-Cooperation the way out of the unnatural state in which both are living. In my humble opinion, non-cooperation with evil is as much a duty as is cooperation with good. But in the past, non-cooperation has been deliberately expressed in violence to the evildoer. I am endeavouring to show to my countrymen that violent non-cooperation only multiplies evil and that as evil can only be sustained by violence, withdrawal of support of evil requires complete abstention from violence. Non-violence implies voluntary submission to the penalty for non-cooperation with evil. I am here, therefore, to invite and submit cheerfully to the highest penalty that can be inflicted upon me for what in law is deliberate crime and what appears to me to be the highest duty of a citizen. The only course open to you, the Judge and the Assessors, is either to resign your posts and thus dissociate yourselves from evil if you feel that the law you are called upon to administer is an evil and that in reality I am innocent, or to inflict on me the severest penalty if you believe that the system and the law you are assisting to administer are good for the people of this country and that my activity is therefore injurious to the public weal.

After his statement before the court, Gandhi was sentenced to six years' imprisonment and thanked the judge for his courtesy. He was imprisoned again in 1930, 1933 and 1942 when he went on hunger strike as part of his campaign of civil disobedience. He eventually collaborated with the English to gain independence for India which was proclaimed twenty-five years later. A saint to many Hindus, he was assassinated in 1948.

•

A. J. BALFOUR
London, 21 June 1922

'*A message to every land where the Jewish race is scattered*'

Arthur Balfour (1848–1930), Conservative prime minister from 1902 to 1906 and foreign secretary in the wartime coalitions, considered the Balfour Declaration of 1917 the most worthwhile act of his long political career. Balfour had been interested in the Jewish national movement since his first meeting with Chaim Weizmann, the leader of British Zionism, in 1906. The declaration affirmed British support for the establishment of a Jewish national home in Palestine provided that safeguards could be reached for the rights of its non-Jewish communities. The declaration formed the basis for the League of Nations mandate for Palestine.

Balfour, according to his niece Blanche Dugdale, thought of the Zionists as guardians of a continuity of religious and racial tradition that made the unassimilated Jew a great conservative force in world politics. He felt strongly about the way the Jewish contribution to culture and religion had for the most part been requited by the Christian world.

That moral indignation was never put more clearly than to the House of Lords in 1922 after Lord Islington had attacked the acceptance of the mandate by Britain.

My noble friend told us in his speech, and I believe him absolutely, that he has no prejudice against the Jews. I think I may say that I have no prejudice in their favour. But their position and their history, their connection with world religion and with world politics, is absolutely unique. There is no parallel to it, there is nothing approaching to a parallel to it, in any other branch of human history. Here you have a small race originally inhabiting a small country, I think of about the size of Wales or Belgium, at any rate of comparable size to those two, at no time in its history wielding anything that can be described as material power, sometimes crushed in between great Oriental monarchies, its inhabitants deported, then scattered, then driven out of the country altogether into every part of the world, and yet maintaining a continuity of religious and racial tradition of which we have no parallel elsewhere.

That, itself, is sufficiently remarkable, but consider – it is not a pleasant consideration, but it is one that we cannot forget – how they have been treated during long centuries, during centuries which in some parts of the world extend to the minute and the hour in which I am speaking; consider how they have been subjected to tyranny and persecution; consider whether the whole culture of Europe, the whole religious organization of Europe, has not from time to time proved itself guilty of great crimes against this race. I quite understand that some members of the race may have given, doubtless did give, occasion for much ill-will, and I do not know how it could be otherwise, treated as they were; but, if you are going to lay stress on that, do not forget what part they have played in the intellectual, the artistic, the philosophic and scientific development of the world. I say nothing of the economic side of their energies, for on that Christian attention has always been concentrated.

I ask your Lordships to consider the other side of their activities. Nobody who knows what he is talking about will deny that they have at least – and I am putting it more moderately than I could do – rowed all their weight in the boat of scientific, intellectual and artistic progress, and they are doing so to this day. You will find them in every University, in every centre of learning; and at the very moment when they were being persecuted, when some of them, at all events, were being persecuted by the Church, their philosophers were developing thoughts which the great doctors of the Church embodied in their religious system. As it was in the Middle Ages, as it was in earlier times, so it is now. And yet, is there anyone here who feels content with the position of the Jews? They have been able, by this extraordinary tenacity of their race, to maintain this continuity, and they have maintained it without having any Jewish Home.

What has been the result? The result has been that they have been described as parasites on every civilization in whose affairs they have mixed themselves – very useful parasites at times I venture to say. But however that may be, do not your Lordships think that if Christendom, not oblivious of all the wrong it has done, can give a chance, without injury to others, to this race of showing whether it can organize a culture in a Home where it will be secured from oppression, that it is not well to say, if we can do it, that we will do it. And, if we can do it, should we not be doing something material to wash out an ancient stain upon our own civilization if we absorb the Jewish race in friendly and effective fashion in those countries in which they are the citizens? We should then have given them what every other nation has, some place, some local habitation, where they can develop the culture and the traditions which are peculiarly their own.

I could defend – I have endeavoured, and I hope not unsuccessfully, to defend – this scheme of the Palestine Mandate from the most material economic view, and from that point of view it is capable of defence. I have endeavoured to defend it from the point of view of the existing population, and I have shown – I hope with some effect – that their prosperity also is intimately bound up with the success of Zionism. But having endeavoured to the best of my ability to maintain those two propositions, I should, indeed, give an inadequate view to your Lordships of my opinions if I sat down without insisting to the utmost of my ability that, beyond and above all this, there is this great ideal at which those who think with me are aiming, and which, I believe, it is within their power to reach.

It may fail. I do not deny that this is an adventure. Are we never to have adventures? Are we never to try new experiments? I hope your Lordships will never sink to that unimaginative depth, and that experiment and adventure will be justified if there is any case or cause for their justification. Surely, it is in order that we may send a message to every land where the Jewish race has been scattered, a message which will tell them that Christendom is not oblivious of their faith, is not unmindful of the service they have rendered to the great religions of the world, and, most of all, to the religion that the majority of your Lordships' House profess, and that we desire to the best of our ability to give them that opportunity of developing, in peace and quietness under British rule, those great gifts which hitherto they have been compelled from the very nature of the case only to bring to fruition in countries which know not their language, and belong not to their race. That is the ideal which I desire to see accomplished, that is the aim which lay at the root of the policy I am trying to defend; and, though it be defensible indeed on every ground, that is the ground which chiefly moves me.

●

STANLEY BALDWIN
London, 6 May 1924

'The sounds of England'

After serving in the governments of Lloyd George and Bonar Law, Stanley Baldwin (1867–1947) succeeded Law as prime minister in May 1923. He resigned when he failed to get a clear majority in the 1923 election but became prime minister again in 1924.

Baldwin was the most self-conscious countryman among British prime ministers of the century, according to his biographer Roy Jenkins. The unchanging nature of English rural life was one of his more effective and frequently recurring oratorical themes, reaching its apogee in this speech to the Royal Society of St George.

This, like many of his other speeches, was prose of a high evocative quality, even though its prophecy was inaccurate in both letter and spirit. 'His romantic nostalgia was wholly genuine, although his dislike of change from the countryside of his boyhood was probably more acute than that of those whose origins and lives were more deeply rooted in it.'

To me, England is the country, and the country is England. And when I ask myself what I mean by England, when I think of England when I am abroad, England comes to me through my various senses – through the ear, through the eye, and through certain imperishable scents. I will tell you what they are, and there may be those among you who feel as I do.

The sounds of England, the tinkle of the hammer on the anvil in the country smithy, the corncrake on a dewy morning, the sound of the scythe against the whetstone, and the sight of a plough team coming over the brow of a hill, the sight that has been seen in England since England was a land, and may be seen in England long after the Empire has perished and every works in England has ceased to function, for centuries the one eternal sight of England. The wild anemones in the woods in April, the last load at night of hay being drawn down a lane as the twilight comes on, when you can scarcely distinguish the figures of the horses as they take it home to the farm, and above all, most subtle, most penetrating and most moving, the smell of wood smoke coming up in an autumn evening, or the smell of the scutch fires: that wood smoke that our ancestors, tens of thousands of years ago, must have caught on the air when they were coming home with the results of the day's forage, when they were still nomads, and when they were still roaming the forests and the plains of the continent of Europe. These things strike down into the very depths of our nature, and touch chords that go back to the beginning of time and the human race, but they are chords that with every year of our life sound a deeper note in our innermost being.

These are the things that make England, and I grieve for it that they are not the childish inheritance of the majority of the people today in our country. They ought to be the inheritance of every child born into this country, but nothing can be more touching than to see how the working man and woman after generations in the towns will have their tiny bit of garden if they can, will go to gardens if they can, to look at something they have never seen as children, but which their ancestors knew and loved. The love of these things is innate and inherent in our people. It makes for that love of home, one of the strongest features of our race, and it is that that makes our race seek its new home in the Dominions overseas, where they have room to see things like this that they can no more see at home. It is that power of making homes, almost peculiar to our people, and it is one of the sources of their greatness. They go overseas, and they take with them what they learned at home: love of justice, love of truth, and the broad humanity that are so characteristic of English people. It may well be that these traits on which we pride ourselves, which we hope to show and try to show in our own lives, may survive – survive among our people so long as they are a people – and I hope and believe this, that just as today more than fifteen centuries since the last of those great Roman legionaries left England, we still speak of the Roman strength, and the Roman work, and the Roman character, so perhaps in the ten thousandth century, long after the Empires of this world as we know them have fallen and others have risen and fallen, and risen and fallen again, the men who are then on this earth may yet speak of those characteristics which we prize as the characteristics of the English, and that long after, maybe, the name of the country has passed away, wherever men are honourable and upright and persevering, lovers of home, of their brethren, of justice and of humanity, the men in the world of that day may say, 'We still have among us the gifts of that great English race.'

•

CLARENCE DARROW
Detroit, 19 May 1926

'The life of the Negro race has been a life of tragedy'

More than a hundred clients of Clarence Darrow (1857–1938) were accused of murder but none was executed. For forty years, the Chicago attorney, a militant agnostic, fanatical humanitarian and spokesman for the underdog, dominated hundreds of courtrooms.

He resigned as general counsel for the Chicago and Northwestern Railway in 1894 to defend Eugene Debs during the Pullman strike. Debs was acquitted and Darrow subsequently became involved in a series of important or sensational cases.

In 1926 some 60,000 blacks in Chicago lived in overcrowded quarters. They were so crowded that some families had moved to the white districts but were regularly driven out. One was Dr Ossian Sweet, who provided himself with guns and ammunition and fired a volley into the street when a big crowd attacked his home. One white man was killed. Sweet and eleven blacks were arrested and Darrow became lawyer for the defence. The jurors could not agree and were dismissed.

A month later the state ordered a retrial, making Henry Sweet, the doctor's brother, who had apparently fired the fatal shot, the sole defendant. Darrow's final plea for Sweet, which lasted eight hours, was perhaps the best appeal to a jury of a brilliant career. Sweet was acquitted.

For Darrow the verdict meant simply that the doctrine that a man's house is his castle applied to blacks as well as whites – probably the first occasion on which that principle had been upheld by a white jury.

We come now to lay this man's case in the hands of a jury of our peers – the first defence and the last defence is the protection of home and life as provided by our law. We are willing to leave it here. I feel, as I look at you, that we will be treated fairly and decently, even understandingly and kindly. You know what this case is. You know why it is. You know that if white men had been fighting their way against colored men, nobody would ever have dreamed of a prosecution. And you know that from the beginning of this case to the end, up to the time you write your verdict, the prosecution is based on race prejudice and nothing else.

Gentlemen, I feel deeply on this subject; I cannot help it. Let us take a little glance at the history of the Negro race. It seems to me that the story would melt hearts of stone. I was born in America. I could have left it if I had wanted to go away. Some other men, reading about this land of freedom that we brag about on the Fourth of July, came voluntarily to America. These men, the defendants, are here because they could not help it. Their ancestors were captured in the jungles and on the plains of Africa, captured as you capture wild beasts, torn from their homes and their kindred; loaded into slave ships, packed like sardines in a box, half of them dying on the ocean passage; some jumping into the sea in their frenzy, when they had a chance to choose death in place of slavery. They were captured and brought there. They could not help it. They were bought and sold as slaves, to work without pay, because they were black. They were subject to all of this for generations, until finally they were given their liberty, so far as the law goes – and that is only a little way, because, after all, every human being's life in this world is inevitably mixed with every other life and, no matter what laws we pass, no matter what precautions we take, unless the people we meet are kindly and decent and human and liberty-loving then there is no liberty. Freedom comes from human beings, rather than from laws and institutions.

Now, that is their history. These people are the children of slavery. If the race that we belong to owes anything to any human being, or to any power in the universe, they owe it to these black men. Above all other men, they owe an obligation and a duty to these black men that can never be repaid. I never see one of them that I do not feel I ought to pay part of the debt of my race – and if you gentlemen feel as you should feel in this case, your emotions will be like mine.

Gentlemen, you are called into this case by chance. It took us a week to find you, a week of culling out prejudice and hatred. Probably we did not cull it all out at that; but we took the best and the fairest that we could find. It is up to you.

Your verdict means something in this case. It means something more than the fate of this boy. It is not often that a case is submitted to twelve men where the decision may mean a milestone in the history of the human race. But this case does. And I hope and I trust that you have a feeling of responsibility that will make you take it and do your duty as citizens of a great nation, and as members of the human family, which is better still.

Let me say just a parting word for Henry Sweet, who has well-nigh been forgotten. I am serious, but it seems almost like a reflection upon this jury to talk as if I doubted your verdict. What has this boy done? This one boy now that I am culling out from all of the rest, and whose fate is in your hands – can you tell me what he has done? Can I believe myself? Am I standing in a court of justice where twelve men on their oaths are asked to take away the liberty of a boy twenty-one years of age, who has done nothing more than what Henry Sweet has done?

Gentlemen, you may think he shot too quick; you may think he erred in judgment; you may think that Dr Sweet should not have gone there prepared to defend his home. But, what of this case of Henry Sweet? What has he done? I want to put it up to you, each one of you, individually. Dr Sweet was his elder brother. He had helped Henry through school. He loved him. He had taken him into his home. Henry had lived with him and his wife; he had fondled his baby. The doctor had promised Henry the money to go through school. Henry was getting his education, to take his place in the world, gentlemen – and this is a hard job. With his brother's help he has worked his way through college up to the last year. The doctor had bought a home. He feared danger. He moved in with his wife and he asked this boy to go with him. And this boy went to defend his brother, and his brother's wife and his child and his home.

Do you think more of him or less of him for that? I never saw twelve men in my life – and I have looked at a good many faces of a good many juries – I never saw twelve men in my life that, if you could get them to understand a human case, were not true and right.

Should this boy have gone along and helped his brother? Or, should he have stayed away? What would you have done? And yet, gentlemen, here is a boy, and the president of his college came all the way from Ohio to tell you what he thinks of him. His teachers have come here, from Ohio, to tell you what they think of him. The Methodist bishop has come here to tell you what he thinks of him.

So, gentlemen, I am justified in saying that this boy is as kindly, as well disposed, as decent a man as one of you twelve. Do you think he ought to be taken out of his school and sent to the penitentiary? All right, gentlemen, if you think so, do it. It's your job, not mine. If you think so, do it. But if you do, gentlemen, if you should ever look into the face of your own boy, or your own brother, or look into your own heart, you will regret it in sackcloth and ashes. You know, if he committed any offence, it was being loyal and true to his brother whom he loved. I know where you will send him and it will not be to a penitentiary.

I do not believe in the law of hate. I may not be true to my ideals always, but I believe in the law of love, and I believe you can do nothing with hatred. I would like to see a time when man loves his fellow man and forgets his color or his creed. We will never be civilized until that time comes. I know the Negro race has a long road to go. I believe that the life of the Negro race has been a life of tragedy, of injustice, of oppression. The law has made him equal, but man has not. And, after all, the last analysis is: what has man done? – and not what has the law done? I know there is a long road ahead of him before he can take the place which I believe he should take. I know that before him there is sorrow, tribulation, and death among the blacks, and perhaps the whites. I am sorry. I would do what I could to avert it. I would advise patience; I would advise tolerance; I would advise understanding; I would advise all those things which are necessary for men who live together.

Gentlemen, what do you think of your duty in this case? I have watched day after day these black, tense faces that have crowded this court. These black faces that now are looking to you twelve whites, feeling that the hopes and fears of a race are in your keeping.

This case is about to end, gentlemen. To them, it is life. Not one of their color sits on this jury. Their fate is in the hands of twelve whites. Their eyes are fixed on you, their hearts go out to you, and their hopes hang on your verdict.

This is all. I ask you, on behalf of this defendant, on behalf of these helpless ones who turn to you, and more than that – on behalf of this great state, and this great city, which must face this problem and face it fairly – I ask you in the name of progress and of the human race, to return a verdict of not guilty in this case!

•

NICOLA SACCO and BARTOLOMEO VANZETTI
Dedham, Massachusetts, 19 April 1927

'*I am never be guilty, never*'

The United States in 1920 was suffering a violent 'Red scare' and organized labour was protesting at the importation of cheap labour from overseas. On 15 April 1920, the paymaster and the guard of a shoe factory at Milford, Massachusetts, were shot dead and robbed. Nicola Sacco (1891–1927) and Bartolomeo Vanzetti (1888–1927), two Italian immigrants who had become anarchists and also dodged the draft, were arrested and charged with the murders.

The trial was held in Dedham and they were found guilty. Associates of Sacco and Vanzetti alerted the Left throughout the world to what seemed a perversion of justice, especially because of the prejudice of the judge who described them as 'anarchist bastards'. After the men had been in prison for seven years, they were finally told they were to be executed. Their last speeches to Judge Webster Thayer were movingly dignified, perhaps because their English was so imperfect.

[*Sacco:*] I am not an orator. It is not very familiar with me the English language, and, as I know, as my friend has told me, my comrade Vanzetti will speak more long, so I thought to give him the chance.

I never know, never heard, even read in history anything so cruel as this court. After seven years prosecuting they still consider us guilty. And these gentle people here are arrayed with us in this court today.

I know the sentence will be between two class, the oppressed class and the rich class, and there will be always collision between one and the other. We fraternize the people with the books, with the literature. You persecute the people, tyrannize over them, and kill them. We try the education of people always. You try to put a path between us and some other nationality that hates each other. That is why I am here today on this bench, for having been the oppressed class. Well, you are the oppressor.

You know it, Judge Thayer – you know all my life, you know why I have been here, and after seven years that you have been persecuting me and my poor wife, and you still today abuse us to death. I would like to tell you my life, but what is the use? You know all about what I say before, and my friend – that is, my comrade – will be talking, because he is more familiar with the language, and I will give him a chance. My comrade, the man kind, the kind man to all the children, you sentence him two times, in the Bridgewater case and the Dedham case, connected with me, and you know he is innocent. You forget all the population that has been with us for seven years, to sympathize and give us all their energy and all their kindness. You do not care for them. Among that peoples and the comrades and the working class there is a big legion of intellectual people which have been with us for seven years, but to not commit the iniquitous sentence, but still the court goes ahead. And I think I thank you all, you peoples, my comrades who have been with me for seven years, with the Sacco–Vanzetti case, and I will give my friend a chance.

I forget one thing which my comrade remember me. As I said before, Judge Thayer know all my life, and he know that I am never be guilty, never – not yesterday nor today nor forever.

[*Vanzetti*:] What I say is that I am innocent, not only of the Braintree crime, but also of the Bridgewater crime. That I am not only innocent of these two crimes, but in all my life I have never stole and I have never killed and I have never spilled blood. That is what I want to say. And it is not all. Not only am I innocent of these two crimes, not only in all my life I have never stole, never killed, never spilled blood, but I have struggled all my life, since I began to reason, to eliminate crime from the earth.

Everybody that knows these two arms knows very well that I did not need to go in between the streets and kill a man to make the money. I can live with my two arms, and live well. But besides that, I can live even without work with my arm for other people. I have had plenty of chance to live independently and to live what the world conceives to be a higher life than not to gain our bread with the sweat of our brow . . .

What I want to say is this: Everybody ought to understand that the first of the defense has been terrible. My first lawyer did not stick to defend us. He had made no work to collect witnesses and evidence in our favor. The record in the Plymouth court is a pity. I am told that they are almost gone – half lost. So the defense had a tremendous work to do in order to collect some evidence, to collect some testimony to offset and to learn what the testimony of the state has done. And in this consideration it take double time of the state without delay, double time that they delay the case it would have been reasonable, whereas it took less than the state.

Well, I have already say that I am not guilty of these two crimes, but I never commit a crime in my life – I have never steal and I have never kill and I have never spilled blood, and I have fought against the crime, and I have fought and I have sacrificed myself even to eliminate the crimes that the law and the church legitimate and sanctify.

That is what I say: I would not wish to a dog or a snake, to the most low and misfortunate creature of the earth – I would not wish to any of them what I have had to suffer for things that I am not guilty of. But my conviction is that I have suffered for things that I am guilty of. I am suffering because I am a radical, and indeed I am a radical; I have suffered because I was an Italian, and indeed I am an Italian; I have suffered more for my family and for my beloved than for myself; but I am so convinced to be right that if you would execute me two times, and if I could be reborn two other times, I would live again to do what I have done already.

Sacco and Vanzetti were electrocuted on 23 August and their execution started riots in London, Paris and Germany. Their case provoked the first serious rebellion against the conservatism of the Republican ascendancy.

•

HERBERT HOOVER
New York, 22 October 1928

'Rugged individualism'

Herbert Hoover (1874–1964) accumulated a personal fortune as a mining engineer before directing relief work in Europe during and after the First World War. He was Secretary of Commerce under Presidents Harding and Coolidge from 1921, when he speeded the modernization of industry which increased the people's prosperity. He became the Republican candidate in the 1928 presidential election, when he was seen as the only man certain to beat the popular Democrat candidate Al Smith, who had been chosen by the liberal, urban element in the party. Smith's record of progressive social reform as Governor of New York compelled Hoover to express the political philosophy that was to dominate Republican thinking in the harsh depression years of his own administration from 1929 to 1933.

His speech on rugged individualism delivered at the very end of the 1928 campaign ranks as a classic statement of American conservatism (even though his philosophy was found tragically inadequate in the Wall Street crash of 1929). He implied that government interference in economic activities must necessarily lead to socialism and insisted that its ultimate effect would be to impair the very basis of liberty and freedom.

After the war, when the Republican Party assumed administration of the country, we were faced with the problem of determination of the very nature of our national life. During one hundred and fifty years we have builded up a form of self-government and a social system which is peculiarly our own. It differs essentially from all others in the world. It is the American system. It is just as definite and positive a political and social system as has ever been developed on earth. It is founded upon a particular conception of self-government in which decentralized local responsibility is the very base. Further than this, it is founded upon the conception that only through ordered liberty, freedom, and equal opportunity to the individual will his initiative and enterprise spur on the march of progress. And in our insistence upon equality of opportunity has our system advanced beyond all the world . . .

When the war closed, the most vital of all issues both in our own country and throughout the world was whether Governments should continue their wartime ownership and operation of many instrumentalities of production and distribution. We were challenged with a peacetime choice between the American system of rugged individualism and a European philosophy of diametrically opposed doctrines – doctrines of paternalism and state socialism. The acceptance of these ideas would have meant the destruction of self-government through centralization of government. It would have meant the undermining of the individual initiative and enterprise through which our people have grown to unparalleled greatness . . .

There is, therefore, submitted to the American people a question of fundamental principle. That is, shall we depart from the principles of our American political and economic system, upon which we have advanced beyond all the rest of the world, in order to adopt methods based on principles destructive of its very foundations? And I wish to emphasize the seriousness of these proposals. I wish to make my position clear; for this goes to the very roots of American life and progress . . .

Bureaucracy is ever desirous of spreading its influence and its power. You cannot extend the mastery of the Government over the daily working life of a people without at the same time making it the master of the people's souls and thoughts. Every expansion of Government in business means that Government in order to protect itself from the political consequences of its errors and wrongs is driven irresistibly without peace to greater and greater control of the nation's press and platform. Free speech does not live many hours after free industry and free commerce die.

It is a false liberalism that interprets itself into the Government operation of commercial business. Every step of bureaucratizing of the business of our country poisons the very roots of liberalism – that is, political equality, free speech, free assembly, free press, and equality of opportunity. It is the road not to more liberty but to less liberty. Liberalism should be found not striving to spread bureaucracy but striving to set bounds to it. True liberalism seeks all legitimate freedom, first in the confident belief that without such freedom the pursuit of all other blessings and benefits is vain. That belief is the foundation of all American progress, political as well as economic.

Liberalism is a force truly of the spirit, a force proceeding from the deep realization that economic freedom cannot be sacrificed if political freedom is to be preserved. Even if governmental conduct of business could give us more efficiency instead of less efficiency, the fundamental objection to it would remain unaltered and unabated. It would destroy political equality. It would increase rather than decrease abuse and corruption. It would stifle initiative and invention. It would undermine the development of leadership. It would cramp and cripple the mental and spiritual energies of our people. It would extinguish equality and opportunity. It would dry up the spirit of liberty and progress. For these reasons primarily it must be resisted. For a hundred and fifty years liberalism has found its true spirit in the American system, not in the European systems . . .

Our people have the right to know whether we can continue to solve our great problems without abandonment of our American system. I know we can. We have demonstrated that our system is responsive enough to meet any new and intricate development in our economic and business life. We have demonstrated that we can meet any economic problem and still maintain our democracy as master in its own house and that we can at the same time preserve equality of opportunity and individual freedom . . .

And what have been the results of our American system? Our country has become the land of opportunity to those born without inheritance, not merely because of the wealth of its resources and industry, but because of this freedom of initiative and enterprise. Russia has natural resources equal to ours. Her people are equally industrious, but she has not had the blessing of one hundred and fifty years of our form of government and of our social system.

By adherence to the principles of decentralized self-government, ordered liberty, equal opportunity, and freedom to the individual our American experiment in human welfare has yielded a degree of well-being unparalleled in all the world. It has come nearer to the abolition of poverty, to the abolition of fear of want, than humanity has ever reached before.

Hoover beat Smith but was reluctant to extend federal power during the Depression and was decisively beaten by Franklin Delano Roosevelt in the 1932 election.

•

OSWALD MOSLEY
London, 28 May 1930

'*The nation has to be mobilized*'

Oswald Mosley (1896–1980) was one of the most tragic personalities of twentieth-century British politics, a charismatic Labour politician who became a figure of ridicule after he founded the British Union of Fascists, which promoted anti-Semitic and Hitlerite policies in the 1930s.

Sitting initially in the House of Commons as an independent MP, he joined the Labour Party in 1924 and entered Ramsay MacDonald's government in 1929. Mosley wanted to solve the Depression by stimulating foreign trade and pumping public funds into industrial projects to create jobs.

The proposals were rejected by the Cabinet. Mosley's resignation speech to parliament was considered as one of the most outstanding oratorical performances of the century. Its admirers included both Lloyd George and Winston Churchill.

We have to face up to this fact, that if men are to be employed on any large scale that employment has to be paid for either by the State or by local authorities. There is a tremendous struggle, an incessant struggle, going on in every Government department to put every penny they can off the taxpayer and on to the ratepayer. What holds up these plans for months is the struggle for these pennies, these minor details. What does it matter? What is the use of shifting the burden from the taxpayer to the ratepayer? What is the use of lifting the burden from the right shoulder to the left? It is the same man who has to carry it, and the economic fact is this, as the Colwyn and every other authoritative inquiry upon the economic side has said, that the burden on the ratepayer is more onerous upon industry than the burden upon the taxpayer. If this burden has to be carried, need we struggle and waste time in deciding whether it is to be carried by the taxpayer or by the ratepayer? . . .

If you are pursuing a deflation policy, restricting the whole basis of credit, there is some force in what is known as the Treasury view, that it is difficult to raise large loans for such purposes as this.

Given, however, a financial policy of stabilization, that Treasury point of view cannot hold water. It would mean that every single new enterprise is going to put as many men out of employment as it will employ. That is a complete absurdity if you pursue that argument to its logical conclusion. If it is true it means that nothing can ever be done by the Government or by Parliament. It means that no Government has any function or any purpose; it is a policy of complete surrender. It has been said rather curiously, in view of the modesty of my programme, that it is the policy of the 'red flag'. I might reply that what is known as the Treasury view is the policy of the 'white' flag. It is a policy of surrender, of negation, by which any policy can be frustrated and blocked in this country.

Hanging all over that policy is the great conception of conversion. There are two ways of achieving conversion. One through the inherent financial strength of your position, leading to a strengthening of Government credit. The other is by the simple process of deflation to make all industrial investments unprofitable and drive your investor into Government securities because he has no other profitable outlet. But there may be another effect of that policy; that the money goes abroad, and then you get the local effect of that policy suggested by the President of the Board of Trade as the only means of solving our industrial problems, when he said on the 14th May: 'During the past fortnight alone £16,000,000 of new capital has been authorized or raised for overseas investment, and so I trust the process will continue.'

Why? Why is it so right and proper and desirable that capital should go overseas to equip factories to compete against us, to build roads and railways in the Argentine or in Timbuctoo, to provide employment for people in those countries while it is supposed to shake the whole basis of our financial strength if anyone dares to suggest the raising of money by the Government of this country to provide employment for the people of this country? If those views are passed without examination or challenge the position of this country is serious indeed. In conclusion let me say that the situation which faces us is, of course, very serious. Everybody knows that; and perhaps those who have been in office for a short time know it even better. It is not, I confidently believe, irreparable, but I feel this from the depths of my being, that the days of muddling through are over, that this time we cannot muddle through.

This nation has to be mobilized and rallied for a tremendous effort, and who can do that except the Government of the day? If that effort is not made we may soon come to crisis, to a real crisis. I do not fear that so much, for this reason, that in a crisis this nation is always at its best. This people knows how to handle a crisis, it cools their heads and steels their nerves. What I fear much more than a sudden crisis is a long, slow, crumbling through the years until we sink to the level of a Spain, a gradual paralysis beneath which all the vigour and energy of this country will succumb. That is a far more dangerous thing, and far more likely to happen unless some effort is made. If the effort is made how relatively easily can disaster be averted. You have in this country resources, skilled craftsmen among the workers, design and technique among the technicians, unknown and unequalled in any other country in the world. What a fantastic assumption it is that a nation which within the lifetime of every one has put forth efforts of energy and vigour unequalled in the history of the world, should succumb before an economic situation such as the present. If the situation is to be overcome, if the great powers of this country are to be rallied and mobilized for a great national effort, then the Government and Parliament must give a lead. I beg the Government tonight to give the vital forces of this country the chance that they await. I beg Parliament to give that lead.

Mosley carried his fight to the Labour Party conference that autumn but was again defeated by MacDonald. In December he published the Mosley Manifesto, *which was backed by seventeen Labour MPs, but he was expelled after founding the progressive socialist New Party.*

Mosley was ruined politically and his ideas were ruined with him. A. J. P.

Taylor describes the rejection of Mosley's programme as a decisive, though negative, event in British history, the moment when the British people resolved to stand on the ancient ways.

•

RAMSAY MacDONALD
Llandudno, 7 October 1930

'*We are not on trial*'

With Keir Hardie, Ramsay MacDonald (1856–1937) was one of the main founders of the British Labour Party. He became an MP in 1906, led the parliamentary Labour Party from 1911, but opposed the First World War and lost his seat in 1918. On re-election in 1922, he again led the party, briefly formed a minority Labour government in 1924 and was again prime minister from 1929.

Confronted by prolonged unemployment and a growing budget deficit, MacDonald's government was beset by economic crisis. Feelers were put out by Lloyd George for a coalition government. The annual Labour Party conference in 1930 met not only against this worsening economic background but also on the day after the R101 airship crash in which forty-eight people died, including Lord Thomson, MacDonald's closest friend in politics.

At the start of his speech, MacDonald paid an emotional tribute to the dead. Then he straightened himself up and launched into a passionate defence of the government and its record.

The Government has fulfilled the confidence that you reposed in it at the last Election. (*Cheers.*) I have no apologies – none whatever. I am not one of those who, standing aside, imagine that pettifogging criticism is either helpful or illuminating. Not at all. The plough, my friends, is in the furrow, and the place for you and me is in the furrow dragging the plough. (*Cheers.*) We have not fulfilled all our pledges – no. Did you expect us to do so? Our pledges are the pledges of men and women who are Socialists, our pledges are the pledges of men and women who know that this system of society cannot and will not work smoothly, and that the great task of statesmen of vision is to transform that system of society from the 'is' until it has become the 'is to be'; and in the course of that transformation, rightly or wrongly, my creed, and, I think, the creed of the great majority, if not all of my colleagues, has been evolution – evolution applied in precisely the same way as the scientific medical man, the scientific healer, applies his knowledge and his art to the frail and the ailing body. He does not prescribe straightaway the final food, the final exercise, the final standard of life, but being a knowing man, a man with an eye, a man not only with scientific knowledge but psychological knowledge, a man who knows how to lead gently and truly as well as to feed accurately, knowing his problem, knowing that it is not a problem of mathematics, not a problem of material things only, but a problem of mental and psychological things, works out a great policy and goes on with it from stage to stage. The men who remain out may say: 'You have not got to your journey's end,' but the men who remain in say, 'No, we have not, but we are going to get there.' (*Cheers . . .*)

It is not the Labour Government that is on trial; it is Capitalism that is being tried. We told you in those days that the time would come when finance would be more powerful than industry. That day has come. We told you in those days that people would say: 'Trade is all right, but finance is all wrong.' That day has come. We told you in those days that the time would come when the man who went into the workshop and into the factory, and his employer as well, would no longer be in the simple relationship of master and man, but that the master would become impersonal, and that powers that have nothing to do with industry would control industry – the powers of gambling with credit. That day has come . . .

So, my friends, we are not on trial; it is the system under which we live. It has broken down, not only in this little island, it has broken down in Europe, in Asia, in America; it has broken down everywhere, as it was bound to break down. And the cure, the new path, the new idea is organization – organization which will protect life, not property; organization which may protect property, but protect property in proper relation to life; organization which will see to it that when science discovers and inventors invent, the class that will be crushed down by reason of knowledge shall not be the working class, but the loafing class. That is the policy that we are going to pursue slowly, steadily, persistently, with knowledge, and with our minds working upon a plan. And I appeal to you, my friends, today, with all that is going on outside – I appeal to you to go back on to your Socialist faith. Do not mix that up with pettifogging patching, either of a Poor Law kind or of Relief Work kind. Construction, ideas, architecture, building line upon line, stone upon stone, storey upon storey: it will not be your happiness, it will certainly not be mine, to see that fabric finished. It will not be your happiness, and it will certainly not be mine, to see that every stone laid in sincerity has been well laid. But I think it will be your happiness, as it is mine, to go on convinced that the great foundations are being well laid, that the ennobling plan is being conceived, and that by skilled craftsmen, confident in each other's goodwill and sincerity, the temple will rise and rise and rise until at last it is complete, and the genius of humanity will find within it an appropriate resting place.

There was tumultuous applause. A later vote of censure was defeated by 1,800,000 votes to 330,000. A year later, after a run on the pound, MacDonald formed a national government with the Conservatives which the majority of Labour MPs refused to support. MacDonald was condemned as a traitor to socialism. Although he had towered over British politics in the 1920s, his reputation thereafter was doomed.

•

JOSEPH STALIN
Moscow, 4 February 1931

'Either we do it – or they crush us'

After assisting Lenin in Petrograd, Joseph Stalin (1879–1953) became the Bolsheviks' first Commissar for Nationalities and helped to defend Petrograd

during the Civil War. At the party congress in 1923 he seized control of the
party machine and manoeuvred to deny power to Trotsky. He succeeded Lenin
and created one of the worst dictatorial tyrannies of the century. In 1928 he
began his policy of achieving Socialism in One Country through the five-year
plans.

About 1,500 big enterprises were built during the first five-year plan, including
the largest power station in Europe; new sectors of industry were established;
thousands of kilometres of roads and canals were constructed; and many new
cities were built. It was a gigantic achievement, won at appalling cost in human
lives.

Yet although there was mounting strain in the country, Stalin was still
unsatisfied with the rate of progress and in this speech to industrial managers
he appealed to the spirit of Russian nationalism to goad workers towards
the social and economic transformation he sought to impose on the
Russians.

His message was simple – either we do it or the West crushes us; and as his
speech turned to the spirit of old Russia his words began to throb with the emotion
that was mostly lacking from his lifeless oratory.

It is sometimes asked whether it is not possible to slow down the
tempo somewhat, to put a check on the movement. No, comrades,
it is not possible! The tempo must not be reduced! On the contrary,
we must increase it as much as is within our powers and possibilities. This is dictated to us by our obligations to the workers and
peasants of the USSR. This is dictated to us by our obligations to
the working class of the whole world.

To slacken the tempo would mean falling behind. And those
who fall behind get beaten. But we do not want to be beaten. No,
we refuse to be beaten! One feature of the history of old Russia
was the continual defeats she suffered because of her backwardness.
She was beaten by the Mongol khans. She was beaten by the
Turkish beys. She was beaten by the Swedish feudal lords. She
was beaten by the Polish and Lithuanian gentry. She was beaten
by the British and French capitalists. She was beaten by the
Japanese barons. All beat her – because of her backwardness,
because of her military backwardness, cultural backwardness, politi-

cal backwardness, industrial backwardness, agricultural backwardness. They beat her because to do so was profitable and could be done with impunity. You remember the words of the pre-revolutionary poet: 'You are poor and abundant, mighty and impotent, Mother Russia.' Those gentlemen were quite familiar with the verses of the old poet. They beat her, saying: 'You are abundant,' so one can enrich oneself at your expense. They beat her, saying: 'You are poor and impotent,' so you can be beaten and plundered with impunity. Such is the law of the exploiters – to beat the backward and the weak. It is the jungle law of capitalism. You are backward, you are weak – therefore you are wrong; hence you can be beaten and enslaved. You are mighty – therefore you are right; hence we must be wary of you.

That is why we must no longer lag behind.

In the past we had no fatherland, nor could we have had one. But now that we have overthrown capitalism and power is in our hands, in the hands of the people, we have a fatherland, and we will uphold its independence. Do you want our socialist fatherland to be beaten and to lose its independence? If you do not want this, you must put an end to its backwardness in the shortest possible time and develop a genuine Bolshevik tempo in building up its socialist economy. There is no other way. That is why Lenin said on the eve of the October Revolution: 'Either perish, or overtake and outstrip the advanced capitalist countries.'

We are fifty or a hundred years behind the advanced countries. We must make good this distance in ten years. Either we do it, or they crush us.

That is what our obligations to the workers and peasants of the USSR dictate to us.

In ten years at most we must make good the distance that separates us from the advanced capitalist countries. We have all the 'objective' possibilities for this. The only thing lacking is the ability to make proper use of these possibilities. And that depends on us. *Only* on us! It is time we learned to make use of these possibilities. It is time to put an end to the rotten line of non-interference in production. It is time to adopt a new line, one corresponding to the present period – the line of *interfering in everything*. If you are a factory manager – interfere in all the affairs of the factory, look into everything, let nothing escape you, learn and learn again. Bolsheviks must master technique. It is time Bolsheviks themselves became experts. In the period of reconstruction, technique decides everything. And a business executive who does not want to study technique, who does not want to master technique, is a joke and not an executive.

It is said that it is hard to master technique. That is not true! There are no fortresses that Bolsheviks cannot capture. We have solved a number of most difficult problems. We have overthrown capitalism. We have assumed power. We have built up a huge socialist industry. We have transferred the middle peasants on to the path of socialism. We have already accomplished what is most important from the point of view of construction. What remains to be done is not so much: to study technique, to master science. And when we have done that we shall develop a tempo of which we dare not even dream at present.

And we shall do it if we really want to.

•

ADOLF HITLER
Düsseldorf, 27 January 1932

'An indomitable aggressive spirit'

By 1932, Adolf Hitler (1889–1945) was within a year of becoming German chancellor. The greatest orator of the twentieth century, albeit allied to its most evil policies, Hitler had discovered his demagogic gifts in open-air tirades against Jews and the Treaty of Versailles after he joined the National Socialist German Workers' Party (the NSDAP, derisively nicknamed 'Nazi') in Munich in 1919. His failed putsch in 1923 won him national fame and imprisonment. While in prison, he wrote Mein Kampf, *which preached a doctrine of racial-nationalist struggle for survival, advocated a German empire in Europe and the purging of the 'Jewish bacillus' from national life.*

One of the Nazis' greatest anxieties in 1932 was the financing of the election campaign. After Hitler's speech to the Industry Club at the Park Hotel in Düsseldorf, arranged by Fritz Thyssen, the anxiety was over. It was the first time that many of the industrialists had met Hitler and his reception was cool and reserved but he spoke for two and a half hours without pause and made one of the best speeches of his life.

In the year 1918, as I considered the position with cool and considered judgement, I was bound to confess: it is an appallingly difficult course to come before the people at such a time and to form for myself a new organization. It is naturally much easier to join one of the existing formations and thence to seek to overcome the inner division of the nation. But is that at all possible when one starts from the existing organizations? Has not every organization in the last resort the spirit, the men who can find satisfaction in its programme and in its struggle? If an organization has continually given way before Marxism and at length one day simply capitulated like a coward, has it not during sixty years been completely filled with a spirit and with men who neither understand the other way nor wish to pursue it? On the contrary, at a period of such confusion, will not the future lie with those who are prepared once more to pass through a sieve the body-politic, which has fallen into such disorder, so that from out of the people a new political leadership can crystallize, which knows how to take the mass of the nation in hand and can avoid the mistakes which led to downfall in the past?

I was naturally forced to say to myself that it would mean an appalling struggle, for I was not so fortunate as to possess an outstanding name; I was only a nameless German soldier, with a very small zinc identification number on my breast. But I came to realize that if a beginning was not made with the smallest cell, if a new body-politic was not thus formed within the nation, a body-politic which could overcome the existing 'ferments of decomposition', then the nation itself as a whole could never rise again. We have indeed in the past had a practical experience of that; it took 150 years before, from the fallen German Reich of ancient days,

Prussia arose to fulfil its historic mission as the germ-cell of a new Reich. And believe me, the case is the same in the question of the internal regeneration of a people. Every idea must draw men to itself. Every idea must step out before the nation, must win from the nation the fighters whom it needs, and must tread alone the difficult way with all its necessary consequences that it may one day gain the strength to turn the course of destiny.

Events have proved that this reasoning was right in the end. For though even today there are many in Germany who believe that we National Socialists would not be capable of constructive work – they deceive themselves! If we were not, already today there would be no more bourgeoisie alive in Germany: the question Bolshevism or not Bolshevism would long ago have been decided . . .

Today that Movement cannot be destroyed: it is there: people must reckon with it, whether they like it or not. (*Loud applause.*) And I am convinced that for all those who still believe in a future for Germany it is clear what their attitude must be. For here they see before them an organization inspired to the highest degree by national sentiment, constructed on the conception of an absolute authority in the leadership in all spheres, at every stage – the solitary party which amongst its members has completely overcome not only the conception of internationalism but also the idea of democracy, which in its entire organization acknowledges only the principles of Responsibility, Command, and Obedience, and which besides all this for the first time has introduced into the political life of Germany a body numbering millions which is built up on the principle of achievement.

Here is an organization which is filled with an indomitable aggressive spirit, an organization which when a political opponent says 'your behaviour we regard as a provocation' for the first time does not see fit immediately to retire from the scene but brutally enforces its own will and hurls against the opponent the retort, 'We fight today! We fight tomorrow! And if you regard our meeting today as a provocation we shall hold yet another next week – until you have learned that it is no provocation when

German Germany also professes its belief!' And when you say 'You must not come into the street' we go into the street in spite of you. And when you say, 'Then we shall kill you', however many sacrifices you force upon us, this young Germany will always continue its marches, and one day it will completely reconquer for the Germans the German street.

And when people cast in our teeth our intolerance, we proudly acknowledge it – yes, we have formed the inexorable decision to destroy Marxism in Germany down to its very last root. And this decision we formed not from any love of brawling: I could easily imagine a life which in itself was fairer than to be hunted through Germany, to be persecuted by countless Government regulations, to stand constantly with one foot in gaol, and to have in the State no right which one can call one's own. I could imagine for myself a fairer destiny than that of fighting a battle which at least at the outset was regarded by all as an insane chimera. Finally I believe that I have the capacity to occupy some post or other in the Social Democratic Party: and one thing is certain: if I had turned my capacity to *this* service, I should today presumably be fit even to enter the Government. But for me it was a greater decision to choose a way on which I was guided by nothing save my own faith, my indestructible confidence in the natural forces – still assuredly present – of our people, and in its importance which with good leadership would one day necessarily reappear.

And now behind us there lie twelve years of fighting. That fight has not been waged in theory only and in the Party alone turned into practice: we are also ready to wage that fight on the larger scale. I cast my mind back to the time when with six other unknown men I founded this association, when I spoke before eleven, twelve, thirteen, fourteen, twenty, thirty, and fifty persons; when I recall how after a year I had won sixty-four members for the Movement, how our small circle kept on growing, I must confess that that which has today been created, when a stream of millions of our German fellow-countrymen is flowing into our Movement, represents something which is unique in German history. The bourgeois parties have had seventy years to work in;

where, I ask you, is the organization which could be compared with ours? Where is the organization which can boast, as ours can, that, at need, it can summon 400,000 men into the street, men who are schooled to blind obedience and are ready to execute any order – provided that it does not violate the law? Where is the organization that in seventy years has achieved what we have achieved in barely twelve years? – and achieved with means which were of so improvised a character that one can hardly avoid a feeling of shame when one confesses to an opponent how poverty-stricken the birth and the growth of this great Movement were in the early days.

Today we stand at the turning-point of Germany's destiny. If the present development continues, Germany will one day of necessity land in Bolshevist chaos, but if this development is broken, then our people must be taken into a school of iron discipline and gradually freed from the prejudices of both camps. A hard schooling, but one we cannot escape!

If one thinks that one can preserve for all time the conceptions of 'bourgeois' and 'proletarian' then one will either preserve the weakness of Germany – which means our downfall – or one ushers in the victory of Bolshevism. If one refuses to surrender those conceptions, then in my judgement a resurrection of the German nation is no longer possible. The chalk line which *Weltanschauungen* have drawn for peoples in the history of the world already more than once has proved to be the death-line. Either we shall succeed in working out a body-politic hard as iron from this conglomerate of parties, associations, unions, and conceptions of the world, from this pride of rank and madness of class, or else, lacking this internal consolidation, Germany will fall in final ruin.

Even if another batch of twenty emergency decrees is rained down on our people, these will not stay the great line which leads to destruction, but if one day the road be rediscovered which leads upwards, then first of all the German people must be bent straight again. That is a process which none can escape! It is no good to say that the proletarians are alone responsible. No, believe me, our whole German people of all ranks has a full measure of responsibility for our collapse – a measure pressed down and running over – some because they willed it and have consciously sought to bring it about, the others because they looked on and were too weak to stop our downfall. In history the failure to act is weighed as strictly as is the purpose or the deed. Today no one can escape the obligation to complete the regeneration of the German body-politic: every one must show his personal sympathy, must take his place in the common effort.

If I speak to you today it is not to ask for your votes or to induce you on my account to do this or that for the Party. No, I am here to expound a point of view, and I am convinced that the victory of this point of view would mean the only possible starting-point for a German recovery; it is indeed the last item standing to the credit of the German people. I hear it said so often by our opponents, 'You, too, will be unable to master the present crisis.' Supposing, gentlemen, that they are right, what would that mean? It would mean that we should be facing a ghastly period and that we should have to meet it with no other defences than a purely materialistic outlook on every side. And then the distress would, simply in its material aspect, be a thousandfold harder to bear, if one had failed to restore to the people any ideal whatsoever.

People say to me so often: 'You are only the drummer of national Germany.' And supposing that I were only the drummer? It would today be a far more statesmanlike achievement to drum once more into this German people a new faith than gradually to squander the only faith they have. Take the case of a fortress, imagine that it is reduced to extreme privations: as long as the garrison sees a possible salvation, believes in it, hopes for it, so long they can bear the reduced ration. But take from the hearts of men their last belief in the possibility of salvation, in a better future – take that completely from them, and you will see how these men suddenly regard their reduced rations as the most important thing in life. The more you bring it home to their consciousness that they are only objects for men to bargain with, that they are only prisoners of world-politics, the more will they, like all prisoners, concentrate their thoughts on purely material interests.

On the other hand, the more you bring back a people into the sphere of faith, of ideals, the more will it cease to regard material distress as the one and only thing which counts. And the weightiest evidence for the truth of that statement is our own German people. We would not ever forget that the German people waged wars of religion for 150 years with prodigious devotion, that hundreds of thousands of men once left their plot of land, their property, and their belongings simply for an ideal, simply for a conviction. We would never forget that during those 150 years there was no trace of even an ounce of material interests. Then you will understand how mighty is the force of an idea, of an ideal.

Only so can you comprehend how it is that in our Movement today hundreds of thousands of young men are prepared at the risk of their lives to withstand our opponents. I know quite well, gentlemen, that when National Socialists march through the streets and suddenly in the evening there arise a tumult and commotion, then the bourgeois draws back the window-curtain, looks out, and says: Once more my night's rest disturbed: no more sleep for me. Why must the Nazis always be so provocative and run about the place at night?

Gentlemen, if everyone thought like that, then no one's sleep at nights would be disturbed, it is true, but then the bourgeois today could not venture into the street. If everyone thought in that way, if these young folk had no ideal to move them and drive them forward, then certainly they would gladly be rid of these nocturnal fights. But remember that it means sacrifice when today many hundred thousands of SA and SS men of the National Socialist Movement every day have to mount on their lorries, protect meetings, undertake marches, sacrifice themselves night after night and then come back in the grey dawn either to workshop and factory or as unemployed to take the pittance of the dole: it means sacrifice when from the little which they possess they have further to buy their uniforms, their shirts, their badges, yes, and even pay their own fares. Believe me, there is already in all this the force of an ideal – a great ideal!

And if the whole German nation today had the same faith in its vocation as these hundred thousands, if the whole nation possessed this idealism, Germany would stand in the eyes of the world otherwise than she stands now! For our situation in the world in its fatal effects is but the result of our own underestimate of German strength. Only when we have once more changed this fatal valuation of ourselves can Germany take advantage of the political possibilities which, if we look far enough into the future, can place German life once more upon a natural and secure basis – and that means either new living-space and the development of a great internal market or protection of German economic life against the world without the utilization of all the concentrated strength of Germany. The labour resources of our people, the capacities, we have them already: no one can deny that we are industrious. But we must first refashion the political pre-conditions: without that, industry and capacity, diligence and economy are in the last resort of no avail, for an oppressed nation will not be able to spend on its own welfare even the fruits of its own economy but must sacrifice them on the altar of exactions and tribute.

And so in contrast to our own official Government I cannot see any hope for the resurrection of Germany if we regard the foreign politics of Germany as the primary factor: the primary necessity is the restoration of a sound national German body-politic armed to strike. In order to realize this end I founded thirteen years ago the National Socialist Movement: that Movement I have led during the last twelve years, and I hope that one day it will accomplish this task and that, as the fairest result of its struggle, it will leave behind it a German body-politic completely renewed internally, intolerant of anyone who sins against the nation and its interests, intolerant against anyone who will not acknowledge its vital interests or who opposes them, intolerant and pitiless against anyone who shall attempt once more to destroy or disintegrate this body-politic, and yet ready

for friendship and peace with anyone who has a wish for peace
and friendship.

*When Hitler sat down, the audience rose and cheered him wildly. Substantial
contributions quickly flowed into the Nazi treasury from heavy industrial
companies. Hitler had won an important victory, says his biographer Alan
Bullock. German industrialists came to see in him the man who would defend their
interests against the threat of Communism and the claims of the trade unions.*

•

STANLEY BALDWIN
London, 10 November 1932

'The bomber will always get through'

*By 1932, the year that Hitler came to power, Baldwin had twice been prime
minister and was now Lord President of the Council in Ramsay MacDonald's
National Government. He had developed a horror of air warfare and bombing,
especially after seeing the results of a study by the Committee of Imperial Defence,
and believed that the League of Nations should ban the building of new military
aircraft. The argument was pursued in Cabinet but inconclusively. Meanwhile
President Hoover had also proposed that bombers should be abolished. Yet by the
autumn Baldwin had decided that Britain could no longer proceed with unilateral
disarmament.*

*On 10 November (moved according to his most recent biographers by a 'truly
daemonic force'), he delivered a short but sensational speech to the Commons
arguing that disarmament by itself would not stop war but that it would reduce the
dangers and opportunities of making war – and ending with an appeal to the
conscience of the young.*

What the world suffers from – and I have said this before – is a
sense of fear, a want of confidence, and it is a fear held instinctively
and without knowledge very often. But in my view, and I have
slowly and deliberately come to this conclusion, there is no one
thing more responsible for that fear – I am speaking now of what

the Hon. Gentleman the Member for Limehouse (Mr Attlee) called the common people of whom I am chief – there is no greater cause of that fear than the fear of the air. Up to the time of the last war, civilians were exempt from the worst perils of war. They suffered sometimes from hunger, sometimes from the loss of sons and relatives serving in the Army, but now, in addition, they suffer from the fear, not only of being killed themselves, but, what is perhaps worse for a man, the fear of seeing his wife and children killed from the air.

These feelings exist among the ordinary people throughout the whole civilized world, and I doubt if many of those who have that fear realize one or two things with reference to its cause. One is the appalling speed which the air has brought into modern warfare. The speed of air attack, compared with the attack of an army, is as the speed of a motor car to that of a four-in-hand and in the next war you will find that any town which is within reach of an aerodrome can be bombed within the first five minutes of war from the air, to an extent which was inconceivable in the last war, and the question will be, whose morale will be shattered quickest by that preliminary bombing? I think it is well also for the man in the street to realize that there is no power on earth that can protect him from being bombed. Whatever people may tell him, the bomber will always get through, and it is very easy to understand that, if you realize the area of space.

I said that any town within reach of an aerodrome could be bombed. Take any large town you like in this island or on the Continent within such reach. For the defence of that town and its suburbs, you have to split up the air into sectors for defence. Calculate that the bombing aeroplanes will be at least 20,000 feet high in the air, and perhaps higher, and it is a matter of simple mathematical calculation – or I will omit the word 'simple' – that you will have sectors of from ten to hundreds of cubic miles to defend.

Now imagine 100 cubic miles covered with cloud and fog, and you can calculate how many aeroplanes you would have to throw into that to have much chance of catching odd aeroplanes as they fly through it. It cannot be done, and there is no expert in Europe who will say that it can. The only defence is in offence, which means that you have to kill more women and children more quickly than the enemy if you want to save yourselves.

I will not pretend that we are not taking our precautions in this country. We have done it. We have made our investigations, much more quietly and hitherto without any publicity, but, considering the years that are required to make your preparations, any Government of this country in the present circumstances of the world would have been guilty of criminal negligence had they neglected to make their preparations. The same is true of other nations. What more potent cause of fear can there be than this kind of thing that is going on on the Continent? And fear is a very dangerous thing. It is quite true that it may act as a deterrent in people's minds against war, but it is much more likely to act to make them want to increase armaments to protect them against the terrors that they know may be launched against them. We have to remember that aerial warfare is still in its infancy, and its potentialities are incalculable and inconceivable.

As far as the air is concerned, there is, as has been most truly said, no way of complete disarmament except the abolition of flying. Now that, again, is impossible. We have never known mankind go back on a new invention. It might be a good thing for this world, as I have heard some of the most distinguished men in the Air Service say, if man had never learned to fly. But he has learned to fly, and there is no more important question, not only before this House, but before every man, woman and child in Europe, than: 'What are we going to do with this power now we have got it?' I make no excuse for bringing this subject forward tonight to ventilate it in this first Assembly in the world, in the hope that perhaps what is said here may be read in other countries and may be considered and pondered, because on the solution of this question hangs not only, in my view, our civilization, but before that terrible day comes there hangs the lesser question, but a difficult one, of the possible rearmament of Germany with an air force. The two things are inextricably wrapped up together.

As long as the air exists, you cannot get rid of the fear of which I spoke, and which I believe to be the parent of many troubles. One cannot help reflecting that, after the hundreds of millions of years during which the human race has been on this earth, it is only within our generation that we have secured the mastery of the air. I certainly do not know how the youth of the world may feel, but it is not a cheerful thought to the older men that, having got that mastery of the air, we are going to defile the earth from the air as we have defiled the soil during all the years that mankind has been on it. This is a question for the younger men far more than it is for us. They are the men who fly in the air. Future generations will fly in the air more and more.

Few of my colleagues around me here, probably, will see another great war. I do not think that we have seen the last great war, but I do not think there will be one just yet; at any rate, if it does come, we shall be too old to be of use to anyone. What about the younger men? How will they investigate this matter? It is they who will have to fight, and it is they who will have to fight out this bloody issue of war. It is really for them to decide. They are the majority upon the earth, and the matter touches them far more closely. The instrument is in their hands. There are some instruments so terrible that mankind has resolved not to use them. I myself happen to know of at least three inventions, deliberately proposed for use in the last war, that were never used – potent to a degree and inhuman.

If the conscience of the young men should ever come to feel with regard to this one instrument that it is evil and should go, the thing will be done; but if they do not feel like that – well, as I say, the future is in their hands. But when the next war comes, and European civilization is wiped out, as it will be and by no force more than by that force, then do not let them lay the blame upon the old men. Let them remember that they, they principally or they alone, are responsible for the terrors that have fallen upon the earth.

Members of parliament were shaken, even moved, by the speech, but its ambiguity left many anxious and perplexed. Where did the speech lead? Churchill asked. There was a sense of fatalism and helplessness about it. 'Tell the truth, tell the truth to the British people.' Although Baldwin had indeed told the truth, albeit in his gnomic manner, the speech did more harm than good because his striking phrase about the bomber always getting through was taken for defeatism and used to prove the futility of rearmament and disarmament alike.

•

FRANKLIN DELANO ROOSEVELT
Washington, DC, 4 March 1933

'*The only thing we have to fear is fear itself*'

On Inauguration Day 1933 all the banks were closed, trading had ceased, and the Depression was at its worst. Widespread unemployment had created a feeling of utter helplessness.

America seemed beyond help – until Franklin D. Roosevelt, crippled since 1921 when he contracted polio and lost the use of both legs, won the 1932 presidential election by a majority of more than 12 million votes, winning 42 states.

Now on a cold March day the crippled Roosevelt (1882–1945), a man of power and vision who knew that he could save his country, took the oath and addressed the millions of Americans listening to their radios. (He had written the first draft in four hours, adding the memorable 'freedom from fear' phrase only the day before the inauguration, perhaps prompted by Henry David Thoreau's "Nothing is so much to be feared as fear". He had just been given a copy of Thoreau's writings.)

His inaugural speech was one of the turning-points of American history, says historian Hugh Brogan. In a few minutes he achieved what had eluded Herbert Hoover for four wearying years: he gave back to his countrymen their hope and energy.

President Hoover, Mr Chief Justice, my friends:

This is a day of national consecration, and I am certain that my fellow-Americans expect that on my induction into the Presidency I will address them with a candor and a decision which the present situation of our nation impels.

This is pre-eminently the time to speak the truth, the whole truth, frankly and boldly. Nor need we shrink from honestly facing conditions in our country today. This great nation will endure as it has endured, will revive and will prosper.

So first of all let me assert my firm belief that the only thing we have to fear is fear itself – nameless, unreasoning, unjustified terror which paralyzes needed efforts to convert retreat into advance.

In every dark hour of our national life a leadership of frankness and vigor has met with that understanding and support of the people themselves which is essential to victory. I am convinced that you will again give that support to leadership in these critical days.

In such a spirit on my part and on yours we face our common difficulties. They concern, thank God, only material things. Values have shrunken to fantastic levels; taxes have risen; our ability to pay has fallen, government of all kinds is faced by serious curtailment of income; the means of exchange are frozen in the currents of trade; the withered leaves of industrial enterprise lie on every side; farmers find no markets for their produce; the savings of many years in thousands of families are gone.

More important, a host of unemployed citizens face the grim problem of existence, and an equally great number toil with little return. Only a foolish optimist can deny the dark realities of the moment.

Yet our distress comes from no failure of substance. We are stricken by no plague of locusts. Compared with the perils which our forefathers conquered because they believed and were not afraid, we have still much to be thankful for. Nature still offers her bounty and human efforts have multiplied it. Plenty is at our doorstep, but a generous use of it languishes in the very sight of the supply.

Primarily, this is because the rulers of the exchange of mankind's goods have failed through their own stubbornness and their own incompetence, have admitted that failure and abdicated. Practices of the unscrupulous money changers stand indicted in the court of public opinion, rejected by the hearts and minds of men.

True, they have tried, but their efforts have been cast in the pattern of an outworn tradition. Faced by failure of credit, they have proposed only the lending of more money.

Stripped of the lure of profit by which to induce our people to follow their false leadership, they have resorted to exhortations, pleading tearfully for restored confidence. They know only the rules of a generation of self-seekers.

They have no vision, and when there is no vision the people perish.

The money changers have fled from their high seats in the temple of our civilization. We may now restore that temple to the ancient truths.

The measure of the restoration lies in the extent to which we apply social values more noble than mere monetary profit.

Happiness lies not in the mere possession of money; it lies in the joy of achievement, in the thrill of creative effort.

The joy and moral stimulation of work no longer must be forgotten in the mad chase of evanescent profits. These dark days will be worth all they cost us if they teach us that our true destiny is not to be ministered unto but to minister to ourselves and to our fellow-men.

Recognition of the falsity of material wealth as the standard of success goes hand in hand with the abandonment of the false belief that public office and high political position are to be valued only by the standards of pride of place and personal profit; and there must be an end to a conduct in banking and in business which too often has given to a sacred trust the likeness of callous and selfish wrongdoing.

Small wonder that confidence languishes, for it thrives only on honesty, on honor, on the sacredness of obligations, on faithful protection, on unselfish performance. Without them it cannot live.

Restoration calls, however, not for changes in ethics alone. This nation asks for action, and action now.

Our greatest primary task is to put people to work. This is no unsolvable problem if we face it wisely and courageously . . .

I favor as a practical policy the putting of first things first. I shall spare no effort to restore world trade by international economic readjustment, but the emergency at home cannot wait on that accomplishment.

The basic thought that guides these specific means of national recovery is not narrowly nationalistic.

It is the insistence, as a first consideration, upon the interdependence of the various elements in, and parts of, the United States – a recognition of the old and permanently important manifestation of the American spirit of the pioneer.

It is the way to recovery. It is the immediate way. It is the strongest assurance that the recovery will endure.

In the field of world policy I would dedicate this nation to the policy of the good neighbor – the neighbor who resolutely respects himself and, because he does so, respects the rights of others – the neighbor who respects his obligations and respects the sanctity of his agreements in and with a world of neighbors.

If I read the temper of our people correctly, we now realize as we have never before, our interdependence on each other; that we cannot merely take, but we must give as well; that if we are to go forward we must move as a trained and loyal army willing to sacrifice for the good of a common discipline, because, without such discipline, no progress is made, no leadership becomes effective.

We are, I know, ready and willing to submit our lives and property to such discipline because it makes possible a leadership which aims at a larger good.

This I propose to offer, pledging that the larger purposes will bind upon us all as a sacred obligation with a unity of duty hitherto evoked only in time of armed strife.

With this pledge taken, I assume unhesitatingly the leadership of this great army of our people, dedicated to a disciplined attack upon our common problems.

Action in this image and to this end is feasible under the forms of government which we have inherited from our ancestors.

Our Constitution is so simple and practical that it is possible always to meet extraordinary needs by changes in emphasis and arrangement without loss of essential form.

That is why our constitutional system has proved itself the most superbly enduring political mechanism the modern world has produced. It has met every stress of vast expansion of territory, of foreign wars, of bitter internal strife, of world relations . . .

I am prepared under my constitutional duty to recommend the measures that a stricken nation in the midst of a stricken world may require.

These measures, or such other measures as the Congress may build out of its experience and wisdom, I shall seek, within my constitutional authority, to bring to speedy adoption.

But in the event that the Congress shall fail to take one of these two courses, and in the event that the national emergency is still critical, I shall not evade the clear course of duty that will then confront me.

I shall ask the Congress for the one remaining instrument to meet the crisis – broad executive power to wage a war against the emergency as great as the power that would be given me if we were in fact invaded by a foreign foe.

For the trust reposed in me I will return the courage and the devotion that befit the time. I can do no less.

We face the arduous days that lie before us in the warm courage of national unity; with the clear consciousness of seeking old and precious moral values; with the clean satisfaction that comes from the stern performance of duty by old and young alike.

We aim at the assurance of a rounded and permanent national life.

We do not distrust the future of essential democracy. The people of the United States have not failed. In their need they have registered a mandate that they want direct, vigorous action.

They have asked for discipline and direction under leadership. They have made me the present instrument of their wishes. In the spirit of the gift I take it.

In this dedication of a nation we humbly ask the blessing of

God. May He protect each and every one of us! May He guide me in the days to come!

By the end of the week half a million letters had been sent to the White House. Here for once were words that were not mere rhetoric, says Hugh Brogan. Words became deeds after 4 March and Roosevelt went on to win four successive elections.

•

ADOLF HITLER
Berlin, 13 July 1934

'*The supreme justiciar of the German people*'

Hitler was made chancellor of Germany on 30 January 1933 and four weeks later the Reichstag Fire gave him the opportunity to establish a one-party system. A little over a year later, on 30 June 1934, he eliminated his rivals on the Night of the Long Knives, when he used Nazi élite units (the SS) in the private army of Himmler, the Nazi police chief, to murder the older and more radical Nazi private army, the Brown-shirts (the SA), led by Ernst Röhm. There were more than one hundred victims of the killings, which made Hitler undisputed leader of the Nazi revolution.

After the blood bath, Joseph Goebbels, Hitler's propagandist, forbade German newspapers to carry obituary notices of the victims, which only fed and intensified rumour, horror and fear. Hitler did not appear before the Reichstag until 13 July, when he spoke for two hours.

Never had Hitler made so evident his contempt for the law or humanity and his determination to preserve his power at any cost.

At one o'clock in the night I received the last dispatches telling me of the alarm summonses; at two o'clock in the morning I flew to Munich. Meanwhile Minister-President Göring had previously received from me the commission that if I proceeded to apply a purge he was to take similar measures at once in Berlin and in Prussia. With an iron fist he beat down the attack on the National Socialist state before it could develop. The necessity for acting with lightning speed meant that in this decisive hour I had very few men with me. In the presence of the Minister Goebbels and of the new Chief of Staff the action of which you are already informed was executed and brought to a close in Munich. Although only a few days before I had been prepared to exercise clemency, at this hour there was no place for any such consideration. Mutinies are suppressed in accordance with laws of iron that are eternally the same. If anyone reproaches me and asks why I did not resort to the regular courts of justice for conviction of the offenders, then all that I can say to him is this: in this hour I was responsible for the fate of the German people, and thereby I became the supreme justiciar of the German people!

Mutinous divisions have in all periods been recalled to order by decimation. Only one state has failed to make any use of its articles of war, and this state paid for that failure by collapse – Germany. I did not wish to deliver up the young Reich to the fate of the old Reich. I gave the order to shoot those who were the ringleaders in this treason, and I further gave the order to burn out down to the raw flesh the ulcers of this poisoning of the wells in our domestic life and of the poisoning of the outside world. And I further ordered that if any of the mutineers should attempt to resist arrest, they were immediately to be struck down with armed force. The nation must know that its existence – and that is guaranteed through its internal order and security – can be threatened by no one with impunity! And everyone must know for all future time that if he raises his hand to strike the state, then certain death is his lot. And every National Socialist must know that no rank and no position can protect him from his personal responsibility and therefore from his punishment. I have prosecuted thousands of our former opponents on account of their corruption. I should in my own mind reproach myself if I were now to tolerate similar offences in our own ranks. No people and no government can help it if creatures arise such as we once knew in Germany, a Kutisker, for example, such as France came to know in a Stavisky, or such as we today have once more experienced – men whose aim is to sin against a nation's interests. But every people is itself guilty if it does not find the strength to destroy such noxious creatures.

If people bring against me the objection that only a judicial procedure could precisely weigh the measure of the guilt and of its expiation, then against this view I lodge my most solemn protest. He who rises against Germany is a traitor to his country: and the traitor to his country is not to be punished according to the range and the extent of his act, but according to the purpose that that act has revealed. He who in his heart purposes to raise a mutiny and thereby breaks loyalty, breaks faith, breaks sacred pledges, he can expect nothing else than that he himself will be the first sacrifice. I have no intention to have the little culprits shot and to spare the great criminals. It is not my duty to inquire whether it was too hard a lot that was inflicted on these conspirators, these agitators and destroyers, these poisoners of the wellsprings of German public opinion and in a wider sense of world opinion: it is not mine to consider which of them suffered too severely: I have only to see to it that Germany's lot should not be intolerable . . .

In these days, which have been days of severe trial both for me and for its members, the SA [storm troopers] has preserved the spirit of loyalty. Thus for the third time the SA has proved that it is mine, just as I will prove at any time that I belong to my SA men. In a few weeks' time the Brown Shirt will once more dominate the streets of Germany and will give to one and all clear evidence that because it has overcome its grievous distress the life of National Socialist Germany is only the more vigorous.

When in March of last year our young revolution stormed through Germany, my highest endeavour was to shed as little blood as possible. To millions of my former opponents, on behalf of the new state and in the name of the National Socialist party, I offered a general amnesty; millions of them have since joined us and are loyally cooperating in the rebuilding of the Reich.

I hoped that it might not be necessary any longer to be forced to defend this state yet again with arms in our hands. But since fate has now none the less put us to this test, all of us wish to pledge ourselves with only the greater fanaticism to hold fast to that which was formerly won at the price of the blood of so many of our best men and which today had to be maintained once more through the blood of German fellow countrymen. Just as one and a half years ago I offered reconciliation to our former opponents, so would I from henceforth also promise forgetfulness to all those who shared in the guilt of this act of madness. Let them bethink themselves, and remembering this melancholy calamity in our new German history let them devote themselves to the task of reparation. May they now recognize with surer insight than before the great task that fate sets us, which civil war and chaos cannot perform. May we all feel responsible for the most precious treasure that there can be for the German people: internal order, internal and external peace, just as I am ready to undertake responsibility at the bar of history for the twenty-four hours in which the bitterest decisions of my life were made, in which fate once again taught me in the midst of anxious care with every thought to hold fast to the dearest thing that has been given us in this world – the German people and the German Reich!

After President von Hindenburg died on 2 August, an announcement was made within an hour that the office of president was being merged with that of the chancellor and that Hitler would become head of the state as well as Supreme Commander of the Armed Forces of the Reich. The same day the officers and men of the German army took their oath of allegiance not to the constitution or to the fatherland but to Hitler himself.

•

BENITO MUSSOLINI
Rome, 2 October 1935

'Italy! Italy! Entirely and universally Fascist!'

Mussolini had been eyeing Eritrea, Ethiopia (Abyssinia) and Somalia as a potential Italian East African empire since he achieved power. After a clash in December 1934 in which 100 Ethiopians were killed and an Italian expeditionary force suffered fifty casualties, attempts to settle the dispute by the League of Nations were rejected by Mussolini, and Italy invaded Ethiopia on 2 October 1935, using aircraft, tanks and poison gas against the primitive Ethiopians.

Standing on his customary balcony in Rome that day, Mussolini rallied Italians for battle at a huge Fascist rally.

Black Shirts of the Revolution! Men and women of all Italy! Italians all over the world – beyond the mountains, beyond the seas! Listen!

A solemn hour is about to strike in the history of the country. Twenty million Italians are at this moment gathered in the squares of all Italy. It is the greatest demonstration that human history records. Twenty millions! One heart alone! One will alone! One decision!

This manifestation signifies that the tie between Italy and Fascism is perfect, absolute, unalterable. Only brains softened by puerile illusions, by sheer ignorance, can think differently because they do not hear what exactly is the Fascist Italy of 1935.

For many months the wheels of destiny under the impulse of our calm determination move towards the goal. In these last hours the rhythm has increased and nothing can stop it now. It is not only an army marching towards its goal, but it is forty-four million Italians marching in unity behind this army because the blackest of injustices is being attempted against them, that of taking from them their place in the sun.

When, in 1915, Italy threw in her fate with that of the Allies, how many cries of admiration, how many promises! But after the common victory, which cost Italy 600,000 dead, 400,000 lost, one million wounded, when peace was being discussed around the table, only the crumbs of the rich colonial booty were left for us to pick up.

For thirteen years we have been patient while the circle tightened around us at the hands of those who wish to suffocate us. We have been patient with Ethiopia for forty years – it is enough now.

Instead of recognizing the rights of Italy, the League of Nations dares talk of sanctions. But until there is proof to the contrary, I refuse to believe that the authentic people of France will join in supporting sanctions against Italy . . .

Until there is proof to the contrary, I refuse to believe that the authentic people of Britain will want to spill blood and send Europe to its catastrophe for the sake of a barbarian country unworthy of ranking among civilized nations.

Just the same, we cannot afford to overlook the possible developments of tomorrow. To economic sanctions we shall answer with our discipline, our spirit of sacrifice, our obedience. To military sanctions we shall answer with militarism. To acts of war we shall answer with acts of war.

A people worthy of their past and their name cannot and never will take a different stand. Let me repeat, in the most categorical manner, the sacred pledge I make at this moment before all the Italians gathered together today, that I should do everything in my power to prevent a colonial conflict from taking on the aspect and weight of a European war.

This conflict may be attractive to certain minds which hope to avenge their disintegrated temples through this new catastrophe. Never, as at this historical hour, have the people of Italy revealed such force of character, and it is against this people, to which mankind owes its greatest conquest, this people of heroes, of poets, of saints, of navigators, of colonizers, that the world dares threaten sanctions.

Italy! Italy! Entirely and universally Fascist! The Italy of the Black Shirt Revolution, rise to your feet, let the cry of your determination rise to the skies and reach our soldiers in East Africa. Let it be a comfort to those who are about to fight. Let it be an encouragement to our friends and a warning to our enemies.

It is the cry of Italy, which goes beyond the mountains and the seas out into the great big world. It is the cry of justice and victory.

Mussolini was given a tumultuous reception. The League of Nations condemned

Mussolini's act of aggression by 50 to 1 and imposed limited sanctions, but Mussolini was undeterred, Stanley Baldwin prevaricated, and the Italians captured Addis Ababa in May 1936. Adolf Hitler drew his own conclusions from the Abyssinian war. Mussolini's triumph was not merely a vindication of his philosophy of force, it was also another demonstration of the decadence of democracy. The League's failure to stop Mussolini was the beginning of the Italo-German alliance.

•

OSWALD MOSLEY
London, 24 March 1935

'England again dares to be great'

Oswald Mosley announced the establishment of the British Union of Fascists in October 1932, three months after Hitler's Nazis had won power in the German elections. 'My duty was to awaken the will to live and to live greatly, to dedicate myself to a national renaissance,' he wrote later. A year later the movement became anti-Semitic and Hitlerite rather than fascist. Dressed in black shirts, riding breeches and jackboots the British fascists staged marches through the streets, particularly in the East End of London, distributing propaganda against democracy and socialism and making vicious attacks on the Jews. Their rallies were attended by thousands and often marked by ugly scenes of violence.

An audience of 8,000 heard this speech at the Albert Hall in which Mosley set out the vision he saw emanating from the 'first instinct of patriotism'.

We count it a privilege to live in an age when England demands that great things shall be done, a privilege to be of the generation which learns to say what can we give instead of what can we take. For thus our generation learns there are greater things than slothful ease; greater things than safety; more terrible things than death.

This shall be the epic generation which scales again the heights of time and history to see once more the immortal lights – the lights of sacrifice and high endeavour summoning through ordeal the soul of humanity to the sublime and the eternal. The alternatives of our age are heroism or oblivion. There are no lesser paths in the history of great nations. Can we, therefore, doubt which path to choose?

Let us tonight at this great meeting give the answer. Hold high the head of England; lift strong the voice of Empire. Let us to Europe and to the world proclaim that the heart of this great people is undaunted and invincible. This flag still challenges the winds of destiny. This flame still burns. This glory shall not die. The soul of Empire is alive, and England again dares to be great.

Mosley's fascist movement was a failure. After riots in London in October 1936 the Public Order Act was passed, banning political uniforms and private armies and limiting the right to march in the streets. Mosley was interned during the war and unsuccessfully fought general elections in 1959 and 1966. He lived in Paris and died in 1980.

•

FRANKLIN DELANO ROOSEVELT
New York, 31 October 1936

The forces of selfishness and of lust for power met their match'

The New Deal had created six million jobs. Roosevelt had given America ideas, leadership and help. The Depression had been mitigated. The spectre of unemployment no longer haunted the land. As Hitler instituted his German dictatorship and Mussolini conquered Abyssinia, Roosevelt had vindicated American democracy and rescued the profit system.

So wherever he spoke during the 1936 presidential campaign, he was greeted as a saviour. His last major speech was in Madison Square Garden in New York City and was considered his best of the campaign. His four speech-writers as well as the president spent more time on it than on any other as he ordered them to take off all gloves. The speech summed up the campaign as well as the record of the previous four years and showed Roosevelt as supremely confident in the creativity of the New Deal and determined to combat and defeat the forces that still opposed him, mainly the business leaders who thought that it was now their turn to rule America again.

The mounting cheers during each shouted sentence of his peroration rose to tumultuous applause as he reached his conclusion.

I submit to you a record of peace; and on that record a well-founded expectation for future peace – peace for the individual, peace for the community, peace for the Nation, and peace with the world.

Tonight I call the roll – the roll of honor of those who stood with us in 1932 and still stand with us today.

Written on it are the names of millions who never had a chance – men at starvation wages, women in sweatshops, children at looms.

Written on it are the names of those who despaired, young men and young women for whom opportunity had become a will-o'-the-wisp.

Written on it are the names of farmers whose acres yielded only bitterness, business men whose books were portents of disaster, home owners who were faced with eviction, frugal citizens whose savings were insecure.

Written there in large letters are the names of countless other Americans of all parties and all faiths, Americans who had eyes to see and hearts to understand, whose consciences were burdened because too many of their fellows were burdened, who looked on these things four years ago and said, 'This can be changed. We will change it.'

We still lead that army in 1936. They stood with us then because in 1932 they believed. They stand with us today because in 1936 they know. And with them stand millions of new recruits who have come to know.

Their hopes have become our record.

We have not come this far without a struggle and I assure you we cannot go further without a struggle.

For twelve years this Nation was afflicted with hear-nothing, see-nothing, do-nothing Government. The Nation looked to Government but the Government looked away. Nine mocking years with the golden calf and three long years of the scourge! Nine crazy years at the ticker and three long years in the breadlines! Nine mad years of mirage and three long years of despair! Powerful influences strive today to restore that kind of government with its doctrine that that Government is best which is most indifferent.

For nearly four years you have had an Administration which instead of twirling its thumbs has rolled up its sleeves. We will keep our sleeves rolled up.

We had to struggle with the old enemies of peace – business and financial monopoly, speculation, reckless banking, class antagonism, sectionalism, war profiteering.

They had begun to consider the Government of the United States as a mere appendage to their own affairs. We know now that Government by organized money is just as dangerous as Government by organized mob.

Never before in all our history have these forces been so united against one candidate as they stand today. They are unanimous in their hate for me – and I welcome their hatred.

I should like to have it said of my first Administration that in it the forces of selfishness and of lust for power met their match. I should like to have it said of my second Administration that in it these forces met their master.

Republican leaders seized on Roosevelt's attack on the forces of reaction that had sought to block his programme and said he was trying to make himself 'master' of the American people, but Roosevelt won every state except Maine and Vermont and polled more than twenty-seven million votes against his opponent Governor Alfred Landon of Kansas who got more than sixteen million votes.

•

WINSTON CHURCHILL
London, 12 November 1936

'The locust years'

By 1936 Winston Churchill, abandoned by his party, betrayed by his friends and stripped of office, was convinced that Germany was stronger in air power than Britain and France combined. He urged Stanley Baldwin to allow a House of Commons debate on defence, during which he delivered this speech, one of the greatest of his career. It was the day that Churchill spoke for all who knew that sooner or later Britain must confront Hitler and he worked on the speech through the night, dictating and revising passages to hone one of his finest philippics – aimed directly at Baldwin.

'He drives his points home with a sledgehammer,' Harold Nicolson recorded as he watched Churchill deliver the speech, which ended with a remarkable peroration in which he damned the House of Commons.

The First Lord of the Admiralty in his speech the other night went even farther. He said, 'We are always reviewing the position.' Everything, he assured us, is entirely fluid. I am sure that that is true. Anyone can see what the position is. The Government simply cannot make up their minds, or they cannot get the Prime Minister to make up his mind. So they go on in strange paradox, decided only to be undecided, resolved to be irresolute, adamant for drift, solid for fluidity, all-powerful to be impotent. So we go on preparing more months and years – precious, perhaps vital to the greatness of Britain – for the locusts to eat. They will say to me, 'A Minister of Supply is not necessary, for all is going well.' I deny it. 'The position is satisfactory.' It is not true. 'All is proceeding according to plan.' We know what that means . . .

Owing to past neglect, in the face of the plainest warnings, we have now entered upon a period of danger greater than has befallen Britain since the U-boat campaign was crushed; perhaps, indeed, it is a more grievous period than that, because at that time at least we were possessed of the means of securing ourselves and of defeating that campaign. Now we have no such assurance. The era of procrastination, of half-measures, of soothing and baffling expedients, of delays, is coming to its close. In its place we are entering a period of consequences. We have entered a period in which for more than a year, or a year and a half, the considerable preparations which are now on foot in Britain will not, as the Minister clearly showed, yield results which can be effective in actual fighting strength; while during this very period Germany may well reach the culminating point of her gigantic military preparations, and be forced by financial and economic stringency to contemplate a sharp decline, or perhaps some other exit from her difficulties. It is this lamentable conjunction of events which seems to present the danger of Europe in its most disquieting form. We cannot avoid this period; we are in it now. Surely, if we can abridge it by even a few months, if we can shorten this period when the German Army will begin to be so much larger than the French Army, and before the British Air Force has come to play its complementary part, we may be the architects who build the peace of the world on sure foundations.

Two things, I confess, have staggered me, after a long Parliamentary experience, in these Debates. The first has been the dangers that have so swiftly come upon us in a few years, and have been transforming our position and the whole outlook of the world. Secondly, I have been staggered by the failure of the House of Commons to react effectively against those dangers. That, I am bound to say, I never expected. I never would have believed that we should have been allowed to go on getting into this plight, month by month and year by year, and that even the Government's own confessions of error would have produced no concentration of Parliamentary opinion and force capable of lifting our efforts to the level of emergency. I say that unless the House resolves to find out the truth for itself it will have committed an act of abdication of duty without parallel in its long history.

•

STANLEY BALDWIN
London, 12 November 1936

'*I shall always trust the instincts of our democratic people*'

Baldwin reacted immediately to Churchill's jibe about the years that the locusts had eaten. He conceded that Britain had cut down the services during 1924–9 because it hoped for disarmament and believed there was no danger of a major war. Nor, he argued, was British public opinion ready for rearmament until 1934–5. Addressing much of his speech to the member for Epping, Churchill, and declaring that he would speak with the 'utmost frankness', he then set out his defence.

Supposing I had gone to the country and said that Germany was rearming and that we must rearm, does anybody think that this pacific democracy would have rallied to that cry at that moment? I cannot think of anything that would have made the loss of the election from my point of view more certain. I think the country itself learned by certain events that took place during the winter of 1934–5 what the perils might be to it. All I did was to take a moment perhaps less unfortunate than another might have been, and we won the election with a large majority; but frankly I could conceive that we should at that time, by advocating certain courses, have been a great deal less successful. We got from the country – with a large majority – a mandate for doing a thing that no one, twelve months before, would have believed possible. It is my firm conviction that had the Government, with this great majority, used that majority to do anything that might be described as arming without a mandate – and they did not do anything, except the slightly increased air programme for which they gave their reasons – had I taken such action as my Right Hon. Friend desired me to take, it would have defeated entirely the end I had in view. I may be wrong, but I put that to the House as an explanation of my action in that respect.

I shall always trust the instincts of our democratic people. They may come a little late, but my word, they come with a certainty when they do come; they come with a unity not imposed from the top, not imposed by force, but a unity that nothing can break. I believe today that, whatever differences there may be among us in the country on various questions – as there must be – the conviction is biting deep into our country, with all its love of peace, that there must be no going back on our resolution for such rearmament as we deem necessary to meet any possible peril from whatever quarter it may come. That feeling is coupled with the feeling which we all have that we are as anxious as ever to see all the countries of Europe considering disarmament, especially in the air. But until that day comes, nothing will shake the resolution either of the Government or of this House or of our people.

It is very easy to be led into supposing that dictatorial methods are necessarily more effective than the coordination of free effort, but we must not imagine that other countries whose governments do not submit their plans for defence to Parliament and do not require the approval of the legislature for the power which they exercise, whose Ministers are never criticized and have not to explain themselves, therefore escape all trouble. The last war showed one thing plainly and it was that at times when we might have suspected that the enemy was prepared to the last button, that all was going happily with him and that he had no difficulties, he was, even then, struggling with handicaps and confusions of which we knew nothing. It is a mistake to suppose that our methods are necessarily inferior to other methods which are largely concealed from the public gaze. My Right Hon. Friend the Member for Epping seldom speaks nowadays without a quotation from the Latin tongue and I rejoice that it should be so. He gave us one today, and I, at this point, would like to give another: 'Omne ignotum pro terribili', which I might translate thus: 'Things you know nothing about are always bogies.'

Experience in the House of Commons has taught me the lesson that more is to be gained in this country by relying on willing cooperation than by adopting dictatorial methods, until they are forced upon you and become essential. The House of Commons and the British people are very alike. The exercise of compulsory powers inevitably involves, at any rate at first, a most serious dislocation of industry, a dislocation which may be out of all proportion to the benefits obtained. It may well be that, instead of being hastened, production for some time may be retarded. But it is certain – and I must repeat this – that it would so dislocate the ordinary free working of industry as to reduce our effective financial strength; and that financial strength, so carefully nursed and looked after through all these years, is one of the strongest weapons we have if war ever comes upon us.

The whole of our efforts in the field of diplomacy and foreign policy will be aimed at bringing agreement and peace to all foreign Powers. At the same time all our efforts will be devoted to this great question of defence – the protection of our own people – and we will not relax our efforts for one moment, because we know that while we shall work for the blessings of peace, there can be no peace, in Europe certainly, unless every country knows that we are prepared for war.

Baldwin's speech, a limp and lame reply, delivered haltingly, haunted his reputation to the grave and increased the sense of unease created by Churchill's speech – but he was to win a triumph the following month when the abdication crisis erupted. He stood accused of acting complacently as Hitler built up German military power. Yet the archives for the era suggest that Baldwin was certainly more aware of the need to build up Britain's defences than his successor Neville Chamberlain.

•

CHAIM WEIZMANN
Jerusalem, 25 November 1936

'The Jews carry Palestine in their hearts'

David Ben-Gurion, the great prime minister of Israel, described Chaim Weizmann (1874–1952) as the most gifted envoy the Jewish people ever produced. 'There was no other Jew in whom the non-Jewish world perceived the embodiment of the Jewish people, with their ability, their will, and their longings,' Ben-Gurion wrote. 'He was perhaps the only truly great ambassador produced by the Jewish people throughout the generations.'

At no moment in his life was Weizmann a greater ambassador for the establishment of a state of Israel than when he addressed the royal commission under Lord Peel, set up by Stanley Baldwin in 1936 to consider the working of the mandate after a series of Arab attacks on Jews. Weizmann was convinced that the Peel Commission offered the hope that a new and possibly decisive phase in the Zionist movement might now be beginning.

As he arrived to meet the commission, there were audible whispers from the spectators on either side of him: 'Ha-shem yatzliach darkecho' (God prosper you on your mission). 'I felt that I would be speaking for generations long since dead, for those who lay buried on Mount Scopus and those whose last resting places were scattered all over the world,' Weizmann wrote in his autobiography. 'I knew that any misstep of mine, any error, however involuntary, would be not mine alone but would redound to the discredit of my people. I was aware of a crushing sense of responsibility.'

Speaking without a prepared text, he began his address in slow measured sentences and sought to put before the commission the permanent principles of the Zionist movement and the immediate urgency of the Jewish problem. He spoke for two and a half hours.

I should like to put before you the Jewish problem as it presents itself today. It is a twofold problem; but its nature can perhaps be expressed in one word: it is the problem of the homelessness of a people. Speaking of homelessness, I should like to state that individual Jews, and individual groups of Jews, may have homes and sometimes very comfortable homes. Indeed, if one thinks of the small communities in the west of Europe beginning with England and continuing further down to the South – France, Switzerland, Italy, Belgium, and Holland – these Jewish communities are, as compared to the Jews in Central, Eastern and South-eastern Europe, in a fairly comfortable position. Then again, the position of the great Jewish community further west in America is, economically, and to a certain extent politically and morally, such that Jews there are free to work and labour without let or hindrance. But if one draws a line and takes the Rhine as the geographical boundary, almost everything to the east of the Rhine is today in a position, politically and economically, which may be described – and I am not given, I think, to exaggeration – as something that is neither life nor death; and one may add that if Europe today were in the same state as it was in 1914 before the War, with the highways and byways of Europe and the world in general open, then we should have witnessed an emigration of Jews that would probably have dwarfed the pre-war emigration – and the pre-war emigration was not by any means small. I think that in the year 1914 alone there emigrated out of Russia, which then included Poland as well, something in the neighbourhood of 120,000 Jews.

They went in the majority of cases to America, where they could readily be absorbed in a highly developed industrial country. The emigrant found his livelihood almost immediately on arrival. This, as Your Lordship and the members of the Commission are well aware, cannot happen today. The world is closed; and we have recently heard it said in authoritative quarters in Geneva, in Poland, and in England, that there are one million Jews too many in Poland. This is not the place to enter into a discussion as to why exactly one million *Jews*? They are citizens of Poland; their fate and their destinies have been bound up with the fate and destinies of Poland for wellnigh a thousand years. They passed through all the vicissitudes of the Polish nation. They desire to make their contribution, good, bad or indifferent – like everybody else – to Polish development. Why should they be singled out as being a million too many?

What does it mean? Where can they go? Is there any place in the world which can rapidly absorb one million people, whoever they may be, Jews or non-Jews? The poor Polish peasant, perhaps ignorant and not very subtle, when he hears people in authority making a pronouncement like that, may possibly interpret it as meaning: here is a superfluous people standing in my way, which must be got rid of somehow.

I do not want to press the point any further. I shall not waste the time of the Commission by describing in any way what is happening in Germany. It is too well known to need elaboration. This accounts for the position of something like 3,600,000 Jews. Poland has slightly over three million; Germany had in 1932 or 1933 something like 600,000, but that number has since diminished. If one goes further afield, and takes the Jewries of Rumania, Latvia, Austria, one sees practically the same picture; and it is no exaggeration on my part to say that today almost six million Jews – I am not speaking of the Jews in Persia and Morocco and such places, who are very inarticulate, and of whom one hears very little – there are in this part of the world six million people pent up in places where they are not wanted, and for whom the world is divided into places where they cannot live, and places into which they may not enter.

Now we think this is not merely a problem which concerns the Jewish community. It is in our view a world problem of considerable importance. Naturally, it is one which affects primarily the Jewish community, and secondarily the state of affairs in that particular part of the world, a part of the world which since the War has moved towards new forms of political and social life, and which is not yet very strong or very mature either politically or economically. These six million people to whom I have referred are condemned to live from hand to mouth, they do not know today what is going to happen tomorrow. I am not speaking now of organized anti-Semitism; even assuming the host-nations were quite friendly, there would still be purely objective reasons in those parts of the world which would tend to grind down the Jewish community and make it into the flotsam and jetsam of the world – grind it into economic dust, so to speak.

Since my early youth, My Lord, I have fought destructive tendencies in Jewry, but it is almost impossible to avoid destructive tendencies amongst a younger generation which lives in the state I have described, unless some hope is given to the young people that one day, some day in some distant future, one in five, one in ten, one in twenty, will find a refuge somewhere where he can work, where he can live, and where he can straighten himself up and look with open eyes at the world and at his fellow men and women. It is no wonder that a certificate for Palestine is considered the highest boon in this part of the world. One in twenty, one in thirty, may get it, and for them it is redemption; it is tantamount to freedom, the opportunity to live and work, and that is why they watch with such intensity all that is going on here, and whether or not the doors of Palestine will remain open or will remain closed.

I could go on dwelling on the tense position in Jewry today, aggravated, as it naturally has been, by the effects of the Great War. This is the moral side of the problem. In all countries we try to do our best, but somehow in many countries we are not entirely accepted as an integral part of the communities to which we belong. This feeling is one of the causes which have prompted Jews throughout the ages, and particularly in the last hundred years, to try to make a contribution towards the solution of the problem and to normalize – to some extent to normalize – the position of the Jews in the world. We are sufficiently strong, My Lord, to have preserved our identity, but an identity which is *sui generis* and not like the identity of other nations. When one speaks of the English or the French or the German nation, one refers to a definite State, a definite organization, a language, a literature, a history, a common destiny; but it is clear that when one speaks of the Jewish people, one speaks of a people which is a minority everywhere, a majority nowhere, which is to some extent identified with the races among which it lives, but still not quite identical. It is, if I may say so, a disembodied ghost of a race, without a body, and it therefore inspires suspicion, and suspicion breeds hatred. There should be one place in the world, in God's wide world, where we could live and express ourselves in accordance with our character, and make our contribution towards the civilized world, in our own way and through our own channels. Perhaps if we had, we would be better understood in ourselves, and our relation to other races and nations would become more normal. We would not have to be always on the defensive or, on the contrary, become too aggressive, as always happened with a minority forced to be constantly on the defensive.

What has produced this particular mentality of the Jews which makes me describe the Jewish race as a sort of disembodied ghost – an entity and yet not an entity in accordance with the usual standards which are applied to define an entity? I believe the main cause which has produced the particular state of Jewry in the world is its attachment to Palestine. We are a stiff-necked people and a people of long memory. We never forget. Whether it is our misfortune or whether it is our good fortune, we have never forgotten Palestine, and this steadfastness, which has preserved the Jew throughout the ages and throughout a career that is almost one long chain of inhuman suffering, is primarily due to some physiological or psychological attachment to Palestine. We have never forgotten it nor given it up. We have survived our Babylonian and Roman conquerors. The Jews put up a fairly severe fight, and the Roman Empire, which digested half of the civilized world, did not digest small Judaea. Whenever they once got a chance, the slightest chance, there the Jews returned, there they created their literature, their villages, towns, and communities. If the Commission would take the trouble to study the post-Roman period of the Jews and the life of the Jews in Palestine, they would find that during the nineteen centuries which have passed since the destruction of Palestine as a Jewish political entity, there was not a single century in which the Jews did not attempt to come back.

It is, I believe, a fallacy to regard those 1,900 years as, so to say, a desert of time; they were not. When the material props of the Jewish commonwealth were destroyed, the Jews carried Palestine in their hearts and in their heads wherever they went. That idea continued to express itself in their ritual and in their prayers. In the East End of London the Jew still prays for dew in the summer and for rain in the winter, and his seasons and festivals are all Palestinian seasons and Palestinian festivals. When Rome destroyed their country, the intellectual leader of the Jewish Community came to the Roman commander and said, 'You have destroyed all our material possessions; give us, I pray, some refuge for our houses of learning.' A refuge was found; the place still exists; it was then a big place, and is now a tiny railway station by the name of Yebna – in Hebrew, *Yabneh*. There were schools there, and there the Jews continued their intellectual output, so that those schools became, so to speak, the spiritual homes, not only of Palestinian Jewry, but of Jewry at large, which was gradually filtering out of Palestine and dispersing all over the world. They replaced the material Palestine, the political Palestine, by a moral Palestine which was indestructible, which remained indestructible; and this yearning found its expression in a mass of literature, sacred and non-sacred, secular and religious.

The Balfour Declaration was issued by His Majesty's Government on 2 November 1917.

It has sometimes glibly been said, 'Here is a document, somewhat vague in its nature, issued in time of war. It was a wartime expedient.' I have a much higher opinion of British statesmen than to attribute to them an act of that kind. It was a solemn act, a promise given to a people, an ancient people, which finds itself in the position which I have described.

What did the Balfour Declaration mean? It meant something quite simple at that time, and I am saying so advisedly. It meant that Judaea was restored to the Jews or the Jews were restored to Judaea. I could submit to the Commission a series of utterances of responsible statesmen and men in every walk of life in England to show that this Declaration was at the time regarded as the Magna Charta of the Jewish people; it was in a sense comparable with another Declaration made thousands of years before, when Cyrus allowed a remnant of the Jews to return from Babylon and to rebuild the Temple. To the ordinary man at that time reading the Declaration, what it meant is broadly indicated by the various speeches at a solemn meeting at the Opera House in London, where (among others) Lord Cecil spoke and said: 'Arabia for the Arabs, Judaea for the Jews, Armenia for the Armenians.' Much water and much blood have flowed under the various bridges of the world since that time, and not all of his predictions have been realized; but we read into the Declaration what the statesmen of Great Britain told us it meant. It meant a National Home, 'national' meaning that we should be able to live like a nation in Palestine, and 'Home' a place where we might live as free men in contradistinction to living on sufferance everywhere else. To English people I need not explain what the word 'home' means, or what it does *not* mean, to us everywhere else.

The meaning is clear, and the Jewry of the world, in the trenches of Europe, in the pogrom-swept area of Russia, saw it like that. Tens of thousands of Jews marched before the house of the British Consul at Odessa at the time. Behind them were half-organized bands of marauders and murderers sweeping the countryside and destroying everything in their wake. But those Jews poured out their hearts in gratitude to the one accessible representative of the British Government, whom they had never seen, of whom they had never heard, whose language they could not speak, whose mentality they could not understand. They felt that here something had been done for us which, after two thousand years of hope and yearning, would at last give us a resting-place in this terrible world.

The Peel Report recommended partition into separate Arab and Jewish states, a drastic solution that was rejected by the Arabs and most Zionists (but accepted by Weizmann). It was never implemented by the British government. The six million Jews for whom Weizmann spoke were exterminated by the Nazis, Israel was established as a Jewish state in Palestine in 1946 and Weizmann was elected president.

•

EDWARD VIII
London, 10 December 1936

'*I have determined to renounce the Throne*'

Edward VIII (1894–1972) succeeded George V as king on 20 January. Within a year and without being crowned, he abdicated rather than give up the woman he loved, Mrs Wallis Simpson, whose divorce had gone through three weeks earlier. A morganatic marriage, denying Mrs Simpson the title of queen but allowing the king to remain on the throne, was considered but rejected by Stanley Baldwin and his government. Given the choice between his throne and Mrs Simpson, the king abdicated, renouncing the throne for himself and his descendants in a personally signed message to Parliament.

After long and anxious consideration, I have determined to renounce the Throne to which I succeeded on the death of My father, and I am now communicating this, My final and irrevocable decision. Realizing as I do the gravity of this step, I can only hope that I shall have the understanding of My peoples in the decision I have taken and the reasons which have led Me to take it. I will not enter now into My private feelings, but I would beg that it should be remembered that the burden which constantly rests upon the shoulders of a Sovereign is so heavy that it can only be borne in circumstances different from those in which I now find Myself. I conceive that I am not overlooking the duty that rests on Me to place in the forefront the public interest, when I declare that I am conscious that I can no longer discharge this heavy task with efficiency or with satisfaction to Myself.

I have accordingly this morning executed an Instrument of Abdication in the terms following:

'I, Edward VIII, of Great Britain, Ireland and the British Dominions beyond the Seas, King, Emperor of India, do hereby declare My irrevocable determination to renounce the Throne for Myself and for My descendants, and My desire that effect should be given to this Instrument of Abdication immediately.

'In token whereof I have hereunto set My hand this tenth day of December, nineteen hundred and thirty-six, in the presence of the witnesses whose signatures are subscribed.

(Signed) EDWARD R I'

My execution of this Instrument has been witnessed by My

three brothers, Their Royal Highnesses the Duke of York, the Duke of Gloucester and the Duke of Kent.

I deeply appreciate the spirit which has actuated the appeals which have been made to Me to take a different decision, and I have, before reaching My final determination, most fully pondered over them. But My mind is made up. Moreover, further delay cannot but be most injurious to the peoples whom I have tried to serve as Prince of Wales and as King and whose future happiness and prosperity are the constant wish of My heart.

I take My leave of them in the confident hope that the course which I have thought it right to follow is that which is best for the stability of the Throne and Empire and the happiness of My peoples. I am deeply sensible of the consideration which they have always extended to Me both before and after My accession to the Throne and which I know they will extend in full measure to My successor.

I am most anxious that there should be no delay of any kind in giving effect to the Instrument which I have executed and that all necessary steps should be taken immediately to secure that My lawful successor, My brother, His Royal Highness the Duke of York, should ascend the Throne.

EDWARD RI

•

STANLEY BALDWIN
London, 10 December 1936

'The House today is a theatre which is being watched by the whole world'

King Edward VIII signed his instrument of abdication on the morning of 10 December. Afterwards Baldwin went to see Queen Mary, the king's mother, and then lunched at 10 Downing Street with his wife. He wrote his speech for the Commons himself, sitting alone, on small scraps of paper. Then he left them behind and they had to be fetched for him. After all that he began by dropping them and spoke extempore from notes that appeared to be in alarming disarray.

'To a quiet attentive House of Commons he made one of his greatest speeches, lasting just under an hour,' say his biographers Keith Middlemas and John Barnes, 'a triumph of art that concealed art, that gave the King the most favourable interpretation ... and which lifted the crisis at last from rumour and scandal on to the high dramatic plane where it has since largely remained.'

The House must remember – it is difficult to realize – that His Majesty is not a boy, although he looks so young. We have all thought of him as our Prince, but he is a mature man, with wide and great experience of life and the world, and he always had before him three, nay, four, things, which in these conversations at all hours, he repeated again and again – That if he went he would go with dignity. He would not allow a situation to arise in which he could not do that. He wanted to go with as little disturbance of his Ministers and his people as possible. He wished to go in circumstances that would make the succession of his brother as little difficult for his brother as possible; and I may say that any idea to him of what might be called a King's party, was abhorrent. He stayed down at Fort Belvedere because he said that he was not coming to London while these things were in dispute, because of the cheering crowds. I honour and respect him for the way in which he behaved at that time.

I have something here which, I think, will touch the House. It is a pencilled note, sent to me by His Majesty this morning, and I have his authority for reading it. It is just scribbled in pencil:

Duke of York. He and the King have always been on the best of terms as brothers and the King is confident that the Duke deserves and will receive the support of the whole Empire.

I would say a word or two on the King's position. The King cannot speak for himself. The King has told us that he cannot carry, and does not see his way to carry, these almost intolerable burdens of Kingship without a woman at his side, and we know that. This crisis, if I may use the word, has arisen now rather than later from that very frankness of His Majesty's character which is one of his many attractions. It would have been perfectly possible for His Majesty not to have told me of this at the date when he did, and not to have told me for some months to come. But he realized the damage that might be done in the interval by gossip, rumours and talk, and he made that declaration to me when he did, on purpose to avoid what he felt might be dangerous, not only here but throughout the Empire, to the moral force of the Crown which we are all determined to sustain.

He told me his intentions, and he has never wavered from them. I want the House to understand that. He felt it his duty to take into his anxious consideration all the representations that his advisers might give him and not until he had fully considered them did he make public his decision. There has been no kind of conflict in this matter. My efforts during these last days have been directed, as have the efforts of those most closely round him, in trying to help him to make the choice which he has not made; and we have failed. The King has made his decision to take this moment to send this Gracious Message because of his confident hope that by that he will preserve the unity of this country and of the whole Empire, and avoid those factious differences which might so easily have arisen.

It is impossible, unfortunately, to avoid talking to some extent today about oneself. These last days have been days of great strain, but it was a great comfort to me, and I hope it will be to the House, when I was assured before I left him on Tuesday night, by that intimate circle that was with him at the Fort that evening, that I had left nothing undone that I could have done to move him from the decision at which he had arrived, and which he has communicated to us. While there is not a soul among us who will not regret this from the bottom of his heart, there is not a soul here today that wants to judge. We are not judges. He has announced his decision. He has told us what he wants us to do, and I think we must close our ranks, and do it . . .

This House today is a theatre which is being watched by the whole world. Let us conduct ourselves with that dignity which His Majesty is showing in this hour of his trial. Whatever our regret at the contents of the Message, let us fulfil his wish, do what he asks, and do it with speed. Let no word be spoken today that the utterer of that word may regret in days to come, let no word be spoken that causes pain to any soul, and let us not forget today the revered and beloved figure of Queen Mary, what all this time has meant to her, and think of her when we have to speak, if speak we must, during this Debate. We have, after all, as the guardians of democracy in this little island to see that we do our work to maintain the integrity of that democracy and of the monarchy, which, as I said at the beginning of my speech is now the sole link of our whole Empire and the guardian of our freedom. Let us look forward and remember our country and the trust reposed by our country in this, the House of Commons, and let us rally behind the new King – (*Hon. Members: 'Hear, hear'*) – stand behind him, and help him; and let us hope that, whatever the country may have suffered by what we are passing through, it may soon be repaired and that we may take what steps we can in trying to make this country a better country for all the people in it.

Baldwin retired six months later and played no further part in public life – but his speech on the abdication crowned his political career with adulation.

•

EDWARD VIII
Windsor, 11 December 1936

'God Save the King'

Seated alone in Windsor Castle, a few miles outside London, after Baldwin's speech to the Commons, the former king broadcast to the nation. It was a poignant

*moment for both the nation and the king, embroiled in one of the great love stories
of the century.*

*A few brushstrokes were added to the speech by Winston Churchill, who
had been one of the king's few supporters in the Commons. The sentence
which speaks of the 'matchless blessing' of a happy home shows the Churchill
touch.*

At long last I am able to say a few words of my own. I have
never wanted to withhold anything, but until now it has not been
constitutionally possible for me to speak.

A few hours ago I discharged my last duty as King and
Emperor, and now that I have been succeeded by my brother, the
Duke of York, my first words must be to declare my allegiance to
him. This I do with all my heart.

You all know the reasons which have impelled me to renounce
the Throne. But I want you to understand that in making up my
mind I did not forget the country or the Empire which as Prince
of Wales, and lately as King, I have for twenty-five years tried to
serve. But you must believe me when I tell you that I have found
it impossible to carry the heavy burden of responsibility and to
discharge my duties as King as I would wish to do without the
help and support of the woman I love.

And I want you to know that the decision I have made has been
mine and mine alone. This was a thing I had to judge entirely for
myself. The other person most nearly concerned has tried up to
the last to persuade me to take a different course. I have made
this, the most serious decision of my life, only upon the single
thought of what would in the end be best for all.

This decision has been made less difficult to me by the sure
knowledge that my Brother, with his long training in the public
affairs of this country and with his fine qualities, will be able to
take my place forthwith, without interruption or injury to the life
and progress of the Empire. And he has one matchless blessing,
enjoyed by so many of you and not bestowed on me – a happy
home with his wife and children.

During these hard days I have been comforted by Her Majesty

my Mother and by my Family. The Ministers of the Crown, and in particular Mr Baldwin, the Prime Minister, have always treated me with full consideration. There has never been any constitutional difference between me and them and between me and Parliament. Bred in the constitutional tradition by my Father, I should never have allowed any such issue to arise.

Ever since I was Prince of Wales, and later on when I occupied the Throne, I have been treated with the greatest kindness by all classes of the people, wherever I have lived or journeyed throughout the Empire. For that I am very grateful.

I now quit altogether public affairs, and I lay down my burden. It may be some time before I return to my native land, but I shall always follow the fortunes of the British race and Empire with profound interest, and if at any time in the future I can be found of service to His Majesty in a private station I shall not fail.

And now we all have a new King. I wish him, and you, his people, happiness and prosperity with all my heart. God bless you all. God Save the King.

After his abdication, Edward VIII was created Duke of Windsor by his successor George VI, his brother. He married Mrs Simpson on 3 June 1937, was governor of the Bahamas during the Second World War, and lived in exile for the rest of his life, mostly in Paris.

●

LEON TROTSKY
New York, 9 February 1937

'*I stake my life*'

Ousted from power and then exiled by Stalin, Trotsky by 1937 had been living in Mexico for a year. The Moscow show trials initiated by Stalin after the assassination of Kirov, the party boss in Leningrad, had started in 1936 with Trotsky chosen to play the part of chief defendant in absentia.

Stalin's aim was to link Trotsky and alleged Trotskyite conspirators such as

Bukharin, Rykov, Zinoviev, Kamenev, Radek and Piatakov (all of them old
Bolsheviks) to the different types of opposition, terror, counter-revolution, wrecking,
espionage and treason in the Soviet Union and to destroy any potential opposition.
The state prosecutor was Andrei Vyshinsky.

More than six thousand people had gathered in the New York Hippodrome,
on 9 February 1937, at a mass meeting called by the American Committee
for the Defence of Leon Trotsky to hear him speak in his own cause. Arrange-
ments had been made for the speech to be transmitted from Mexico direct
to the hall. The meeting was to have been Trotsky's first opportunity of speak-
ing directly to a large audience in defence of the accused in the Moscow
trials.

For reasons which are still unknown the speech could not be heard – but it was
a passionate, eloquent and prophetic denunciation of Stalin.

Dear Listeners, Comrades, and Friends: Why does Moscow so
fear the voice of a single man? Only because I know the truth,
the whole truth. Only because I have nothing to hide. Only
because I am ready to appear before a public and impartial commission of inquiry with documents, facts, and testimonies in my hands,
and to disclose the truth to the very end. I declare: if this commission decides that I am guilty in the slightest degree of the crimes
which Stalin imputes to me, I pledge in advance to place myself
voluntarily in the hands of the executioners of the GPU. That, I
hope, is clear. Have you all heard? I make this declaration before
the entire world. I ask the Press to publish my words in the
farthest corners of our planet. But if the commission establishes –
do you hear me? – that the Moscow trials are a conscious and
premeditated frame-up, constructed with the bones and nerves of
human beings, I will not ask my accusers to place themselves
voluntarily before a firing-squad. No, the eternal disgrace in the
memory of human generations will be sufficient for them! Do the
accusers of the Kremlin hear me? I throw my defiance in their
faces. And I await their reply!

At the heart of the Moscow trials is an absurdity. According to
the official version, the Trotskyists had been organizing the most
monstrous plot since 1931. However, all of them, as if by com-

mand, spoke and wrote in one way but acted in another. In spite
of the hundreds of persons implicated in the plot, over a period of
five years, not a trace of it was revealed: no splits, no denuncia-
tions, no confiscated letters, until the hour of the general confessions arrived! Then a new miracle came to pass. People who had
organized assassinations, prepared war, divided the Soviet Union,
these hardened criminals suddenly confessed in August 1936 not
under the pressure of proofs – no, because there were no proofs –
but for certain mysterious reasons, which hypocritical psycho-
logists declare are peculiar attributes of the 'Russian soul'. Just
think: yesterday they carried out railroad wrecking and poisoning
of workers – by unseen order of Trotsky. Today they are Trotsky's
accusers and heap upon him their pseudo-crimes. Yesterday they
dreamed only of killing Stalin. Today they all sing hymns of praise
to him. What is it: a madhouse? No, they tell us, it is not a
madhouse, but the 'Russian soul'. You lie, gentlemen, about the
Russian soul. You lie about the human soul in general.

The miracle consists not only in the simultaneity and the
universality of the confessions. The miracle, above all, is that,
according to the general confessions, the conspirators did
something which was fatal precisely to their own political interests,
but extremely useful to the leading clique. Once more the conspirators before the tribunal said just what the most servile agents of
Stalin would have said. Normal people, following the dictates of
their own will, would never have been able to conduct themselves
as Zinoviev, Kamenev, Radek, Piatakov, and the others did. Devotion to their ideas, political dignity, the simple instinct of self-
preservation would force them to struggle for themselves, for
their personalities, for their interests, for their lives. The only
reasonable and fitting question is this: Who led these people into a
state in which all human reflexes are destroyed, and how did he do
it? There is a very simple principle in jurisprudence, which holds
the key to many secrets: *is fecit cui prodest*; he who benefits by it, he
is the guilty one. The entire conduct of the accused has been
dictated from beginning to end, not by their own ideas and
interests, but by the interests of the ruling clique. And the pseudo-

plot, and the confessions, the theatrical judgement and the entirely real executions, all were arranged by one and the same hand. Whose? *Cui prodest?* Who benefits? The hand of Stalin! The rest is deceit, falsehood, the idle babbling about the 'Russian soul'! In the trials there did not figure fighters, nor conspirators, but puppets in the hands of the GPU. They played assigned roles. The aim of the disgraceful performance: to eliminate the whole opposition, to poison the very source of critical thought, to definitely ensconce the totalitarian regime of Stalin.

We repeat: the accusation is a premeditated frame-up. This frame-up must inevitably appear in each of the defendants' confessions, if they are examined alongside the facts. The prosecutor Vyshinsky knows this very well. That is why he did not address a single concrete question to the accused, which would have embarrassed them considerably. The names, documents, dates, places, means of transportation, circumstances of the meetings – around these decisive facts Vyshinsky has placed a cloak of shame, or to be more exact, a shameless cloak. Vyshinsky dealt with the accused, not in the language of the jurist, but in the conventional language of the past-master of frame-up, in the jargon of the thief. The insinuating character of Vyshinsky's questions – along with the complete absence of material proofs – this represents the second crushing evidence against Stalin.

Among you, dear listeners, there must be not a few people who freely say: 'The confessions of the accused are false, that is clear; but how was Stalin able to obtain such confessions; therein lies the secret!' In reality the secret is not so profound. The Inquisition, with a much more simple technique, extorted all sorts of confessions from its victims. That is why the democratic penal law renounced the methods of the Middle Ages, because they led not to the establishment of the truth, but to a simple confirmation of the accusations dictated by the inquiring judge. The GPU trials have a thoroughly inquisitorial character: that is the simple secret of the confessions! . . .

Let him who has a particle of imagination picture to himself an unfortunate Soviet citizen, an oppositionist, isolated and persecuted, a pariah, who is constrained to write, not telegrams of salutation to Stalin, but dozens and scores of confessions of his crimes. Perhaps in this world there are many heroes who are capable of bearing all kinds of tortures, physical or moral, which are inflicted on themselves, their wives, their children. I do not know . . . My personal observations inform me that the capacities of the human nervous system are limited. Through the GPU Stalin can trap his victim in an abyss of black despair, humiliation, infamy, in such a manner that he takes upon himself the most monstrous crimes, with the prospect of imminent death or a feeble ray of hope for the future as the sole outcome. If, indeed, he does not contemplate suicide.

Suicide or moral prostration: there is no other choice! But do not forget that in the prisons of the GPU even suicide is often an inaccessible luxury!

The Moscow trials do not dishonour the revolution, because they are the progeny of reaction. The Moscow trials do not dishonour the old generation of Bolsheviks; they only demonstrate that even Bolsheviks are made of flesh and blood, and that they do not resist endlessly when over their heads swings the pendulum of death. The Moscow trials dishonour the political regime which has conceived them: the regime of Bonapartism, without honour and without conscience! All of the executed died with curses on their lips for this regime.

The Moscow trials are a signal. Woe to them who do not heed! The Reichstag trial surely had a great importance. But it concerned only vile Fascism, this embodiment of all the vices of darkness and barbarism. The Moscow trials are perpetrated under the banner of socialism. We will not concede this banner to the masters of falsehood! If our generation happens to be too weak to establish socialism over the earth, we will hand the spotless banner down to our children. The struggle which is in the offing transcends by far the importance of individuals, factions, and parties. It is the struggle for the future of all mankind. It will be severe. It will be lengthy. Whoever seeks physical comfort and spiritual calm, let him step aside. In time of reaction it is more convenient to lean

on the bureaucracy than on the truth. But all those for whom
the word socialism is not a hollow sound but the content of
their moral life – forward! Neither threats nor persecutions nor
violations can stop us! Be it even over our bleaching bones, the
truth will triumph! We will blaze the trail for it. It will conquer!
Under all the severe blows of fate, I shall be happy, as in the
best days of my youth, if together with you I can contribute to
its victory! Because, my friends, the highest human happiness is
not the exploitation of the present but the cooperation of the
future.

The show trials went on, culminating in the trial of Bukharin and Rykov in 1938.
On a single day in December 1938 Stalin sanctioned the execution of 3,167
prisoners. On 20 August 1940, Trotsky was battered to death in his Mexican
home by one of Stalin's agents.

•

MARTIN NIEMÖLLER
Berlin-Dahlem, 27 June 1937

'*The oppression is growing*'

As Martin Niemöller (1892–1984) celebrated Holy Communion on Friday,
25 June 1937, he was incensed to discover that three members of the Gestapo
were present. He had also heard that Hans Asmussen, theological adviser to
the council of the German church, had gone into hiding from the Nazis.

On the following Sunday, the subject of Niemöller's sermon was Rabbi Gamaliel
who, according to Acts 5, had persuaded the Jewish Sanhedrin to show tolerance to
the teaching of St Peter and his fellow Christians. The result was that the apostles
were released from custody. Neutrality was impossible, Niemöller preached.
Persecution had begun.

(The Lord shall yet comfort Zion) Acts 5: 33–42:
Jesus Christ says: 'Blessed are ye when men shall revile you and
persecute you for My sake.' And faith hears that, and faith clings

to that promise, and faith is happy and comforted, as Jesus bade it: 'Rejoice and be exceeding glad!'

But, brothers and sisters, can this *really* be so? Can we be happy and comforted in our faith? We see today that this matter of a happy and comforted faith is no child's play, that it is not enough to be able to quote passages from the Bible; that we do not go far with a little inspired protestation and our usual normal measure of inextinguishable optimism, and that we have reached the point where we cannot resist alone, without help.

The oppression is growing, and anyone who has had to submit to the Tempter's machine-gun fire during this last week thinks differently from what he did even three weeks ago. I have in mind how on Wednesday the Secret Police forced their way into the locked church at Friedrichwerder and in the vestry arrested eight members of the Reich Council of Brethren who were holding a meeting there, and took them away. I have in mind how yesterday at Saarbrücken six women and a male member of the congregation were taken into custody because they were distributing an election leaflet of the Confessional Church, at the request of the Council of Brethren. I say to you: anyone who knows these things and who has actually had to suffer these things, is not far from uttering the Prophet's words – indeed such a one would fain say with the Prophet: 'It is enough – no, it is too much! – now, O Lord, take away my life!'

And anyone who has the experience I had the night before last at an evening Communion service and sees beside him nothing less than three young members of the Secret Police who have come in their official capacity to spy upon the community of Jesus Christ in their praying, singing and preaching – three young men who were also assuredly baptized once upon a time in the name of the Lord Jesus Christ and who also assuredly vowed loyalty to their Saviour at the confirmation altar, and whose office and duty it now is to set traps for the community of Jesus Christ – anyone who sees that cannot escape so easily from the shame of the Church; he cannot pass the matter off with a pious phrase and an inspired protest: such a sight may cost him a sleepless and most

certainly a restless night, and he may even cry from the depths of
his despair: 'Lord, have mercy upon me!'

*Niemöller never again preached in Dahlem church until after the death of
Adolf Hitler. On 1 July, he was arrested by the secret police. A year later he
was taken to Sachsenhausen Concentration Camp, and then to Dachau. He
spent four years in solitary confinement before being liberated by the Allies in
1945.*

•

ADOLF HITLER
Berlin, 26 September 1938

'My patience is now at an end'

*Among all the millions of words of twentieth-century oratory, none are more
chilling than the seven that Hitler uttered at the Berlin Sportspalast in
September 1938: 'My patience is now at an end.'*

*The British prime minister Neville Chamberlain had visited Hitler twice in the
previous ten days but had been snubbed, even after offering a plan agreed by Britain
and France and accepted by the Czechs – but later repudiated by the British
Cabinet – for the Sudeten districts of Czechoslovakia to be transferred to Germany
without a plebiscite.*

*Chamberlain refused to give up hope and dispatched Sir Horace Wilson to
Germany with a personal appeal to Hitler suggesting direct negotiations between
the German and Czech governments, with the British present as a third party, in
the hope of persuading him to moderate the tone of the speech he was due to make
in the Sportspalast.*

*When Wilson arrived three hours before the speech was due, Hitler was in
his most intransigent mood, working his resentment, hatred and opposition up
to the pitch where they would provide the necessary stimulus for his speech.*

*Three hours later, Chamberlain and Beneš, the Czech president, got their
answer.*

And now before us stands the last problem that must be solved and will be solved. It is the last territorial claim which I have to make in Europe, but it is the claim from which I will not recede and which, God willing, I will make good.

The history of the problem is as follows: in 1918 under the watchword 'The Right of the Peoples to Self-determination' Central Europe was torn in pieces and was newly formed by certain crazy so-called 'statesmen'. Without regard for the origin of the peoples, without regard for either their wish as nations or for economic necessities Central Europe at that time was broken up into atoms and new so-called States were arbitrarily formed. To this procedure Czechoslovakia owes its existence. This Czech State began with a single lie and the father of this lie was named Beneš. This Mr Beneš at that time appeared in Versailles and he first of all gave the assurance that there was a Czechoslovak nation. He was forced to invent this lie in order to give to the slender number of his own fellow-countrymen a somewhat greater range and thus a fuller justification. And the Anglo-Saxon statesmen, who were, as always, not very adequately versed in respect of questions of geography or nationality, did not at that time find it necessary to test these assertions of Mr Beneš. Had they done so, they could have established the fact that there is no such thing as a Czechoslovak nation but only Czechs and Slovaks and that the Slovaks did not wish to have anything to do with the Czechs but . . . (*the rest of the sentence was drowned in a tumultuous outburst of applause*).

So in the end through Mr Beneš these Czechs annexed Slovakia. Since this State did not seem fitted to live, out of hand three and a half million Germans were taken in violation of their right to self-determination and their wish for self-determination. Since even that did not suffice, over a million Magyars had to be added, then some Carpathian Russians, and at last several hundred thousand Poles.

That is this State which then later proceeded to call itself Czechoslovakia – in violation of the right of the peoples to self-determination, in violation of the clear wish and will of the nations to which this violence had been done . . .

Now the shameless part of this story begins. This State whose Government is in the hands of a minority compels the other nationalities to cooperate in a policy which will oblige them one of these days to shoot at their own brothers. Mr Beneš demands of the German: 'If I wage war against Germany, then you have to shoot against the Germans. And if you refuse to do this, you are a traitor against the State and I will have you yourself shot.' And he makes the same demand of Hungary and Poland. He demands of the Slovaks that they should support aims to which the Slovak people are completely indifferent. For the Slovak people wishes to have peace – and not adventures. Mr Beneš thus actually turns these folk either into traitors to their country or traitors to their people. Either they betray their people, are ready to fire on their fellow-countrymen, or Mr Beneš says: 'You are traitors to your country and you will be shot for that by me.' Can there be anything more shameless than to compel folk of another people, in certain circumstances, to fire on their own fellow-countrymen only because a ruinous, evil, and criminal Government so demands it? I can here assert: when we had occupied Austria, my first order was: no Czech needs to serve, rather he must not serve, in the German Army. I have not driven him to a conflict with his conscience . . .

Mr Beneš now places his hopes on the world! And he and his diplomats make no secret of the fact. They state: it is our hope that Chamberlain will be overthrown, that Daladier will be removed, that on every hand revolutions are on the way. They place their hope on Soviet Russia. He still thinks then that he will be able to evade the fulfilment of his obligations.

And then I can say only one thing: now two men stand arrayed one against the other: there is Mr Beneš and here stand I. We are two men of a different make-up. In the great struggle of the peoples while Mr Beneš was sneaking about through the world, I as a decent German soldier did my duty. And now today I stand over against this man as the soldier of my people!

I have only a few statements still to make: I am grateful to Mr Chamberlain for all his efforts. I have assured him that the German people desires nothing else than peace, but I have also told him that I cannot go back behind the limits set to our patience. I have further assured him, and I repeat it here, that when this problem is solved there is for Germany no further territorial problem in Europe. And I have further assured him that at the moment when Czechoslovakia solves her problems, that means when the Czechs have come to terms with their other minorities, and that peaceably and not through oppression, then I have no further interest in the Czech State. And that is guaranteed to him! We want no Czechs!

But in the same way I desire to state before the German people that with regard to the problem of the Sudeten Germans my patience is now at an end! I have made Mr Beneš an offer which is nothing but the carrying into effect of what he himself has promised. The decision now lies in his hands: Peace or War! He will either accept this offer and now at last give to the Germans their freedom or we will go and fetch this freedom for ourselves. The world must take note that in four and a half years of war and through the long years of my political life there is one thing which no one could ever cast in my teeth: I have never been a coward!

Now I go before my people as its first soldier and behind me – that the world should know – there marches a people and a different people from that of 1918!

If at that time a wandering scholar was able to inject into our people the poison of democratic catchwords – the people of today is no longer the people that it was then. Such catchwords are for us like wasp-stings: they cannot hurt us: we are now immune.

In this hour the whole German people will unite with me! It will feel my will to be its will. Just as in my eyes it is its future and its fate which give me the commission for my action.

And we wish now to make our will as strong as it was in the time of our fight, the time when I, as a simple unknown soldier, went forth to conquer a Reich and never doubted of success and final victory.

Then there gathered close about me a band of brave men and brave women, and they went with me. And so I ask you my

German people to take your stand behind me, man by man, and woman by woman.

In this hour we all wish to form a common will and that will must be stronger than every hardship and every danger.

And if this will is stronger than hardship and danger then one day it will break down hardship and danger.

We are determined!

Now let Mr Beneš make his choice!

Alan Bullock, the distinguished Hitler biographer, describes this speech as a masterpiece of invective which even Hitler never surpassed. Rarely, he said, had the issue of war or peace been so nakedly reduced to the personal resentment and vanity of one man.

Chamberlain tried yet again. Three days later a settlement of the crisis was reached in Munich by the heads of government of Germany, Britain, France and Italy (Hitler, Chamberlain, Daladier and Mussolini) and the Sudetenland was annexed to Germany.

On 1 October German troops marched into the Sudetenland. The Second World War started on 3 September the following year.

•

NEVILLE CHAMBERLAIN
London, 30 September 1938

'Peace for our time'

If Hitler's declaration that his patience was at an end was the most ominous sentence of the century, Neville Chamberlain's belief that he had won peace from Hitler was the most complacent. After conferring with Hitler, Mussolini and Daladier, Chamberlain (1869–1940), British prime minister since May 1937, had signed the Munich Pact and returned to London a hero.

He addressed the cheering crowd from a first-floor window at 10 Downing Street.

My good friends, this is the second time in our history that there has come back from Germany to Downing Street peace with honour. (*After the cheering stopped, Chamberlain continued.*) I believe it is peace for our time. We thank you from the bottom of our hearts. (*To this the crowd responded: 'We thank you. God bless you.' Then a pause until Chamberlain said:*) And now I recommend you to go home and sleep quietly in your beds.

●

WINSTON CHURCHILL
London, 5 October 1938

'A total and unmitigated defeat'

A prolonged four-day debate in the House of Commons followed the signing of the Munich Pact. Chamberlain was so popular that his majority was never in doubt.

Nevertheless, several powerful speeches lamenting British humiliation and weakness were made by prominent Conservatives, including Anthony Eden, who had resigned as Chamberlain's foreign secretary because of his policy of appeasement, and Duff Cooper, First Lord of the Admiralty, who resigned after declaring that Britain should have gone to war to prevent one country dominating the continent by 'brute force'.

Speaking on the third day, Churchill made the most damning indictment of all of Chamberlain's policies.

When I think of the fair hopes of a long peace which still lay before Europe at the beginning of 1933 when Herr Hitler first obtained power, and of all the opportunities of arresting the growth of the Nazi power which have been thrown away, when I think of the immense combinations and resources which have been neglected or squandered, I cannot believe that a parallel exists in the whole course of history. So far as this country is concerned the responsibility must rest with those who have had the undisputed control of our political affairs. They neither prevented Germany from rearming, nor did they rearm ourselves in time. They quarrelled with Italy without saving Ethiopia. They exploited and discredited the vast institution of the League of Nations and they neglected to make alliances and combinations which might have repaired previous errors, and thus they left us in the hour of trial without adequate national defence or effective international security . . .

Many people, no doubt, honestly believe that they are only giving away the interests of Czechoslovakia, whereas I fear we shall find that we have deeply compromised, and perhaps fatally endangered, the safety and even the independence of Great Britain and France. This is not merely a question of giving up the German colonies, as I am sure we shall be asked to do. Nor is it a question only of losing influence in Europe. It goes far deeper than that. You have to consider the character of the Nazi movement and the rule which it implies. The Prime Minister desires to see cordial relations between this country and Germany. There is no difficulty at all in having cordial relations between the peoples. Our hearts go out to them. But they have no power. But never will you have friendship with the present German Government. You must have diplomatic and correct relations, but there can never be friendship between the British democracy and the Nazi power, that power which spurns Christian ethics, which cheers its onward course by a barbarous paganism, which vaunts the spirit of aggression and conquest, which derives strength and perverted pleasure from persecution, and uses, as we have seen, with pitiless brutality the threat of murderous force. That power cannot ever be the trusted friend of the British democracy.

What I find unendurable is the sense of our country falling into the power, into the orbit and influence of Nazi Germany, and of our existence becoming dependent upon their good will or pleasure. It is to prevent that that I have tried my best to urge the maintenance of every bulwark of defence – first, the timely creation of an Air Force superior to anything within striking distance of our shores; secondly, the gathering together of the collective strength of many nations; and thirdly, the making of alliances and military conventions, all within the Covenant, in order to gather together forces at any rate to restrain the onward movement of this power. It has all been in vain. Every position has been successfully undermined and abandoned on specious and plausible excuses.

We do not want to be led upon the high road to becoming a satellite of the German Nazi system of European domination. In a very few years, perhaps in a very few months, we shall be confronted with demands with which we shall no doubt be invited to comply. Those demands may affect the surrender of territory or the surrender of liberty. I foresee and foretell that the policy of submission will carry with it restrictions upon the freedom of speech and debate in Parliament, on public platforms, and discussions in the Press, for it will be said – indeed, I hear it said sometimes now – that we cannot allow the Nazi system of dictatorship to be criticized by ordinary, common English politicians. Then, with a Press under control, in part direct but more potently indirect, with every organ of public opinion doped and chloroformed into acquiescence, we shall be conducted along further stages of our journey . . .

I have been casting about to see how measures can be taken to protect us from this advance of the Nazi power, and to secure those forms of life which are so dear to us. What is the sole method that is open? The sole method that is open for us is to regain our old island independence by acquiring that supremacy in the air which we were promised, that security in our air defences which we were assured we had, and thus to make ourselves an island once again. That, in all this grim outlook, shines out as the overwhelming fact. An effort at rearmament the like of which has not been seen ought to be made forthwith, and all the resources of this country and all its united strength should be bent to that task . . .

I do not begrudge our loyal, brave people, who were ready to do their duty no matter what the cost, who never flinched under the strain of last week – I do not grudge them the natural, spontaneous outburst of joy and relief when they learned that the hard ordeal would no longer be required of them at the moment;

but they should know the truth. They should know that there has been gross neglect and deficiency in our defences; they should know that we have sustained a defeat without a war, the consequences of which will travel far with us along our road; they should know that we have passed an awful milestone in our history, when the whole equilibrium of Europe has been deranged, and that the terrible words have for the time being been pronounced against the Western democracies: 'Thou art weighed in the balance and found wanting.' And do not suppose that this is the end. This is only the beginning of the reckoning. This is only the first sip, the first foretaste of a bitter cup which will be proffered to us year by year unless by a supreme recovery of moral health and martial vigour, we arise again and take our stand for freedom as in the olden time.

Chamberlain won the vote but the abstention of thirty Conservative MPs was the most convincing demonstration yet of the opposition to his policies among his own supporters. Churchill was condemned by The Times *as treating the Commons to prophecies that made Jeremiah appear an optimist.*

•

NEVILLE CHAMBERLAIN
Birmingham, 17 March 1939

'Is this an attempt to dominate the world by force?'

Already diminished by Munich, Czechoslovakia fell to Hitler on 15 March 1939. Two days later, Neville Chamberlain addressed his own people, the Birmingham Conservative Association. His prepared speech was an elaborate defence of Munich – but at the last moment he threw in a reference to what had happened two days before. The audience applauded his protest and with each roar Chamberlain's improvisations grew stronger.

With this speech, appeasement and Munich were eclipsed. Chamberlain turned British foreign policy upside down.

Surely as a joint signatory of the Munich Agreement I was entitled, if Herr Hitler thought it ought to be undone, to that consultation which is provided for in the Munich declaration. Instead of that he has taken the law into his own hands. Before even the Czech President was received, and confronted with demands which he had no power to resist, the German troops were on the move, and within a few hours they were in the Czech capital.

According to the proclamation which was read out in Prague yesterday Bohemia and Moravia have been annexed to the German Reich. Non-German inhabitants, who of course include the Czechs, are placed under the German Protector in the German Protectorate. They are to be subject to the political, military, and economic needs of the Reich. They are called self-governing States, but the Reich is to take charge of their foreign policy, their Customs and their Excise, their bank reserves, and the equipment of the disarmed Czech forces. Perhaps most sinister of all, we hear again of the appearance of the Gestapo, the secret police, followed by the usual tale of wholesale arrests of prominent individuals, with consequences with which we are all familiar.

Every man and woman in this country who remembers the fate of the Jews and the political prisoners in Austria must be filled today with distress and foreboding. Who can fail to feel his heart go out in sympathy to the proud and brave people who have so suddenly been subjected to this invasion, whose liberties are curtailed, whose national independence has gone? What has become of this declaration of, 'No further territorial ambition'? What has become of the assurance, 'We don't want Czechs in the Reich'? What regard had been paid here to that principle of self-determination on which Herr Hitler argued so vehemently with me at Berchtesgaden when he was asking for the severance of Sudetenland from Czecho-Slovakia and its inclusion in the German Reich?

Now we are told that this seizure of territory has been necessitated by disturbances in Czecho-Slovakia. We are told that the proclamation of this new German Protectorate against the will of its inhabitants has been rendered inevitable by disorders which threatened the peace and security of her mighty neighbour. If there were disorders, were they not fomented from without? (*Cheers.*) And can anybody outside Germany take seriously the idea that they could be a danger to that great country, that they could provide any justification for what has happened?

Does not the question inevitably arise in our minds, if it is so easy to discover good reasons for ignoring assurances so solemnly and so repeatedly given, what reliance can be placed upon any other assurances that come from the same source?

There is another set of questions which almost inevitably must occur in our minds and to the minds of others, perhaps even in Germany herself. Germany, under her present regime, has sprung a series of unpleasant surprises upon the world. The Rhineland, the Austrian *Anschluss*, the severance of Sudetenland – all these things shocked and affronted public opinion throughout the world. Yet, however much we might take exception to the methods which were adopted in each of those cases, there was something to be said, whether on account of racial affinity or of just claims too long resisted – there was something to be said for the necessity of a change in the existing situation.

But the events which have taken place this week in complete disregard of the principles laid down by the German Government itself, seem to fall into a different category, and they must cause us all to be asking ourselves, 'Is this the end of an old adventure, or is it the beginning of a new? Is this the last attack upon a small State, or is it to be followed by others? Is this, in fact, a step in the direction of an attempt to dominate the world by force?'

Those are grave and serious questions. I am not going to answer them tonight. But I am sure they will require the grave and serious consideration, not only of Germany's neighbours but of others, perhaps even beyond the confines of Europe. Already there are indications that the process has begun, and it is obvious that it is likely now to be speeded up.

We ourselves will naturally turn first to our partners in the British Commonwealth of Nations – (*cheers*) – and to France – (*cheers*) – to whom we are so closely bound, and I have no doubt that others, too, knowing that we are not disinterested in what goes on in South-Eastern Europe, will wish to have our counsel and advice.

In our own country we must all review the position with that sense of responsibility which its gravity demands. Nothing must be excluded from that review which bears upon the national safety. Every aspect of our national life must be looked at again from that angle. The Government, as always, must bear the main responsibility, but I know that all individuals will wish to review their own position, too, and to consider again if they have done all they can to offer their service to the State.

I do not believe there is anyone who will question my sincerity when I say there is hardly anything I would not sacrifice for peace. (*Cheers.*) But there is one thing that I must except, and that is the liberty that we have enjoyed for hundreds of years, and which we will never surrender. (*Loud cheers.*) That I, of all men, should feel called upon to make such a declaration – that is the measure of the extent to which these events have shattered the confidence which was just beginning to show its head and which, if it had been allowed to grow, might have made this year memorable for the return of all Europe to sanity and stability.

It is only six weeks ago that I was speaking in this city, and that I alluded to rumours and suspicions which I said ought to be swept away. I pointed out that any demand to dominate the world by force was one which the democracies must resist, and I added that I could not believe that such a challenge was intended, because no Government with the interests of its own people at heart could expose them for such a claim to the horrors of world war.

And indeed, with the lessons of history for all to read, it seems incredible that we should see such a challenge. I feel bound to repeat that, while I am not prepared to engage this country by new unspecified commitments operating under conditions which cannot now be foreseen, yet no greater mistake could be made than to suppose that, because it believes war to be a senseless and cruel thing, this nation has so lost its fibre that it will not take part to the utmost of its power, resisting such a challenge if it ever were made. For that declaration I am convinced that I have not merely the support, the sympathy, the confidence of my fellow-countrymen and countrywomen, but I shall have also the approval of the whole British Empire and of all other nations who value peace indeed, but who value freedom even more.

The speech was described in the London Times *as 'momentous'. It was broadcast and heard throughout the British Empire and the United States and also broadcast fully in German. Chamberlain declared war on Germany on 3 September (see next speech).*

•

NEVILLE CHAMBERLAIN
London, 3 September 1939

'*This country is at war with Germany*'

I am speaking to you from the Cabinet Room at 10 Downing Street.

This morning the British Ambassador in Berlin handed the German Government a final Note stating that, unless we heard from them by 11 o'clock that they were prepared at once to withdraw their troops from Poland, a state of war would exist between us.

I have to tell you now that no such undertaking has been received, and that consequently this country is at war with Germany.

You can imagine what a bitter blow it is to me that all my long struggle to win peace has failed. Yet I cannot believe that there is anything more or anything different that I could have done and that would have been more successful.

Up to the very last it would have been quite possible to have arranged a peaceful and honourable settlement between Germany and Poland, but Hitler would not have it. He had evidently made up his mind to attack Poland whatever happened, and although he now says he put forward reasonable proposals which were rejected by the Poles, that is not a true statement.

The proposals were never shown to the Poles, nor to us, and, though they were announced in a German broadcast on Thursday night, Hitler did not wait to hear comments on them, but ordered his troops to cross the Polish frontier. His action shows convincingly that there is no chance of expecting that this man will ever give up his practice of using force to gain his will. He can only be stopped by force.

We and France are today, in fulfilment of our obligations, going to the aid of Poland, who is so bravely resisting this wicked and unprovoked attack on her people. We have a clear conscience. We have done all that any country could do to establish peace. The situation in which no word given by Germany's ruler could be trusted and no people or country could feel themselves safe has become intolerable. And now that we have resolved to finish it, I know that you will all play your part with calmness and courage.

At such a moment as this the assurances of support that we have received from the Empire are a source of profound encouragement to us.

When I have finished speaking certain detailed announcements will be made on behalf of the Government. Give these your closest attention. The Government have made plans under which it will be possible to carry on the work of the nation in the days of stress and strain that may be ahead. But these plans need your help.

You may be taking your part in the fighting services or as a volunteer in one of the branches of Civil Defence. If so you will report for duty in accordance with the instructions you have received. You may be engaged in work essential to the prosecution of war for the maintenance of the life of the people – in factories, in transport, in public utility concerns, or in the supply of other necessaries of life. If so, it is of vital importance that you should carry on with your jobs.

Now may God bless you all. May He defend the right. It is the evil things that we shall be fighting against – brute force, bad

faith, injustice, oppression and persecution – and against them I
am certain that the right will prevail.

•

LEO AMERY
London, 7 May 1940

'In the name of God, go'

*By 1940, Leo Amery (1873–1955) was almost at the end of his political career,
during which he had been First Lord of the Admiralty, colonial secretary and
Dominions secretary in the 1920s. Now a distinguished elder statesman, he was a
fierce critic of Chamberlain's vacillation and weak leadership. On the day before
war was declared, it was Amery who had shouted to Arthur Greenwood, the
former Labour leader, to 'Speak for England' when he rose to speak after
Chamberlain.*

*On 7 May 1940, Chamberlain opened a debate on the disastrous Norwegian
campaign. Among the younger Conservative MPs, there were many territorial
officers who spoke for the units which had suffered in Norway. Among them,
wearing the uniform of Admiral of the Fleet, was Sir Roger Keyes, who denounced
the government.*

*Then Amery, a friend and colleague of Chamberlain's for many years and a
fellow Birmingham MP, stood up to speak. He was called during the dinner hour
but the House quickly filled up as he moved the target of Chamberlain's critics
from the navy towards the prime minister and his conduct of the war. Sensing the
mood of the Commons, and with devastating effect, he ended his speech with the
angry words used by Oliver Cromwell to the Long Parliament in the seventeenth
century. As he uttered them, he pointed at the prime minister and delivered his
pitiless attack. It was one of the most dramatic moments in the tumultuous two-
day debate.*

Believe me, as long as the present methods prevail, all our valour
and all our resources are not going to see us through. Above all,
so long as they prevail, time is not going to be on our side,
because they are methods which, inevitably and inherently, waste

time and weaken decisions. What we must have, and have soon, is a supreme war directorate of a handful of men free from administrative routine, free to frame policy among themselves, and with the task of supervising, inspiring, and impelling a group of departments clearly allocated to each one of them. That is the only way. We learned that in the last war. My Right Hon. Friend the Member for Carnarvon Boroughs (Mr Lloyd George) earned the undying gratitude of the nation for the courage he showed in adopting what was then a new experiment. The experiment worked, and it helped to win the war. After the war years, the Committee of Imperial Defence laid it down as axiomatic that, while in a minor war you might go on with an ordinary Cabinet, helped perhaps by a War Committee, in a major war you must have a War Cabinet – meaning precisely the type of Cabinet that my Right Hon. Friend introduced then. The overwhelming opinion of this House and of the public outside has been demanding that for a long while. We are told that there would be no particular advantage in it at the present time. I ask, Is this or is this not a major war?

We must have, first of all, a right organization of government. What is no less important today is that the Government shall be able to draw upon the whole abilities of the nation. It must represent all the elements of real political power in this country, whether in this House or not. The time has come when Hon. and Right Hon. Members opposite must definitely take their share of the responsibility. The time has come when the organization, the power and influence of the Trades Union Congress cannot be left outside. It must, through one of its recognized leaders, reinforce the strength of the national effort from inside. The time has come, in other words, for a real National Government . . .

Just as our peacetime system is unsuitable for war conditions, so does it tend to breed peacetime statesmen who are not too well fitted for the conduct of war. Facility in debate, ability to state a case, caution in advancing an unpopular view, compromise and procrastination are the natural qualities – I might almost say, virtues – of a political leader in time of peace. They are fatal qualities

in war. Vision, daring, swiftness and consistency of decision are
the very essence of victory. In our normal politics, it is true,
the conflict of party did encourage a certain combative spirit. In
the last war we Tories found that the most perniciously aggressive
of our opponents, the Right Hon. Member for Carnarvon
Boroughs, was not only aggressive in words, but was a man of
action. In recent years the normal weakness of our political life has
been accentuated by a coalition based upon no clear political
principles. It was in fact begotten of a false alarm as to the
disastrous results of going off the Gold Standard. It is a coalition
which has been living ever since in a twilight atmosphere between
Protection and Free Trade and between unprepared collective
security and unprepared isolation. Surely, for the Government of
the last ten years to have bred a band of warrior statesmen would
have been little short of a miracle. We have waited for eight
months, and the miracle has not come to pass. Can we afford to
wait any longer?

Somehow or other we must get into the Government men who
can match our enemies in fighting spirit, in daring, in resolution
and in thirst for victory. Some three hundred years ago, when this
House found that its troops were being beaten again and again by
the dash and daring of the Cavaliers, by Prince Rupert's Cavalry,
Oliver Cromwell spoke to John Hampden. In one of his speeches
he recounted what he said. It was this:

'I said to him, "Your troops are most of them old, decayed
serving men and tapsters and such kind of fellows . . . You
must get men of a spirit that are likely to go as far as they
will go, or you will be beaten still."'

It may not be easy to find these men. They can be found only by
trial and by ruthlessly discarding all who fail and have their failings
discovered. We are fighting today for our life, for our liberty, for
our all; we cannot go on being led as we are. I have quoted certain
words of Oliver Cromwell. I will quote certain other words. I do
it with great reluctance, because I am speaking of those who are

old friends and associates of mine, but they are words which, I think, are applicable to the present situation. This is what Cromwell said to the Long Parliament when he thought it was no longer fit to conduct the affairs of the nation:

'You have sat too long here for any good you have been doing. Depart, I say, and let us have done with you. In the name of God, go.'

•

DAVID LLOYD GEORGE
London, 7 May 1940

'Sacrifice the seals of office'

Leo Amery had pointed his finger at Neville Chamberlain and used Cromwell's words: 'In the name of God, go.' Then, as one of the most memorable debates in British history went into its second day, the Labour Party decided to call for a vote of censure.

Chamberlain was startled, angry, and taken unawares. He jumped up and declared: 'I do not seek to evade criticism but I say to my friends in the House, and I have friends in the House, no government can prosecute a war efficiently unless it has public and parliamentary support. I accept this challenge. I welcome it indeed. At least I shall see who is with us and who is against us and I call on my friends to support us in the lobby tonight.'

Chamberlain's intervention was a major miscalculation and provoked an unforgettable speech – the last decisive intervention in the House of Commons by Lloyd George. Aroused by Chamberlain's appeal to his 'friends' and the prime minister's cheapening of the office he had held with such distinction during the last world war, he now had his revenge for years of exclusion from power.

The situation is a grave one – I agree with what was said about that by the Prime Minister – and it would be a fatal error on our part not to acknowledge it. In such experience as I have had of war direction I have never tried to minimize the extent of a disaster. I try to get the facts, because unless you really face the facts you cannot overcome the difficulties and restore the position. There is no case, in my judgement, for panic. I say that deliberately, after a good deal of reflection, but there is a grave case for pulling ourselves together. We cannot do that unless we tell the country the facts. They must realize the magnitude of our jeopardy. We have two immense Empires federated in the struggle for liberty, the two greatest Empires in the world, the British Empire and the French Empire, with almost inexhaustible resources but not easily mobilized, not easily roused, especially ours.

You are not going to rouse the British Empire – because you will have to do it not merely in Britain but throughout the world – to put forth the whole of its strength unless and until you tell it the facts and realities of the peril that confronts it. At the cost of unpleasantness, I am going to do that, not with a view to terrifying them or spreading dismay and consternation, but with a view to rousing real action and not sham action such as we have had. It is no use saying that the balance of advantage is in our favour, or adding up the numbers of ships sunk on either side. That kind of petty-cash balance-sheet is not the thing to look at. There are more serious realities than that.

We promised Poland; we promised Czecho-Slovakia. We said: 'We will defend your frontiers if you will revise them.' There was a promise to Poland, to Norway, and to Finland. Our promissory notes are now rubbish on the market. (*Hon. Members:* '*Shame.*') Tell me one country at the present moment, one neutral country, that would be prepared to stand up and finance us on a mere promise from us? What is the use of not facing facts? . . .

The Hon. Member for Stockton-on-Tees (Mr Harold Macmillan) gave the whole of the facts, and they have never been answered yet. That is the situation with regard to our strategical position. What is the use of denying it? It is one of the facts that we have to face. We have to restore that prestige in the world if we are to win this war. There is also the fact that the state of our preparations is known to the world. We started these preparations five years ago, in 1935. In 1935 a promise of rearmament was made; in 1936 active proposals were submitted to this House and were passed without a Division. The Government said they would commit us to £1,500 million. If they had asked for more and had said that it was necessary, there was no party in this House which would have challenged it. (*Interruption.*) If any party had challenged it, you had your majority. What has been done? Is there anyone in this House who will say that he is satisfied with the speed and efficiency of the preparations in any respect for air, for Army, yea, for Navy? Everybody is disappointed. Everybody knows that whatever was done was done half-heartedly, ineffectively, without drive and unintelligently. For three or four years I thought to myself that the facts with regard to Germany were exaggerated by the First Lord, because the then Prime Minister – not this Prime Minister – said that they were not true. The First Lord was right about it. Then came the war. The tempo was hardly speeded up. There was the same leisureliness and inefficiency. Will anybody tell me that he is satisfied with what we have done about aeroplanes, tanks, guns, especially anti-aircraft guns? Is anyone here satisfied with the steps we took to train an Army to use them? Nobody is satisfied. The whole world knows that. And here we are in the worst strategic position in which this country has ever been placed.

Sir Patrick Hannon (Birmingham, Moseley): We have our sea power.

Mr J. J. Davidson (Glasgow, Maryhill): And your dividends.

Mr Lloyd George: I wish we had used it in some parts of Norway. I do not think that the First Lord was entirely responsible for all the things that happened there.

Mr Churchill: I take complete responsibility for everything that has been done by the Admiralty, and I take my full share of the burden.

Mr Lloyd George: The Right Hon. Gentleman must not allow himself to be converted into an air-raid shelter to keep the splinters from hitting his colleagues. But that is the position, and we must face it. I agree with the Prime Minister that we must face it as a people and not as a party, nor as a personal issue. The Prime Minister is not in a position to make his personality in this respect inseparable from the interests of the country.

The Prime Minister: What is the meaning of that observation? I have never represented that my personality – (*Hon. Members: 'You did!'*) On the contrary, I took pains to say that personalities ought to have no place in these matters.

Mr Lloyd George: I was not here when the Right Hon. Gentleman made the observation, but he definitely appealed on a question which is a great national, Imperial and world issue. He said, 'I have got my friends.' It is not a question of who are the Prime Minister's friends. It is a far bigger issue. The Prime Minister must remember that he has met this formidable foe of ours in peace and in war. He has always been worsted. He is not in a position to appeal on the grounds of friendship. He has appealed for sacrifice. The nation is prepared for every sacrifice so long as it has leadership, so long as the Government show clearly what they are aiming at and so long as the nation is confident that those who are leading it are doing their best. I say solemnly that the Prime Minister should give an example of sacrifice, because there is nothing which can contribute more to victory in this war than that he should sacrifice the seals of office.

When the Commons voted, the government's majority was reduced to 81 from its usual figure of 200. Forty-one Tories voted with the opposition and some sixty abstained. As Chamberlain left the House, a few Tory rebels, among them Harold Macmillan (who was later to be prime minister) sang 'Rule Britannia!' and shouted 'Go, Go, Go!' Winston Churchill became prime minister of a coalition government on 10 May.

•

WINSTON CHURCHILL
London, 13 May 1940

'*I have nothing to offer but blood, toil, tears and sweat*'

On becoming prime minister, Churchill mobilized the language and made it fight. The first occasion occurred only three days after he had formed his coalition Cabinet. It was Whit Monday and Churchill made a short speech to the House of Commons. Yet on entering the chamber it was Chamberlain who got more cheers than Churchill, whose support was mostly on the Labour benches.

The speech was unforgettable, imposing Churchill's character and resolve on the Commons whether they liked it or not. The effect was electrifying, says Robert Rhodes James, one of his biographers. As he walked out of the chamber, he said to one of his aides: 'That got the SODS, didn't it!'

Churchill's war speeches, with their bulldog spirit, their refusal to acknowledge the prospect of defeat, rallied the British at the most critical period of the war when Hitler was advancing to Dunkirk and threatening to invade England.

It must be remembered that we are in the preliminary stage of one of the greatest battles in history, that we are in action at many points in Norway and in Holland, that we have to be prepared in the Mediterranean, that the air battle is continuous and that many preparations have to be made here at home. In this crisis I hope I may be pardoned if I do not address the House at any length today. I hope that any of my friends and colleagues, or former colleagues, who are affected by the political reconstruction, will make all allowance for any lack of ceremony with which it has been necessary to act. I would say to the House, as I said to those who have joined the Government: 'I have nothing to offer but blood, toil, tears and sweat.'

We have before us an ordeal of the most grievous kind. We have before us many, many long months of struggle and of suffering. You ask, what is our policy? I will say: It is to wage war, by sea, land and air, with all our might and with all the strength that God can give us: to wage war against a monstrous tyranny, never surpassed in the dark, lamentable catalogue of human crime. That is our policy. You ask, What is our aim? I can answer in one word: Victory – victory at all costs, victory in spite of all terror, victory, however long and hard the road may be; for without victory, there is no survival. Let that be realized; no survival for the British Empire; no survival for all that the British Empire has stood for, no survival for the urge and impulse of the ages, that mankind will move forward towards its goal. But I take up my task with buoyancy and hope. I feel sure that our cause will not be suffered to fail among men. At this time I feel entitled to claim the aid of all, and I say, 'Come, then, let us go forward together with our united strength.'

•

WINSTON CHURCHILL
BBC Radio, 19 May 1940

'*Be ye men of valour*'

Churchill's war of words began in earnest when he made his first broadcast to the nation as prime minister on 19 May. The Germans had invaded Holland and Belgium and broken through the French defences at Sedan. It was clear that French resistance could not long continue and that the position of British troops on the continent was perilous.

After only three hours to compose the speech, Churchill broadcast live and warned that a German attack on Britain might be imminent. It was a call to arms that caught the imagination of the nation.

Our task is not only to win the battle – but to win the War. After this battle in France abates its force, there will come the battle for our island – for all that Britain is, and all that Britain means. That will be the struggle. In that supreme emergency we shall not hesitate to take every step, even the most drastic, to call forth from our people the last ounce and the last inch of effort of which they are capable. The interests of property, the hours of labour, are nothing compared with the struggle for life and honour, for right and freedom, to which we have vowed ourselves.

I have received from the Chiefs of the French Republic, and in particular from its indomitable Prime Minister, M. Reynaud, the most sacred pledges that whatever happens they will fight to the end, be it bitter or be it glorious. Nay, if we fight to the end, it can only be glorious.

Having received His Majesty's commission, I have found an administration of men and women of every party and of almost every point of view. We have differed and quarrelled in the past; but now one bond unites us all – to wage war until victory is won, and never to surrender ourselves to servitude and shame, whatever the cost and the agony may be. This is one of the most awe-striking periods in the long history of France and Britain. It is also beyond doubt the most sublime. Side by side, unaided except by their kith and kin in the great Dominions and by the wide Empires which rest beneath their shield – side by side, the British and French peoples have advanced to rescue not only Europe but mankind from the foulest and most soul-destroying tyranny which has ever darkened and stained the pages of history. Behind them – behind us – behind the armies and fleets of Britain and France – gather a group of shattered States and bludgeoned races: the Czechs, the Poles, the Norwegians, the Danes, the Dutch, the Belgians – upon all of whom the long night of barbarism will descend, unbroken even by a star of hope, unless we conquer, as conquer we must; as conquer we shall.

Today is Trinity Sunday. Centuries ago words were written to be a call and a spur to the faithful servants of Truth and Justice: 'Arm yourselves, and be ye men of valour, and be in readiness for the conflict; for it is better for us to perish in battle than to look upon the outrage of our nation and our altar. As the Will of God is in Heaven, even so let it be.'

•

WINSTON CHURCHILL
London, 18 June 1940

'This was their finest hour'

The crumbling French resistance to Hitler could not be maintained much longer. On 10 June, the government left Paris; on 16 June Marshal Pétain formed a new government. The next day France sued for peace. As Churchill predicted in this House of Commons speech, the Battle of France was over and the Battle of Britain had begun. Britain, he declared, was now resolved to fight on alone.

The defiant words were heard by millions when it was broadcast four hours later and it is probably the best remembered Churchill speech of the war, particularly for the magnificent peroration. Even so, as Churchill wrote later, rhetoric was no guarantee of survival.

We do not yet know what will happen in France or whether the French resistance will be prolonged, both in France and in the French Empire overseas. The French Government will be throwing away great opportunities and casting adrift their future if they do not continue the war in accordance with their Treaty obligations, from which we have not felt able to release them. The House will have read the historic declaration in which, at the desire of many Frenchmen – and of our own hearts – we have proclaimed our willingness at the darkest hour in French history to conclude a union of common citizenship in this struggle. However matters may go in France or with the French Government, or other French Governments, we in this island and in the British Empire will never lose our sense of comradeship with the French people. If we are now called upon to endure what they have been suffering, we shall emulate their courage, and if final victory rewards our toils they shall share the gains, aye, and freedom shall be restored to all. We abate nothing of our just demands: not one jot or tittle do we recede. Czechs, Poles,

Norwegians, Dutch, Belgians have joined their causes to our own. All these shall be restored.

What General Weygand called the Battle of France is over. I expect that the Battle of Britain is about to begin. Upon this battle depends the survival of Christian civilization. Upon it depends our own British life, and the long continuity of our institutions and our Empire. The whole fury and might of the enemy must very soon be turned on us. Hitler knows that he will have to break us in this island or lose the war. If we can stand up to him, all Europe may be free and the life of the world may move forward into broad, sunlit uplands. But if we fail, then the whole world, including the United States, including all that we have known and cared for, will sink into the abyss of a new Dark Age made more sinister, and perhaps more protracted, by the lights of perverted science. Let us therefore brace ourselves to our duties and so bear ourselves that, if the British Empire and its Commonwealth last for a thousand years, men will still say, 'This was their finest hour.'

•

CHARLES DE GAULLE
London, 18–19 June 1940

'*The flame of French resistance*'

A veteran of the First World War, when he served under Colonel Pétain, General de Gaulle (1890–1970) successfully commanded an armoured division in May 1940 and briefly held the junior post of under-secretary for war under Paul Reynaud, the French prime minister. When the French armies collapsed, Reynaud sent for Pétain, who soon became premier himself and made arrangements for surrender and an armistice. De Gaulle escaped to England to organize the Free French movement and was sentenced to death in absentia *by a French court.*

The Battle of France was over, the Battle of Britain about to begin and the fortunes of the allies against Hitler stood at their lowest ebb as the tall French officer stood before the microphone to rally Frenchmen throughout the world.

I

The leaders who, for many years past, have been at the head of the French armed forces have set up a government.

Alleging the defeat of our armies, this government has entered into negotiations with the enemy with a view to bringing about a cessation of hostilities. It is quite true that we were, and still are, overwhelmed by enemy mechanized forces, both on the ground and in the air. It was the tanks, the planes, and the tactics of the Germans, far more than the fact that we were outnumbered, that forced our armies to retreat. It was the German tanks, planes, and tactics that provided the element of surprise which brought our leaders to their present plight.

But has the last word been said? Must we abandon all hope? Is our defeat final and irremediable? To those questions I answer – No!

Speaking in full knowledge of the facts, I ask you to believe me when I say that the cause of France is not lost. The very factors that brought about our defeat may one day lead us to victory.

For, remember this, France does not stand alone. She is not isolated. Behind her is a vast empire, and she can make common cause with the British Empire, which commands the seas and is continuing the struggle. Like England, she can draw unreservedly on the immense industrial resources of the United States.

This war is not limited to our unfortunate country. The outcome of the struggle has not been decided by the Battle of France. This is a world war. Mistakes have been made, there have been delays and untold suffering, but the fact remains that there still exists in the world everything we need to crush our enemies someday. Today we are crushed by the sheer weight of mechanized force hurled against us, but we can still look to a future in which even greater mechanized force will bring us victory. The destiny of the world is at stake.

I, General de Gaulle, now in London, call on all French officers and men who are at present on British soil, or may be in the future, with or without their arms; I call on all engineers and skilled workmen from the armaments factories who are at present on British soil, or may be in the future, to get in touch with me.

Whatever happens, the flame of French resistance must not and shall not die.

Tomorrow I shall broadcast again from London.

II

Frenchmen must now be fully aware that all ordinary forms of authority have disappeared.

Faced by the bewilderment of my countrymen, by the disintegration of a government in thrall to the enemy, by the fact that the institutions of my country are incapable, at the moment, of functioning, I, General de Gaulle, a French soldier and military leader, realize that I now speak for France.

In the name of France, I make the following solemn declaration:

It is the bounden duty of all Frenchmen who still bear arms to continue the struggle. For them to lay down their arms, to evacuate any position of military importance, or agree to hand over any part of French territory, however small, to enemy control, would be a crime against our country. For the moment I refer particularly to French North Africa – to the *integrity* of French North Africa.

The Italian armistice is nothing but a clumsy trap. In the Africa of Clauzel, Bugeaud, Lyautey, and Noguès, honour and duty strictly enjoin that the French should refuse to carry out the conditions imposed by the enemy.

The thought that the panic of Bordeaux could make itself felt across the sea is not to be borne.

Soldiers of France, wherever you may be, arise!

De Gaulle acted as an inspiration to the French resistance. In June 1943 he became head of the French Committee of National Liberation in Algiers. He landed in Normandy a week after D-Day and marched into Paris on 25 August 1944, while German sharpshooters were still on the roofs.

•

J. B. PRIESTLEY
London, 1940

'This little steamer'

Churchill did not speak alone after Dunkirk. J. B. Priestley, the British novelist, commanded almost as big an audience for his Postscript broadcasts on BBC Radio with their cheerful, chatty understatements.

Priestley, the author of Good Companions *and* English Journey, *captured not only the mood of defiance of the British but also their deeply held inner conviction that they would triumph over 'little old Hitler' as well as the quintessential English spirit (echoing Stanley Baldwin's speech on England, page 90) that eventually conquered Hitler – as these two short Postscripts demonstrate.*

Here at Dunkirk is another English epic. And to my mind what was most characteristically English about it – so typical of us, so absurd and yet so grand and gallant that you hardly know whether to laugh or to cry when you read about them – was the part played in the difficult and dangerous embarkation – not by the warships, magnificent though they were – but by the little pleasure-steamers. We've known them and laughed at them, these fussy little steamers, all our lives. We have called them 'the shilling sicks'. We have watched them load and unload their crowds of holiday passengers – the gents full of high spirits and bottled beer, the ladies eating pork pies, the children sticky with peppermint rock. Sometimes they only went as far as the next seaside resort. But the boldest of them might manage a Channel crossing, to let everybody have a glimpse of Boulogne. They were usually paddle steamers, making a great deal more fuss with all their churning than they made speed; and they weren't proud, for they let you see their works going round. They liked to call themselves *Queens* and *Belles*; and even if they were new, there was always something old-fashioned, a Dickens touch, a mid-Victorian air, about them. They seemed to belong to the same ridiculous holiday world as pierrots and piers, sand castles, ham-and-egg teas, palmists, automatic machines, and crowded sweating promenades. But they were called out of that world – and, let it be noted – they were called out in good time and good order. Yes, those 'Brighton Belles' and 'Brighton Queens' left that innocent foolish world of theirs – to sail into the inferno, to defy bombs, shells, magnetic mines, torpedoes, machine-gun fire – to rescue our soldiers. Some of them – alas – will never return. Among those paddle steamers that will never return was one that I knew well, for it was the pride of our ferry service to the Isle of Wight – none other than the good ship *Gracie Fields*. I tell you, we were proud of the *Gracie Fields*, for she was the glittering queen of our local line, and instead of taking an hour over her voyage, used to do it, churning like mad, in forty-five minutes. And now never again will we board her at Cowes and go down into her dining saloon for a fine breakfast of bacon and eggs. She has paddled and churned away – for ever. But now – look – this little steamer, like all her brave and battered sisters, is immortal. She'll go sailing proudly down the years in the epic of Dunkirk. And our great-grandchildren, when they learn how we began this War by snatching glory out of defeat, and then swept on to victory, may also learn how the little holiday steamers made an excursion to hell and came back glorious.

I think the countryman knows, without being told, that we hold our lives here, as we hold our farms, upon certain terms. One of those terms is that while wars still continue, while one nation is ready to hurl its armed men at another, you must if necessary stand up and fight for your own. And this decision comes from the natural piety of simple but sane men. Such men, you will notice, are happier now than the men who have lost that natural piety.

Well, as we talked on our post on the hilltop, we watched the dusk deepen in the valleys below, where our women-folk listened to the news as they knitted by the hearth, and we remembered that these were our homes and that now at any time they might be blazing ruins, and that half-crazy German youths, in whose empty eyes the idea of honour and glory seems to include every form of beastliness, might soon be let loose down there. The sentries took their posts. There was a mist coming over the down. Nothing much happened for a time. A green light that seemed to defy all black-out regulations turned out to be merely an extra large and luminous glow-worm; the glow-worms, poor ignorant little creatures, don't know there's a war on and so continue lighting themselves up. A few searchlights went stabbing through the dusk and then faded. The mist thickened, and below in all the valleys, there wasn't the faintest glimmer of light. You heard the ceaseless high melancholy singing of the telegraph wires in the wind.

So we talked about what happened to us in the last war, and about the hay and the barley, about beef and milk and cheese and tobacco. Then a belt of fog over to the left became almost silvery, because somewhere along there all the searchlights were sweeping the sky. Then somewhere behind that vague silveriness, there was a sound as if gigantic doors were being slammed to. There was the rapid stabbing noise of anti-aircraft batteries, and far away some rapping of machine-guns. Then the sirens went, in our two nearest towns, as if all that part of the darkened countryside, like a vast trapped animal, were screaming at us.

J. B. Priestley was included among the 2,820 people who were to be rounded up by the Nazis as dangerous adversaries after they had conquered Britain. They also included Noël Coward, Virginia Woolf, Aldous Huxley, E. M. Forster, H. G. Wells and Bertrand Russell.

•

FRANKLIN DELANO ROOSEVELT
Washington, DC, 29 December 1940

'The arsenal of democracy'

Although the Battle of Britain had been won, the Battle of the Atlantic was intensifying. Vessels were being sunk faster than British shipyards could replace them. Money was running out and soon Britain would not be able to pay for the supplies she needed.

Apart from responding to Britain's plight by increasing American naval activity in the Atlantic, Roosevelt aired the idea of Lend-Lease. 'If your neighbour's house is on fire and he wants to borrow your garden hose, you don't ask to be paid, you just want your hose back.' Roosevelt also educated the American public about what was at stake in the war in some of his most dramatic speeches. One of them was this fireside chat.

The experience of the past two years has proven beyond doubt that no nation can appease the Nazis. No man can tame a tiger into a kitten by stroking it. There can be no appeasement with ruthlessness. There can be no reasoning with an incendiary bomb. We know now that a nation can have peace with the Nazis only at the price of total surrender . . .

The people of Europe who are defending themselves do not ask us to do their fighting. They ask us for the implements of war, the planes, the tanks, the guns, the freighters which will enable them to fight for their liberty and for our security. Emphatically we must get these weapons to them in sufficient volume and quickly enough, so that we and our children will be saved the agony and suffering of war which others have had to endure.

Let not the defeatists tell us that it is too late. It will never be earlier. Tomorrow will be later than today.

Certain facts are self-evident.

In a military sense Great Britain and the British Empire are today the spearhead of resistance to world conquest. They are putting up a fight which will live forever in the story of human gallantry.

There is no demand for sending an American Expeditionary Force outside our own borders. There is no intention by any member of your Government to send such a force. You can, therefore, nail any talk about sending armies to Europe as deliberate untruth.

Our national policy is not directed toward war. Its sole purpose is to keep war away from our country and our people . . .

Democracy's fight against world conquest is being greatly aided, and must be more greatly aided, by the rearmament of the United States and by sending every ounce and every ton of munitions and supplies that we can possibly spare to help the defenders who are in the front lines. It is no more unneutral for us to do that than it is for Sweden, Russia and other nations near Germany, to send steel and ore and oil and other war materials into Germany every day of the week.

We are planning our own defence with the utmost urgency; and in its vast scale we must integrate the war needs of Britain and the other free nations which are resisting aggression . . .

No pessimistic policy about the future of America shall delay the immediate expansion of those industries essential to defence. We need them. It is the purpose of the nation to build now with all possible speed every machine, every arsenal, every factory that we need to manufacture our defence material. We have the men – the skill – the wealth – and above all, the will.

I am confident that if and when production of consumer or luxury goods in certain industries requires the use of machines and raw materials that are essential for defence purposes, then such production must yield, and will gladly yield, to our primary and compelling purpose.

I appeal to the owners of plants – to the managers – to the workers – to our own Government employees – to put every ounce of effort into producing these munitions swiftly and without stint. With this appeal I give you the pledge that all of us who are officers of your Government will devote ourselves to the same whole-hearted extent to the great task that lies ahead.

As planes and ships and guns and shells are produced, your Government, with its defence experts, can then determine how best to use them to defend this hemisphere. The decision as to how much shall be sent abroad and how much shall remain at home must be made on the basis of our over-all military necessities.

We must be the great arsenal of democracy. For us this is an emergency as serious as war itself. We must apply ourselves to our task with the same resolution, the same sense of urgency, the same spirit of patriotism and sacrifice as we would show were we at war.

This fireside chat was the most successful that Roosevelt had ever given. According to opinion polls, more than sixty per cent of Americans agreed with what he said.

•

FRANKLIN DELANO ROOSEVELT
Washington, DC, 6 January 1941

'The four freedoms'

Only eight days after promising to make America the arsenal of democracy, Roosevelt addressed Congress and made perhaps the most famous speech of his career, in which he declared that America would support all nations that struggled on behalf of four essential freedoms: freedom of speech and religion and freedom from want and fear (an echo of his inaugural address).

Roosevelt was again offering implicit support to Britain and coaxing Americans towards a war that he was convinced they would sooner or later be forced to enter.

Every realist knows that the democratic way of life is at this moment being directly assailed in every part of the world – assailed either by arms, or by secret spreading of poisonous propaganda by those who seek to destroy unity and promote discord in nations that are still at peace.

During sixteen long months this assault has blotted out the whole pattern of democratic life in an appalling number of independent nations, great and small. The assailants are still on the march, threatening other nations, great and small.

Therefore, as your President, performing my constitutional duty to 'give to the Congress information of the state of the Union', I find it, unhappily, necessary to report that the future and the safety of our country and of our democracy are overwhelmingly involved in events far beyond our borders.

Armed defence of democratic existence is now being gallantly waged in four continents. If that defence fails, all the population and all the resources of Europe, Asia, Africa and Australasia will be dominated by the conquerors. Let us remember that the total of those populations and their resources in those four continents greatly exceeds the sum total of the population and the resources of the whole of the Western Hemisphere many times over.

In times like these it is immature – and incidentally, untrue – for anybody to brag that an unprepared America, single-handed, and with one hand tied behind its back, can hold off the whole world.

No realistic American can expect from a dictator's peace international generosity, or return of true independence, or world disarmament, or freedom of expression, or freedom of religion, or even good business.

Such a peace would bring no security for us or for our neighbours. 'Those, who would give up essential liberty to purchase a little temporary safety, deserve neither liberty nor safety.'

As a nation, we may take pride in the fact that we are soft-hearted; but we cannot afford to be soft-headed.

We must always be wary of those who with sounding brass and a tinkling cymbal preach the 'ism' of appeasement.

We must especially beware of that small group of selfish men who would clip the wings of the American eagle in order to feather their own nests.

I have recently pointed out how quickly the tempo of modern warfare could bring into our very midst the physical attack which we must eventually expect if the dictator nations win this war.

There is much loose talk of our immunity from immediate and direct invasion from across the seas. Obviously, as long as the British Navy retains its power, no such danger exists. Even if there were no British Navy, it is not probable that any enemy would be stupid enough to attack us by landing troops in the

United States from across thousands of miles of ocean, until it had acquired strategic bases from which to operate.

But we learn much from the lessons of the past years in Europe – particularly the lesson of Norway, whose essential seaports were captured by treachery and surprise built up over a series of years.

As long as the aggressor nations maintain the offensive, they – not we – will choose the time and the place and the method of their attack.

That is why the future of all the American Republics is today in serious danger.

That is why this Annual Message to the Congress is unique in our history.

That is why every member of the Executive Branch of the Government and every member of the Congress faces great responsibility and great accountability.

The need of the moment is that our actions and our policy should be devoted primarily – almost exclusively – to meeting this foreign peril. For all our domestic problems are now a part of the great emergency.

Just as our national policy in internal affairs has been based upon a decent respect for the rights and the dignity of all our fellow men within our gates, so our national policy in foreign affairs has been based on a decent respect for the rights and dignity of all nations, large and small. And the justice of morality must and will win in the end.

Our national policy is this:

First, by an impressive expression of the public will and without regard to partisanship, we are committed to all-inclusive national defence.

Second, by an impressive expression of the public will and without regard to partisanship, we are committed to full support of all those resolute peoples, everywhere, who are resisting aggression and are thereby keeping war away from our Hemisphere. By this support, we express our determination that the democratic cause shall prevail; and we strengthen the defence and the security of our own nation.

Third, by an impressive expression of the public will and without regard to partisanship, we are committed to the proposition that principles of morality and considerations for our own security will never permit us to acquiesce in a peace dictated by aggressors and sponsored by appeasers. We know that enduring peace cannot be bought at the cost of other people's freedom.

In the future days, which we seek to make secure, we look forward to a world founded upon four essential human freedoms.

The first is freedom of speech and expression – everywhere in the world.

The second is freedom of every person to worship God in his own way – everywhere in the world.

The third is freedom from want – which, translated into world terms, means economic understandings which will secure to every nation a healthy peacetime life for its inhabitants – everywhere in the world.

The fourth is freedom from fear – which, translated into world terms, means a world-wide reduction of armaments to such a point and in such a thorough fashion that no nation will be in a position to commit an act of physical aggression against any neighbour – anywhere in the world.

That is no vision of a distant millennium. It is a definite basis for a kind of world attainable in our own time and generation. That kind of world is the very antithesis of the so-called new order of tyranny which the dictators seek to create with the crash of a bomb.

To that new order we oppose the greater conception – the moral order. A good society is able to face schemes of world domination and foreign revolutions alike without fear.

Since the beginning of our American history, we have been engaged in change – in a perpetual peaceful revolution – a revolution which goes on steadily, quietly adjusting itself to changing conditions – without the concentration camp or the quick-lime in the ditch. The world order which we seek is the cooperation of free countries, working together in a friendly, civilized society.

This nation has placed its destiny in the hands and heads and hearts of its millions of free men and women; and its faith in freedom under the guidance of God. Freedom means the supremacy of human rights everywhere. Our support goes to those who struggle to gain those rights or keep them. Our strength is our unity of purpose.

To that high concept there can be no end save victory.

•

JOSEPH STALIN
Moscow, 3 July 1941

'A grave danger hangs over our country'

Stalin was taken by surprise in 1941 when Hitler tore up the Nazi–Soviet Pact, launched Operation Barbarossa and invaded Russia. For the first week, he suffered some kind of mental breakdown, especially when he realized the speed with which the Germans were advancing. When members of the Politburo arrived to meet him at Kuntsevo on 30 June, he seems to have thought they had come to arrest him. Only after being urged to establish a state defence committee under his chairmanship did Stalin begin to recover his self-confidence and to reappear in the Kremlin.

Once he had overcome his own fears, he emerged once again as the indispensable leader – and on 3 July spoke to the people over the radio. Appealing to Russian patriotism, he made an awe-inspiring call to the people to destroy everything if forced to retreat – to scorch the earth. It was as if the Russia of 1812 had been resurrected and spoken through Stalin's mouth, said one commentator.

Comrades! Citizens! Brothers and Sisters! Men of our Army and Navy!

I am addressing you, my friends!

The perfidious military attack on our fatherland, begun on 22 June by Hitler's Germany, is continuing.

In spite of heroic resistance of the Red Army, and although the enemy's finest divisions and finest air-force units have already been smashed and have met their doom on the field of battle, the enemy continues to push forward, hurling fresh forces into the attack.

Hitler's troops have succeeded in capturing Lithuania, a considerable part of Latvia, the western part of White Russia, and a part of the western Ukraine.

The Fascist air force is extending the range of operations of its bombers and is bombing Murmansk, Orsha, Mogilev, Smolensk, Kiev, Odessa, and Sevastopol.

A grave danger hangs over our country.

How could it have happened that our glorious Red Army surrendered a number of our cities and districts to the Fascist armies?

Is it really true that German Fascist troops are invincible, as is ceaselessly trumpeted by boastful Fascist propagandists? Of course not!

History shows that there are no invincible armies, and never have been. Napoleon's army was considered invincible, but it was beaten successively by Russian, English, and German armies. Kaiser Wilhelm's German army in the period of the first imperialist war was also considered invincible, but it was beaten several times by Russian and Anglo-French forces, and was finally smashed by Anglo-French forces.

The same must be said of Hitler's German Fascist army today. This army has not yet met with serious resistance on the Continent of Europe. Only on our territory has it met serious resistance, and if as a result of this resistance the finest divisions of Hitler's German Fascist army have been defeated by our Red Army, it means that this army, too, can be smashed and will be smashed as were the armies of Napoleon and Wilhelm.

There can be no doubt that this short-lived military gain for Germany is only an episode, while the tremendous political gain of the USSR is a serious and lasting factor that is bound to form the basis for development of decisive military successes of the Red Army in the war with Fascist Germany . . .

In case of a forced retreat of Red Army units, all rolling stock must be evacuated; to the enemy must not be left a single engine, a single railway car, not a single pound of grain or a gallon of fuel.

Collective farmers must drive off all their cattle and turn over their grain to the safekeeping of state authorities for transportation to the rear. All valuable property including nonferrous metals, grain, and fuel which cannot be withdrawn must without fail be destroyed.

In areas occupied by the enemy, guerrilla units, mounted and foot, must be formed, diversionist groups must be organized to combat enemy troops, to foment guerrilla warfare everywhere, to blow up bridges, roads, damage telephone and telegraph lines, and to set fire to forests, stores, and transports.

In occupied regions conditions must be made unbearable for the enemy and all his accomplices. They must be hounded and annihilated at every step and all their measures frustrated.

This war with Fascist Germany cannot be considered an ordinary war. It is not only a war between two armies, it is also a great war of the entire Soviet people against the German Fascist forces.

The aim of this national war in defence of our country against the Fascist oppressors is not only elimination of the danger hanging over our country, but also aid to all European peoples groaning under the yoke of German Fascism.

In this war of liberation we shall not be alone.

In this great war we shall have loyal allies in the peoples of Europe and America, including German people who are enslaved by Hitlerite despots.

Our war for the freedom of our country will merge with the struggle of the peoples of Europe and America for their independence, for democratic liberties. It will be a united front of peoples standing for freedom and against enslavement and threats of enslavement by Hitler's Fascist armies.

In this connection the historic utterance of British Prime Minister Churchill regarding aid to the Soviet Union and the declaration of the USA government signifying readiness to render aid to our country, which can only evoke a feeling of gratitude in the hearts of the peoples of the Soviet Union, are fully comprehensible and symptomatic.

Comrades, our forces are numberless. The overweening enemy will soon learn this to his cost. Side by side with the Red Army and Navy thousands of workers, collective farmers, and intellectuals are rising to fight the enemy aggressor. The masses of our people will rise up in their millions. The working people of Moscow and Leningrad already have commenced to form vast popular levies in support of the Red Army.

Such popular levies must be raised in every city that is in danger of an enemy invasion; all working people must be roused to defend our freedom, our honour, our country – in our patriotic war against German Fascism.

In order to insure a rapid mobilization of all forces of the peoples of the USSR, and to repulse the enemy who treacherously attacked our country, a State Committee of Defence has been formed in whose hands the entire power of the state has been vested.

The State Committee of Defence has entered into its functions and calls upon all our people to rally around the party of Lenin–Stalin and around the Soviet government so as self-denyingly to support the Red Army and Navy, demolish the enemy, and secure victory.

All our forces for the support of our heroic Red Army and our glorious Red Navy!

All the forces of the people – for the demolition of the enemy!

Forward, to our victory!

•

REINHARD HEYDRICH
Wannsee, 20 January 1942

'The final solution'

One of the most important events in the history of the twentieth century occurred at a villa on the banks of the Wannsee, a lake near Berlin, on 20 January 1942.

It was a conference under the chairmanship of Reinhard Heydrich, head of the SS Intelligence Service, at which Hitler's Nazis planned the final solution, the extermination of about eleven million Jews in Europe. Heydrich had been appointed 'Plenipotentiary for the Preparation of the Final Solution of the European Jewish Question'.

This was his address to the senior civil servants.

We have the means, the methods, the organization, experience and people. And we have the will. This is a historic moment in the struggle against Jewry. The Führer has declared his determination . . . to destroy European Jewry. The Führer sees himself . . . as exterminating fatal bacteria to save the organism. It is them or us. What has happened so far? Step by step we have forced the Jews out of all levels of German life . . .

We have forced them out of the *Lebensraum* of the people partly by transfers to concentration camps, and partly due to Obersturmbannführer Eichmann's organization by permitting 537,000 Jews to emigrate before the war; and finally

We have seen since the beginning of the war the liquidation of hundreds of thousands of Polish, Baltic and Russian Jews. You gentlemen from the Party Chancellery, the Reich Chancellery, the Foreign Office, General Government and Ministry for the East have been kept informed by Gestapo reports of the Action groups' activities . . .

The Reichsführer SS has forbidden any further emigration of Jews. The Jews remaining in the Reich and all European Jews in our present and future spheres of influence will be evacuated to the East for the final solution . . .

We shall work effectively but silently. Total cooperation will be required in this matter of life or death for the Reich. So that we can all envisage what the Jewish question in the Reich involves (*pointing to a map of Europe*) the red area shows the Reich on the eve of war. This is the Eastern front. Behind in white conquered Eastern territories under Germany's civilian rule. In pink territories subject to the Reich – in vertical red stripes occupied territories in the rest of Europe. Horizontal red stripes, our Allies or countries under our influence. The dots on the map like fly spots represent the density of the Jewish population. That is our problem the further we advance between Riga and Odessa.

We must deal with the settlements of our Jewish opponents. They've made themselves comfortable there for centuries. In my own home town of Odessa there are more than 70,000 Jewish inhabitants. There were, used to be (*laughter*). To sum up gentlemen, our Action groups following hard on the heels of our troops have virtually eliminated the Jewish concentrations. We have influenced the old anti-Semitism by certain procedural measures.

Now the rough work has been done we begin the period of finer work. We need to work in harmony with the civil administration. We count on you gentlemen as far as the final solution is concerned. What is to be resolved will be resolved here (*pointing to the East*), at the world's arse, as my men say. War and gunsmoke have made immense achievements possible. It is the Reichsführer SS's will that the Jewish question is settled there in one clean sweep. The total Jews concerned – 11,000,000.

This breaks down as follows:

In the old Reich – 130,000
In Austria – 43,000
In the Protectorate – 75,000
In the General Government – 2,500,000
In the Balkans – 1,600,000
In Occupied France – 165,000
In Unoccupied France – 740,000 (Quite a task!)
In the New Europe for which we shall be responsible,
    in foreign unoccupied countries, like England – 330,000
In neutral countries like Switzerland – 18,000 of the Chosen
    People.

In the final solution we will use the Jews as labour in the East. They will be marched, both sexes segregated, in columns, building roads on the way, breaking rocks, draining marshes. We'll give them every opportunity to find out what work means, on the extensive industrial plants now being constructed by Comrade Pohl of the SS's Economic Office . . .

Of course, most of these Jews will succumb to natural wastage: the remainder, the toughest, will have to be processed accordingly. Why? Because it is the survival of the fittest. Otherwise they'd seed a new Jewish resurrection. Look at history!

Heydrich was wounded in Prague on 27 May 1942 by two Czechs parachuted in from Britain. He died eight days later. His death was revenged by the massacre at Lidice. Wherever Heydrich went, a trail of blood was always left behind. He was correctly described as a butcher and a hangman.

•

CHAIM RUMKOWSKI
Łódź ghetto, 4 September 1942

'Give me your children'

At the Łódź ghetto in Poland, which the Germans used to incarcerate the old and sick and other unwanted Jews from the cities of western Europe, Chaim Rumkowski, aged sixty, a widower without children and Elder of the ghetto, believed he was ruling a Jewish state. He loved the ghetto, where more than 160,000 Jews were contained. It was his dominion and he tried to point out the value of ghettoization, a partial fulfilment of the Zionist goals he embraced. He repeatedly told Jews at Łódź that when the war was over he would be chosen to run a protectorate that the Nazis would establish to contain all the Jews of Europe.

Although Rumkowski bargained with the Germans to minimize deportations from the ghetto, his Faustian pact with the Nazis obliged him to fulfil an unending series of deportation orders imposed on him by the Nazis: ten thousand, fifteen thousand, twenty thousand – and then ten thousand more. Finally the entire ghetto was gone.

The most chilling of all his exhortations to the inhabitants of Łódź ghetto (perhaps indeed the most horrifying speech in this anthology) was this address in which he urged the Jews to give up their children to the Nazis – and the gas ovens.

In The Drowned and the Saved, *Primo Levi describes Rumkowski's oratorical style as unmistakable. He adopted the technique of Mussolini and Hitler, the style of inspired recitation, pseudo-colloquy with the crowd, the creation of consent through subjugation and plaudit. 'The man who has throne and sceptre, who is not afraid of being contradicted or derided, speaks like this.'*

A grievous blow has struck the ghetto. They are asking us to give up the best we possess – the children and the elderly. I was unworthy of having a child of my own, so I gave the best years of my life to children. I've lived and breathed with children. I never imagined that I would be forced to deliver this sacrifice to the altar with my own hands. In my old age I must stretch out my hands and beg: Brothers and sisters, hand them over to me! Fathers and mothers, give me your children! (*Horrible, terrifying wailing among the assembled crowd.*)

I had a suspicion something was about to befall us. I anticipated 'something' and was always like a watchman on guard to prevent it. But I was unsuccessful because I did not know what was threatening us. I did not know the nature of the danger. The taking of the sick from the hospitals caught me completely by surprise. And I give you the best proof there is of this: I had my own nearest and dearest among them, and I could do nothing for them.

I thought that that would be the end of it, that after that they'd leave us in peace, the peace for which I long so much, for which I've always worked, which has been my goal. But something else, it turned out, was destined for us. Such is the fate of the Jews: always more suffering and always worse suffering, especially in times of war.

Yesterday afternoon, they gave me the order to send more than 20,000 Jews out of the ghetto, and if not – 'We will do it!' So, the question became: 'Should we take it upon ourselves, do it ourselves, or leave it for others to do?' Well, we – that is, I and my closest associates – thought first not about 'How many will perish?' but 'How many is it possible to save?' And we reached the conclusion that, however hard it would be for us, we should take the implementation of this order into our own hands.

I must perform this difficult and bloody operation – I must cut off limbs in order to save the body itself! – I must take children because, if not, others may be taken as well, God forbid.

(*Horrible wailing.*)

I have no thought of consoling you today. Nor do I wish to calm you. I must lay bare your full anguish and pain. I come to you like a bandit, to take from you what you treasure most in your hearts! I have tried, using every possible means, to get the order revoked. I tried – when that proved to be impossible – to soften the order. Just yesterday I ordered a list of children aged nine – I wanted, at least, to save this one age group, the nine- to ten-year-olds. But I was not granted this concession. On only one point did I succeed, in saving the ten-year-olds and up. Let this be a consolation in our profound grief.

There are, in the ghetto, many patients who can expect to live only a few days more, maybe a few weeks. I don't know if the idea is diabolical or not, but I must say it: 'Give me the sick. In their place, we can save the healthy.' I know how dear the sick are to any family, and particularly to Jews. However, when cruel demands are made, one has to weigh and measure: who shall, can and may be saved? And common sense dictates that the saved must be those who can be saved and those who have a chance of being rescued, not those who cannot be saved in any case.

We live in the ghetto, mind you. We live with so much restriction that we do not have enough even for the healthy, let alone for the sick. Each of us feeds the sick at the expense of our own health: we give our bread to the sick. We give them our meagre ration of sugar, our little piece of meat. And what's the result? Not enough to cure the sick, and we ourselves become ill. Of course, such sacrifices are the most beautiful and noble. But there are times when one has to choose: sacrifice the sick, who haven't the slightest chance of recovery and who also may make others ill, or rescue the healthy.

I could not deliberate over this problem for long; I had to resolve it in favour of the healthy. In this spirit, I gave the appropriate instructions to the doctors, and they will be expected to deliver all incurable patients, so that the healthy, who want and are able to live, will be saved in their place.

(*Horrible weeping.*)

I understand you, mothers; I see your tears, all right. I also feel what you feel in your hearts, you fathers who will have to go to work the morning after your children have been taken from you, when just yesterday you were playing with your dear little ones. I know and feel all this. Since four o'clock yesterday, when I first found out about the order, I have been utterly broken. I share your pain. I suffer because of your anguish, and I don't know how I'll survive this – where I'll find the strength.

I must tell you a secret: they requested 24,000 victims, 3,000 a day for eight days. I succeeded in reducing the number to 20,000, but only on the condition that these would be children below the age of ten. Children ten and older are safe. Since the children and the aged together equal only some 13,000 souls, the gap will have to be filled with the sick.

I can barely speak. I am exhausted; I only want to tell you what I am asking of you: Help me carry out this action! I am trembling. I am afraid that others, God forbid, will do it themselves . . .

A broken Jew stands before you. Do not envy me. This is the most difficult of all the orders I've ever had to carry out at any time. I reach out to you with my broken, trembling hands and I beg: Give into my hands the victims, so that we can avoid having further victims, and a population of a hundred thousand Jews can be preserved. So they promised me: if we deliver our victims by ourselves, there will be peace . . .

(*Shouts: 'We all will go!' 'Mr Chairman, an only child should not be taken; children should be taken from families with several children!'*)

These are empty phrases! I don't have the strength to argue with you! If the authorities were to arrive, none of you would shout.

I understand what it means to tear off a part of the body.

Yesterday I begged on my knees, but it didn't work. From small villages with Jewish populations of seven to eight thousand, barely a thousand arrived here. So which is better? What do you want: that eighty to ninety thousand Jews remain, or, God forbid, that the whole population be annihilated?

You may judge as you please; my duty is to preserve the Jews who remain. I do not speak to hotheads. I speak to your reason and conscience. I have done and will continue doing everything possible to keep arms from appearing in the streets and blood from being shed. The order could not be undone; it could only be reduced.

One needs the heart of a bandit to ask from you what I am asking. But put yourself in my place, think logically, and you'll reach the conclusion that I cannot proceed any other way. The part that can be saved is much larger than the part that must be given away.

By 1 September 1944, nearly all the Jews of Łódź had been murdered. Rumkowski was told he could remain in the ghetto. He declined the offer and joined the last transport for Auschwitz where he too was murdered. Soviet troops liberated the ghetto on 19 January 1945. Of the 160,000 original inhabitants, there remained 870 starving human beings.

•

GENERAL BERNARD MONTGOMERY
Cairo, 13 August 1942

'*We will stand and fight* here'

The fame of Bernard Montgomery (1887–1976) as a field commander was established with the British Eighth Army from July 1942 to January 1944 as the Desert Rats fought Erwin Rommel, the brilliant German general, from Alamein across north Africa and then into Sicily and southern Italy.

Monty, as he was universally known, was an inspiring leader who cared for his soldiers' morale. He could play with an audience of British troops like a fanatical ecclesiastic launching a crusade, said one contemporary observer. Monty arrived in Cairo on 12 August 1942, and assumed command of the Eighth Army the next day, when he made this address to his demoralized officers.

I want first of all to introduce myself to you. You do not know me. I do not know you. But we have got to work together; therefore we must understand each other, and we must have confidence each in the other. I have only been here a few hours. But from what I have seen and heard since I arrived I am prepared to say, here and now, that I have confidence in you. We will then work together as a team; and together we will gain the confidence of this great Army and go forward to final victory in Africa.

I believe that one of the first duties of a commander is to create what I call 'atmosphere', and in that atmosphere his staff, subordinate commanders, and troops will live and work and fight.

I do not like the general atmosphere I find here. It is an atmosphere of doubt, of looking back to select the next place to which to withdraw, of loss of confidence in our ability to defeat Rommel, of desperate defence measures by reserves in preparing positions in Cairo and the Delta.

All that must cease.

Let us have a new atmosphere.

The defence of Egypt lies here at Alamein and on the Ruweisat Ridge. What is the use of digging trenches in the Delta? It is quite useless; if we lose this position we lose Egypt; all the fighting troops now in the Delta must come here at once, and will. *Here* we will stand and fight; there will be no further withdrawal. I have ordered that all plans and instructions dealing with further withdrawal are to be burnt, and at once. We will stand and fight *here*.

If we can't stay here alive, then let us stay here dead.

I want to impress on everyone that the bad times are over. Fresh Divisions from the UK are now arriving in Egypt, together with ample reinforcements for our present Divisions. We have 300 to 400 Sherman new tanks coming and these are actually being unloaded at Suez *now*. Our mandate from the Prime Minister is to destroy the Axis forces in North Africa; I have seen it, written on half a sheet of notepaper. And it will be done. If anyone here thinks it can't be done, let him go at once; I don't want any doubters in this party. It can be done, and it will be done: beyond any possibility of doubt.

Now I understand that Rommel is expected to attack at any moment. Excellent. Let him attack.

I would sooner it didn't come for a week, just give me time to sort things out. If we have two weeks to prepare we will be sitting pretty; Rommel can attack as soon as he likes, after that, and I hope he does.

Meanwhile, we ourselves will start to plan a great offensive; it will be the beginning of a campaign which will hit Rommel and his Army for six right out of Africa.

But first we must create a reserve Corps, mobile and strong in armour, which we will train *out of the line*. Rommel has always had such a force in his Africa Corps, which is never used to hold the line but which is always in reserve, available for striking blows. Therein has been his great strength. We will create such a Corps ourselves, a British Panzer Corps; it will consist of two armoured Divisions and one motorized Division; I gave orders yesterday for it to begin to form, back in the Delta.

I have no intention of launching our great attack until we are completely ready; there will be pressure from many quarters to attack soon; *I will not attack until we are ready*, and you can rest assured on that point.

Meanwhile, if Rommel attacks while we are preparing, let him do so with pleasure; we will merely continue with our own preparations and *we* will attack when *we* are ready, and not before.

I want to tell you that I always work on the Chief of Staff system. I have nominated Brigadier de Guingand as Chief of Staff Eighth Army. I will issue orders through him. Whatever he says will be taken as coming from me and will be acted on *at once*. I understand there has been a great deal of 'bellyaching' out here.

By bellyaching I mean inventing poor reasons for *not* doing what one has been told to do.

All this is to stop at once.

I will tolerate no bellyaching.

If anyone objects to doing what he is told, then he can get out of it: and at once. I want that made very clear right down through the Eighth Army.

I have little more to say just at present. And some of you may think it is quite enough and may wonder if I am mad.

I assure you I am quite sane.

I understand there are people who often think I am slightly mad; so often that I now regard it as rather a compliment.

All I have to say to that is that if I am slightly mad, there are a large number of people I could name who are raving lunatics!!

What I have done is to get over to you the 'atmosphere' in which we will now work and fight; you must see that that atmosphere permeates right through the Eighth Army to the most junior private soldier. All the soldiers must know what is wanted; when they see it coming to pass there will be a surge of confidence throughout the Army.

I ask you to give me your confidence and to have faith that what I have said will come to pass.

There is much work to be done.

The orders I have given about no further withdrawal will mean a complete change in the layout of our dispositions; also, we must begin to prepare for our great offensive.

The first thing to do is to move our HQ to a decent place where we can live in reasonable comfort and where the Army Staff can all be together and side by side with the HQ of the Desert Air Force. This is a frightful place here, depressing, unhealthy and a rendezvous for every fly in Africa; we shall do no good work here. Let us get over there by the sea where it is fresh and healthy. If officers are to do good work they must have decent messes, and be comfortable. So off we go on the new line.

The Chief of Staff will be issuing orders on many points very shortly, and I am always available to be consulted by the senior officers of the staff. The great point to remember is that we are going to finish with this chap Rommel once and for all. It will be quite easy. There is no doubt about it.

He is definitely a nuisance. Therefore we will hit him a crack and finish with him.

Montgomery's speech to his officers marked one of the turning points of the war. Rommel's offensive at Alam Halfa began on the night of 30–31 August. The attack was held. Monty had gained the initiative and at El Alamein in October he won a decisive victory. He went on to command allied ground troops in the Normandy landings and he played a decisive role in checking the German counter-offensive in the Ardennes in 1944. On 4 May 1945 he formally accepted the surrender of all German forces in north-western Europe at Lüneburg Heath.

●

ÉAMON DE VALERA
Dublin, 17 March 1943

'The vision of such an Ireland'

Guerrilla commander, political prisoner, successful revolutionary, a partisan in civil war, Éamon de Valera (1882–1975) was prime minister of Ireland for more than twenty years and president for fourteen years until he retired in 1973 at the age of ninety. He was elected president of Sinn Féin, the Irish republican party in 1917, but subsequently founded Fianna Fáil and formed a government in 1932. As prime minister he gradually cut the links binding Dublin to British rule. A new constitution in 1937 created the sovereign democratic state of Eire.

As Roy Foster, the historian of Ireland, says, Fianna Fáil Ireland was a nation set apart by Catholicism and nationality: the interlocking relationships of Church and politics helped to define a unique, God-given way of life. There was also revealed a fierce suspicion of cosmopolitanism and what it stood for, as revealed in de Valera's St Patrick's Day broadcasts on the new national radio station.

The most celebrated of those broadcasts was made in 1943 when he called up a vision of an Ireland characterized by cosy homesteads, athletic youths and comely maidens.

Before the present war began I was accustomed on St Patrick's Day to speak to our kinsfolk in foreign lands, particularly those in the United States, and to tell them year by year of the progress being made towards building up the Ireland of their dreams and ours – the Ireland that we believe is destined to play, by its example and its inspiration, a great part as a nation among the nations.

Acutely conscious though we all are of the misery and desolation in which the greater part of the world is plunged, let us turn aside for a moment to that ideal Ireland that we would have. That Ireland which we dreamed of would be the home of a people who valued material wealth only as the basis of right living, of a people who were satisfied with frugal comfort and devoted their leisure to the things of the spirit – a land whose countryside would be bright with cosy homesteads, whose fields and villages would be joyous with the sounds of industry, with the romping of sturdy children, the contests of athletic youths and the laughter of comely maidens, whose firesides would be forums for the wisdom of serene old age. It would, in a word, be the home of a people living the life that God desires that man should live.

With the tidings that make such an Ireland possible, St Patrick came to our ancestors 1,500 years ago, promising happiness here as well as happiness hereafter. It was the pursuit of such an Ireland that later made our country worthy to be called the Island of Saints and Scholars. It was the idea of such an Ireland, happy, vigorous, spiritual, that fired the imagination of our poets, that made successive generations of patriotic men give their lives to win religious and political liberty, and that will urge men in our own and future generations to die, if need be, so that these liberties may be preserved.

One hundred years ago the Young Irelanders, by holding up the vision of such an Ireland before the people, inspired our nation and moved it spiritually as it had hardly been moved since the golden age of Irish civilization. Fifty years after the Young Irelanders, the founders of the Gaelic League similarly inspired and moved the people of their day, as did later the leaders of the Volunteers. We of this time, if we have the will and the active enthusiasm, have the opportunity to inspire and move our generation in like manner. We can do so by keeping this thought of a noble future for our country constantly before our minds, ever seeking in action to bring that future into being, and ever remembering that it is to our nation as a whole that future must apply.

For many the pursuit of the material is a necessity. Man, to express himself fully and to make the best use of the talents God has given him, needs a certain minimum of comfort and leisure. A section of our people have not yet this minimum. They rightly strive to secure it, and it must be our aim and the aim of all who are just and wise to assist in the effort. But many have got more than is required and are free, if they choose, to devote themselves more completely to cultivating the things of the mind, and in particular those which mark us out as a distinct nation.

The first of these latter is the national language. It is for us what no other language can be. It is our very own. It is more than a symbol; it is an essential part of our nationhood. It has been moulded by the thought of a hundred generations of our forebears. In it is stored the accumulated experience of a people, our people, who even before Christianity was brought to them were already cultured and living in a well-ordered society. The Irish language spoken in Ireland today is the direct descendant without break of the language our ancestors spoke in those far-off days.

As a vehicle of three thousand years of our history, the language is for us precious beyond measure. As the bearer to us of a philosophy, of an outlook on life deeply Christian and rich in practical wisdom, the language today is worth far too much to dream of letting it go. To part with it would be to abandon a great part of ourselves, to lose the key of our past, to cut away the roots from the tree. With the language gone we could never aspire again to being more than half a nation.

For my part, I believe that this outstanding mark of our nationhood can be preserved and made forever safe by this generation. I am indeed certain of it, but I know that it cannot be saved without understanding and cooperation and effort and sacrifice. It would be wrong to minimize the difficulties. They are not slight. The task of restoring the language as the everyday speech of our people is a task as great as any nation ever undertook. But it is a noble task. Other nations have succeeded in it, though in their case, when the effort was begun, their national language was probably more widely spoken among their people than is ours with us. As long as the language lives, however, on the lips of the people as their natural speech in any substantial part of this land we are assured of success if – *if* we are in earnest.

•

GENERAL GEORGE PATTON
England and France, 1943–4

'That son of a bitch Patton again'

'Old Blood and Guts' was the nickname given to General George Patton (1885–1945) by his troops during the Second World War as a testimony to his reputation for recklessness and hot-headed daring.

That daring was shown at its most flamboyant in 1944 when his Third Army advanced across France in a sweep through Brittany, round Paris, up the Marne and the Moselle, across the Rhine and eventually into Czechoslovakia in April 1945.

As they went into battle, Patton, puffing his cigar, was given to making short, sharp, morale-boosting addresses at his staff conferences and to his men.

The three published here were given to his troops in England and Normandy. The third was his welcome to the 761st 'Black Panther' Tank Battalion. They show that you don't need to be long-winded to be eloquent or to allow your audience to get the message, and raised profanity to a fine art.

I am not supposed to be commanding this Army – I am not even supposed to be in England. Let the first bastards to find out be the goddam Germans. Some day I want them to rise on their hind legs and howl: 'Jesus Christ, it's that goddam Third Army and that son of a bitch Patton again' . . . There's one great thing that you men can say when it's all over and you're home once more. You can thank God that twenty years from now when you're sitting by the fireside with your grandson on your knee, and he asks you what you did in the war, you won't have to shift him to the other knee, cough and say, 'I shovelled crap in Louisiana.'

Now, gentlemen, doubtless from time to time there will be some complaints that we are pushing people too hard. I don't give a good Goddamn about such complaints. I believe in the old and sound rule that an ounce of sweat is worth a gallon of blood. The harder we push, the more Germans we'll kill, and gentlemen, the more Germans we kill, the fewer of our men will be killed. Pushing means fewer casualties. I want you to remember that.

There's another thing I want you to remember. Forget this Goddamn business of worrying about our flanks. We must guard our flanks, but not to the extent that we don't do anything else. Some Goddamned fool once said that flanks must be secured and since then sons of bitches all over the world have been going crazy guarding their flanks. We don't want any of that in the Third Army. Flanks are something for the enemy to worry about, not us.

Also, I don't want to get any messages saying, 'I'm holding my position.' We're not holding anything! Let the Hun do that. We are advancing constantly and are not interested in holding anything, except the enemy. We're going to hold on to him and kick the hell out of him all the time.

Our basic plan of operation is to advance and to keep on advancing regardless of whether we have to go over, under, or through the enemy. We have one motto, *'L'audace, l'audace, toujours l'audace!'* Remember that, gentlemen. From here on out, until we win or die in the attempt, we will always be audacious.

Men, you are the first Negro tankers ever to fight in the American army. I would never have asked for you if you were not good. I have nothing but the best in my army. I don't care what colour you are as long as you go up there and kill those Kraut sons-of-bitches. Everyone has their eyes on you and are expecting great things from you. Most of all, your race is looking forward to your success. Don't let them down, and, damn you, don't let me down!

If you want me you can always find me in the lead tank.

Patton was killed in a road accident while commanding the US Fifth Army in occupied Germany in December 1945.

•

BISHOP GEORGE BELL
London, 9 February 1944

'Obliteration is not a justifiable act of war'

The Anglican churchman George Bell (1893–1958) was Dean of Canterbury and then Bishop of Chichester from 1929 to 1958. Bell was a bishop with an international outlook and moral courage. That courage was demonstrated when he exposed the anti-Christian trend of Hitlerism at its beginnings, for which he was sharply criticized. It was shown again during the Second World War when he attacked the Allied policy of bombing cities and civilian homes in Germany, as in this House of Lords speech. His criticism made him deeply unpopular but he did not flinch from his moral position.

I turn to the situation in February 1944, and the terrific devastation by Bomber Command of German towns. I do not forget the Luftwaffe, or its tremendous bombing of Belgrade, Warsaw, Rotterdam, London, Portsmouth, Coventry, Canterbury and many other places of military, industrial and cultural importance. Hitler is a barbarian. There is no decent person on the Allied side who is likely to suggest that we should make him our pattern or attempt to be competitors in that market. It is clear enough that large-scale bombing of enemy towns was begun by the Nazis. I am not arguing that point at all. The question with which I am concerned is this. Do the Government understand the full force of what area bombardment is doing and is destroying now? Are they alive not only to the vastness of the material damage, much of which is irreparable, but also to the harvest they are laying up for the future relationships of the peoples of Europe as well as to its moral implications? The aim of Allied bombing from the air, said the Secretary of State for Air at Plymouth on 22 January, is to paralyse German war industry and transport. I recognize the legitimacy of concentrated attack on industrial and military objectives, on airfields and air bases, in view especially of the coming of the Second Front. I fully realize that in attacks on centres of war industry and transport the killing of civilians when it is the result of bona-fide military activity is inevitable. But there must be a fair balance between the means employed and the purpose achieved. To obliterate a whole town because certain portions contain military and industrial establishments is to reject the balance.

Let me take two crucial instances, Hamburg and Berlin. Hamburg has a population of between one and two million people. It contains targets of immense military and industrial importance. It also happens to be the most democratic town in Germany where the anti-Nazi opposition was strongest. Injuries to civilians resulting from bona-fide attacks on particular objectives are legitimate according to International Law. But owing to the methods used the whole town is now a ruin. Unutterable destruction and devastation were wrought last autumn. On a very conservative estimate, according to the early German statistics, 28,000 persons were killed. Never before in the history of air warfare was an attack of such weight and persistence carried out against a single industrial concentration. Practically all the buildings, cultural, military, residential, industrial, religious – including the famous University Library with its 800,000 volumes, of which three-quarters have perished – were razed to the ground.

Berlin, the capital of the Reich, is four times the size of

Hamburg. The offices of the Government, the military, industrial, war-making establishments in Berlin are a fair target. Injuries to civilians are inevitable. But up to date half Berlin has been destroyed, area by area, the residential and the industrial portions alike. Through the dropping of thousands of tons of bombs, including fire-phosphorus bombs, of extraordinary power, men and women have been lost, overwhelmed in the colossal tornado of smoke, blast and flame. It is said that 74,000 persons have been killed and that three million are already homeless. The policy is obliteration, openly acknowledged. That is not a justifiable act of war. Again, Berlin is one of the greatest centres of art collections in the world. It has a large collection of Oriental and classical sculpture. It has one of the best picture galleries in Europe, comparable to the National Gallery. It has a gallery of modern art better than the Tate, a museum of ethnology without parallel in this country, one of the biggest and best organized libraries – State and university, containing two and a half million books – in the world. Almost all these non-industrial, non-military buildings are grouped together near the old Palace and in the Street of the Linden. The whole of that street, which has been constantly mentioned in the accounts of the raids, has been demolished. It is possible to replace flat houses by mass production. It is not possible so quickly to rebuild libraries or galleries or churches or museums. It is not very easy to rehouse those works of art which have been spared. Those works of art and those libraries will be wanted for the re-education of the Germans after the war. I wonder whether your Lordships realize the loss involved in that.

How is it, then, that this wholesale destruction has come about? The answer is that it is the method used, the method of area bombing. The first outstanding raid of area bombing was, I believe, in the spring of 1942, directed against Lübeck, then against Rostock, followed by the thousand-bomber raid against Cologne at the end of May 1942. The point I want to bring home, because I doubt whether it is sufficiently realized, is that it is no longer definite military and industrial objectives which are the aim of the bombers, but the whole town, area by area, is plotted carefully out. This area is singled out and plastered on one night; that area is singled out and plastered on another night; a third, a fourth, a fifth area is similarly singled out and plastered night after night, till, to use the language of the Chief of Bomber Command with regard to Berlin, the heart of Nazi Germany ceases to beat. How can there be discrimination in such matters when civilians, monuments, military objectives and industrial objectives all together form the target? How can the bombers aim at anything more than a great space when they see nothing and the bombing is blind?

Is it a matter for wonder that anti-Nazis who long for help to overthrow Hitler are driven to despair? I have here a telegram, which I have communicated to the Foreign Office, sent to me on 27 December last by a well-known anti-Nazi Christian leader who had to flee from Germany for his life long before the war. It was sent from Zürich, and puts what millions inside Germany must feel. He says:

'Is it understood that present situation gives us no sincere opportunity for appeal to people because one cannot but suspect effect of promising words on practically powerless population convinced by bombs and phosphor that their annihilation is resolved?'

If we wish to shorten the war, as we must, then let the Government speak a word of hope and encouragement both to the tortured millions of Europe and to those enemies of Hitler to whom in 1939 Mr Churchill referred as 'millions who stand aloof from the seething mass of criminality and corruption constituted by the Nazi Party machine'.

Why is there this blindness to the psychological side? Why is there this inability to reckon with the moral and spiritual facts? Why is there this forgetfulness of the ideals by which our cause is inspired? How can the War Cabinet fail to see that this progressive devastation of cities is threatening the roots of civilization? How can they be blind to the harvest of even fiercer warring and desolation, even in this country, to which the present destruction will inevitably lead when the members of the War Cabinet have long passed to their rest? How can they fail to realize that this is not the way to curb military aggression and end war? This is an extraordinarily solemn moment. What we do in war – which, after all, lasts a comparatively short time – affects the whole character of peace, which covers a much longer period. The sufferings of Europe, brought about by the demoniac cruelty of Hitler and his Nazis, and hardly imaginable to those in this country who for the last five years have not been out of this island or had intimate association with Hitler's victims, are not to be healed by the use of power only, power exclusive and unlimited. The Allies stand for something greater than power. The chief name inscribed on our banner is 'Law'. It is of supreme importance that we who, with our Allies, are the liberators of Europe should so use power that it is always under the control of law. It is because the bombing of enemy towns – this area bombing – raises this issue of power unlimited and exclusive that such immense importance is bound to attach to the policy and action of His Majesty's Government. I beg to move.

Bell was the natural choice to become Archbishop of Canterbury, but was ignored by Winston Churchill, who had disliked his attacks on British war policy.

•

J. ROBERT OPPENHEIMER
Los Alamos, New Mexico, 2 November 1945

'Our deep moral dependence'

Ever since the discovery of nuclear fission, Julius Robert Oppenheimer (1904– 67), one of the world's greatest nuclear scientists, carried in his mind the possibility of powerful explosives based on it. He realized how much it might do for the Allies in the Second World War and how much it might change the course of history – and also how ominous the developments could be for the future of the human race.

He became the first director of the Los Alamos atomic-bomb project in 1943 and led the scientists who produced the atomic bombs that fell on Hiroshima and Nagasaki.

He resigned in 1945 and made this speech, as a fellow scientist and 'fellow worrier', to the Association of Los Alamos Scientists – a defence of the atomic bomb that was permeated with uneasiness about how it might now be used.

The reason that we did this job is because it was an organic necessity. If you are a scientist you cannot stop such a thing. If you are a scientist you believe that it is good to find out how the world works; that it is good to find out what the realities are; that it is good to turn over to mankind at large the greatest possible power to control the world and to deal with it according to its lights and its values.

There has been a lot of talk about the evil of secrecy, of concealment, of control, of security. Some of that talk has been on a rather low plane, limited really to saying that it is difficult or inconvenient to work in a world where you are not free to do what you want. I think that the talk has been justified, and that the almost unanimous resistance of scientists to the imposition of control and secrecy is a justified position, but I think that the reason for it may lie a little deeper. I think that it comes from the fact that secrecy strikes at the very root of what science is, and what it is for. It is not possible to be a scientist unless you believe that it is good to learn. It is not good to be a scientist, and it is not possible, unless you think that it is of the highest value to share your knowledge, to share it with anyone who is interested. It is not possible to be a scientist unless you believe that the knowledge of the world, and the power which this gives, is a thing which is of intrinsic value to humanity, and that you are using it to help in the spread of knowledge, and are willing to take the consequences. And, therefore, I think that this resistance which we feel and see all around us to anything which is an attempt to treat science of the future as though it were rather a dangerous thing, a thing that must be watched and managed, is resisted not because of its inconvenience – I think that we are in a position where we must be willing to take any inconveniences – but resisted because it is based on a philosophy incompatible with that by which we live, and learned to live in the past.

There are many people who try to wriggle out of this. They say the real importance of atomic energy does not lie in the weapons that have been made; the real importance lies in all the great benefits which atomic energy, which the various radiations, will bring to mankind. There may be some truth in this. I am sure that there is truth in it, because there has never in the past been a new field opening up where the real fruits of it have not been invisible at the beginning. I have a very high confidence that the fruits – the so-called peacetime applications – of atomic energy will have in them all we think, and more. There are others who try to escape the immediacy of this situation by saying that, after all, war has always been very terrible; after all, weapons have always gotten worse and worse; that this is just another weapon and it doesn't create a great change; that they are not so bad; bombings have been bad in this war and this is not a change in that – it just adds a little to the effectiveness of bombing; that some sort of protection will be found. I think that these efforts to diffuse and weaken the nature of the crisis make it only more dangerous. I think it is for us to accept it as a very grave crisis, to realize that these atomic weapons which we have started to make are very terrible, that they involve a change, that they are not just a slight modification: to accept this, and to accept with it the necessity for those transformations in the world that will make it possible to integrate these developments into human life.

As scientists I think we have perhaps a little greater ability to accept change, and accept radical change, because of our experiences in the pursuit of science. And that may help us – that, and the fact that we have lived with it – to be of some use in understanding these problems . . .

The control of atomic weapons cannot be in itself the unique end of such operation [of international collaboration]. The only unique end can be a world that is united, and a world in which war will not occur. But those things don't happen overnight, and in this field it would seem that one could get started, and get started without meeting those insuperable obstacles which history has so often placed in the way of any effort of cooperation. Now this is not an easy thing, and the point I want to make, the one point I want to hammer home, is what an enormous change in spirit is involved. There are things which we hold very dear, and I think rightly hold very dear; I would say that the word democracy perhaps stood for some of them as well as any other word. There are many parts of the world in which there is no democracy. There are other things which we hold dear, and which we rightly should. And when I speak of a new spirit in international affairs I mean that even to these deepest of things which we cherish, and for which Americans have been willing to die – and certainly most of us would be willing to die – even in these deepest things, we realize that there is something more profound than that; namely, the common bond with other men everywhere. It is only if you do that that this makes sense; because if you approach the problem and say, 'We know what is right and we would like to use the atomic bomb to persuade you to agree with us,' then you are in a very weak position and you will not succeed, because under those conditions you will not succeed in delegating responsibility for the survival of men. It is a purely unilateral statement; you will find yourselves attempting by force of arms to prevent a disaster.

I want to express the utmost sympathy with the people who have to grapple with this problem and in the strongest terms to urge you not to underestimate its difficulty. I can think of an analogy, and I hope it is not a completely good analogy: in the days in the first half of the nineteenth century there were many people, mostly in the North, but some in the South, who thought that there was no evil on earth more degrading than human slavery, and nothing that they would more willingly devote their lives to than its eradication. Always when I was young I wondered why it was that when Lincoln was President he did not declare that the war against the South, when it broke out, was a war that slavery should be abolished, that this was the central point, the rallying point, of that war. Lincoln was severely criticized by many of the Abolitionists as you know, by many then called radicals, because he seemed to be waging a war which did not hit the thing that was most important. But Lincoln realized, and I have only in the last months come to appreciate the depth and wisdom of it, that beyond the issue of slavery was the issue of the community of the people of the country, and the issue of the Union. I hope that today this will not be an issue calling for war; but I wanted to remind you that in order to preserve the Union Lincoln had to subordinate the immediate problem of the eradication of slavery, and trust – and I think that if he had had his way it would have gone so – to the conflict of these ideas in a united people to eradicate it . . .

It is everywhere felt that the fraternity between us and scientists in other countries may be one of the most helpful things for the future; yet it is apparent that even in this country not all of us who are scientists are in agreement. There is no harm in that; such disagreement is healthy. But we must not lose the sense of fraternity because of it; we must not lose our fundamental confidence in our fellow scientists.

I think that we have no hope at all if we yield in our belief in the value of science, in the good that it can be to the world to know about reality, about nature, to attain a gradually greater and greater control of nature, to learn, to teach, to understand. I think that if we lose our faith in this we stop being scientists, we sell out our heritage, we lose what we have most of value for this time of crisis.

But there is another thing: we are not only scientists; we are men, too. We cannot forget our dependence on our fellow men. I mean not only our material dependence, without which no science would be possible, and without which we could not work; I mean also our deep moral dependence, in that the value of science must lie in the world of men, that all our roots lie there. These are the strongest bonds in the world, stronger than those even that bind us to one another, these are the deepest bonds – that bind us to our fellow men.

Oppenheimer became chairman of the Atomic Energy Commission but opposed the hydrogen bomb. His career ended after he was brought before Joseph McCarthy's UnAmerican Affairs Committee, labelled as a poor security risk and kept from seeing classified information.

•

WINSTON CHURCHILL
Fulton, Missouri, 5 March 1946

The 'iron curtain'

Winston Churchill had lost the British general election in 1945 and was now leader of the Opposition. In 1946 he decided to absent himself from parliament for a few months and accepted an invitation to deliver an address at Westminster College in Fulton, Missouri, the home state of President Truman. Truman and Churchill travelled together in the president's special train.

At Fulton, Churchill made the most important and influential of his post-war speeches, in which he advocated a United Nations peace-keeping force and the strengthening of the 'special relationship' between Britain and the United States. The speech is remembered most, however, for Churchill's description of the 'iron curtain' that had descended across Europe.

A shadow has fallen upon the scenes so lately lighted by the Allied victory. Nobody knows what Soviet Russia and its Communist international organization intends to do in the immediate future, or what are the limits, if any, to their expansive and proselytizing tendencies. I have a strong admiration and regard for the valiant Russian people and for my wartime comrade, Marshal Stalin. There is deep sympathy and goodwill in Britain – and I doubt not here also – towards the peoples of all the Russias and a resolve to persevere through many differences and rebuffs in establishing lasting friendships. We understand the Russian need to be secure on her western frontiers by the removal of all possibility of German aggression. We welcome Russia to her rightful place among the leading nations of the world. We welcome her flag upon the seas.

Above all, we welcome constant, frequent and growing contacts between the Russian people and our own people on both sides of the Atlantic. It is my duty, however, for I am sure you would wish me to state the facts as I see them to you, to place before you certain facts about the present position in Europe.

From Stettin in the Baltic to Trieste in the Adriatic, an iron curtain has descended across the Continent. Behind that line lie all the capitals of the ancient states of Central and Eastern Europe. Warsaw, Berlin, Prague, Vienna, Budapest, Belgrade, Bucharest and Sofia, all these famous cities and the populations around them lie in what I must call the Soviet sphere, and all are subject in one form or another, not only to Soviet influence but to a very high and, in many cases, increasing measure of control from Moscow. Athens alone – Greece with its immortal glories – is free to decide its future at an election under British, American and French observation. The Russian-dominated Polish Government has been encouraged to make enormous and wrongful inroads upon Germany, and mass expulsions of millions of Germans on a scale grievous and undreamed-of are now taking place. The Communist parties, which were very small in all these Eastern states of Europe, have been raised to pre-eminence and power far beyond their numbers and are seeking everywhere to obtain totalitarian control. Police governments are prevailing in nearly every case, and so far, except in Czechoslovakia, there is no true democracy.

Turkey and Persia [Iran] are both profoundly alarmed and disturbed at the claims which are being made upon them and at the pressure being exerted by the Moscow Government. An attempt is being made by the Russians in Berlin to build up a quasi-Communist party in their zone of Occupied Germany by showing special favours to groups of left-wing German leaders. At the end of the fighting last June, the American and British Armies withdrew westwards, in accordance with an earlier agreement, to a depth at some points of one hundred and fifty miles upon a front of nearly four hundred miles, in order to allow our Russian allies to occupy this vast expanse of territory which the Western Democracies had conquered.

If now the Soviet Government tries, by separate action, to build up a pro-Communist Germany in their areas, this will cause new serious difficulties in the British and American zones, and will give the defeated Germans the power of putting themselves up to auction between the Soviets and the Western Democracies. Whatever conclusions may be drawn from these facts – and facts they are – this is certainly not the Liberated Europe we fought to build up. Nor is it one which contains the essentials of permanent peace.

The safety of the world requires a new unity in Europe, from which no nation should be permanently outcast. It is from the quarrels of the strong parent races in Europe that the world wars we have witnessed, or which occurred in former times, have sprung. Twice in our own lifetime we have seen the United States, against their wishes and their traditions, against arguments, the force of which it is impossible not to comprehend, drawn by irresistible forces, into these wars in time to secure the victory of the good cause, but only after frightful slaughter and devastation had occurred. Twice the United States has had to send several millions of its young men across the Atlantic to find the war; but now war can find any nation, wherever it may dwell between dusk and dawn. Surely we should work with conscious purpose for a grand pacification of Europe, within the structure of the United Nations and in accordance with its Charter. That I feel is an open cause of policy of very great importance.

Churchill became prime minister in 1951 and resigned office in 1955. He was made an honorary citizen of the United States in 1963 – a unique distinction – and won the Nobel Prize for Literature in 1953. He died in 1965 and was given a state funeral.

•

GEORGE MARSHALL
Cambridge, Massachusetts, 5 June 1947

'Our policy is directed against hunger, poverty, desperation and chaos'

Although he was chief of staff of the US Army throughout the Second World War, General George Marshall (1880–1959) is mainly remembered today for the Marshall Plan, which was launched by this speech at Harvard's Memorial Church. It was made six months after President Truman appointed him Secretary of State and proposed to offer American financial aid for a programme of European economic recovery on condition that European governments themselves took the first steps towards collaboration.

The truth of the matter is that Europe's requirements for the next three or four years of foreign food and other essential products – principally from America – are so much greater than her present ability to pay that she must have substantial additional help, or face economic, social and political deterioration of a very grave character.

The remedy lies in breaking the vicious circle and restoring the confidence of the European people in the economic future of their own countries and of Europe as a whole. The manufacturer and the farmer throughout wide areas must be able and willing to exchange their products for currencies, the continuing value of which is not open to question.

Aside from the demoralizing effect on the world at large and the possibilities of disturbances arising as a result of the desperation of the people concerned, the consequences to the economy of the United States should be apparent to all. It is logical that the United States should do whatever it is able to do to assist in the return of normal economic health in the world, without which there can be no political stability and no assured peace.

Our policy is directed not against any country or doctrine but against hunger, poverty, desperation and chaos. Its purpose should be the revival of a working economy in the world so as to permit the emergence of political and social conditions in which free institutions can exist. Such assistance, I am convinced, must not be on a piecemeal basis as various crises develop. Any assistance that this Government may render in the future should provide a cure rather than a mere palliative.

Any government that is willing to assist in the task of recovery will find full cooperation, I am sure, on the part of the United States Government. Any government which manoeuvres to block the recovery of other countries cannot expect help from us. Furthermore, governments, political parties or groups which seek to perpetuate human misery in order to profit therefrom politically or otherwise will encounter the opposition of the United States.

It is already evident that, before the United States Government can proceed much further in its efforts to alleviate the situation and help start the European world on its way to recovery, there must be some agreement among the countries of Europe as to the requirements of the situation and the part those countries themselves will take in order to give proper effect to whatever action might be undertaken by this Government. It would be neither fitting nor efficacious for this Government to undertake to draw up unilaterally a programme designed to place Europe on its feet economically. This is the business of the Europeans. The initiative, I think, must come from Europe. The role of this country should consist of friendly aid in the drafting of a European programme and of later support of such a programme so far as it may be practical for us to do so. The programme should be a joint one, agreed to by a number, if not all European nations.

An essential part of any successful action on the part of the United States is an understanding on the part of the people of America of the character of the problem and the remedies to be applied. Political passion and prejudice should have no part. With foresight, and a willingness on the part of our people to face up to the vast responsibility which history has clearly placed upon our country, the difficulties I have outlined can and will be overcome.

The Organization for European Economic Cooperation, representing eighteen European countries, as well as Canada and the USA, was set up in 1948. Marshall Aid totalling $17,000 million was administered through the OEEC and American dollars speeded the recovery of Europe from the devastation of war. Marshall did almost as much to shape the post-war world as Churchill and Roosevelt.

•

JAWAHARLAL NEHRU
Delhi, 14 August 1947

'The noble mansion of free India'

Jawaharlal Nehru (1889–1964) became active in the Indian Congress movement in 1919 and spent the next twenty-eight years at the forefront of the struggle for Indian independence, spending nine years in gaol and long periods under partial restraint. He became president of the Congress movement in 1929 with the support of Gandhi and was subsequently re-elected four times.

Now in August 1947 he had helped to negotiate India's freedom from the British government of Clement Attlee and it was the eve of independence. At this moment of triumph, Nehru made two great speeches, the first to the Indian parliament, the second to the nation over the radio.

I

Long years ago we made a tryst with destiny, and now the time comes when we shall redeem our pledge, not wholly or in full measure, but very substantially. At the stroke of the midnight hour, when the world sleeps, India will awake to life and freedom. A moment comes, which comes but rarely in history, when we step out from the old to the new, when an age ends, and when the soul of a nation, long suppressed, finds utterance. It is fitting that at this solemn moment we take the pledge of dedication to the service of India and her people and to the still larger cause of humanity.

At the dawn of history India started on her unending quest, and trackless centuries are filled with her striving and the grandeur of her success and her failures. Through good and ill fortune alike she has never lost sight of that quest or forgotten the ideals which gave her strength. We end today a period of ill fortune and India discovers herself again. The achievement we celebrate today is but a step, an opening of opportunity, to the greater triumphs and achievements that await us. Are we brave enough and wise enough to grasp this opportunity and accept the challenge of the future?

Freedom and power bring responsibility. The responsibility rests upon this Assembly, a sovereign body representing the sovereign people of India. Before the birth of freedom we have endured all the pains of labour and our hearts are heavy with the memory of this sorrow. Some of those pains continue even now. Nevertheless, the past is over and it is the future that beckons to us now.

That future is not one of ease or resting but of incessant striving so that we may fulfil the pledges we have so often taken and the one we shall take today. The service of India means the service of the millions who suffer. It means the ending of poverty and ignorance and disease and inequality of opportunity. The ambition of the greatest man of our generation has been to wipe every tear from every eye. That may be beyond us, but as long as there are tears and suffering, so long our work will not be over.

And so we have to labour and to work, and work hard, to give reality to our dreams. Those dreams are for India, but they are also for the world, for all the nations and peoples are too closely knit together today for any one of them to imagine that it can live apart. Peace has been said to be indivisible; so is freedom, so is prosperity now, and so also is disaster in this One World that can no longer be split into isolated fragments.

To the people of India, whose representatives we are, we make an appeal to join us with faith and confidence in this great adventure. This is no time for petty and destructive criticism, no time for ill-will or blaming others. We have to build the noble mansion of free India where all her children may dwell.

II

The appointed day has come – the day appointed by destiny – and India stands forth again, after long slumber and struggle, awake, vital, free and independent. The past clings on to us still in some measure and we have to do much before we redeem the pledges we have so often taken. Yet the turning-point is past, and history begins anew for us, the history which we shall live and act and others will write about.

It is a fateful moment for us in India, for all Asia and for the world. A new star rises, the star of freedom in the East, a new hope comes into being, a vision long cherished materializes. May the star never set and that hope never be betrayed!

We rejoice in that freedom, even though clouds surround us, and many of our people are sorrow-stricken and difficult problems encompass us. But freedom brings responsibilities and burdens and we have to face them in the spirit of a free and disciplined people.

On this day our first thoughts go to the architect of this freedom, the Father of our Nation [Gandhi], who, embodying the old spirit of India, held aloft the torch of freedom and lighted up the darkness that surrounded us. We have often been unworthy followers of his and have strayed from his message, but not only we but succeeding generations will remember this message and bear the imprint in their hearts of this great son of India, magnificent in his faith and strength and courage and humility. We shall never allow that torch of freedom to be blown out, however high the wind or stormy the tempest.

Our next thoughts must be of the unknown volunteers and soldiers of freedom who, without praise or reward, have served India even unto death.

We think also of our brothers and sisters who have been cut off from us by political boundaries and who unhappily cannot share at present in the freedom that has come. They are of us and will remain of us whatever may happen, and we shall be sharers in their good [or] ill fortune alike.

The future beckons to us. Whither do we go and what shall be our endeavour? To bring freedom and opportunity to the common man, to the peasants and workers of India; to fight and end poverty and ignorance and disease; to build up a prosperous, democratic and progressive nation, and to create social, economic and political institutions which will ensure justice and fullness of life to every man and woman.

We have hard work ahead. There is no resting for any one of us till we redeem our pledge in full, till we make all the people of India what destiny intended them to be. We are citizens of a great country, on the verge of bold advance, and we have to live up to that high standard. All of us, to whatever religion we may belong, are equally the children of India with equal rights, privileges and obligations. We cannot encourage communalism or narrow-mindedness, for no nation can be great whose people are narrow in thought or in action.

To the nations and peoples of the world we send greetings and pledge ourselves to cooperate with them in furthering peace, freedom and democracy.

And to India, our much-loved motherland, the ancient, the eternal and the ever-new, we pay our reverent homage and we bind ourselves afresh to her service. JAI HIND.

Nehru became an international statesman, mediating in Korea (1951) and Vietnam (1954) as well as sending Indian troops on United Nations peace-keeping missions in Palestine, the Congo and Cyprus. He rationalized Hindu laws and won acceptance of plans for a mixed economy. His death in 1964 deprived India of moral leadership of the developing Third World, but Nehru founded a dynasty. He was succeeded by his daughter, Indira Gandhi (1917–84), who was, in turn, succeeded by her son Rajiv Gandhi in 1984.

●

JAWAHARLAL NEHRU
Delhi, 30 January 1948

'The light has gone out of our lives'

When Gandhi was assassinated by a Hindu nationalist, the world mourned one of the greatest figures of the twentieth century. The Indian government received more than 3,400 unsolicited messages of sympathy from foreign governments. The United Nations lowered its flag to half-mast.

'Mahatma Gandhi was the spokesman for the conscience of all mankind,' said General George Marshall, United States Secretary of State. 'Gandhi had demonstrated that a powerful human following can be assembled . . . through the cogent example of a morally superior conduct of life,' asserted Professor Albert Einstein.

There were expressions of sympathy from the Pope, the Dalai Lama, the Archbishop of Canterbury, the Chief Rabbi of London, King George VI, President Truman, Chiang Kai-shek and the president of France.

No tribute, however, was more simply or movingly expressed than this radio speech by Gandhi's disciple, the prime minister of the independent India that Gandhi worked to achieve throughout his life.

Friends and comrades, the light has gone out of our lives and there is darkness everywhere. I do not know what to tell you and how to say it. Our beloved leader, Bapu as we called him, the father of the nation, is no more. Perhaps I am wrong to say that. Nevertheless, we will not see him again as we have seen him for these many years. We will not run to him for advice and seek solace from him, and that is a terrible blow, not to me only, but to millions and millions in this country, and it is a little difficult to soften the blow by any other advice that I or anyone else can give you.

The light has gone out, I said, and yet I was wrong. For the light that shone in this country was no ordinary light. The light that has illumined this country for these many years will illumine this country for many more years, and a thousand years later that light will still be seen in this country and the world will see it and it will give solace to innumerable hearts. For that light represented the living truth . . . the eternal truths, reminding us of the right path, drawing us from error, taking this ancient country to freedom.

All this has happened when there was so much more for him to do. We could never think that he was unnecessary or that he had done his task. But now, particularly, when we are faced with so many difficulties, his not being with us is a blow most terrible to bear.

A madman has put an end to his life, for I can only call him mad who did it, and yet there has been enough of poison spread in this country during the past years and months, and this poison has had effect on people's minds. We must face this poison, we must root out this poison, and we must face all the perils that encompass us and face them not madly or badly but rather in the way that our beloved teacher taught us to face them. The first thing to remember now is that no one of us dare misbehave because we are angry. We have to behave like strong and determined people, determined to face all the perils that surround us, determined to carry out the mandate that our great teacher and our great leader has given us, remembering always that if, as I believe, his spirit looks upon us and sees us, nothing would displease his soul so much as to see that we have indulged in any small behaviour or any violence.

So we must not do that. But that does not mean that we should be weak, but rather that we should in strength and in unity face all the troubles that are in front of us. We must hold together, and all our petty troubles and difficulties and conflicts must be ended in the face of this great disaster. A great disaster is a symbol to us to remember all the big things of life and forget the small things, of which we have thought too much.

•

JOSEPH McCARTHY
Wheeling, West Virginia, 20 February 1950

'*I have in my hand . . .*'

Joseph McCarthy (1908–57), the junior Republican senator from Wisconsin, began his career as America's leading Red hunter on 9 February 1950, when he made this speech at the McLure Hotel in Wheeling.

McCarthy's accusation that fifty-seven members of the State Department were card-carrying members of the Communist Party instantly became national news and provoked denials from the President and the State Department.

Controversy about what McCarthy really said raged for years. This version of his infamous speech is taken from the statement he made on the Senate floor on 20 February, when he put into the Congressional record a copy of what he really said at Wheeling.

Today we are engaged in a final, all-out battle between communistic atheism and Christianity. The modern champions of communism have selected this as the time. And, ladies and gentlemen, the chips are down – they are truly down . . .

Can there be anyone here tonight who is so blind as to say that the war is not on? Can there be anyone who fails to realize that the Communist world has said, 'The time is now' – that this is the time for the show-down between the democratic Christian world and the Communist atheistic world?

Unless we face this fact, we shall pay the price that must be paid by those who wait too long.

Six years ago, at the time of the first conference to map out the peace – Dumbarton Oaks – there was within the Soviet orbit 180 million people. Lined up on the antitotalitarian side there were in the world at that time roughly 1,625 million people. Today, only six years later, there are 800 million people under the absolute domination of Soviet Russia – an increase of over 400 percent. On our side, the figure has shrunk to around 500 million. In other words, in less than six years the odds have changed from 9 to 1 in our favour to 8 to 5 against us. This indicates the swiftness of the tempo of Communist victories and American defeats in the cold war. As one of our outstanding historical figures once said, 'When a great democracy is destroyed, it will not be because of enemies from without, but rather because of enemies from within.'

The truth of this statement is becoming terrifyingly clear as we see this country each day losing on every front.

At war's end we were physically the strongest nation on earth and, at least potentially, the most powerful intellectually and morally. Ours could have been the honour of being a beacon in the desert of destruction, a shining living proof that civilization was not ready to destroy itself. Unfortunately, we have failed miserably and tragically to arise to the opportunity.

The reason why we find ourselves in a position of impotency is not because our only powerful potential enemy has sent men to invade our shores, but rather because of the traitorous actions of those who have been treated so well by this Nation. It has not been the less fortunate or members of minority groups who have been selling this Nation out, but rather those who have had all the benefits that the wealthiest nation on earth has had to offer – the finest homes, the finest college education, and the finest jobs in Government we can give.

This is glaringly true in the State Department. There the bright young men who are born with silver spoons in their mouths are the ones who have been worst . . .

I have in my hand fifty-seven cases of individuals who would appear to be either card-carrying members or certainly loyal to the Communist Party, but who nevertheless are still helping to shape our foreign policy . . .

One of the important reasons for the graft, the corruption, the dishonesty, the disloyalty, the treason in high Government positions – one of the most important reasons why this continues is a lack of moral uprising on the part of the 140 million American people. In the light of history, however, this is not hard to explain.

It is the result of an emotional hang-over and a temporary moral lapse which follows every war. It is the apathy to evil which people who have been subjected to the tremendous evils of war feel. As the people of the world see mass murder, the destruction of defenseless and innocent people, and all of the crime and lack of morals which go with war, they become numb and apathetic. It has always been thus after war.

However, the morals of our people have not been destroyed. They still exist. This cloak of numbness and apathy has only needed a spark to rekindle them. Happily, this spark has finally been supplied.

As you know, very recently the Secretary of State [Dean Acheson] proclaimed his loyalty to a man guilty of what has always been considered as the most abominable of all crimes – of being a traitor to the people who gave him a position of great trust [Alger Hiss]. The Secretary of State in attempting to justify his continued devotion to the man who sold out the Christian world to the atheistic world, referred to Christ's Sermon on the Mount as a justification and reason therefor, and the reaction of the American people to this would have made the heart of Abraham Lincoln happy.

When this pompous diplomat in striped pants, with a phony British accent, proclaimed to the American people that Christ on the Mount endorsed communism, high treason, and betrayal of a sacred trust, the blasphemy was so great that it awakened the dormant indignation of the American people.

He has lighted the spark which is resulting in a moral uprising and will end only when the whole sorry mess of twisted, warped thinkers are swept from the national scene so that we may have a new birth of national honesty and decency in Government.

The smear tactics of McCarthy and his philistine contempt for intellectuals did untold damage to the American tradition of freedom of thought. He even denounced General George Marshall as a front man for Communism.

McCarthyism, the practice of accusing individuals of belonging to Communist front organizations with little evidence for the accusation, destroyed the careers of many men and women and created a sense of Red menace which won the 1952 election for the Republicans.

Then McCarthy sought to discredit the Army. The Army demonstrated that McCarthy had sought preferential treatment for one of his aides. A Senate motion of censure condemned McCarthy's conduct in 1954 and he finally discredited his cause a few days later by attacking President Eisenhower by name.

•

WILLIAM FAULKNER
Stockholm, 10 December 1950

'The agony and the sweat'

When William Faulkner (1897–1962), the creator of Yoknapatawpha County and author of As I Lay Dying *and* The Sound and the Fury, *won the Nobel Prize, he bought his first dress suit for the occasion and decided to go to Stockholm for the prize-giving.*

At the state banquet, the quiet farmer from Oxford, Mississippi, appeared before a microphone and television camera for the first time and said that he declined to accept the end of man.

I feel that this award was not made to me as a man, but to my work – a life's work in the agony and sweat of the human spirit, not for glory and least of all for profit, but to create out of the materials of the human spirit something which did not exist before. So this award is only mine in trust. It will not be difficult to find a dedication for the money part of it commensurate with the purpose and significance of its origin. But I would like to do the same with the acclaim too, by using this moment as a pinnacle from which I might be listened to by the young men and women already dedicated to the same anguish and travail, among whom is already that one who will someday stand here where I am standing.

Our tragedy today is a general and universal physical fear so long sustained by now that we can even bear it. There are no longer problems of the spirit. There is only the question: when will I be blown up? Because of this, the young man or woman writing today has forgotten the problems of the human heart in conflict with itself which alone can make good writing because only that is worth writing about, worth the agony and the sweat.

He must learn them again. He must teach himself that the basest of all things is to be afraid; and, teaching himself that, forget it forever, leaving no room in his workshop for anything but the old verities and truths of the heart, the old universal truths lacking which any story is ephemeral and doomed – love and honour and pity and pride and compassion and sacrifice. Until he does so, he labours under a curse. He writes not of love but of lust, of defeats in which nobody loses anything of value, of victories without hope, and, worst of all, without pity or compassion. His griefs grieve on no universal bones, leaving no scars. He writes not of the heart but of the glands.

Until he relearns these things, he will write as though he stood among and watched the end of man. I decline to accept the end of man. It is easy enough to say that man is immortal simply because he will endure; that when the last ding-dong of doom has clanged and faded from the last worthless rock hanging tideless in the last red and dying evening, that even then there will still be one more sound: that of his puny inexhaustible voice, still talking. I refuse to accept this. I believe that man will not merely endure: he will prevail. He is immortal, not because he alone among creatures has an inexhaustible voice, but because he has a soul, a spirit capable of compassion and sacrifice and endurance. The poet's, the writer's, duty is to write about these things. It is his privilege to help man endure by lifting his heart, by reminding him of the courage and honour and hope and pride and compassion and pity and sacrifice which have been the glory of his past. The poet's voice need not merely be the record of man; it can be one of the props, the pillars, to help him endure and prevail.

•

ANEURIN BEVAN
London, 23 April 1951

'*There is only one hope for mankind*'

Aneurin Bevan (1897–1960) was the son of a miner who left school at thirteen to work on the coal-face and rose to become the spokesman for the South Wales

*miners during the General Strike of 1926. He became an MP in 1929, was the
most constructive of Churchill's critics during the Second World War and was one
of the greatest Labour orators.*

*As minister of health from 1945 to 1951, he was the founder of the British
National Health Service – but he resigned from the government on 21 April 1951
in protest at the imposition of health-service charges to meet defence costs. He told
Clement Attlee, the prime minister, that he could not carry out policies which
were 'repugnant' to his conscience.*

*Two days later he made his resignation speech to the Commons. He stood
almost alone. There was no sympathy on the Conservative benches and Labour
MPs feared he would destroy the government.*

The western world has embarked upon a campaign of arms production upon a scale, so quickly, and of such an extent that the
foundations of political liberty and Parliamentary democracy will
not be able to sustain the shock. This is a very grave matter
indeed. I have always said that the defence programme must always
be consistent with the maintenance of the standard of life of the
British people and the maintenance of the social services, and that
as soon as it became clear we had engaged upon an arms
programme inconsistent with those considerations, I could no
longer remain a Member of the Government.

I therefore beg the House and the country, and the world, to
think before it is too late. It may be that on such an occasion as
this the dramatic nature of a resignation might cause even some of
our American friends to think before it is too late. It has always
been clear that the weapons of the totalitarian States are, first,
social and economic, and only next military; and if in attempting
to meet the military effect of those totalitarian machines, the
economies of the western world are disrupted and the standard of
living is lowered or industrial disturbances are created, then Soviet
Communism establishes a whole series of Trojan horses in every
nation of the western economy . . .

This great nation has a message for the world which is distinct
from that of America or that of the Soviet Union. Ever since 1945
we have been engaged in this country in the most remarkable

piece of social reconstruction the world has ever seen. By the end of 1950 we had assumed the moral leadership of the world. (*Interruption.*) It is no use Hon. Members opposite sneering, because when they come to the end of the road it will not be a sneer which will be upon their faces. There is only one hope for mankind, and that hope still remains in this little island. It is from here that we tell the world where to go and how to go there, but we must not follow behind the anarchy of American competitive capitalism which is unable to restrain itself at all, as is seen in the stockpiling that is now going on, and which denies to the economy of Great Britain even the means of carrying on our civil production . . .

The Chancellor of the Exchequer in this year's Budget proposes to reduce the Health expenditure by £13 million – only £13 million out of £4,000 million.

If he finds it necessary to mutilate, or begin to mutilate, the Health Services for £13 million out of £4,000 million, what will he do next year? Or are you next year going to take your stand on the upper denture? The lower half apparently does not matter, but the top half is sacrosanct. Is that right? If my Hon. Friends are asked questions at meetings about what they will do next year, what will they say?

The Chancellor of the Exchequer is putting a financial ceiling on the Health Service. With rising prices the Health Service is squeezed between that artificial figure and rising prices. What is to be squeezed out next year? Is it the upper half? When that has been squeezed out and the same principle holds good, what do you squeeze out the year after? Prescriptions? Hospital charges? Where do you stop? I have been accused of having agreed to a charge on prescriptions. That shows the danger of compromise. Because if it is pleaded against me that I agreed to the modification of the Health Service, then what will be pleaded against my Right Hon. Friends next year, and indeed what answer will they have if the vandals opposite come in? What answer? The Health Service will be like Lavinia – all the limbs cut off and eventually her tongue cut out, too.

I should like to ask my Right Hon. and Hon. Friends, where are they going? (*Hon. Members: 'Where are you going?'*) Where am I going? I am where I always was. Those who live their lives in mountainous and rugged countries are always afraid of avalanches, and they know that avalanches start with the movement of a very small stone. First, the stone starts on a ridge between two valleys – one valley desolate and the other valley populous. The pebble starts, but nobody bothers about the pebble until it gains way, and soon the whole valley is overwhelmed. That is how the avalanche starts, that is the logic of the present situation, and that is the logic my Right Hon. and Hon. Friends cannot escape. Why, therefore, has it been done in this way?

After all, the National Health Service was something of which we were all very proud, and even the Opposition were beginning to be proud of it. It only had to last a few more years to become a part of our traditions, and then the traditionalists would have claimed the credit for all of it. Why should we throw it away? In the Chancellor's Speech there was not one word of commendation for the Health Service – not one word. What is responsible for that?

Why has the cut been made? He cannot say, with an overall surplus of over £220 million and a conventional surplus of £39 million, that he had to have the £13 million. That is the arithmetic of Bedlam. He cannot say that his arithmetic is so precise that he must have the £13 million, when last year the Treasury were £247 million out. Why?

What is the cause of it? Why has it been done? . . .

I say this, in conclusion. There is only one hope for mankind – and that is democratic Socialism. There is only one party in Great Britain which can do it – and that is the Labour Party. But I ask them carefully to consider how far they are polluting the stream. We have gone a long way – a very long way – against great difficulties. Do not let us change direction now. Let us make it clear, quite clear, to the rest of the world that we stand where we stood, that we are not going to allow ourselves to be diverted from our path by the exigencies of the immediate situation. We shall do what is necessary to defend ourselves – defend ourselves by arms, and not only with arms but with the spiritual resources of our people.

The speech stunned the House of Commons. Newspapers jeered and even the miners of Durham were critical. Bevan was defeated by Hugh Gaitskell (the chancellor who imposed the health charges) in the contest for the Labour leadership of 1955 but then became official spokesman on foreign affairs.

•

ADLAI STEVENSON
Illinois, 26 July 1952

'Let's talk sense to the American people'

When the Republicans selected General Eisenhower as their presidential candidate in 1952, the Democrats responded by nominating their best man, Governor Adlai Stevenson (1900–1965) of Illinois, who had proved himself an effective reforming governor.

Until then, few Americans had heard of Stevenson, although he had served in government, been a delegate to the UN General Assembly and was elected governor of Illinois by a record-breaking half million votes in 1948.

As Stevenson accepted the Democratic nomination, the nation heard for the first time the eloquence that made him so memorable a speaker.

The ordeal of the twentieth century – the bloodiest, most turbulent era of the Christian age – is far from over. Sacrifice, patience, understanding, and implacable purpose may be our lot for years to come.

Let's face it. Let's talk sense to the American people. Let's tell them the truth, that there are no gains without pains, that we are now on the eve of great decisions, not easy decisions, like resistance when you're attacked, but a long, patient, costly struggle which alone can assure triumph over the great enemies of man – war, poverty, and tyranny – and the assaults upon human dignity which are the most grievous consequences of each.

Let's tell them that the victory to be won in the twentieth century, this portal to the golden age, mocks the pretensions of individual acumen and ingenuity. For it is a citadel guarded by thick walls of ignorance and mistrust which do not fall before the trumpets' blast or the politicians' imprecations or even a general's baton. They are, my friends, walls that must be directly stormed by the hosts of courage, morality, and of vision, standing shoulder to shoulder, unafraid of ugly truth, contemptuous of lies, half-truths, circuses, and demagoguery.

The people are wise – wiser than the Republicans think. And the Democratic party is the people's party, not the labour party, not the farmers' party, not the employers' party – it is the party of no one because it is the party of everyone.

That, I think, is our ancient mission. Where we have deserted it we have failed. With your help there will be no desertion now. Better we lose the election than mislead the people; and better we lose than misgovern the people.

Help me do the job in this autumn of conflict and of campaign; help me to do the job in these years of darkness, of doubt, and of crisis which stretch beyond the horizon of tonight's happy vision, and we will justify our glorious past and the loyalty of silent millions who look to us for compassion, for understanding, and for honest purpose. Thus we will serve our great tradition greatly.

I ask of you all you have; I will give to you all I have, even as he who came here tonight and honoured me, as he has honoured you – the Democratic party – by a lifetime of service and bravery that will find him an imperishable page in the history of the Republic and of the Democratic party – President Harry S. Truman.

And finally, my friends, in the staggering task that you have assigned me, I shall always try 'to do justly, to love mercy, and walk humbly with my God.'

Eisenhower won the election by a landslide and Stevenson lost again in 1956–

but his liberalism captured a generation of Democrats, saved the Republicans from falling back into the clutches of the Southern conservatives, and prepared the way for the reformers of the Kennedy and Johnson administrations.

•

DWIGHT D. EISENHOWER
Washington, DC, 16 April 1953

'*A theft from those who hunger*'

General Dwight D. Eisenhower (1890–1969) was commander-in-chief of the Allied armies of liberation in the West during the Second World War. That supremely challenging task called for qualities of mind and character which Eisenhower possessed to a unique degree and which gave him in 1952 an easy election to the presidency – the first Republican since Hoover in 1928.

Eisenhower had a general's approach to the presidency. He delegated power and believed that the president should reign rather than rule. His approach provoked criticism that America lacked leadership and direction.

After the death of Stalin and three months after his inauguration, he interrupted his golfing holiday and flew back to Washington to speak to the American Society of Newspaper Editors. He made a serious appeal to the new leaders of the Soviet Union for a political settlement of the issues between them and the Free World. The speech made clear how far the United States was prepared to go as well as what it was prepared to surrender and laid down the conditions for coexistence.

So it has come to pass that the Soviet Union itself has shared and suffered the very fears it has fostered in the rest of the world.

This has been the way of life forged by eight years of fear and force.

What can the world, or any nation in it, hope for if no turning is found on this dread road?

The worst to be feared and the best to be expected can be simply stated.

The *worst* is atomic war.

The *best* would be this: a life of perpetual fear and tension; a burden of arms draining the wealth and the labour of all peoples; a wasting of strength that defies the American system or the Soviet system or any system to achieve true abundance and happiness for the peoples of this earth.

Every gun that is made, every warship launched, every rocket fired signifies, in the final sense, a theft from those who hunger and are not fed, those who are cold and are not clothed.

This world in arms is not spending money alone.

It is spending the sweat of its labourers, the genius of its scientists, the hopes of its children.

The cost of one modern heavy bomber is this: a modern brick school in more than thirty cities.

It is two electric power plants, each serving a town of 60,000 population.

It is two fine, fully equipped hospitals.

It is some fifty miles of concrete highway.

We pay for a single fighter plane with a half million bushels of wheat.

We pay for a single destroyer with new homes that could have housed more than 8,000 people.

This, I repeat, is the best way of life to be found on the road the world has been taking.

This is not a way of life at all, in any true sense. Under the cloud of threatening war, it is humanity hanging from a cross of iron.

These plain and cruel truths define the peril and point the hope that come with this spring of 1953.

This is one of those times in the affairs of nations when the gravest choices must be made, if there is to be a turning towards a just and lasting peace.

It is a moment that calls upon the governments of the world to speak their intentions with simplicity and with honesty.

It calls upon them to answer the question that stirs the hearts of all sane men: *is there no other way the world may live?*

The world knows that an era ended with the death of Joseph

Stalin. The extraordinary thirty-year span of his rule saw the Soviet Empire expand to reach from the Baltic Sea to the Sea of Japan, finally to dominate 800 million souls.

The Soviet system shaped by Stalin and his predecessors was born of one World War. It survived with stubborn and often amazing courage a second World War. It has lived to threaten a third.

Now a new leadership has assumed power in the Soviet Union. Its links to the past, however strong, cannot bind it completely. Its future is, in great part, its own to make.

This new leadership confronts a free world aroused, as rarely in its history, by the will to stay free . . .

I know of only one question upon which progress waits. It is this:

What is the Soviet Union ready to do?

Whatever the answer be, let it be plainly spoken.

Again we say: the hunger for peace is too great, the hour in history too late, for any government to mock men's hopes with mere words and promises and gestures.

The test of truth is simple. There can be no persuasion but by deeds.

Is the new leadership of the Soviet Union prepared to use its decisive influence in the Communist world, including control of the flow of arms, to bring not merely an expedient truce in Korea but genuine peace in Asia?

Is it prepared to allow other nations, including those of Eastern Europe, the free choice of their own forms of government?

Is it prepared to act in concert with others upon serious disarmament proposals to be made firmly effective by stringent UN control and inspection?

If not, where then is the concrete evidence of the Soviet Union's concern for peace?

The test is clear.

There is, before all peoples, a precious chance to turn the black tide of events. If we failed to strive to seize this chance, the judgement of future ages would be harsh and just.

If we strive but fail and the world remains armed against itself, it at least need be divided no longer in its clear knowledge of who has condemned humankind to this fate.

The purpose of the United States in stating these proposals is simple and clear.

These proposals spring – without ulterior purpose or political passion – from our calm conviction that a hunger for just peace is in the hearts of all peoples – those of Russia, and of China, no less than of our own country.

They conform to our firm faith that God created men to enjoy, not to destroy, the fruits of the earth and of their own toil.

They aspire to this: the lifting from the backs and from the hearts of men, of their burden of arms and of fears, so that they may find before them a golden age of freedom and of peace.

The arms race between the two superpowers continued and there was no lessening of their mutual mistrust. Eisenhower was re-elected in 1956.

•

KWAME NKRUMAH
Accra, 10 July 1953

'*The motion of destiny*'

After graduating from Achimoto College at Lincoln University in Pennsylvania and the London School of Economics, Kwame Nkrumah (1909–72) returned to his homeland and founded the Convention People's Party in 1949. He sought immediate self-government for the Gold Coast, which he renamed Ghana. During his ten years in America he had acquired a strong sense of black solidarity and a burning vision of an independent United States of Africa.

His party won an overwhelming election victory in 1951 and Nkrumah, who had been imprisoned by the British for sedition, was released to head the government. He cooperated with the British governor in a peaceful transfer of power. A white paper on constitutional reform was published in July 1953 – and on 10 July

Nkrumah moved his independence motion, known popularly as 'The motion of destiny'.

I am asking you to give my Government the power to bring to fruition the longing hopes, the ardent dreams, the fervent aspirations of the chiefs and people of our country. Throughout a century of alien rule our people have, with ever increasing tendency, looked forward to that bright and glorious day when they shall regain their ancient heritage, and once more take their place rightly as free men in the world.

Mr Speaker, we have frequent examples to show that there comes a time in the history of all colonial peoples when they must, because of their will to throw off the hampering shackles of colonialism, boldly assert their God-given right to be free of a foreign ruler. Today we are here to claim this right to our independence . . .

The right of a people to decide their own destiny, to make their way in freedom, is not to be measured by the yardstick of colour or degree of social development. It is an inalienable right of peoples which they are powerless to exercise when forces, stronger than they themselves, by whatever means, for whatever reasons, take this right away from them. If there is to be a criterion of a people's preparedness for self-government, then I say it is their readiness to assume the responsibilities of ruling themselves. For who but a people themselves can say when they are prepared? How can others judge when that moment has arrived in the destiny of a subject people? What other gauge can there be?

Mr Speaker, never in the history of the world has an alien ruler granted self-rule to a people on a silver platter. Therefore, Mr Speaker, I say that a people's readiness and willingness to assume the responsibilities of self-rule is the single criterion of their preparedness to undertake those responsibilities . . .

In the very early days of the Christian era, long before England had assumed any importance, long even before her people had united into a nation, our ancestors had attained a great empire, which lasted until the eleventh century, when it fell before the attacks of the Moors of the North. At its height that empire stretched from Timbuktu to Bamako, and even as far as to the Atlantic. It is said that lawyers and scholars were much respected in that empire and that the inhabitants of Ghana wore garments of wool, cotton, silk and velvet. There was trade in copper, gold and textile fabrics, and jewels and weapons of gold and silver were carried.

Thus may we take pride in the name of Ghana, not out of romanticism, but as an inspiration for the future. It is right and proper that we should know about our past. For just as the future moves from the present so the present has emerged from the past. Nor need we be ashamed of our past. There was much in it of glory. What our ancestors achieved in the context of their contemporary society gives us confidence that we can create, out of that past, a glorious future, not in terms of war and military pomp, but in terms of social progress and of peace. For we repudiate war and violence. Our battles shall be against the old ideas that keep men trammelled in their own greed; against the crass stupidities that breed hatred, fear and inhumanity. The heroes of our future will be those who can lead our people out of the stifling fog of disintegration through serfdom, into the valley of light where purpose, endeavour and determination will create that brotherhood which Christ proclaimed two thousand years ago, and about which so much is said, but so little done . . .

Honourable Members, you are called, here and now, as a result of the relentless tide of history, by Nemesis as it were, to a sacred charge, for you hold the destiny of our country in your hands. The eyes and ears of the world are upon you; yea, our oppressed brothers throughout this vast continent of Africa and the New World are looking to you with desperate hope, as an inspiration to continue their grim fight against cruelties which we in this corner of Africa have never known – cruelties which are a disgrace to humanity, and to the civilization which the white man has set himself to teach us. At this time, history is being made; a colonial people in Africa has put forward the first definite claim for independence. An African colonial people proclaim that they are ready to assume the stature of free men and to prove to the world that they are worthy of the trust.

I know that you will not fail those who are listening for the mandate that you will give to your Representative Ministers. For we are ripe for freedom, and our people will not be denied. They are conscious that the right is theirs, and they know that freedom is not something that one people can bestow on another as a gift. They claim it as their own and none can keep it from them.

As long as we remain subject to an alien power, too much of our energy is diverted from constructive enterprise. Oppressive forces breed frustration. Imperialism and colonialism are a twofold evil. This theme is expressed in the truism that 'no nation which oppresses another can itself be free'. Thus we see that this evil not only wounds the people which is subject, but the dominant nation pays the price in a warping of their finer sensibilities through arrogance and greed. Imperialism and colonialism are a barrier to true friendship . . .

In our daily lives, we may lack those material comforts regarded as essential by the standards of the modern world, because so much of our wealth is still locked up in our land; but we have the gifts of laughter and joy, a love of music, a lack of malice, an absence of the desire for vengeance for our wrongs, all things of intrinsic worth in a world sick of injustice, revenge, fear and want.

We feel that there is much the world can learn from those of us who belong to what we might term the pre-technological societies. These are values which we must not sacrifice unheedingly in pursuit of material progress. That is why we say that self-government is not an end in itself.

We have to work hard to evolve new patterns, new social customs, new attitudes to life, so that while we seek the material, cultural and economic advancement of our country, while we raise their standards of life, we shall not sacrifice their fundamental happiness. That, I should say, Mr Speaker, has been the greatest tragedy of Western society since the industrial revolution.

In harnessing the forces of nature, man has become the slave of the machine, and of his own greed. If we repeat these mistakes and suffer the consequences which have overtaken those that made them, we shall have no excuse. This is a field of exploration for the young men and women now in our schools and colleges, for our sociologists and economists, for our doctors and our social welfare workers, for our engineers and town planners, for our scientists and our philosophers.

Mr Speaker, when we politicians have long passed away and been forgotten, it is upon their shoulders that will fall the responsibility of evolving new forms of social institutions, new economic instruments to help build in our rich and fertile country a society where men and women may live in peace, where hate, strife, envy and greed, shall have no place.

Mr Speaker, we can only meet the challenge of our age as a free people. Hence our demand for our freedom, for only free men can shape the destinies of their future.

Mr Speaker, Honourable Members, we have great tasks before us. I say, with all seriousness, that it is rarely that human beings have such an opportunity for service to their fellows.

Mr Speaker, for my part, I can only re-echo the words of a great man: 'Man's dearest possession is life, and since it is given him to live but once, he must so live as not to be besmeared with the shame of a cowardly existence and trivial past, so live that dying he might say: all my life and all my strength were given to the finest cause in the world – the liberation of mankind.'

Mr Speaker, 'Now God be thank'd, Who has match'd us with His hour!' I beg to move.

'The acclamation that burst forth was such that one expected the roof and walls to collapse,' Nkrumah wrote later. Nkrumah became president when Ghana became a republic on 1 July 1960. He was respected as a Pan-African leader but once in power became increasingly dictatorial at home and was overthrown in a military coup in 1966. A statue was erected and a park opened in his memory in Accra in 1992. His body was reinterred in a mausoleum.

•

FIDEL CASTRO
Santiago, Cuba, 16 October 1953

'History will absolve me'

On 26 July 1953 Fidel Castro, a Cuban lawyer and defender of the poor in Havana, led an unsuccessful armed revolt against the Moncada Barracks. A mass trial of Castro and 122 other defendants started in the Santiago Palace of Justice on 21 September. Castro was eventually confined to prison and his trial was held in virtual secrecy in a small nurses' lodge at the Saturnino Lora hospital – a decision made to perpetuate the official fiction that he was too ill to attend the Palace of Justice.

Castro's speech from the dock, inspired by his hero José Martí, the Cuban philosopher, remains the fundamental document of the subsequent Cuban revolution and the most venerated scripture of the rebel movement. The speech built up history's case to justify taking up arms against tyrants, summoning up the spirit of Luther and Calvin, Montesquieu and Rousseau, Milton, Locke, Paine and Balzac.

Castro practised the delivery of his speech in his cell until dawn. Then he went before the judges and declared: 'When men carry the same ideals in their hearts, nothing can isolate them – neither prison walls nor the sod of cemeteries. For a single memory, a single spirit, a single conscience, a single dignity will sustain them all.'

Honourable Judges: If there is in your hearts a vestige of love for your country, love for humanity, love for justice, listen carefully. I know that I will be silenced for many years; I know that the regime will try to suppress the truth by all possible means; I know that there will be a conspiracy to bury me in oblivion. But my voice will not be stilled – it will rise from my breast even when I feel most alone, and my heart will give it all the fire that callous cowards deny it . . .

From a shack in the mountains on Monday, July the 27th, I listened to the dictator's voice on the air while there were still eighteen of our men in arms against the government. Those who have never experienced similar moments will never know that kind of bitterness and indignation. While the long cherished hopes of freeing our people lay in ruins about us we heard those crushed hopes gloated over by a tyrant more vicious, more arrogant than ever. The endless stream of lies and slanders, poured forth in his crude, odious, repulsive language, may only be compared to the endless stream of clean young blood which had flowed since the previous night – with his knowledge, consent, complicity and approval – being spilled by the most inhuman gang of assassins it is possible to imagine.

To have believed him for a single moment would have sufficed to fill a man of conscience with remorse and shame for the rest of his life. At that time I could not even hope to brand his miserable forehead with the mark of truth which condemns him for the rest of his days and for all time to come. Already a circle of more than a thousand men, armed with weapons more powerful than ours and with peremptory orders to bring in our bodies, was closing in around us. Now that the truth is coming out, now that speaking before you I am carrying out the mission I set for myself, I may die peacefully and content. So I shall not mince any words about those savage murderers . . .

Moncada Barracks were turned into a workshop of torture and death. Some shameful individuals turned their uniforms into butchers' aprons. The walls were splattered with blood. The bullets imbedded in the walls were encrusted with singed bits of skin, brains and human hair, the grisly reminders of rifle shots fired full in the face. The grass around the barracks was dark and sticky with human blood. The criminal hands that are guiding the destiny of Cuba had written for the prisoners at the entrance of that den of death the very inscription of Hell: 'Forsake all hope.'

They did not even attempt to cover appearances. They did not bother in the least to conceal what they were doing. They thought they had deceived the people with their lies and they ended up deceiving themselves. They felt themselves lords and masters of the universe, with power over life and death. So the fear they had experienced upon our attack at daybreak was dissipated in a feast of corpses, in a drunken orgy of blood . . .

Dante divided his *Inferno* into nine circles. He put the criminals in the seventh, the thieves in the eighth and the traitors in the ninth. Difficult dilemma the devils will be faced with, when they try to find an adequate spot for this man's soul – if this man has a soul. The man who instigated the atrocious acts in Santiago de Cuba doesn't even have a heart.

In every society there are men of base instincts. The sadists, brutes, conveyors of all the ancestral atavisms go about in the guise of human beings, but they are monsters, only more or less restrained by discipline and social habit. If they are offered a drink from a river of blood, they will not be satisfied until they drink the river dry. All these men needed was the order. At their hands the best and noblest Cubans perished: the most valiant, the most honest, the most idealistic. The tyrant called them mercenaries. There they were dying as heroes at the hands of men who collect a salary from the Republic and who, with the arms the Republic gave them to defend her, serve the interests of a clique and murder her best citizens.

Throughout their torturing of our comrades, the Army offered them the chance to save their lives by betraying their ideology and falsely declaring that Prío had given them money. When they indignantly rejected that proposition, the Army continued with its horrible tortures. They crushed their testicles and they tore out their eyes. But no one yielded. No complaint was heard nor a favour asked. Even when they had been deprived of their virile organs, our men were still a thousand times more men than all their tormentors together. Photographs, which do not lie, show the bodies torn to pieces. Other methods were used. Frustrated by the valour of the men, they tried to break the spirit of our women. With a bleeding human eye in their hands, a sergeant and several other men went to the cell where our comrades Melba Hernández and Haydée Santamaría were held. Addressing the latter, and showing her the eye, they said: 'This eye belonged to your brother. If you will not tell us what he refused to say, we will tear out the other.' She, who loved her valiant brother above all things, replied full of dignity: 'If you tore out an eye and he did not speak, much less will I.' Later they came back and burned their arms with lit cigarettes until at last, filled with spite, they told the young Haydée Santamaría: 'You no longer have a fiancé because we have killed him too.' But, still imperturbable, she answered: 'He is not dead, because to die for one's country is to live forever.' Never had the heroism and the dignity of Cuban womanhood reached such heights . . .

We are Cubans and to be Cuban implies a duty; not to fulfil that duty is a crime, is treason. We are proud of the history of our country; we learned it in school and have grown up hearing of freedom, justice and human rights. We were taught to venerate the glorious example of our heroes and martyrs. Céspedes, Agramonte, Maceo, Gómez, and Martí were the first names engraved in our minds. We were taught that the Titan once said that liberty is not begged for but won with the blade of a machete. We were taught that for the guidance of Cuba's free citizens, the Apostle wrote in his book *The Golden Age*: 'The man who abides by unjust laws and permits any man to trample and mistreat the country in which he was born, is not an honourable man . . . In the world there must be a certain degree of honour just as there must be a certain amount of light. When there are many men without honour, there are always others who bear in themselves the honour of many men. These are the men who rebel with great force against those who steal the people's freedom, that is to say, against those who steal human honour itself. In those men thousands more are contained, an entire people is contained, human dignity is contained . . .' We were taught that the 10th of October and the 24th of February are glorious anniversaries of national rejoicing because they mark days on which Cubans rebelled against the yoke of infamous tyranny. We were taught to cherish and defend the beloved flag of the lone star, and to sing every afternoon the verses of our National Anthem: 'To live in chains is to live in disgrace and in opprobrium' and 'To die for one's homeland is to live forever!' All this we learned and will never forget, even though today in our land there is murder and prison for the men who practise the ideas taught to them since the cradle. We were born in a free country that our parents bequeathed to us and the Island will sink into the sea before we consent to be slaves of anyone.

It seemed that the Apostle would die during his Centennial. It seemed that his memory would be extinguished forever. So great was the affront! But he is alive; he has not died. His people are rebellious. His people are worthy. His people are faithful to his memory. There are Cubans who have fallen defending his doctrines. There are young men who in magnificent selflessness came to die beside his tomb, giving their blood and their lives so that he could keep on living in the heart of his nation. Cuba, what would have become of you had you let your Apostle die?

I come to the close of my defence plea but I will not end it as lawyers usually do, asking that the accused be freed. I cannot ask freedom for myself while my comrades are already suffering in the ignominious prison of the Isle of Pines. Send me there to join them and to share their fate. It is understandable that honest men should be dead or in prison in a Republic where the President is a criminal and a thief . . .

I know that imprisonment will be harder for me than it has ever been for anyone, filled with cowardly threats and hideous cruelty. But I do not fear prison, as I do not fear the fury of the miserable tyrant who took the lives of seventy of my comrades. Condemn me. It does not matter. History will absolve me.

Castro was sentenced to fifteen years but was freed two years later and went into exile. He returned to Cuba with his brother Raúl and Che Guevara in December 1956 and conducted guerrilla operations from the Sierra Maestra. On 8 January 1959, he entered Havana in triumph and became prime minister a year later. Castro and Guevara became worldwide symbols of rebellion during the student revolts of the 1960s in the United States and Europe.

•

BERTRAND RUSSELL
BBC Radio, London, 30 December 1954

'Shall we choose death?'

Bertrand Russell's claim to be remembered by history rests on his work in mathematical and symbolic logic and his profound influence on philosophy. Yet he was also constantly involved in political affairs. Russell (1872–1970) was deprived of his fellowship at Trinity College, Cambridge, during the First World War because of his pacifism. He was imprisoned in 1918. During the Second World War, however, he abandoned his pacifism because of his hatred of Fascism. When the atom bomb was followed by the hydrogen bomb, he became a campaigner for nuclear disarmament – and this speech on BBC Radio was a characteristic example of the powerful rhetoric he used against the arms race that built up between the United States and the Soviet Union, the two great superpowers, and which, he argued, was endangering the human race.

The broadcast was made after the explosion of the first H-bomb, his thin singsong voice charged with the detached intensity of a prophet.

I am speaking not as a Briton, not as a European, not as a member of a western democracy, but as a human being, a member of the species Man, whose continued existence is in doubt. The world is full of conflicts: Jews and Arabs; Indians and Pakistanis; white men and Negroes in Africa; and, overshadowing all minor conflicts, the titanic struggle between communism and anti-communism.

Almost everybody who is politically conscious has strong feelings about one or more of these issues; but I want you, if you can, to set aside such feelings for the moment and consider yourself only as a member of a biological species which has had a remarkable history and whose disappearance none of us can desire. I shall try to say no single word which should appeal to one group rather than to another. All, equally, are in peril, and, if the peril is understood, there is hope that they may collectively avert it. We have to learn to think in a new way. We have to learn to ask ourselves not what steps can be taken to give military victory to whatever group we prefer, for there no longer are such steps. The question we have to ask ourselves is: What steps can be taken to prevent a military contest of which the issue must be disastrous to all sides?

The general public, and even many men in positions of authority, have not realized what would be involved in a war with hydrogen bombs. The general public still thinks in terms of the obliteration of cities. It is understood that the new bombs are more powerful than the old and that, while one atomic bomb could obliterate Hiroshima, one hydrogen bomb could obliterate the largest cities such as London, New York, and Moscow. No doubt in a hydrogen-bomb war great cities would be obliterated. But this is one of the minor disasters that would have to be faced. If everybody in London, New York, and Moscow were exterminated, the world might, in the course of a few centuries, recover from the blow. But we now know, especially since the Bikini test, that hydrogen bombs can gradually spread destruction over a much wider area than had been supposed. It is stated on very good authority that a bomb can now be manufactured which will be 25,000 times as powerful as that which destroyed Hiroshima. Such a bomb, if exploded near the ground or under water, sends radioactive particles into the upper air. They sink gradually and reach the surface of the earth in the form of a deadly dust or rain. It was this dust which infected the Japanese fishermen and their catch of fish although they were outside what American experts believed to be the danger zone. No one knows how widely such lethal radioactive particles might be diffused, but the best authorities are unanimous in saying that a war with hydrogen bombs is quite likely to put an end to the human race. It is feared that if many hydrogen bombs are used there will be universal death – sudden only for a fortunate minority, but for the majority a slow torture of disease and disintegration . . .

Here, then, is the problem which I present to you, stark and dreadful and inescapable: Shall we put an end to the human race; or shall mankind renounce war? People will not face this alternative because it is so difficult to abolish war. The abolition of war will demand distasteful limitations of national sovereignty. But what perhaps impedes understanding of the situation more than anything else is that the term 'mankind' feels vague and abstract. People scarcely realize in imagination that the danger is to themselves and their children and their grandchildren, and not only to a dimly apprehended humanity. And so they hope that perhaps war may be allowed to continue provided modern weapons are prohibited. I am afraid this hope is illusory. Whatever agreements not to use hydrogen bombs had been reached in time of peace, they would no longer be considered binding in time of war, and both sides would set to work to manufacture hydrogen bombs as soon as war broke out, for if one side manufactured the bombs and the other did not, the side that manufactured them would inevitably be victorious . . .

As geological time is reckoned, Man has so far existed only for a very short period – one million years at the most. What he has achieved, especially during the last 6,000 years, is something utterly new in the history of the Cosmos, so far at least as we are acquainted with it. For countless ages the sun rose and set, the moon waxed and waned, the stars shone in the night, but it was only with the coming of Man that these things were understood. In the great world of astronomy and in the little world of the atom, Man has unveiled secrets which might have been thought undiscoverable. In art and literature and religion, some men have shown a sublimity of feeling which makes the species worth preserving. Is all this to end in trivial horror because so few are able to think of Man rather than of this or that group of men? Is our race so destitute of wisdom, so incapable of impartial love, so blind even to the simplest dictates of self-preservation, that the last proof of its silly cleverness is to be the extermination of all life on our planet? – for it will be not only men who will perish, but also the animals, whom no one can accuse of communism or anti-communism.

I cannot believe that this is to be the end. I would have men forget their quarrels for a moment and reflect that, if they will allow themselves to survive, there is every reason to expect the triumphs of the future to exceed immeasurably the triumphs of the past. There lies before us, if we choose, continual progress in happiness, knowledge, and wisdom. Shall we, instead, choose death, because we cannot forget our quarrels? I appeal, as a human being to human beings: remember your humanity, and forget the rest. If you can do so, the way lies open to a new Paradise; if you cannot, nothing lies before you but universal death.

Russell reiterated his prophetic message for the rest of his life. He helped to found the Campaign for Nuclear Disarmament in 1958 and became its president. He was imprisoned in 1961 for inciting the public to commit a breach of the peace as part of the protest movement against nuclear weapons. During the Cuban missile crisis of 1962 he corresponded directly with President Kennedy and President Khrushchev.

•

MARTIN LUTHER KING
Montgomery, Alabama, 5 December 1955

'*There comes a time when people get tired*'

Martin Luther King (1929–68), a black American Baptist pastor, was the right man in the right place at a moment when history demanded a man of stature to become the leader of his people. That moment occurred in 1954, when King led the victorious campaign against segregated seating in Montgomery's buses. Never before in American history had any black leader succeeded in carrying out a prolonged and victorious attack upon oppression by white people. King subsequently led the civil-rights movement, insisting, like Gandhi, on non-violence.

About a thousand black Americans packed Holt Street Baptist Church on the night of 5 December 1955, the day when the first campaign started. Outside, another five thousand, mainly labourers and servants, listened to the speeches over loudspeakers. With only twenty minutes to prepare his speech, King wrote later that he decided that he would seek to arouse his followers to action by insisting their self-respect was at stake and that if they accepted such injustices without protesting they would betray their own sense of dignity and the eternal edicts of God himself. 'But I would balance this with a strong affirmation of the Christian doctrine of love.'

As King and Ralph Abernathy entered the church together, all heads turned. King led the congregation in singing 'Onward Christian Soldiers' and 'Leaning on the Everlasting Arms'. After prayers and a reading from the Scriptures, he advanced to the lectern. As the audience applauded and television cameras began to shoot from all sides, the crowd grew quiet. Then King, speaking without notes or a manuscript, delivered the speech that first drew him to national attention.

We're here this evening for serious business. We're here in a general sense because first and foremost, we are American citizens, and we are determined to acquire our citizenship to the fullness of its meaning. We are here also because of our deep-seated belief that democracy transformed from thin paper to thick action is the greatest form of government on earth.

There comes a time that people get tired. We are here this evening to say to those who have mistreated us so long that we are tired – tired of being segregated and humiliated; tired of being kicked about by the brutal feet of oppression.

There comes a time my friends when people get tired of being plunged across the abyss of humiliation, when they experience the bleakness of nagging despair. There comes a time when people get tired of being pushed out of the glimmering sunlight of last July and left standing amid the piercing chill of an Alpine November.

We had no alternative but to protest. For many years, we have shown amazing patience. We have sometimes given our white brothers the feeling that we liked the way we were being treated. But we come here tonight to be saved from that patience that makes us patient with anything less than freedom and justice.

One of the great glories of democracy is the right to protest for right.

These organizations [White Citizens' Councils and the Ku Klux Klan] are protesting for the perpetuation of injustice in the community, we are protesting for the birth of justice in the community. Their methods lead to violence and lawlessness. But in our protest there will be no cross burnings. No white person will be taken from his home by a hooded Negro mob and brutally murdered. There will be no threats and intimidation. We will be guided by the highest principles of law and order.

Our method will be that of persuasion, not coercion. We will only say to the people, 'Let your conscience be your guide.' Our actions must be guided by the deepest principles of our Christian faith. Love must be our regulating ideal. Once again we must hear the words of Jesus echoing across the centuries ('Love your enemies, bless them that curse you, and pray for them that despitefully use you'). If we fail to do this our protest will end up as a meaningless drama on the stage of history, and its memory will be shrouded with the ugly garments of shame. In spite of the mistreatment that we have confronted we must not become bitter, and end up by hating our white brothers. As Booker T. Washington said, 'Let no man pull you so low as to make you hate him.'

We are not wrong in what we are doing. If we are wrong, the Supreme Court of this nation is wrong. If we are wrong, the Constitution of the United States is wrong. If we are wrong, God Almighty is wrong. If we are wrong, Jesus of Nazareth was merely a Utopian dreamer who never came down to earth.

If you will protest courageously, and yet with dignity and Christian love, when the history books are written in future generations, the historians will have to pause and say, 'There lived a great people – a black people – who injected new meaning and dignity into the veins of civilization.' This is our challenge and our overwhelming responsibility.

•

NIKITA KHRUSHCHEV
Moscow, 25 February 1956

'We must abolish the cult of the individual'

Six months after the death of Stalin, Nikita Khrushchev (1894–1971) became first secretary of the Communist Party and started to build his power at the top of the Soviet Union. He secured the succession of his nominee, Bulganin, to the premiership in 1955.

The twentieth congress of the party, in 1956, held at the Kremlin with 1,355 voting delegates, was the first since Stalin's death. At the first meeting, the delegates noticed that there was no photograph of Stalin in the conference hall. Khrushchev gave his seven-hour report with hardly any allusion to Stalin. After the regular session on 24 February, the delegates were summoned to a closely guarded night meeting. At this secret meeting, Khrushchev made one of the most sensational speeches of the century in which he attacked the cult of personality during Stalin's reign of terror and introduced an era of liberalization in which many of Stalin's victims were rehabilitated.

Comrades! In the report of the Central Committee of the party at the twentieth Congress, in a number of speeches by delegates to the Congress, and also formerly during the plenary CC-CPSU sessions, quite a lot has been said about the cult of the individual and about its harmful consequences.

After Stalin's death the Central Committee of the party began to implement a policy of explaining concisely and consistently that it is impermissible and foreign to the spirit of Marxism-Leninism to elevate one person, to transform him into a super-man possessing supernatural characteristics akin to those of a god. Such a man supposedly knows everything, sees everything, thinks for everyone, can do anything, is infallible in his behaviour.

Such a belief about a man, and specifically about Stalin, was cultivated among us for many years . . .

In December 1922, in a letter to the Party Congress, Vladimir Ilyich wrote:

> After taking over the position of Secretary-General Comrade Stalin accumulated in his hands immeasurable power and I am not certain whether he will be always able to use this power with the required care.

This letter – a political document of tremendous importance, known in the party history as Lenin's 'testament' – was distributed among the delegates to the twentieth Party Congress. You have read it, and will undoubtedly read it again more than once. You might reflect on Lenin's plain words, in which expression is given to Vladimir Ilyich's anxiety concerning the party, the people, the State, and the future direction of party policy.

Vladimir Ilyich said:

> Stalin is excessively rude, and this defect, which can be freely tolerated in our midst and in contacts among us Communists, becomes a defect which cannot be tolerated in one holding the position of the Secretary-General. Because of this I propose that the comrades consider the method by which Stalin would be removed from this position and by which another man would be selected for it, a man who, above all, would differ from Stalin in only one quality, namely, greater tolerance, greater loyalty, greater kindness and more considerate attitude towards the comrades, a less capricious temper, &c.

This document of Lenin's was made known to the delegates at the thirteenth Party Congress, who discussed the question of transferring Stalin from the position of Secretary-General. The delegates declared themselves in favour of retaining Stalin in this post, hoping that he would heed the critical remarks of Vladimir Ilyich and would be able to overcome the defects which caused Lenin serious anxiety . . .

As later events have proven, Lenin's anxiety was justified: in the first period after Lenin's death Stalin still paid attention to his advice, but later he began to disregard the serious admonitions of Vladimir Ilyich.

When we analyse the practice of Stalin in regard to the direction of the party and of the country, when we pause to consider everything which Stalin perpetrated, we must be convinced that Lenin's fears were justified. The negative characteristics of Stalin, which, in Lenin's time, were only incipient, transformed themselves during the last years into a grave abuse of power by Stalin, which caused untold harm to our party.

We have to consider seriously and analyse correctly this matter in order that we may preclude any possibility of a repetition in any form whatever of what took place during the life of Stalin, who absolutely did not tolerate collegiality in leadership and in work, and who practised brutal violence, not only towards everything which opposed him but also towards that which seemed to his capricious and despotic character contrary to his concepts.

Stalin acted not through persuasion, explanation, and patient cooperation with people, but by imposing his concepts and demanding absolute submission to his opinion. Whoever opposed this concept or tried to prove his viewpoint, and the correctness of his position, was doomed to removal from the leading collective and to subsequent moral and physical annihilation. This was especially true during the period following the seventeenth Party Congress, when many prominent party leaders and rank-and-file party workers, honest and dedicated to the cause of Communism, fell victim to Stalin's despotism . . .

Stalin originated the concept 'enemy of the people'. This term automatically rendered it unnecessary that the ideological errors of a man or men engaged in a controversy be proven: this term made possible the usage of the most cruel repression, violating all norms of revolutionary legality, against anyone who in any way disagreed with Stalin, against those who were only suspected of hostile intent, against those who had bad reputations. This concept, 'enemy of the people', actually eliminated the possibility of any kind of ideological fight or the making of one's views known on this or that issue, even those of a practical character. In the main, and in actuality, the only proof of guilt used, against all norms of current legal science, was the 'confession' of the accused himself: and, as subsequent probing proved, 'confessions' were acquired through physical pressures against the accused.

This led to glaring violations of revolutionary legality, and to the fact that many entirely innocent persons, who in the past had defended the party line, became victims. We must assert that in regard to those persons who in their time had opposed the party line, there were often no sufficiently serious reasons for their physical annihilation. The formula 'enemy of the people' was specifically introduced for the purpose of physically annihilating such individuals.

Everyone knows how irreconcilable Lenin was with the ideological enemies of Marxism, with those who deviated from the correct party line. At the same time, however, Lenin, as is evident from the given document, in his practice of directing the party demanded the most intimate party contact with people who had shown indecision or temporary nonconformity with the party line, but whom it was possible to return to the party path. Lenin advised that such people should be patiently educated without the application of extreme methods. Lenin's wisdom in dealing with people was evident in his work with cadres.

An entirely different relationship with people characterized Stalin. Lenin's traits – patient work with people; stubborn and painstaking education of them; the ability to induce people to follow him without using compulsion, but rather through the ideological influence on them of the whole collective – were entirely foreign to Stalin. He discarded the Leninist method of convincing and educating: he abandoned the method of ideological struggle for that of administrative violence, mass repressions, and terror. He acted on an increasingly larger scale and more stubbornly through punitive organs, at the same time often violating all existing norms of morality and of Soviet laws.

Arbitrary behaviour by one person encouraged and permitted

arbitrariness in others. Mass arrests and deportations of many thousands of people, execution without trial and without normal investigation . . .

Lenin used severe methods only in the most necessary cases, when the exploiting classes were still in existence and were vigorously opposing the Revolution, when the struggle for survival was decidedly assuming the sharpest forms, even including a Civil War.

Stalin, on the other hand, used extreme methods and mass repressions at a time when the Revolution was already victorious, when the Soviet State was strengthened, when the exploiting classes were already liquidated and Socialist relations were rooted solidly in all phases of national economy, when our party was politically consolidated and had strengthened itself both numerically and ideologically. It is clear that here Stalin showed in a whole series of cases his intolerance, his brutality, and his abuse of power. Instead of proving his political correctness and mobilizing the masses, he often chose the path of repression and physical annihilation, not only against actual enemies but also against individuals who had not committed any crimes against the party and the Soviet Government. Here we see no wisdom but only a demonstration of the brutal force which had once so alarmed V. I. Lenin . . .

I recall the first days when the conflict between the Soviet Union and Yugoslavia began artificially to be blown up. Once, when I came from Kiev to Moscow, I was invited to visit Stalin who, pointing to the copy of a letter lately sent to Tito, asked me: 'Have you read this?'

Not waiting for my reply, he answered: 'I will shake my little finger – and there will be no more Tito. He will fall.'

We have dearly paid for this 'shaking of the little finger'. This statement reflected Stalin's mania for greatness, but he acted just that way: 'I will shake my little finger – and there will be no Kossior'; 'I will shake my little finger once more and Postyshev and Chubar will be no more'; 'I will shake my little finger again – Voznesensky, Kuznetsov and many others will disappear.'

But this did not happen to Tito. No matter how much or how

little Stalin shook, not only his little finger but everything else that he could shake, Tito did not fall. Why? The reason was that, in this case of disagreement with the Yugoslav comrades, Tito had behind him a State and a people who had gone through a severe school of fighting for liberty and independence, a people which gave support to its leaders.

You see to what Stalin's mania for greatness led. He had completely lost consciousness of reality; he demonstrated his suspicion and haughtiness not only in relation to individuals in the USSR but in relation to whole parties and nations.

Stalin's reluctance to consider life's realities and the fact that he was not aware of the real state of affairs in the provinces can be illustrated by his direction of agriculture. All those who interested themselves even a little in the national situation saw the difficult situation in agriculture, but Stalin never even noted it. Did we tell Stalin about this? Yes, we told him, but he did not support us. Why? Because Stalin never travelled anywhere, did not meet city and kolkhoz workers; he did not know the actual situation in the provinces. He knew the country and agriculture only from films. And these films had dressed up and beautified the existing situation in agriculture.

Many films so pictured kolkhoz life that the tables were bending from the weight of turkeys and geese. Evidently Stalin thought that it was actually so.

Vladimir Ilyich Lenin looked at life differently; he was always close to the people; he used to receive peasant delegates, and often spoke at factory gatherings; he used to visit villages and talk with the peasants.

Stalin separated himself from the people and never went anywhere. This went on for dozens of years. The last time he visited a village was in January 1928, when he went to Siberia in connection with grain deliveries. How then could he have known the situation in the provinces?

We should in all seriousness consider the question of the cult of the individual. We cannot let this matter get out of the party, especially not to the press. It is for this reason that we are considering it here at a closed congress session. We should know the limits: we should not give ammunition to the enemy: we should not wash our dirty linen before their eyes. I think that the delegates to the congress will understand and assess properly all these proposals. (*Tumultuous applause.*)

Comrades! We must abolish the cult of the individual decisively, once and for all; we must draw the proper conclusions concerning both ideological-theoretical and practical work.

It is necessary for this purpose:

First, in a Bolshevik manner, to condemn and to eradicate the cult of the individual as alien to Marxism-Leninism and not consonant with the principles of party leadership and the norms of party life, and to fight inexorably all attempts at bringing back this practice in one form or another.

To return to and actually practise in all our ideological work the most important theses of Marxist-Leninist science about the people as the creator of history and as the creator of all material and spiritual good of humanity, about the decisive role of the Marxist party in the revolutionary fight for the transformation of society, about the victory of communism.

Comrades: The twentieth Congress of the Communist Party of the Soviet Union has manifested with a new strength the unshakable unity of our party, its cohesiveness around the Central Committee, its resolute will to accomplish the great task of building communism. (*Tumultuous applause.*) And the fact that we present in all their ramifications the basic problems of overcoming the cult of the individual which is alien to Marxism-Leninism, as well as the problem of liquidating its burdensome consequences, is evidence of the great moral and political strength of our party. (*Prolonged applause.*)

We are absolutely certain that our party, armed with the historical resolutions of the twentieth congress, will lead the Soviet people along the Leninist path to new successes, to new victories. (*Tumultuous, prolonged applause.*)

Long live the victorious banner of our party – Leninism! (*Tumultuous, prolonged applause ending in standing ovation.*)

Although delivered in secret, the speech reached other Communist countries and eventually leaked out in the West. It encouraged restlessness in Poland, revolt in Hungary and hastened the rift with Chairman Mao and Peking, the main reasons for Khrushchev's downfall in 1964, two years after the United States and the Soviet Union nearly came to war over the Cuban missile crisis.

•

ANEURIN BEVAN
London, 5 December 1956

'We have to act up to different standards'

The Suez Crisis of 1956, initiated after President Nasser of Egypt national-ized the Suez Canal Company, divided British public opinion more bitterly than any other post-war dispute – and also diverted British and American attention from Soviet intervention to suppress the Hungarian national uprising. An Anglo-French invasion of Egypt started on 5 November but was halted two days later after being condemned by the United Nations, as well as the United States.

Aneurin Bevan, now the official Labour spokesman on foreign affairs, was the fiercest British critic of Suez. The first inquest on the disaster was held in the Commons on 5 December, when Bevan, according to his biographer Michael Foot, made what many considered the greatest speech of his life: 'Bevan welded the scattered indictment into a single, glittering synthesis; the wit merged with the wisdom and the wisdom with the wit, like two edges of the same sword.' This was the peroration.

The social furniture of modern society is so complicated and fragile that it cannot support the jackboot. We cannot run the processes of modern society by attempting to impose our will upon nations by armed force. If we have not learned that we have learned nothing. Whatever may have been the morality of the Government's action – and about that there is no doubt – there is no doubt about its imbecility. There is not the slightest shadow of doubt that we have attempted to use methods which were bound to destroy the objectives we had, and, of course, this is what we have discovered.

It has been proved over and over again now in the modern world that men and women are often prepared to put up with material losses for things that they really think worth while. It has been shown in Budapest, and it could be shown in the Middle East. That is why I beg Hon. Members to turn their backs on this most ugly chapter and realize that if we are to live in the world and are to be regarded as a decent nation, decent citizens in the world, we have to act up to different standards than the one that we have been following in the last few weeks.

I resent most bitterly this unconcern for the lives of innocent men and women. It may be that the dead in Port Said are 100, 200 or 300. If it is only one, we had no business to take it. Do Hon. Members begin to realize how this is going to revolt the world when it passes into the imagination of men and women everywhere, and in this country, that we, with eight million here in London, the biggest single civilian target in the world, with our crowded island exposed, as no nation in the world is exposed, to the barbarism of modern weapons, we ourselves set the example.

We ourselves conscript our boys and put guns and aeroplanes in their hands and say, 'Bomb there.' Really, this is so appalling that human language can hardly describe it. And for what? The Government resorted to epic weapons for squalid and trivial ends, and that is why all through this unhappy period Ministers – all of them – have spoken and argued and debated well below their proper form – because they have been synthetic villains. They are not really villains. They have only set off on a villainous course, and they cannot even use the language of villainy.

It is no use Hon. Members consoling themselves that they have more support in the country than many of them feared they might have. Of course they have support in the country. They have support among many of the unthinking and unreflective who still react to traditional values, who still think that we can solve all these problems in the old ways. Of course they have. Not all the human race has grown to adult state yet. But do not let them take comfort in that thought. The Right Hon. Member for Woodford (Sir Winston Churchill) has warned them before. In the first volume of his *Second World War*, he writes about the situation before the war and he says this:

> Thus an Administration more disastrous than any in our history saw all its errors and shortcomings acclaimed by the nation. There was however a bill to be paid, and it took the new House of Commons nearly ten years to pay it.

The speech was acclaimed both inside and outside the House of Commons and made even Bevan's former critics believe that he should be the next Foreign Secretary.

•

ANEURIN BEVAN
Brighton, 3 October 1957

'Naked into the conference chamber'

Why has he done it? Why, why, why? was the angry, bemused reaction of the Bevanites, Aneurin Bevan's allies on the left of the Labour Party, after the speech to the party conference in which he opposed resolution 24 calling for unilateral British disarmament.

His speech in the 1957 H-bomb debate was the bravest of Bevan's career: he was siding with his old enemy, Hugh Gaitskell, and denouncing the views of his closest political friends. 'I have thought about this very anxiously,' he said. 'I knew that I was going to make a speech that would offend and even hurt many of my friends.' He was interrupted by cries of protest. 'But do you think I am afraid?' There was no answer. 'I shall say what I believe.' This is what Bevan then said.

If you carry this resolution and follow out all its implications and do not run away from it you will send a British Foreign Secretary, whoever he may be, naked into the conference chamber. Able to preach sermons, of course; he could make good sermons. But action of that sort is not necessarily the way in which you take the menace of this bomb from the world. It might be that action of that sort will still be there available to us if our other actions fail. It is something you can always do. You can always, if the influence you have upon your allies and upon your opponents is not yielding any fruits, take unilateral action of that sort. (*A cry of 'Do it now.'*) 'Do it now,' you say. This is the answer I give from the platform. Do it now as a Labour Party Conference? You cannot do it now. It is not in your hands to do it. All you can do is pass a resolution. What you are saying is that a British Foreign Secretary gets up in the United Nations, without consultation – mark this; this is a responsible attitude! – without telling any members of the Commonwealth, without concerting with them, that the British Labour movement decides unilaterally that this country contracts out of all its commitments and obligations entered into with other countries and members of the Commonwealth – without consultation at all. And you call that statesmanship? I call it an emotional spasm . . .

If any Socialist Foreign Secretary is to have a chance he must be permitted to substitute good policies for bad policies. Do not disarm him diplomatically, intellectually, and in every other way before he has a chance to turn round.

This country could be destroyed merely as an incident of a war between Russia and the USA. It is not necessary for any bombs to drop on us. If war broke out between the USA and the Soviet Union, this country would be poisoned with the rest of mankind. What we have, therefore, to consider is how far the policies we are considering can exert an influence and a leverage over the policies of the USA and of the Soviet Union . . .

I do seriously believe in the rejection of the bomb. But that is not the issue. That is what I am telling you. If resolution 24 only meant that we would have very little difficulty with it. But if resolution 24 is read with its implications it means that as decent folk you must immediately repudiate all the protection and all the alliances and all the entanglements you have with anybody who uses or possesses or manufactures hydrogen bombs. That is our dilemma. I find it a very, very serious dilemma. This problem is without precedent in the history of the world. I consider that it is not only a question of practical statesmanship . . .

No nation is entitled to try to exterminate an evil by invoking a greater evil than the one it is trying to get rid of. The hydrogen bomb is, of course, a greater evil than any evil it is intended to meet. But, unfortunately, the USSR and the USA are in possession of this weapon, and we are in danger of being exterminated as a consequence of their rivalries and their antagonisms. What I would like to have is the opportunity of exerting influence upon the policies of those countries, but this is not the way to do it. You do not give us a chance. It was said to me during the week, 'What is the use of getting up on the platform and saying you are going to stop or suspend the tests?' We have said that already. Are we thinking merely in terms of stronger and stronger resolutions accompanied by no action at all?

I am begging and praying our comrades here to reconsider the demands they have made, because I agree that those who support resolution No. 24 do it with complete sincerity. They do it because they believe that the resolution embodies their detestation of the bomb. But I am sure that in your secret hearts you will admit that you have not fully thought out the implications of that. You have not realized that the consequence of passing that resolution would be to drive Great Britain into a diplomatic purdah.

Bevan became deputy leader of the Labour Party in 1959.

●

HENDRIK VERWOERD
Cape Town, 20 May 1959

'We have now come to a fateful hour'

'South Africa is a white man's country and he must remain the master here': Hendrik Verwoerd (1901–66) advocated his master plan for apartheid from the moment he entered the South African parliament in 1948. He believed he had a

divine mission and spent the next eighteen years, first as minister of native affairs and then as prime minister from 1958, putting separate development of the black and white races into practice.

The South African Senate in May 1959 was debating a bill promoting 'Bantu' self-government. Attacking the leader of the opposition United Party, Verwoerd set out his policy of separate development, under which 'the Bantu' would obtain independence when they were capable of it.

The United Party has said over and over: Nothing else is possible but a common South Africa, a multiracial country, although numerically the Bantu will outnumber the Whites three or four times. I repeat, with candour and in the best interests of the White people of South Africa, that I choose an assured White state in South Africa, whatever happens to the other areas, rather than to have my people absorbed in one integrated state in which the Bantu must eventually dominate. One Bantustan for the whole of South Africa is the inevitable consequence of the policy of the United Party.

Therefore to talk about partition and subdivision as being a distasteful pattern is utterly nonsensical, because in terms of both policies there will be Black areas, and in terms of the policy of apartheid the White man will at least control his own area, whatever the difficulties might be and however hard it might be. He at least has the opportunity to save himself, which under a multiracially controlled state he will not have . . .

What would happen in Britain if Britain were to allow Jamaicans to enter the country to seek work to such an extent that in the end they would be in the majority (if immigration on such a scale were possible in such a small country). Would the British just quietly say: We will not stop the inflow, and as soon as they number seventy million or eighty million and we are only fifty-nine million (or whatever the figure may be), then they are in the majority, and because everybody should have equal rights therefore England in future will belong to them! That is ridiculous, but it is in line with what now has to happen in South Africa according to the argument of the United Party. The inflowing Black workers have increased in number to such an extent that a multiracial Government must follow and in that way they will become the conquerors of White South Africa, just as the Jamaicans would be in England if they were permitted to do the same thing that the Leader of the Opposition says took place here since the First World War. That is the most peculiar argument I have ever heard as a plea for the granting of political rights to the Bantu, as is the statement that we should not protect ourselves and should not keep the government of the country in our own hands.

If the Hon. Leader of the Opposition wants to frighten people, however – then my reply to this type of reasoning is that in the long run I would prefer to have a smaller White state in South Africa which will control its own army, its own navy, its own police, its own defence force, and which will stand as a bulwark for White civilization in the world and which, in the event of an emergency and a clash with ideologies in neighbouring states, will also have the support of the outside world to enable it to maintain itself (in other words, rather a White nation which can fight for its survival), than a bigger state which has already been surrendered to Bantu domination.

I propose now to sketch the consequences, in terms of this same type of reasoning, of the United Party's policy. What would be the (remember this) eventual position – because after all the Hon. Leader of the Opposition argues in terms of the situation which will eventually arise when our policy is carried out – what would be the eventual situation in the event of his policy being carried out? Then you would have a multiracial community and a multiracial state with ever-expanding control by, and a joint say on the part of, continually developing Natives in one joint country, with the Natives outnumbering the Whites four to one.

What would that involve? A South African army and a South African police force under black generals; an air force under a Black air-marshal; a government with Black Cabinet Ministers; a Parliament with Black Members of Parliament; administrators and mayors, all Black! Now I ask the Hon. Leader of the Opposition: With such an end in view, what hope would there be for the White man? Not only would he not have his own army, his own defence force and his own diplomatic channels to protect himself against foreign ideologies, if there is an emergency, but he would already be under the domination and under the superior power of the army, navy, air force, police service, government – nation-wide – of the Black man. Is that the eventual picture which the Leader of the Opposition wants South Africa to choose?

We are faced with the choice of either giving the White man his own area and the Bantu his, or having one state for all in which the Bantu will govern. The struggle in Africa is for the Natives to control their own areas. The Bantu do not want mixed governments . . .

I believe that we have now come to a fateful hour in which a final choice has to be made. It is not an easy choice, because, in whichever way one regards the future, there are difficulties to be surmounted. But amongst the alternatives is the choice of separate Bantu development in line with the development in Africa and in line with the objects of the world at large, viz. to give the Bantu self-government in their own areas. Then, however, we can also tell the world and Africa with even more justice: Also give us, the White people, the right to retain and to govern our own area . . .

The policy of the National Party is to strive for a permanent White South Africa, whatever dangers are threatening it, whilst being prepared to develop the areas where the Bantu control may be extended under the leadership of the White man as the guardian, and on the understanding that even if it should lead to Bantu independence, it would be ensured by wise statesmanship; that that development takes place in such a spirit and in such a way that friendship will remain possible although the White man will never be under any form of Bantu control, whether in federal form or in the form of Union. That is the choice.

Until his assassination in 1966, Verwoerd led South Africa down the path of a police state and intensified the policies of apartheid.

•

ANEURIN BEVAN
Blackpool, 29 November 1959

'An ugly society, a vulgar society, a meretricious society'

The Labour Party, led by Hugh Gaitskell, had lost the 1959 general election to the Conservatives, led by Harold Macmillan. As it met for a special inquest on its defeat, Labour was once again divided over its commitment to nationaliza-tion, with the revisionist Gaitskell urging that the constitution should be brought 'up to date' and arguing that public ownership was no longer the be-all and end-all of party policy.

The next day, overcoming his sickness of the previous months, Aneurin Bevan, now deputy leader, reopened the socialist argument, yet preserved the unity of the party. 'It was the classic Bevan speech,' says Michael Foot, his biographer, 'shaped to secure an immediate end and yet elevating the party debate to the realm of political philosophy . . . Samson's locks had grown again but he used his strength not to destroy but to sustain.'

If it is said that we lost the election because of our belief in public ownership, then 12,250,000 people voted for us because they believed in public ownership. It is not a bad start-off, is it? Now you may say: 'Ah, but they did not vote for you because they believed in public ownership.' Well, you cannot have it both ways, can you? Or even suppose you were allowed to have it both ways, then you must conclude that 12,250,000 people did vote for us despite their distaste for public ownership. That is the biggest single vote ever given for public ownership in any country in the whole world. Then why the hell this defeatism? Why all this talk that we have actually gone back? Of course it is true that in the present-day affluent society a very large number of people are not as discontented as they were, and because we are a Party that stands for the redress of discontent and the wrongs caused by discontent, the absence of so much discontent therefore has reduced our popularity. But you know, comrades, I have been in this movement now for many years. I was in this movement in between the war years when there were two million unemployed, and still the Tories got a majority. You would have thought that there was some spontaneous generation of Socialist conviction; but we lost before the war years. Even the unemployed voted against us. Even in the areas where there was as much as 20 per cent and 30 per cent of unemployment we lost seats. Should we not therefore have voted in favour of unemployment?

The fact is – and that is accepted, and derive your lessons from it – that a very considerable number of young men and women in the course of the last five or ten years have had their material conditions improved and their status has been raised in consequence and their discontents have been reduced, so that temporarily their personalities are satisfied with the framework in which they live. They are not conscious of constriction; they are not conscious of frustration or of limitation as formerly they were, in exactly the same way as even before the war large numbers of workers were not sufficiently conscious of frustration and of limitation, even on unemployment benefit, to vote against the Tories.

What is the lesson for us? It is that we must enlarge and expand those personalities, so that they can become again conscious of limitation and constriction. The problem is one of education, not of surrender! This so-called affluent society is an ugly society still. It is a vulgar society. It is a meretricious society. It is a society in which priorities have gone all wrong. I once said – and I do not want to quote myself too frequently – that the language of priorities was the religion of Socialism, and there is nothing wrong with that statement either, but you can only get your priorities right if you have the power to put them right, and the argument, comrades, is about power in society. If we managed to get a majority in Great Britain by the clever exploitation of contemporary psychology, and we did not get the commanding heights of the economy in our power, then we did not get the priorities right. The argument is about power and only about power, because only by the possession of power can you get the priorities correct . . .

Frank Pakenham made a speech here yesterday in which he said that his beliefs were derived from his religion. I do not claim to be a very religious man; I never have. But I must remind Frank Pakenham that Christ drove the money-changers from the Temple. He did not open the doors wide for them to enter. He drove them away. If we go on to apply the principles of Christianity to contemporary British society, they have been done elsewhere rather better than they have been done here. I think there is something evil, something abominable, something disgraceful in a country that can turn its back on Hola, that can turn its back on the old-age pensioners, that can starve the Health Service, and reap £1,500 million from the Stock Exchange boom immediately after the election is over.

What are we going to say, comrades? Are we going to accept the defeat? Are we going to say to India, where Socialism has been adopted as the official policy despite all the difficulties facing the Indian community, that the British Labour movement has dropped Socialism here? What are we going to say to the rest of the world? Are we going to send a message from this great Labour movement, which is the father and mother of modern democracy and modern Socialism, that we in Blackpool in 1959 have turned our backs on our principles because of a temporary unpopularity in a temporarily affluent society?

Let me give you a personal confession of faith. I have found in my life that the burdens of public life are too great to be borne for trivial ends. The sacrifices are too much, unless we have something really serious in mind; and therefore, I hope we are going to send from this Conference a message of hope, a message of encouragement, to the youth and to the rest of the world that is listening very carefully to what we are saying.

I was rather depressed by what Denis Healey [a fellow Labour MP] said. I have a lot of respect for him: but you know, Denis, you are not going to be able to help the Africans if the levers of power are left in the hands of their enemies in Britain. You cannot do it! Nor can you inject the principles of ethical Socialism into an economy based upon private greed. You cannot do it! You cannot mix them, and therefore I beg and pray that we should wind this Conference up this time on a message of hope, and we should say to India and we should say to Africa and Indonesia, and not only to them, but we should say to China and we should say to Russia, that the principles of democratic Socialism have not been extinguished by a temporary defeat at the hands of the Tories a few weeks ago!

You know, comrades, parliamentary institutions have not been destroyed because the Left was too vigorous; they have been destroyed because the Left was too inert. You cannot give me a single illustration in the Western world where Fascism conquered because Socialism was too violent. You cannot give me a single illustration where representative government has been undermined because the representatives of the people asked for too much. But I can give you instance after instance we are faced with today where representative government has been rendered helpless because the representatives of the people did not ask enough. We have never suffered from too much vitality; we have suffered from too little. That is why I say that we are going to go from this Conference a united Party. We are going to go back to the House of Commons, and we are going to fight the Tories. But we are not only going to fight them there; we are going to fight them in the constituencies and inside the trade unions. And we are going to get the youth! Let them start. Do not let them wait for the Executive, for God's sake! Start getting your youth clubs, go in and start now! Go back home and start them, and we will give all the help and encouragement that we can.

I have enough faith in my fellow creatures in Great Britain to believe that when they have got over the delirium of the television, when they realize that their new homes that they have been put into are mortgaged to the hilt, when they realize that the moneylender has been elevated to the highest position in the land, when they realize that the refinements for which they should look are not there, that it is a vulgar society of which no decent person could be proud, when they realize all those things, when the years go by and they see the challenge of modern society not being met by the Tories who can consolidate their political powers only on the basis of national mediocrity, who are unable to exploit the resources of their scientists because they are prevented by the greed of their capitalism from doing so, when they realize that the flower of our youth goes abroad today because they are not being given opportunities of using their skill and their knowledge properly at home, when they realize that all the tides of history are flowing in our direction, that we are not beaten, that we represent the future: then, when we say it and mean it, then we shall lead our people to where they deserve to be led!

This characteristically emotional affirmation of British democratic socialism was almost Bevan's last speech and he won a tumultuous reception. He died the following summer.

•

HAROLD MACMILLAN
Cape Town, 3 February 1960

'The wind of change'

Harold Macmillan (1894–1986) had been British prime minister for three years when in January 1960 he left for a tour of Africa that took him through Ghana, Nigeria, Rhodesia, and Nyasaland and then to the apartheid state of South Africa, where he made the most famous speech of his life.

The speech to both houses of parliament was the most important event of the tour. 'I approached this ordeal with much trepidation,' Macmillan wrote in his memoirs. 'I knew that much of what I would be constrained to say would be disagreeable to many of my hearers.' Dr Hendrik Verwoerd, the South African prime minister [and also one of the prime movers of apartheid], had seen the outlines of the text and what Macmillan was to say had come as a shock.

Standing in the chamber of the Old Cape Colony parliament, Macmillan, who had encouraged independence in Britain's former colonies, delivered a fifty-minute speech in which he made plain Britain's deep distaste for the racial policies of his hosts, who were still then members of the British Commonwealth.

Ever since the break-up of the Roman Empire one of the constant facts of political life in Europe has been the emergence of independent nations. They have come into existence over the centuries in different forms, with different kinds of Government, but all have been inspired by a deep, keen feeling of nationalism, which has grown as the nations have grown.

In the twentieth century, and especially since the end of the war, the processes which gave birth to the nation states of Europe have been repeated all over the world. We have seen the awakening of national consciousness in peoples who have for centuries lived in dependence upon some other power. Fifteen years ago this movement spread through Asia. Many countries there of different races and civilizations pressed their claim to an independent national life. Today the same thing is happening in Africa, and the most striking of all the impressions I have formed is of the strength of this African national consciousness. In different places it takes different forms, but it is happening everywhere. The wind of change is blowing through this continent, and, whether we like it or not, this growth of national consciousness is a political fact. We must all accept it as a fact, and our national policies must take account of it.

Of course, you understand this better than anyone. You are sprung from Europe, the home of nationalism, and here in Africa you have yourselves created a new nation. Indeed, in the history of our times yours will be recorded as the first of the African nationalisms, and this tide of national consciousness which is now rising in Africa is a fact for which you and we and the other nations of the Western World are ultimately responsible. For its causes are to be found in the achievements of Western civilization, in the pushing forward of the frontiers of knowledge, in the applying of science in the service of human needs, in the expanding of food production, in the speeding and multiplying of the means of communication, and perhaps, above all, the spread of education . . .

As I see it the great issue in this second half of the twentieth century is whether the uncommitted peoples of Asia and Africa will swing to the East or to the West. Will they be drawn into the Communist camp? Or will the great experiments in self-government that are now being made in Asia and Africa, especially within the Commonwealth, prove so successful, and by their example so compelling, that the balance will come down in favour of freedom and order and justice?

The struggle is joined, and it is a struggle for the minds of men. What is now on trial is much more than our military strength or our diplomatic and administrative skill. It is our way of life. The uncommitted nations want to see before they choose.

What can we show them to help them choose right? Each of the independent members of the Commonwealth must answer that question for itself. It is a basic principle of our modern Commonwealth that we respect each other's sovereignty in matters of internal policy. At the same time we must recognize that in this shrinking world in which we live today the internal policies of one nation may have effects outside it. We may sometimes be tempted to say to each other, 'Mind your own business,' but in these days I would myself expand the old saying so that it runs: 'Mind your own business, but mind how it affects my business, too.'

Let me be very frank with you, my friends. What Governments and Parliaments in the United Kingdom have done since the war in according independence to India, Pakistan, Ceylon, Malaya and Ghana, and what they will do for Nigeria and other countries now nearing independence, all this, though we take full and sole responsibility for it, we do in the belief that it is the only way to establish the future of the Commonwealth and of the Free World on sound foundations. All this of course is also of deep and close concern to you for nothing we do in this small world can be done in a corner or remain hidden. What we do today in West, Central and East Africa becomes known tomorrow to everyone in the

Union, whatever his language, colour or traditions. Let me assure you, in all friendliness, that we are well aware of this and that we have acted and will act with full knowledge of the responsibility we have to all our friends.

Nevertheless I am sure you will agree that in our own areas of responsibility we must each do what we think right. What we think right derives from a long experience both of failure and success in the management of our own affairs. We have tried to learn and apply the lessons of our judgement of right and wrong. Our justice is rooted in the same soil as yours – in Christianity and in the rule of law as the basis of a free society. This experience of our own explains why it has been our aim in the countries for which we have borne responsibility, not only to raise the material standards of living, but also to create a society which respects the rights of individuals, a society in which men are given the opportunity to grow to their full stature – and that must in our view include the opportunity to have an increasing share in political power and responsibility, a society in which individual merit and individual merit alone is the criterion for a man's advancement, whether political or economic . . .

The attitude of the United Kingdom towards this problem was clearly expressed by the Foreign Secretary, Mr Selwyn Lloyd, speaking at the United Nations General Assembly on 17 September 1959. These were his words:

In those territories where different races or tribes live side by side the task is to ensure that all the people may enjoy security and freedom and the chance to contribute as individuals to the progress and well being of these countries. We reject the idea of any inherent superiority of one race over another. Our policy therefore is non-racial. It offers a future in which Africans, Europeans, Asians, the peoples of the Pacific and others with whom we are concerned, will all play their full part as citizens in the countries where they live, and in which feelings of race will be submerged in loyalty to new nations.

I have thought you would wish me to state plainly and with full candour the policy for which we in Britain stand. It may well be that in trying to do our duty as we see it we shall sometimes make difficulties for you. If this proves to be so we shall regret it. But I know that even so you would not ask us to flinch from doing our duty.

As a fellow member of the Commonwealth it is our earnest desire to give South Africa our support and encouragement, but I hope you won't mind my saying frankly that there are some aspects of your policies which make it impossible for us to do this without being false to our own deep convictions about the political destinies of free men to which in our own territories we are trying to give effect. I think we ought, as friends, to face together, without seeking to apportion credit or blame, the fact that in the world of today this difference of outlook lies between us . . .

The fact is that in this modern world no country, not even the greatest, can live for itself alone. Nearly two thousand years ago, when the whole of the civilized world was comprised within the confines of the Roman Empire, St Paul proclaimed one of the great truths of history – we are all members one of another. During this twentieth century that eternal truth has taken on a new and exciting significance. It has always been impossible for the individual man to live in isolation from his fellows, in the home, the tribe, the village, or the city. Today it is impossible for nations to live in isolation from one another. What Dr John Donne said of individual men three hundred years ago is true today of my country, your country, and all the countries of the world:

Any man's death diminishes me, because I am involved in Mankind. And therefore never send to know for whom the bell tolls; it tolls for thee.

All nations now are interdependent one upon another, and this is generally realized throughout the Western World . . . Those of us who by grace of the electorate are temporarily in charge of affairs in your country and in mine, we fleeting transient phantoms on the great stage of history, we have no right to sweep aside on this account the friendship that exists between our countries, for that is the legacy of history. It is not ours alone to deal with as we wish. To adapt a famous phrase, it belongs to those who are living, but it also belongs to those who are dead and to those who are yet unborn. We must face the differences, but let us try to see beyond them down the long vista of the future.

I hope – indeed, I am confident – that in another fifty years we shall look back on the differences that exist between us now as matters of historical interest, for as time passes and one generation yields to another, human problems change and fade. Let us remember these truths. Let us resolve to build, not to destroy, and let us remember always that weakness comes from division, strength from unity.

Verwoerd made an impromptu defence of 'justice for the white man' within his official vote of thanks. White South Africans voted eight months later to leave the British Commonwealth and the Independent Republic of South Africa was formed on 31 May 1961.

•

EUGENE McCARTHY
Los Angeles, 13 July 1960

'Do not reject this man'

There were five strong candidates for the Democratic nomination for the presidential election in 1960: Adlai Stevenson, Stuart Symington, Hubert Humphrey, Lyndon Baines Johnson and John F. Kennedy.

Stevenson had lost the two previous elections to Eisenhower but was still keen for the nomination that was to be denied to him when the convention opted for Kennedy. Among those who were thinking uneasily of deserting Stevenson for Kennedy, there were many who nevertheless thought Stevenson alone had the intellectual stature and integrity required by the next American president – and this address by Senator Eugene McCarthy of Minnesota, an eloquent and moving tribute to Stevenson's distinguished career in American politics, stood out from the other nomination speeches for its dramatic boldness.

These times, men say, are out of joint. They say these are the worst of times without being the best of times – this may be true. But I say to you these external signs, these practical problems which face us, are nothing compared to the problems of the mind and of the spirit which face the United States and the free world today.

If the mind is clouded and if the will is confused and uncertain, there can be no sound decision and no sound action.

There's demagoguery abroad in the land at all times, and demagoguery, I say to you, takes many forms. There's that which says 'here is wealth, and here is material comfort.' We suffer a little from that in the United States.

There's demagoguery which promises people power, which is used for improper purposes and ends. And we have seen in this century and in this generation what happens when power is abused.

I say to you there's a subtle kind of demagoguery which erodes the spirit. And this is the demagoguery which has affected this United States in the last eight years.

What are we told? What have we been told? We've been told that we can be strong without sacrifice. This is what we've been told. We've been told that we can be good without any kind of discipline if we just say we're humble and sincere – this is the nature of goodness. We've been told that we can be wise without reflection. We can be wise without study, we've been told. I say this is the erosion of the spirit which has taken place in this United States in the last eight years. And I say to you that the time has come to raise again the cry of the ancient prophet. What did he say? He said the prophets prophesy falsely and the high priests, he said, ruled by their word, and my people love to have it so. But what will be the end?

I say to you the political prophets have prophesied falsely in these eight years. And the high priests of government have ruled by that false prophecy. And the people seemed to have loved it so.

But there was one man – there was one man who did not prophesy falsely, let me remind you. There was one man who said: Let's talk sense to the American people.

What did the scoffers say? The scoffers said: Nonsense. They said: Catastrophic nonsense. But we know it was the essential and the basic and the fundamental truth that he spoke to us.

There was a man who talked sense to the American people. There was one man who said: This is a time for self-examination. This is a time for us to take stock, he said. This is a time to decide where we are and where we're going.

This, he said, is a time for virtue. But what virtues did he say we needed? Oh yes, he said we need the heroic virtues – we always do. We need fortitude; we need courage; we need justice. Everyone cheers when you speak out for those virtues.

But what did he say in addition to that? He said we need the unheroic virtues in America. We need the virtue, he said, of patience. There were those who said we've had too much of patience.

We need, he said, the virtue of tolerance. We need the virtue of forbearance. We need the virtues of patience and understanding.

This was what the prophet said. This is what he said to the American people. I ask you, did he prophesy falsely? Did he prophesy falsely?

He said this is a time for greatness. This is a time for greatness for America. He did not say he possessed it. He did not even say he was destined for it. He did say that the heritage of America is one of greatness.

And he described the heritage to us. And he said the promise of America is a promise of greatness. And he said, this promise we must fulfill.

This was his call to greatness. This was the call to greatness that was issued in 1952.

He did not seek power for himself in 1952. He did not seek power in 1956.

He does not seek it for himself today.

This man knows – this man knows, as all of us do from history, that power often comes to those who seek it. But history does not prove that power is always well used by those who seek it.

On the contrary, the whole history of democratic politics is to this end, that power is best exercised by those who are sought out by the people, by those to whom power is given by a free people.

And so I say to you Democrats here assembled: Do not turn away from this man. Do not reject this man. He has fought gallantly. He has fought courageously. He has fought honorably. In 1952 in the great battle. In 1956 he fought bravely. And between those years and since, he has stood off the guerrilla attacks of his enemies and the sniping attacks of those who should have been his friends. Do not reject this man who has made us all proud to be called Democrats. Do not reject this man who, his enemies said, spoke above the heads of the people, but they said it only because they didn't want the people to listen. He spoke to the people. He moved their minds and stirred their hearts, and this was what was objected to. Do not leave this prophet without honour in his own party. Do not reject this man.

I submit to you a man who is not the favorite son of any one state. I submit to you the man who is the favorite son of fifty states.

And not only of fifty states but the favorite son of every country in the world in which he is known – the favorite son in every country in which he is unknown but in which some spark even though unexpressed of desire for liberty and freedom still lives.

This favorite son I submit to you: Adlai E. Stevenson of Illinois.

Stevenson became ambassador to the United Nations in the Kennedy administration. McCarthy challenged President Johnson in 1968 and got forty per cent of the vote in the New Hampshire primary – which caused Robert Kennedy to declare and persuaded Johnson to stand down. After the assassination of Kennedy, Hubert Humphrey won the nomination.

JOHN F. KENNEDY
Los Angeles, 15 July 1960

'A new frontier'

After the stolid, dull Eisenhower years, Senator John Fitzgerald Kennedy (1917–63) offered new horizons and new hope to Americans, summoning them to join him on the new frontier.

At the Democratic Convention in Los Angeles he had defeated Hubert Humphrey, Stuart Symington, Lyndon Johnson and Adlai Stevenson to win the nomination for the presidential election. As he spoke at the ceremony of acceptance, he was flanked by his mother and sister, and by his defeated rivals. As the sun set he spoke, facing west, to 80,000 Democrats in the Los Angeles Coliseum – and to thirty-five million Americans watching him on television.

His face was tired and haggard after a year of strain and a week of sleeplessness. His voice was high and sad.

The American people expect more from us than cries of indignation and attack. The times are too grave, the challenge too urgent, and the stakes too high – to permit the customary passions of political debate. We are not here to curse the darkness, but to light the candle that can guide us through that darkness to a safe and sane future. As Winston Churchill said on taking office some twenty years ago:

'If we open a quarrel between the present and the past, we shall be in danger of losing the future.'

Today our concern must be with that future. For the world is changing. The old era is ending. The old ways will not do.

All over the world, particularly in the newer nations, young men are coming to power – men who are not bound by the traditions of the past – men who are not blinded by the old fears and hates and rivalries – young men who can cast off the old slogans and delusions and suspicions.

The Republican nominee-to-be,* of course, is also a young man. But his approach is as old as McKinley. His party is the party of the past. His speeches are generalities from Poor Richard's Almanac. Their platform, made up of left-over Democratic planks, has the courage of our old convictions. Their pledge is a pledge to the status quo – and today there can be no status quo.

For I stand tonight facing west on what was once the last frontier. From the lands that stretch 3,000 miles behind me, the pioneers of old gave up their safety, their comfort and sometimes their lives to build a new world here in the West.

They were not the captives of their own doubts, the prisoners of their own price tags. Their motto was not 'every man for himself' – but 'all for the common cause.' They were determined to make that new world strong and free, to overcome its hazards and its hardships, to conquer the enemies that threatened from without and within.

Today some would say that those struggles are all over – that all the horizons have been explored – that all the battles have been won – that there is no longer an American frontier.

But I trust that no one in this assemblage will agree with those sentiments. For the problems are not all solved and the battles are not all won – and we stand today on the edge of a new frontier – the frontier of the 1960s – a frontier of unknown opportunities and perils – a frontier of unfulfilled hopes and threats.

Woodrow Wilson's New Freedom promised our nation a new political and economic framework. Franklin Roosevelt's New Deal promised security and succour to those in need. But the New Frontier of which I speak is not a set of promises – it is a set of challenges. It sums up not what I intend to offer the American people, but what I intend to ask of them. It appeals to their pride, not their pocketbook – it holds out the promise of more sacrifice instead of more security.

But I tell you the New Frontier is here, whether we seek it or not. Beyond that frontier are uncharted areas of science and space,

* Richard Nixon.

unsolved problems of peace and war, unconquered pockets of ignorance and prejudice, unanswered questions of poverty and surplus.

It would be easier to shrink back from that frontier, to look to the safe mediocrity of the past, to be lulled by good intentions and high rhetoric – and those who prefer that course should not cast their votes for me, regardless of party.

But I believe the times demand invention, innovation, imagination, decision. I am asking each of you to be new pioneers on that New Frontier. My call is to the young in heart, regardless of age – to the stout in spirit, regardless of party – to all who respond to the scriptural call:

'Be strong and of good courage; be not afraid, neither be thou dismayed.'

For courage – not complacency – is our need today – leadership – not salesmanship. And the only valid test of leadership is the ability to lead, and lead vigorously. A tired nation, said David Lloyd George, is a tory nation – and the United States today cannot afford to be either tired or tory.

There may be those who wish to hear more – more promises to this group or that – more harsh rhetoric about the men in the Kremlin – more assurances of a golden future, where taxes are always low and subsidies ever high. But my promises are in the platform you have adopted. Our ends will not be won by rhetoric and we can have faith in the future only if we have faith in ourselves.

For the harsh facts of the matter are that we stand on this frontier at a turning-point in history. We must prove all over again whether this nation – or any nation so conceived – can long endure – whether our society – with its freedom of choice, its breadth of opportunity, its range of alternatives – can compete with the single-minded advance of the Communist system.

Can a nation organized and governed such as ours endure? That is the real question. Have we the nerve and the will? Can we carry through in an age where we will witness not only new breakthroughs in weapons of destruction – but also a race for mastery of the sky and the rain, the ocean and the tides, the far side of space and the inside of men's minds?

Are we up to the task? Are we equal to the challenge? Are we willing to match the Russian sacrifice of the present for the future? Or must we sacrifice our future in order to enjoy the present?

That is the question of the New Frontier. That is the choice our nation must make – a choice that lies not merely between two men or two parties, but between the public interest and private comfort – between national greatness and national decline – between the fresh air of progress and the stale, dank atmosphere of 'normalcy' – between determined dedication and creeping mediocrity.

All mankind waits upon our decision. A whole world looks to see what we will do. We cannot fail their trust; we cannot fail to try.

John Kennedy won the election by a narrow margin over Richard Nixon and became in January the following year the youngest – and first Roman Catholic – president in US history.

•

JOHN F. KENNEDY
Washington, DC, January 1961

'*The torch has been passed to a new generation of Americans*'

For men and women born during or after the Second World War, John Kennedy's inaugural address, signalling the arrival in power of a new generation and a forty-four-year-old president, still burns in the memory. The new president instructed his speechwriter, Theodore Sorensen, to find the secret of Abraham Lincoln's Gettysburg address. Kennedy adopted the cadences of Lincoln. Most Lincolnesque of all was his use of the oratorical 'Let', a device used to start eight sentences. Many phrases were made memorable by his use of contra-puntalism, as in 'Let us never negotiate out of fear. But let us never fear to negotiate.'

Critics have since ranked Kennedy's inaugural with Jefferson (the first), Lincoln (the second), Wilson (the first) and Franklin D. Roosevelt (first and second). According to the American student of oratory William Safire, Kennedy set the standard by which modern presidential inaugurals are judged.

We observe today not a victory of party but a celebration of freedom, symbolizing an end as well as a beginning, signifying renewal as well as change. For I have sworn before you and Almighty God the same solemn oath our forebears prescribed nearly a century and three-quarters ago.

The world is very different now. For man holds in his mortal hands the power to abolish all forms of human poverty and all forms of human life. And yet the same revolutionary belief for which our forebears fought is still at issue around the globe, the belief that the rights of man come not from the generosity of the state but from the hand of God.

We dare not forget today that we are the heirs of that first revolution. Let the word go forth from this time and place, to friend and foe alike, that the torch has been passed to a new generation of Americans, born in this century, tempered by war, disciplined by a hard and bitter peace, proud of our ancient heritage, and unwilling to witness or permit the slow undoing of these human rights to which this nation has always been committed, and to which we are committed today at home and around the world.

Let every nation know, whether it wishes us well or ill, that we shall pay any price, bear any burden, meet any hardship, support any friend, oppose any foe to assure the survival and the success of liberty . . . to those nations who would make themselves our adversary, we offer not a pledge but a request: that both sides begin anew the quest for peace, before the dark powers of destruction unleashed by science engulf all humanity in planned or accidental self-destruction.

We dare not tempt them with weakness. For only when our arms are sufficient beyond doubt can we be certain beyond doubt that they will never be employed.

But neither can two great and powerful groups of nations take comfort from our present course – both sides overburdened by the cost of modern weapons, both rightly alarmed by the steady spread of the deadly atom, yet both racing to alter that uncertain balance of terror that stays the hand of mankind's final war.

So let us begin anew, remembering on both sides that civility is not a sign of weakness, and sincerity is always subject to proof. Let us never negotiate out of fear, but let us never fear to negotiate.

Let both sides explore what problems unite us instead of belabouring those problems which divide us.

Let both sides, for the first time, formulate serious and precise proposals for the inspection and control of arms, and bring the absolute power to destroy other nations under the absolute control of all nations.

Let both sides seek to invoke the wonders of science instead of its terrors. Together let us explore the stars, conquer the deserts, eradicate disease, tap the ocean depths and encourage the arts and commerce.

Let both sides unite to heed in all corners of the earth the command of Isaiah to 'undo the heavy burdens . . . [and] let the oppressed go free.'

And if a beachhead of cooperation may push back the jungle of suspicion, let both sides join in creating a new endeavour, not a new balance of power, but a new world of law, where the strong are just and the weak secure and the peace preserved.

All this will not be finished in the first one hundred days. Nor will it be finished in the first one thousand days, nor in the life of this Administration, nor even perhaps in our lifetime on this planet. But let us begin.

In your hands, my fellow citizens, more than mine, will rest the final success or failure of our course. Since this country was founded, each generation of Americans has been summoned to give testimony to its national loyalty. The graves of young Americans who answered the call to service surround the globe.

Now the trumpet summons us again – not as a call to bear

arms, though arms we need; not as a call to battle, though embattled we are; but a call to bear the burden of a long twilight struggle, year in and year out, 'rejoicing in hope, patient in tribulation,' a struggle against the common enemies of man: tyranny, poverty, disease and war itself.

Can we forge against these enemies a grand and global alliance, North and South, East and West, that can assure a more fruitful life for all mankind? Will you join in that historic effort?

In the long history of the world, only a few generations have been granted the role of defending freedom in its hour of maximum danger. I do not shrink from this responsibility; I welcome it. I do not believe that any of us would exchange places with any other people or any other generation. The energy, the faith, the devotion which we bring to this endeavour will light our country and all who serve it, and the glow from that fire can truly light the world.

And so, my fellow Americans, ask not what your country can do for you; ask what you can do for your country.

My fellow citizens of the world, ask not what America will do for you, but what together we can do for the freedom of man.

Finally, whether you are citizens of America or citizens of the world, ask of us here the same high standards of strength and sacrifice which we ask of you. With a good conscience our only sure reward, with history the final judge of our deeds, let us go forth to lead the land we love, asking His blessing and His help, but knowing that here on earth God's work must truly be our own.

●

GIDEON HAUSNER
Jerusalem, 17–18 April 1961

'That man was Eichmann'

As a young Nazi SS officer, Adolf Eichmann (1906–62) was appointed head of the Central Office for Jewish Emigration in Vienna in 1938 and from 1942 assumed responsibility for the extinction of unwanted Jewish internees.

He supervised the deportation of slave labourers from among them. After the war he fled to South America. He was kidnapped in Argentina by Israeli agents in 1960 and charged with crimes against the Jewish people at his trial in Jerusalem in 1961.

As Attorney-General of the State of Israel, Gideon Hausner, at the age of forty-six, led the prosecution of Eichmann – the spokesman for six million Jews. He spoke for ten hours.

The following extracts are from his speeches at the opening and conclusion of the trial.

When I stand before you, O Judges of Israel, to lead the prosecution of Adolf Eichmann, I do not stand alone. With me here are six million accusers. But they cannot rise to their feet and point their finger at the man in the dock with the cry *'J'accuse'* on their lips. For they are now only ashes – ashes piled high on the hills of Auschwitz and the fields of Treblinka and strewn in the forests of Poland. Their graves are scattered throughout Europe. Their blood cries out, but their voice is stilled. Therefore will I be their spokesman. In their name will I unfold this terrible indictment . . .

. . . never, down the long, bloodstained road travelled by this people, never since the first days of its nationhood, has any man arisen who succeeded in dealing so grievous a blow as did Hitler and his regime, and Adolf Eichmann, as its executive arm for the destruction of Jewry. Human history knows no other example of a man against whom could be drawn up such a bill of indictment.

The deeds of those classic figures of barbarism, Nero, Attila, Genghis Khan, pale into insignificance when set against the abominations, the murderous horrors, which will be presented to you in this trial . . . only in our generation has an organized state set upon an entire defenceless and peaceful population, men, women, and children, greybeards and babies, incarcerated them behind electrified fences, imprisoned them in concentration camps, and resolved to destroy them utterly . . .

In this trial, we shall encounter a new kind of killer, the kind that exercises his bloody craft behind a desk, and only occasionally does the deed with his own hands . . . But it was his word that put gas chambers into action; he lifted the telephone, and railway trains left for the extermination centres; his signature it was that sealed the doom of tens of thousands. He had but to give the order, and troopers took off to rout Jews out of their homes, to beat and torture them and drive them into ghettos, to steal their property and, after brutality and pillage, after all had been wrung from them, when even their hair had been taken, to transport them en masse to their slaughter. Even their dead bodies were not immune. Gold teeth were extracted and wedding rings torn from fingers . . .

Eichmann was the one who *planned, initiated and organized,* who instructed others to spill this ocean of blood, and to use all the means of murder, theft and torture. He is responsible, therefore, as though he with his own hands had knotted the hangman's noose, lashed the victims into the gas chambers, shot and thrust into the open pits every single one of the millions who were murdered. Such is his responsibility in the eyes of the law. And such is his responsibility by every standard of conscience and morality. His accomplices in the crime were . . . the leaders of a nation – including professors and scholars, robed dignitaries with academic degrees, educated persons, the 'intelligentsia.' We shall encounter them – the doctors and lawyers, scholars, bankers and economists – in those councils which resolved to exterminate the Jews, and among them officers and directors of the work of murder in all its terrible phases . . .

... words exist to express what man's reason can conceive and his heart contain, and here we are dealing with actions which transcend our human grasp. Yet this is what did happen: millions were condemned to death, not for any crime, not for anything they had done, but only because they belonged to the Jewish people. The development of technology placed at the disposal of the destroyers efficient equipment for the execution of their appalling designs ...

... there was only one man who had been concerned almost entirely with the Jews, whose business had been their destruction, whose role in the establishment of the iniquitous regime had been limited to them. That man was Adolf Eichmann. If we charge him also with crimes against people who were not Jews, committed, as it were, 'by the way', this is because we make no ethnic distinctions. But we should remember that the mission of the accused, in which for years he saw his destiny and calling, and to which he devoted himself with enthusiasm and endless zeal, was the destruction of the Jews ...

Eichmann will tell you that he carried out the orders of his superiors. But the conscience of the world, speaking with the voice of the International Military Tribunal, has declared that orders contrary to the principles of conscience and morality, orders that violate the essential imperatives on which human society is based and negate the basic rules without which men cannot live together – such orders constitute no defence, legal or moral. Therefore, in the light of the ruling, our own law in Israel has denied the accused the legal right to submit such a defence. But that is by no means all. We shall prove to the court that he went far beyond his actual orders, that he took the initiative in extermination operations for which he had been given no orders whatsoever, and carried them out only because of his devotion to the task in which he saw his life's mission ...

... the first and principal means of repression used by the SS was the concentration camp, in which were developed and perfected systems of terror employing all the resources available to modern technology. The Nazi, the romantic mystic, the family man, who on the surface seemed to be a loving husband to his wife and a merciful father to his children, the lover of nature, was revealed in the concentration camps as a monster of insane brutality, who did not hesitate to trample on human beings, without blinking an eye, as if they were insects. One of the shocking chapters in *Commandant of Auschwitz*, the story of Rudolf Hoess, is the part where Hoess describes his own peaceful family life at home: the education he gave his sons, his affectionate regard for his wife – and all this going on just on the other side of the high-tension barbed-wire fence of the terrible extermination camp in which between five and ten thousand people were being put to death *each day* – and sometimes even more.

The Gestapo knew well how to exploit all the human frailties of their victims. They knew that starvation and torture, given time, can break even strong men; that by brutality and humiliation it is possible to efface the divine image, leaving a man insensitive, inert, an obedient robot doing as he is told, even when he is ordered to dig his own grave . . . Every means of humiliation was deliberately employed to destroy the Jew's faith in himself. When a man is whipped across the face and he is unable to react; when he is deprived of food until he aches with hunger; when men and women, boys and girls, are given orders to perform their excretory functions in full sight of one another, like beasts; when women are made to run naked before the guards; when, morning and night, executions by shooting and hanging prove that the lives of Jews are absolutely worthless; when senseless butchery takes place before your eyes for the sport of capricious guards; when twenty times a day you are made aware that you are abandoned and defenseless, your life dependent on the mood of any one of the SS men on that particular day – under such circumstances it was not difficult to create a condition in which most of these unfortunates were stripped of all faith and feeling, bereft for the most part of any will to go on living, their supreme desire being a speedy and painless death . . .

The Nazis . . . were skilled in lies and chicanery. They knew how to use every expedient to deceive their victims. After every manhunt, in which thousands and tens of thousands of Jews would be sent to their deaths and others would manage to hide or escape, a rumour would be deliberately spread by the Nazis that this was the last operation of its kind, and that the survivors would no longer be touched, that there would be no more transports. Many individuals of the type that cling to hope, those who could not or would not believe that the fate of all the Jews had indeed been sealed, or who were exhausted by hunger, misery and suffering, would venture out of their hiding places or return from the forests, only to be captured by their persecutors in a new manhunt. The tiger played with his victims at his own sweet will. We shall find some Jews among those carrying out Nazi orders, in the Jewish police in the ghettos and in the Councils of Elders. Even at the entrance to the gas chambers there were often Jews whose task it was to calm the victims and persuade them that they were merely going to showers. This was one of the most satanic aspects of the entire program: to deaden men's senses, to deprive them of all emotional and intellectual vigor, to leave no more than a terrified and lifeless robot, so that it was possible to use the prisoners in the camps themselves as part of the murder machine against their own people . . .

You will hear evidence of deeds which the mind of man does not want to believe. You will hear about little ones thrown out of windows of hospitals when they failed to respond to orders that they report for parade.

We shall present to you the instructions issued by Eichmann and his office about the transport of children. One of these said that the children were to be divided among the transports intended for Auschwitz. Children of fourteen were considered 'independent' for purposes of transport to the extermination camps. Nor can we say who suffered the more terrible fate: those who died, or those who concealed themselves in every conceivable hiding-place and crevice, who lived in perpetual terror of expulsion, who survived through the kindness of Christian neighbors who agreed to hide them. Children would come home from the schools and centres organized by the community to find their parents' home was empty, for they had been sent by some 'aktion' or 'operation' to their deaths; and the apartment had in the meantime been occupied by others.

You will hear evidence of tender infants pressed by their mothers to their bodies in the gas chambers so that they should not inhale the poisonous gas, until the executioners came and threw them alive into the furnaces or the waiting graves.

Those unhappy children who lived for years in fear of the beating of a rifle butt on their door; who had been sent by their parents to the woods in an attempt to save them, who had been taught to choke their tears and sighs because a weeping child would be shot on the spot; who had been ordered to deny their origins and pretend to be Christians; who saw their fathers being lashed with whips before their eyes; in front of whom 'discussions' would be carried on by the German executioners as to who should be killed first – the father or the son; who went to the open grave with 'Hear, O Israel!' on their lips – these children and youths . . . are the very soul and hard core of the indictment. Those Anne Franks and Justine Drangers and a million others.

We shall present the pictures of some of those children swollen with hunger, frightened and crushed, with eyes frozen with terror. We shall show you the photographs of their starved bodies thrown into manure wagons, of the helpless little ones on the threshold of the extermination chambers.

At Auschwitz the killings were carried out by every method, shooting, hanging, and beating, but mainly in the massive gas chambers. In each such chamber 2,000 people were herded together for a 'shower' – a flow of poison gas. The death factory operated unceasingly. The extermination of 2,000 people lasted 25 minutes, after which the bodies were taken to one of the five giant furnaces. Medical experiments were made on human beings as if they were guinea pigs. Parts of female sex organs were cut out, or limbs were subjected to X-rays until the unfortunate creatures writhed in pain prior to their death. Men were castrated. Experiments were made on the influence of paraffin and petrol injections on human skin and the effects of chemical substances on mental resistance. The methods of punishment would not have shamed the most cruel barbarians in history. Beating on the naked body was a comparatively light punishment. Water was poured into people's ears, fingernails were extracted, prisoners starved until they went out of their minds. In the bunker of those sentenced for punishment by starvation a dead prisoner was found, bent over whom was a second prisoner, also dead, grasping the liver from the corpse of the first. He had died while tearing at the liver of a fellow human being. The Nazi contribution to European culture was the reintroduction of cannibalism . . .

We shall prove that the accused performed all these deeds with the set purpose of destroying the Jewish people, wholly or in part. Adolf Eichmann will enjoy a privilege which he did not accord to a single one of his victims. He will be able to defend himself before the court. His fate will be decided according to law and according to the evidence, with the burden of proof resting upon the prosecution. And the judges of Israel will pronounce true and righteous judgment.

It is no wonder that the German Foreign Ministry passed on for Eichmann's information the warning, broadcast by London Radio, that those responsible for the murders in Auschwitz would be brought to judgment. Even on the verge of the German collapse in April 1945, in that atmosphere of the twilight of the gods, when the Allies from the East, West and South were closing in – Eichmann still told a German Red Cross representative that he could not agree to the more humanitarian methods of dealing with Jews then being considered by Himmler.

Many millions of non-Jews also perished in the Great War. We shall not attempt to decide here, at this trial, which of the acts of hostility were contrary to the laws and customs of war as laid down by international law. But we shall say, with all the emphasis at our command, that the extermination of the Jewish people was not connected with any military action. It cannot be compared with the bombing of cities or with submarine warfare. These were acts of war, and whether they were legitimate or not they were carried out in connection with and in the process of waging war.

The extermination of the Jews had no connection with the war effort of Germany and her allies. The extermination was carried out *at the time* of the war, when the battle-smoke to some extent covered and concealed the atrocities; but it was not done in pursuit of war, nor was it impelled by the needs or necessities of war.

Eichmann was hanged on 31 May 1962.

•

HUGH GAITSKELL
Scarborough, 5 October 1961

'We will fight, fight and fight again'

As leader of the Labour Party since 1955, Hugh Gaitskell (1906–63) had led opposition to the Suez invasion of 1956 but clashed with his left wing over nationalization and unilateral nuclear disarmament.

At the 1961 party conference, he faced a challenge to his leadership from Harold Wilson (which he defeated) as well as a resolution seeking to commit Labour to unilateral disarmament.

His speech was therefore the most important of his political life. He had not slept the previous night and wrote the peroration at 4 a.m. Gaitskell thought he would lose and be forced to resign the leadership. As he rose to speak he looked overtired and white with tension and he was continually interrupted by boos and howls of protest, particularly when he referred to 'fellow travellers'.

I would not wish for one day to remain a Leader who had lost the confidence of his colleagues in Parliament. It is perfectly reasonable to try to get rid of somebody, to try to get rid of a man you do not agree with, who you think perhaps is not a good Leader. But there are ways of doing this. What would be wrong, in my opinion, and would not be forgiven, is if, in order to get rid of a man, you supported a policy in which you did not wholeheartedly believe, a policy which, as far as the resolution is concerned, is not clear.

Before you take the vote on this momentous occasion, allow me a last word. Frank Cousins [leader of the unilateralist Transport and General Workers' Union] has said this is not the end of the problem. I agree with him. It is not the end of the problem because Labour Members of Parliament will have to consider what they do in the House of Commons. What do you expect of them? You know how they voted in June overwhelmingly for the policy statement. It is not in dispute that the vast majority of Labour Members of Parliament are utterly opposed to unilateralism and neutralism. So what do you expect them to do? Change their minds overnight? To go back on the pledges they gave to the people who elected them from their constituencies? And supposing they did do that. Supposing all of us, like well-behaved sheep, were to follow the policies of unilateralism and neutralism, what kind of an impression would that make upon the British people? You do not seem to be clear in your minds about it, but I will tell you this. I do not believe that the Labour Members of Parliament are prepared to act as time servers. I do not believe they will do this, and I will tell you why: because they are men of conscience and honour. People of the so-called Right and so-called Centre have every justification for having a conscience, as well as people of the so-called Left. I do not think they will do this because they are honest men, loyal men, steadfast men, experienced men, with a lifetime of service to the Labour Movement.

There are other people too, not in Parliament, in the Party who share our convictions. What sort of people do you think they are? What sort of people do you think we are? Do you think we can simply accept a decision of this kind? Do you think that we can become overnight the pacifists, unilateralists and fellow travellers that other people are? How wrong can you be? As wrong as you are about the attitude of the British people.

In a few minutes the Conference will make its decision. Most of the votes, I know, are predetermined and we have been told what is likely to happen. We know how it comes about. I sometimes think, frankly, that the system we have, by which great unions decide their policy before even their conferences can consider the

Executive recommendation, is not really a very wise one or a good one. Perhaps in a calmer moment this situation could be looked at.

I say this to you: we may lose the vote today and the result may deal this Party a grave blow. It may not be possible to prevent it, but I think there are many of us who will not accept that this blow need be mortal, who will not believe that such an end is inevitable. There are some of us, Mr Chairman, who will fight and fight and fight again to save the Party we love. We will fight and fight and fight again to bring back sanity and honesty and dignity, so that our Party with its great past may retain its glory and its greatness.

It is in that spirit that I ask delegates who are still free to decide how they vote, to support what I believe to be a realistic policy on defence, which yet could so easily have united the great Party of ours, and to reject what I regard as the suicidal path of unilateral disarmament which will leave our country defenceless and alone.

Gaitskell was greeted by the biggest ovation of his life and one journalist wrote that this was his finest hour. Although the left won the vote, the margin was only 300,000 instead of the expected million or more. Gaitskell's political courage and integrity and his appeal to those 'still free to decide' switched votes and turned a triumph into a hollow victory.

●

IAIN MACLEOD
Brighton, 11 October 1961

'The brotherhood of man'

As British Colonial Secretary from 1959 to 1961, Iain Macleod (1913–70) pursued a historic policy of granting independence to the British colonies in Africa more quickly than many Conservatives wished and defying some of the most powerful sectors of the Tory Party. Although he was woundingly described as 'too clever by half' (by the Marquess of Salisbury), he achieved his purpose in ensuring that Britain's withdrawal from most parts of Africa was accomplished with more speed and good will than it otherwise would have been.

Speaking to the Conservative conference on the day before Harold Macmillan made him chairman of the party and leader of the House of Commons, Macleod defined the British imperial mission and the moral principles on which it was based. Its most memorable phrase was based on Robert Burns:

> *That man to man the whole world o'er*
> *Shall brothers be for a' that.*

Many contemporaries considered Macleod, with his rasping voice, with scorn or passion controlled, the best parliamentary debater of his generation – and this speech to an audience in which many disagreed violently with his policy was one of his finest.

At the end of the last war, something like 630 million people lived in the dependent territories of the Crown. Now, that figure is about 40 million. Indeed, when this week started, the figure was 30 million. Think, then, of that change from 630 million and reflect that at the same time, over the same period, Russian imperialism has shackled 100 million men and women who once were free. And when you compare those two records, I hope you will share my indignation that in international forums, in the United Nations itself, most of all in the countries where tyranny itself reigns, our British colonial record should be attacked . . .

It has fallen to me to be Colonial Secretary during two of the most tremendous years of advance that the world has ever seen. You must be in no doubt that you are watching one of the great dramas of history, as so many countries thrust forwards through nationalism towards their independence . . .

The tightrope of timing which the Colonial Secretary has to walk in every territory every week, sometimes almost every day, is the most difficult of all his tasks – how you try to reconcile the emerging nationalism of these countries with the need for the surest possible protection for the minority. As you walk this tightrope, you must realize that if you fall from it it will bring disaster and perhaps bloodshed to so many people to whom you stand in a position of trustee.

How, then, do you go forward? On what moral principles should you base your policy, for be very sure that in this field, as in every other field, if your policies are not based on principle they will fail? I can only give you my own personal belief. First, I believe in the rights and duties of men, and that means of all men. But do not ever fall into the error of assuming that, because you give a man better housing, because you give a man better education, because you improve the health services, somehow that will satisfy his craving for basic political rights. It cannot do. Indeed, it is bound to sharpen it.

Remember also that however great your services may have been to a country, however noble the contribution we have made in the five continents of the world to the developing countries has been – and it has been noble – that will never always be accepted as a reason why automatically you should govern. We would never have accepted – we did not accept – this from the Romans. The Irish never accepted it from us. Be quite sure that the inheritors of the British Empire equally would not accept it from our people. But yet there is a way. Let me remind you of something that I said at last year's Conference when I quoted the Prime Minister of Nigeria. He was referring to the British Colonial record in Nigeria. He said that we had been, first, masters, then leaders, and finally partners, but always friends. This is the answer – in partnership and in friendship. This can be done.

Secondly, I believe in what our grandfathers would have called the British Imperial mission. It is not yet completed. Since the world began, empires have grown and flourished and decayed, some into a sort of genteel obscurity, some leaving little heritage and culture behind them, some even no more than stones covered by the sand. They are one with Nineveh and Tyre, but we are the only empire leaving behind us a coherent political scheme of development. We are the only people who, with all the hesitations and failures that there have been, are genuinely resolved on turning, to use Harold Macmillan's phrase, an empire into a commonwealth and a commonwealth into a family. This is what we are doing.

... The third principle is that I believe quite simply in the brotherhood of man – men of all races, of all colours, of all creeds. I think it is this that must be in the centre of our thinking.

And now what lies ahead in this event? It is perhaps strange to an English and to a Welsh audience to quote the greatest of our Scottish native poets, but nobody has put this in simpler or finer words than Burns:

> It is coming yet for a' that,
> That man to man the whole world o'er,
> Shall brothers be for a' that.

And this is coming. There are foolish men who will deny it, but they will be swept away; but if we are wise then indeed the task of bringing these countries towards their destiny of free and equal partners and friends with us in the Commonwealth of Nations can be a task as exciting, as inspiring and as noble as the creation of empire itself.

Macleod became Chancellor of the Exchequer when Edward Heath was elected prime minister in 1970 but died within a month of taking office.

•

DOUGLAS MACARTHUR
West Point, New York, 12 May 1962

'Duty – Honor – Country'

As Supreme Allied Commander in the south-west Pacific during the Second World War, General Douglas MacArthur (1880–1964) halted the advance of the Japanese and then, as commander of the occupation forces in Japan from 1945 to 1957, was virtually a pro-consul, organizing the rehabilitation of the defeated nation.

After becoming commander-in-chief of US forces in the Korean War, he was relieved of command by President Truman in 1951 after advocating carrying the war into China.

On his return to America he was given a hero's welcome and made a moving speech to Congress which he concluded by saying:

'*When I joined the Army even before the turn of the century, it was the fulfillment of all my boyish hopes and dreams. The world has turned over many times since I took the oath on the Plain at West Point, and the hopes and dreams have long since vanished. But I still remember the refrain of one of the most popular barrack ballads of that day which proclaimed most proudly that –*

'*Old soldiers never die, they just fade away.*

'*And like the old soldier of that ballad, I now close my military career and just fade away – an old soldier who tried to do his duty as God gave him the light to see that duty.*

'*Good-by.*'

Three weeks later MacArthur was awarded the Sylvanus Thayer Medal, the highest honour of the United States Military Academy. He reviewed the Corps of Cadets on the Plain at West Point and then, speaking without preparation, responded to the presentation. This speech was the real soldier's farewell. After this speech, MacArthur really did fade away.

Duty – Honor – Country. Those three hallowed words reverently dictate what you ought to be, what you can be, what you will be. They are your rallying points; to build courage when courage seems to fail; to regain faith when there seems to be little cause for faith; to create hope when hope becomes forlorn. Unhappily, I possess neither that eloquence of diction, that poetry of imagination, nor that brilliance of metaphor to tell you all that they mean. The unbelievers will say they are but words, but a slogan, but a flamboyant phrase. Every pedant, every demagogue, every cynic, every hypocrite, every troublemaker, and, I am sorry to say, some others of an entirely different character, will try to downgrade them even to the extent of mockery and ridicule.

But these are some of the things they do. They build your basic character; they mold you for your future roles as custodians of the nation's defense; they make you strong enough to know when you are weak, and brave enough to face yourself when you are afraid. They teach you to be proud and unbending in honest failure, but humble and gentle in success, not to substitute words for actions, not to seek the path of comfort, but to face the stress and spur of difficulty and challenge; to learn to stand up in the storm but to have compassion on those who fail; to master yourself before you seek to master others; to have a heart that is clean, a goal that is high; to learn to laugh yet never forget how to weep; to reach into the future yet never neglect the past; to be serious yet never to take yourself too seriously; to be modest so that you will remember the simplicity of true greatness, the open mind of true wisdom, the meekness of true strength. They give you a temper of the will, a quality of the imagination, a vigor of the emotions, a freshness of the deep springs of life, a temperamental predominance of courage over timidity, an appetite for adventure over love of ease. They create in your heart the sense of wonder, the unfailing hope of what next, and the joy and inspiration of life. They teach you in this way to be an officer and a gentleman.

And what sort of soldiers are those you are to lead? Are they reliable, are they brave, are they capable of victory? Their story is known to all of you; it is the story of the American man-at-arms. My estimate of him was formed on the battlefield many years ago, and has never changed. I regarded him then as I regard him now – as one of the world's noblest figures, not only as one of the finest military characters, but also as one of the most stainless. His name and fame are the birthright of every American citizen. In his youth and strength, his love and loyalty, he gave all that mortality can give. He needs no eulogy from me or from any other man. He has written his own history and written it in red on his enemy's breast. But when I think of his patience under adversity, of his courage under fire, and of his modesty in victory, I am filled with an emotion of admiration I cannot put into words. He belongs to history as furnishing one of the greatest examples of successful patriotism; he belongs to posterity as the instructor of future generations in the principles of liberty and freedom; he belongs to the present, to us, by his virtues and by his achievements. In twenty campaigns, on a hundred battlefields, around a thousand campfires, I have witnessed that enduring fortitude, that patriotic self-abnegation, and that invincible determination which have carved his status in the hearts of his people. From one end of the world to the other he has drained deep the chalice of courage.

As I listened to those songs of the glee club, in memory's eye I could see those staggering columns of the First World War, bending under soggy packs, on many a weary march from dripping dusk to drizzling dawn, slogging ankle deep through the mire of shell-shocked roads, to form grimly for the attack, blue-lipped, covered with sludge and mud, chilled by the wind and rain, driving home to their objective, and, for many, to the judgment seat of God. I do not know the dignity of their birth but I do know the glory of their death. They died unquestioning, uncomplaining, with faith in their hearts, and on their lips the hope that we would go on to victory. Always for them – Duty – Honor – Country; always their blood and sweat and tears as we sought the way and the light and the truth.

And twenty years after, on the other side of the globe, again the filth of murky foxholes, the stench of ghostly trenches, the slime of dripping dugouts; those broiling suns of relentless heat, those torrential rains of devastating storm, the loneliness and utter desolation of jungle trails, the bitterness of long separation from those they loved and cherished, the deadly pestilence of tropical disease, the horror of stricken areas of war; their resolute and determined defense, their swift and sure attack, their indomitable purpose, their complete and decisive victory – always victory – always through the bloody haze of their last reverberating shot, the vision of gaunt, ghastly men reverently following your password of Duty – Honor – Country.

The code which those words perpetrate embraces the highest moral laws and will stand the test of any ethics or philosophies ever promulgated for the uplift of mankind. Its requirements are for the things that are right, and its restraints are from the things that are wrong. The soldier, above all other men, is required to practice the greatest act of religious training – sacrifice. In battle and in the face of danger and death, he discloses those divine attributes which his Maker gave when He created man in His own image. No physical courage and no brute instinct can take the place of the Divine help which alone can sustain him. However horrible the incidents of war may be, the soldier who is called upon to offer and to give his life for his country is the noblest development of mankind.

You now face a new world – a world of change. The thrust into outer space of the satellites, spheres and missiles marked the beginning of another epoch in the long story of mankind – the chapter of the space age. In the five or more billions of years the scientists tell us it has taken to form the earth, in the three or more billion years of development of the human race, there has never been a greater, a more abrupt or staggering evolution. We deal now not with things of this world alone, but with the illimitable distances and as yet unfathomed mysteries of the universe. We are reaching out for a new and boundless frontier. We speak in strange terms: of harnessing the cosmic energy; of making winds and tides work for us; of creating unheard-of synthetic materials to supplement or even replace our old standard basics; of purifying sea water for our drink; of mining ocean floors for new fields of wealth and food; of disease preventatives to expand life into the hundreds of years; of controlling the weather for a more equitable distribution of heat and cold, of rain and shine; of space ships to the moon; of the primary target in war, no longer limited to the armed forces of an enemy, but instead to include his civil populations; of ultimate conflict between a united human race and the sinister forces of some other planetary galaxy; of such dreams and fantasies as to make life the most exciting of all time.

And through all this welter of change and development, your mission remains fixed, determined, inviolable – it is to win our wars. Everything else in your professional career is but a corollary to this vital dedication. All other public purposes, all other public projects, all other public needs, great or small, will find others for their accomplishment; but you are the ones who are trained to fight; yours is the profession of arms – the will to win, the sure knowledge that in war there is no substitute for victory; that if you lose, the nation will be destroyed; that the very obsession of your public service must be Duty – Honor – Country. Others will debate the controversial issues, national and international, which divide man's minds; but serene, calm, aloof, you stand as the nation's war guardian, as its lifeguard from the raging tides of international conflict; as its gladiator in the arena of battle. For a century and a half, you have defended, guarded, and protected its hallowed traditions of liberty and freedom, of right and justice. Let civilian voices argue the merits or demerits of our processes of government; whether our strength is being sapped by deficit financing, indulged in too long; by federal paternalism grown too mighty; by power groups grown too arrogant; by politics grown too corrupt; by crime grown too rampant; by morals grown too low; by taxes grown too high; by extremists grown too violent; whether our personal liberties are as thorough and complete as they should be. These great national problems are not for your professional participation or military solution. Your guidepost stands out like a tenfold beacon in the night – Duty – Honor – Country.

You are the leaven which binds together the entire fabric of our national system of defence. From your ranks come the great captains who hold the nation's destiny in their hands the moment the war tocsin sounds. The Long Gray Line has never failed us. Were you to do so, a million ghosts in olive drab, in brown khaki, in blue and gray, would rise from their white crosses thundering those magic words – Duty – Honor – Country.

This does not mean that you are war mongers. On the contrary, the soldier, above all other people, prays for peace, for he must suffer and bear the deepest wounds and scars of war. But always in our ears ring the ominous words of Plato, that wisest of all philosophers, 'Only the dead have seen the end of war.'

The shadows are lengthening for me. The twilight is here. My days of old have vanished tone and tint; they have gone glimmering through the dreams of things that were. Their memory is one of wondrous beauty, watered by tears, and coaxed and caressed by the smiles of yesterday. I listen vainly, but with thirsty ear, for the witching melody of faint bugles blowing reveille, of far drums beating the long roll. In my dreams I hear again the crash of guns, the rattle of musketry, the strange mournful mutter of the battle-field. But in the evening of my memory, always I come back to West Point. Always there echoes and re-echoes in my ears – Duty – Honor – Country.

●

HUGH GAITSKELL
Brighton, 3 October 1962

'The end of a thousand years of history'

Hugh Gaitskell was a fighter, a politician with a stubborn faith in the power of reasoned argument. A year earlier he had defeated a challenge to his leadership and won acceptance for his opposition to unilateral disarmament. Now he was determining the policy of the Labour Party on joining the European Common Market, the issue that has dominated and divided British politics ever since. To the anguish of his right-wing supporters, most of whom backed entry into Europe, Gaitskell swung the party into a position of hostility towards the Common Market.

No other living British politician could have so dominated a mass conference by the sheer force of intellect and personality, said Anthony Crosland, one of Gaitskell's friends. Yet Dora, Gaitskell's wife, observed during the standing ovation: 'All the wrong people are cheering.'

I understand and deeply sympathize with the people of France and of Germany in their desire to get rid of the conflicts which have so often broken out between them and which indeed are all too fresh in our minds. But I sometimes wonder whether the great problems of the world today are to be found in the unity or disunity of Western Europe. I would have said there were two problems outstanding above all others: the problem of peace and the problems of poverty; the problem of East–West relations that plagues us and the problem of the division of the world into the 'haves' and the 'have nots'.

I know some will say with great sincerity: 'But we recognize that and we believe that by Britain going into Europe a great contribution can be made to these problems.' Maybe so, but it is for them to submit the proof. So far it is hard to be convinced. For although, of course, Europe has had a great and glorious civilization, although Europe can claim Goethe and Leonardo, Voltaire and Picasso, there have been evil features in European history too – Hitler and Mussolini and today the attitude of some Europeans to the Congo problem, the attitude of at least one European government to the United Nations. You cannot say what this Europe will be: it has its two faces and we do not know as yet which is the one which will dominate.

But here is another question we have to ask; what exactly is involved in the concept of political union? We hear a lot about it; we are told that the Economic Community is not just a customs union, that all who framed it saw it as a stepping stone towards political integration. We ought to be told what is meant by that, for if this be true our entry into the Common Market carries with it some very serious political obligations. But when you ask it is not easy to get a clear answer . . .

I can see only three possibilities outside the obligations that we accept specifically in the Treaty of Rome. It may mean that there is no obligation upon the Government of Britain to do more than talk, consult more frequently with the President of France and the Chancellor of Germany. I see no harm in these talks, but I am not terribly optimistic about what they will produce . . .

But what else? If it is not just talking, what is it? The second possibility is majority decisions on political issues, just as we are to have majority decisions on economic issues. Do we want that? Well, I suppose you might say we would be able somehow or other to outvote those we disagree with. I would like to be very sure of that before I committed myself.

Then, of course, there is the idea and the ideal of Federal

Europe. Now I know it will be said by some, 'Why bring up federation? It is not immediate, it is not imposed upon us, it may not happen.' But we would be foolish to deny, not to recognize and indeed sympathize with the desire of those who created the Economic Community for political federation. That is what they mean, that is what they are after when they admit freely that under the present constitution of EEC the Assembly has no powers except the very far-reaching, overriding one, which they are most unlikely to use, of dismissing the Commission by a two-thirds majority. When it is pointed out that the Commission is a body which has powers but is not responsible or under anybody's control, what is the answer? The answer they give us: 'That is why we should set up a Federal Assembly with powers over them.' This is what they are arguing.

What does federation mean? It means that powers are taken from national governments and handed over to federal governments and to federal parliaments. It means – I repeat it – that if we go into this we are no more than a state (as it were) in the United States of Europe, such as Texas and California. They are remarkably friendly examples, you do not find every state as rich or having such good weather as those two! But I could take others: it would be the same as in Australia, where you have Western Australia, for example, and New South Wales. We should be like them. This is what it means; it does mean the end of Britain as an independent nation state. It may be a good thing or a bad thing but we must recognize that this is so . . .

We must be clear about this: it does mean, if this is the idea, the end of Britain as an independent European state. I make no apology for repeating it. It means the end of a thousand years of history. You may say, 'Let it end,' but, my goodness, it is a decision that needs a little care and thought. And it does mean the end of the Commonwealth. How can one really seriously suppose that if the mother country, the centre of the Commonwealth, is a province of Europe (which is what federation means) it could continue to exist as the mother country of a series of independent nations? It is sheer nonsense.

Although nobody knew it at the time, Gaitskell was making his last speech to a Labour Party conference. He died unexpectedly early the following year and his epitaph from his political allies was that he was the greatest prime minister who never was.

•

JOHN F. KENNEDY
Berlin, 11 June 1963

'Ich bin ein Berliner'

When President Kennedy went to West Berlin for an eight-hour visit in 1963, his motorcade was cheered every foot of the way. He got his first sight of the Berlin Wall as he approached the Brandenburg Gate. He had been scheduled to gaze over the wall through the gate on to the Unter den Linden, once the main avenue of the German capital, but the five arches of the gate were covered by red banners blocking his view of East Berlin.

Kennedy's speech that day, from the city where the Iron Curtain showed the great divide between communist East and capitalist West at its most cruel in the symbolism of the Berlin Wall, struck a chord that reverberated around the world.

Two thousand years ago the proudest boast was 'civis Romanus sum'. Today in the world of freedom the proudest boast is 'Ich bin ein Berliner.'

There are many people in the world who really don't understand – or say they don't – what is the great issue between the free world and the Communist world. Let them come to Berlin.

There are some who say that Communism is the wave of the future. Let them come to Berlin.

And there are some who say in Europe and elsewhere 'we can work with the Communists.' Let them come to Berlin.

And there are even a few who say that it's true that Communism is an evil system but it permits us to make economic progress. Let them come to Berlin.

Freedom has many difficulties and democracy is not perfect. But we have never had to put a wall up to keep our people in, to prevent them from leaving us.

I want to say on behalf of my countrymen who live many miles away on the other side of the Atlantic, who are far distant from you, that they take the greatest pride that they have been able to share with you, even from a distance the story of the last eighteen years.

I know of no town, no city that has been besieged for eighteen years that still lives with the vitality and the force and the hope and the determination of the City of West Berlin.

While the wall is the most obvious and vivid demonstration of the failures of the Communist system, all the world can see we take no satisfaction in it, for it is, as your Mayor has said, an offence not only against history, but an offence against humanity, separating families, dividing husbands and wives and brothers and sisters and dividing a people who wish to be joined together.

What is true of this city is true of Germany. Real lasting peace in Europe can never be assured as long as one German out of four is denied the elementary right of free men, and that is to make a free choice.

In eighteen years of peace and good faith this generation of Germans has earned the right to be free, including the right to unite their families and their nation in lasting peace with goodwill to all people.

You live in a defended island of freedom, but your life is part of the main. So let me ask you as I close, to lift your eyes beyond the dangers of today to the hopes of tomorrow, beyond the freedom merely of this city of Berlin and all your country of Germany to the advance of freedom everywhere, beyond the wall to the day of peace with justice, beyond yourselves and ourselves to all mankind.

Freedom is indivisible and when one man is enslaved who are free? When all are free, then we can look forward to that day when this city will be joined as one and this country and this great continent of Europe in a peaceful and hopeful globe.

When that day finally comes, as it will, the people of West Berlin can take sober satisfaction in the fact that they were in the front lines for almost two decades.

All free men, wherever they may live, are citizens of Berlin. And therefore, as a free man, I take pride in the words 'Ich bin ein Berliner.'

•

NIGEL BIRCH
London, 17 June 1963

'Never glad confident morning again'

The Profumo scandal of 1963 arose after John Profumo, Secretary of State for War, was forced to resign after admitting to an affair with Christine Keeler, a call-girl who was simultaneously involved with a Russian naval attaché, about which he had lied to the House of Commons.

In a statement to the Commons, Harold Macmillan, the prime minister, emphasized that Profumo was dismissed from the government for lying – but the general effect of his speech and his conduct throughout the scandal was to show Macmillan as naïve and out of touch.

Nigel Birch, who had resigned from Macmillan's government in 1958 in protest at increases in government spending, was one of the most accomplished speakers in the Commons. He was pithy, with a coruscating wit, and his interventions often turned a parliamentary debate into an occasion.

The most notable was when he attacked Macmillan in the Profumo debate and ended his speech with a quotation from Robert Browning, as deadly a use of quotation as Leo Amery's dismissal of Neville Chamberlain.

We know a deal more now about Profumo than we did at the time of the statement, but we have all known him pretty well for a number of years in this House. I must say that he never struck me as a man at all like a cloistered monk; and Miss Keeler was a professional prostitute . . . Here one had an active, busy man and a professional prostitute. On his own admission, Profumo had a number of meetings with her, and, if we are to judge by the published statements, she is not a woman who would be intellectually stimulating. Is it really credible that the association had no sexual content? There seems to me to be a certain basic improbability about the proposition that their relationship was purely platonic. What are whores about? Yet Profumo's word was accepted. It was accepted from a colleague. Would that word have been accepted if Profumo had not been a colleague or even if he had been a political opponent? Everyone must, I think, make his own judgement about that.

We were told that special consideration ought to have been given to Profumo because he was a colleague. It is certainly true that a Prime Minister owes to his subordinates all the help, comfort and protection that he can give them. But surely that help, that comfort and that protection must stop short of condoning a lie in a personal statement to this House.

Then we are told that special weight ought to have been given to Profumo's words because he was a Privy Councillor and a Secretary of State. I am a Privy Councillor and I have been a Secretary of State, but when I sustained the burden of both offices I did not feel that any sea change had taken place in my personality. I remained what I was, what I had always been and what I am today; and I do not believe it reasonable to suppose that any sea change took place in Mr Profumo's personality.

He was not a man who was ever likely to tell the absolute truth in a tight corner, and at the time the statement was made he was in a very tight corner indeed. There are people – and it is to the credit of our poor, suffering humanity that it is so – who will tell the whole truth about themselves whatever the consequences may be. Of such are saints and martyrs, but most of us are not like that. Most people in a tight corner either prevaricate – or, as in this case, they lie.

This lie was accepted. I have meditated very deeply on this, and though I have given some rather tough reasons for not accepting

that Profumo's statement was credible, I have after deep consideration come to the conclusion that my Right Hon. Friend did
absolutely genuinely believe it. I will give my reasons now for
taking that view, and these reasons concern the competence and
the good sense with which the affair was handled.

Profumo on his own admission had been guilty of a very
considerable indiscretion, for a Minister at any rate. He was not a
particularly successful Minister. He had no great place in this
House or in the country. I cannot really see that the Prime Minister
was under any obligation whatever to retain his services, nor do I
think that getting rid of Mr Profumo would, in fact, have made
the political situation any worse than it then was. On the other
hand, to retain him entailed a colossal risk and a colossal gamble.
The difficulties and dangers were obvious enough. The Press were
in full cry. They were in possession of letters. They were hardly
likely to have bought letters unless they had something of interest
in them. Miss Keeler was pretty certain to turn up again, and if
she did, editors were sure to make use of her literary talent. The
dangers were enormous, and yet this colossal gamble was taken,
and in this gamble, as it seems to me, the possible gain was
negligible and the possible loss devastating.

The conclusion that I draw from that is that the course adopted
by my Right Hon. Friend the Prime Minister could have been
adopted only by someone who genuinely and completely believed
the statements of Profumo, and therefore, I absolutely acquit my
Right Hon. Friend of any sort of dishonour. On the other hand,
on the question of competence and good sense I cannot think that
the verdict can be favourable.

What is to happen now? I cannot myself see at all that we can
go on acting as if nothing had happened. We cannot just have
business as usual. I myself feel that the time will come very soon
when my Right Hon. Friend ought to make way for a much
younger colleague. I feel that that ought to happen. I certainly will
not quote at him the savage words of Cromwell, but perhaps some
of the words of Browning might be appropriate in his poem on
'The Lost Leader', in which he wrote:

> . . . let him never come back to us!
> There would be doubt, hesitation and pain.
> Forced praise on our part – the glimmer of twilight,
> Never glad confident morning again!

'Never glad confident morning again!' – so I hope that the change will not be too long delayed.

Ahead of us we have a Division. We have the statement of my Right Hon. and noble Friend Lord Hailsham, in a personal assurance on television, that a Whip is not a summons to vote but a summons to attend. I call the Whips to witness that I at any rate have attended.

The speech electrified the Commons. The publicity it received and its effect on Birch's fellow Tories weakened Macmillan's hold over the Tory Party. Macmillan retired four months later. Birch was created a life peer and became Lord Rhyl in 1970.

•

MARTIN LUTHER KING
Washington, DC, 28 August 1963

'*I have a dream*'

As the centenary of Abraham Lincoln's emancipation proclamation was celebrated in 1963, the National Association for the Advancement of Colored People, using the slogan 'Free by '63', launched a massive campaign for justice for America's blacks. The most important demonstrations were in Birmingham, Alabama (where Martin Luther King, 1929–68, led a march on the city hall, was twice thrown into gaol but won substantial measures of desegregation) and in Selma where a grand march of protest to Montgomery was addressed by King and Ralph Bunche, until then the only black American winner of the Nobel Peace Prize.

Then Philip Randolph, dean of the black American leaders, proposed a march on Washington for jobs and freedom. 'There was no precedent for a convocation of national scope and gargantuan size,' King wrote later. 'Complicating the situation were innumerable prophets of doom who feared that the slightest incident of violence would alienate Congress and destroy all hope of legislation.'

Yet 210,000 gathered at the Washington Monument in August and marched to the Lincoln Memorial, where the high point of the day was the speech by Martin Luther King, the voice of black Americans. He had written it in longhand the night before and did not finish it until 4 a.m. Now, standing before the marchers, King rose to the drama of the occasion, and delivered one of the most memorable speeches of the century. No public figure of his generation could match the skill with which he made a mastery of the spoken word the servant of his cause.

Five score years ago, a great American, in whose symbolic shadow we stand, signed the Emancipation Proclamation. This momentous decree came as a great beacon light of hope to millions of Negro slaves who had been seared in the flames of withering injustice. It came as a joyous daybreak to end the long night of captivity.

But one hundred years later, we must face the tragic fact that the Negro is still not free. One hundred years later, the life of the Negro is still sadly crippled by the manacles of segregation and the chains of discrimination. One hundred years later, the Negro lives on a lonely island of poverty in the midst of a vast ocean of material prosperity. One hundred years later, the Negro is still languished in the corners of American society and finds himself an exile in his own land. So we have come here today to dramatize an appalling condition.

In a sense we have come to our nation's Capital to cash a check. When the architects of our republic wrote the magnificent words of the Constitution and the Declaration of Independence, they were signing a promissory note to which every American was to fall heir. This note was a promise that all men would be guaranteed the unalienable rights of life, liberty, and the pursuit of happiness.

It is obvious today that America has defaulted on this promissory note insofar as her citizens of color are concerned. Instead of honoring this sacred obligation, America has given the Negro people a bad check; a check which has come back marked 'insufficient funds.' But we refuse to believe that the bank of justice is bankrupt. We refuse to believe that there are insufficient funds in the great vaults of opportunity of this nation. So we have come to cash this check – a check that will give us upon demand the riches of freedom and the security of justice. We have also come to this hallowed spot to remind America of the fierce urgency of *now*. This is no time to engage in the luxury of cooling off or to take the tranquilizing drug of gradualism.

Now is the time to make real the promises of Democracy.

Now is the time to rise from the dark and desolate valley of segregation to the sunlit path of racial justice.

Now is the time to open the doors of opportunity to all of God's children.

Now is the time to lift our nation from the quicksands of racial injustice to the solid rock of brotherhood.

It would be fatal for the nation to overlook the urgency of the moment and to underestimate the determination of the Negro. This sweltering summer of the Negro's legitimate discontent will not pass until there is an invigorating autumn of freedom and equality. Nineteen sixty-three is not an end, but a beginning. Those who hope that the Negro needed to blow off steam and will now be content will have a rude awakening if the nation returns to business as usual. There will be neither rest nor tranquillity in America until the Negro is granted his citizenship rights. The whirlwinds of revolt will continue to shake the foundations of our nation until the bright day of justice emerges.

But there is something that I must say to my people who stand on the warm threshold which leads into the palace of justice. In the process of gaining our rightful place we must not be guilty of wrongful deeds. Let us not seek to satisfy our thirst for freedom by drinking from the cup of bitterness and hatred. We must forever conduct our struggle on the high plane of dignity and discipline. We must not allow our creative protest to degenerate into physical violence. Again and again we must rise to the majestic heights of meeting physical force with soul force. The marvelous new militancy which has engulfed the Negro community must not lead us to a distrust of all white people, for many of our white brothers, as evidenced by their presence here today, have come to realize that their destiny is tied up with our destiny and their freedom is inextricably bound to our freedom. We cannot walk alone.

And as we walk, we must make the pledge that we shall march ahead. We cannot turn back. There are those who are asking the devotees of civil rights, 'When will you be satisfied?' We can never be satisfied as long as the Negro is the victim of the unspeakable horrors of police brutality. We can never be satisfied as long as our bodies, heavy with the fatigue of travel, cannot gain lodging in the motels of the highways and the hotels of the cities. We cannot be satisfied as long as the Negro's basic mobility is from a smaller ghetto to a larger one. We can never be satisfied as long as a Negro in Mississippi cannot vote and a Negro in New York believes he has nothing for which to vote. No, no, we are not satisfied, and we will not be satisfied until justice rolls down like waters and righteousness like a mighty stream.

I am not unmindful that some of you have come here out of great trials and tribulations. Some of you have come fresh from narrow jail cells. Some of you have come from areas where your quest for freedom left you battered by the storms of persecution and staggered by the winds of police brutality. You have been the veterans of creative suffering. Continue to work with the faith that unearned suffering is redemptive.

Go back to Mississippi, go back to Alabama, go back to South Carolina, go back to Georgia, go back to Louisiana, go back to the slums and ghettos of our northern cities, knowing that somehow this situation can and will be changed. Let us not wallow in the valley of despair.

I say to you today, my friends, that in spite of the difficulties and frustrations of the moment I still have a dream. It is a dream deeply rooted in the American dream.

I have a dream that one day this nation will rise up and live out the true meaning of its creed: 'We hold these truths to be self-evident; that all men are created equal.'

I have a dream that one day on the red hills of Georgia the sons of former slaves and the sons of former slaveowners will be able to sit down together at the table of brotherhood.

I have a dream that one day even the state of Mississippi, a desert state sweltering with the heat of injustice and op-pression, will be transformed into an oasis of freedom and justice.

I have a dream that my four little children will one day live in a nation where they will not be judged by the color of their skin but by the content of their character.

I have a dream today.

I have a dream that one day the state of Alabama, whose governor's lips are presently dripping with the words of interposi-tion and nullification, will be transformed into a situation where little black boys and black girls will be able to join hands with little white boys and white girls and walk together as sisters and brothers.

I have a dream today.

I have a dream that one day every valley shall be exalted, every hill and mountain shall be made low, the rough places will be made plains, and the crooked places will be made straight, and the glory of the Lord shall be revealed, and all flesh shall see it together.

This is our hope. This is the faith with which I return to the South. With this faith we will be able to hew out of the mountain of despair a stone of hope. With this faith we will be able to transform the jangling discords of our nation into a beautiful symphony of brotherhood. With this faith we will be able to work together, to pray together, to struggle together, to go to jail together, to stand up for freedom together, knowing that we will be free one day.

This will be the day when all of God's children will be able to sing with new meaning

My country, 'tis of thee,
Sweet land of liberty,
    Of thee I sing:
Land where my fathers died,
Land of the pilgrims' pride,
From every mountainside
    Let freedom ring.

And if America is to be a great nation this must become true. So let freedom ring from the prodigious hilltops of New Hampshire. Let freedom ring from the mighty mountains of New York. Let freedom ring from the heightening Alleghenies of Pennsylvania!

Let freedom ring from the snowcapped Rockies of Colorado!

Let freedom ring from the curvacious peaks of California!

But not only that; let freedom ring from Stone Mountain of Georgia!

Let freedom ring from Lookout Mountain of Tennessee!

Let freedom ring from every hill and molehill of Mississippi. From every mountainside, let freedom ring.

When we let freedom ring, when we let it ring from every village and every hamlet, from every state and every city, we will be able to speed up that day when all of God's children, black men and white men, Jews and Gentiles, Protestants and Catholics, will be able to join hands and sing in the words of the old Negro spiritual, 'Free at last! free at last! thank God almighty, we are free at last!'

James Reston, one of America's most distinguished journalists, described the speech as 'an anguished echo from all the old American reformers' – from Roger Williams calling for religious liberty, Sam Adams for political liberty and Thoreau denouncing coercion to William Lloyd Garrison demanding emancipation and Eugene V. Debs crying for economic equality. King echoed them all.

Martin Luther King was Time's *Man of the Year in 1963 and was awarded the Nobel Peace Prize in 1964. Civil-rights Acts, initiated by President Kennedy, were put on the statute book by President Johnson in 1964 and*

1965. King was assassinated on a civil-rights mission to Memphis, Tennessee, on 4 April 1968.

•

HAROLD WILSON
Scarborough, 1 October 1963

'The white heat of technology'

Harold Wilson (1916–) became leader of the Labour Party in 1963 after the death of Hugh Gaitskell. His challenge to the Tories, now led after the retirement of Harold Macmillan by the aristocratic Sir Alec Douglas-Home, was mounted with dramatic effect at the Labour Party Conference, an annual platform for a major speech by the party leader.

In a speech that was rewritten during the small hours of the morning, Wilson summoned Labour to embrace the cult of the new and to harness the white heat of the technological revolution, and identified himself with the technicians and white-coat workers. There should be more scientists in government, he urged, more investment in scientific research and a new minister of technology. There was no room in the Labour movement for Luddites or antique working practices.

The contrast between Wilson and Douglas-Home, who confessed to doing his sums with matchsticks, was dramatic. 'We are living in the jet age,' Wilson said in other speeches, 'but we are governed by an Edwardian establishment mentality.' Wilson's message swept the political board. After twelve years of Tory rule, it chimed with the public mood and was compared to President Kennedy's 'new frontier'.

We are redefining and we are restating our Socialism in terms of the scientific revolution. But that revolution cannot become a reality unless we are prepared to make far-reaching changes in economic and social attitudes which permeate our whole system of society.

The Britain that is going to be forged in the white heat of this revolution will be no place for restrictive practices or for outdated methods on either side of industry. We shall need a totally new attitude to the problems of apprenticeship, of training and retraining for skill. If there is one thing where the traditional philosophy of capitalism breaks down it is in training for apprenticeship, because quite frankly it does not pay any individual firm, unless it is very altruistic or quixotic or farsighted, to train apprentices if it knows at the end of the period of training they will be snapped up by some unscrupulous firm that makes no contribution to apprenticeship training. That is what economists mean when they talk about the difference between marginal private cost and net social cost.

So we are going to need a new attitude. In some industries we shall have to get right away from the idea of apprenticeship to a single firm. There will have to be apprenticeship with the industry as a whole, and the industry will have to take responsibility for it. Indeed, if we are going to end demarcation and snobbery in our training for skill and for science why should not these apprenticeship contracts be signed with the State itself? Then again, in the Cabinet room and the board room alike those charged with the control of our affairs must be ready to think and to speak in the language of our scientific age.

For the commanding heights of British industry to be controlled today by men whose only claim is their aristocratic connections or the power of inherited wealth or speculative finance is as irrelevant to the twentieth century as would be the continued purchase of commissions in the armed forces by lordly amateurs. At the very time that even the MCC has abolished the distinction between amateurs and professionals, in science and industry we are content to remain a nation of Gentlemen in a world of Players.

For those of us who have studied the formidable Soviet challenge in the education of scientists and technologists, and above all, in the ruthless application of scientific techniques in Soviet industry, know that our future lies not in military strength alone but in the efforts, the sacrifices, and above all the energies which a free people can mobilize for the future greatness of our country. Because we are democrats, we reject the methods which

Communist countries are deploying in applying the results of scientific research to industrial life, but because we care deeply about the future of Britain, we must use all the resources of democratic planning, all the latent and underdeveloped energies and skills of our people, to ensure Britain's standing in the world. That is the message which I believe will go out from this Conference to the people of Britain and to the people of the world.

The speech was greeted with a long standing ovation. Almost every correspondent was instantly seduced by Wilson's pseudo-scientific jargon, a disenchanted critic wrote later. Yet it had a big impact on floating middle-class voters and Wilson became prime minister in 1964. He won two subsequent elections in 1966 and 1974 and retired in 1976.

•

LYNDON B. JOHNSON
Washington, DC, 27 November 1963

'Let us continue'

According to the historian Theodore White, there was no word less than superb to describe the performance of Lyndon Johnson (1908–73) as he became president of the United States after the assassination of John Kennedy. All accounts of his behaviour through that week of tragedy endowed him with 'superlative grace'. At his inauguration, Kennedy had declared: 'Let us begin.' Now Johnson used the healing words: 'Let us continue' and proceeded to make continuity the watchword of Washington.

On the Sunday after the assassination, Johnson detailed some of the best brains of Kennedy's staff – Theodore Sorensen, McGeorge Bundy and J. K. Galbraith – to draft his first speech to Congress, adding to the team his old friend Abe Fortas, a Washington lawyer, and Bill Moyers and Horace Busby from his personal staff to add ideas.

He laboured on the speech throughout the next two days, changing words and phrases as he sought the right tone. When Bundy and Moyers brought him the finished speech, he pencilled in freshly the words that came from his own heart – 'For thirty-two years Capitol Hill has been my home' – and was ready to deliver the address that made his personal policy into national policy.

Mr Speaker, Mr President, Members of the House, Members of the Senate, my fellow Americans:

All I have I would have given gladly not to be standing here today.

The greatest leader of our time has been struck down by the foulest deed of our time. Today John Fitzgerald Kennedy lives on in the immortal words and works that he left behind. He lives on in the mind and memories of mankind. He lives on in the hearts of his countrymen.

No words are sad enough to express our sense of loss. No words are strong enough to express our determination to continue the forward thrust of America that he began.

The dream of conquering the vastness of space – the dream of partnership across the Atlantic – and across the Pacific as well – the dream of a Peace Corps in less developed nations – the dream of education for all of our children – the dream of jobs for all who seek them and need them – the dream of care for our elderly – the dream of an all-out attack on mental illness – and above all, the dream of equal rights for all Americans, whatever their race or color – these and other American dreams have been vitalized by his drive and by his dedication.

And now the ideas and the ideals which he so nobly represented must and will be translated into effective action.

Under John Kennedy's leadership, this Nation has demonstrated that it has the courage to seek peace, and it has the fortitude to risk war. We have proved that we are a good and reliable friend to those who seek peace and freedom. We have shown that we can also be a formidable foe to those who reject the path of peace and those who seek to impose upon us or our allies the yoke of tyranny.

This Nation will keep its commitments from South Viet-Nam

to West Berlin. We will be unceasing in the search for peace; resourceful in our pursuit of areas of agreement even with those with whom we differ; and generous and loyal to those who join with us in common cause.

In this age when there can be no losers in peace and no victors in war, we must recognize the obligation to match national strength with national restraint. We must be prepared at one and the same time for both the confrontation of power and the limitation of power. We must be ready to defend the national interest and to negotiate the common interest. This is the path that we shall continue to pursue. Those who test our courage will find it strong, and those who seek our friendship will find it honourable. We will demonstrate anew that the strong can be just in the use of strength; and the just can be strong in the defence of justice.

And let all know we will extend no special privilege and impose no persecution. We will carry on the fight against poverty and misery, and disease and ignorance, in other lands and in our own.

We will serve all the Nation, not one section or one sector, or one group, but all Americans. These are the United States – a united people with a united purpose.

Our American unity does not depend upon unanimity. We have differences; but now, as in the past, we can derive from those differences strength, not weakness, wisdom, not despair. Both as a people and a government, we can unite upon a programme, a programme which is wise and just, enlightened and constructive.

For thirty-two years Capitol Hill has been my home. I have shared many moments of pride with you, pride in the ability of the Congress of the United States to act, to meet any crisis, to distil from our differences strong programmes of national action.

An assassin's bullet has thrust upon me the awesome burden of the Presidency. I am here today to say I need your help; I cannot bear this burden alone. I need the help of all Americans, and all America. This Nation has experienced a profound shock, and in this critical moment, it is our duty, yours and mine, as the Government of the United States, to do away with uncertainty and doubt and delay, and to show that we are capable of decisive action; that from the brutal loss of our leader we will derive not weakness, but strength; that we can and will act and act now.

From this chamber of representative government, let all the world know and none misunderstand that I rededicate this Government to the unswerving support of the United Nations, to the honourable and determined execution of our commitments to our allies, to the maintenance of military strength second to none, to the defence of the strength and the stability of the dollar, to the expansion of our foreign trade, to the reinforcement of our programmes of mutual assistance and cooperation in Asia and Africa, and to our Alliance for Progress in this hemisphere.

On the 20th day of January, in 1961, John F. Kennedy told his countrymen that our national work would not be finished 'in the first thousand days, nor in the life of this administration, nor even perhaps in our lifetime on this planet. But,' he said, 'let us begin.'

Today, in this moment of new resolve, I would say to all my fellow Americans, let us continue.

This is our challenge – not to hesitate, not to pause, not to turn about and linger over this evil moment, but to continue on our course so that we may fulfil the destiny that history has set for us.

•

NELSON MANDELA
Johannesburg, 20 April 1964

'An ideal for which I am prepared to die'

After being sentenced to life imprisonment in 1964, Nelson Mandela (1918–) became a worldwide symbol of heroic black resistance to the apartheid regime of South Africa. He was described as the Black Pimpernel.

He joined the African National Congress in 1952 and became a member of a small action group whose main task was to launch Umkhonto we Sizwe (Spear of the Nation) or MK. From a safe house in Rivonia, MK planned sabotage of strategic targets – after its first terrorist attacks in 1961 bombs exploded in Johannesburg, Port Elizabeth and Durban.

When the ANC was banned in 1961, Mandela evaded arrest for a year but was gaoled for five years in 1962 and sent to Robben Island. His prison term was interrupted by the Rivonia trial, brought after a police raid on ANC headquarters in 1963. Mandela and his colleagues were charged under the Suppression of Communism Act.

The trial opened on 9 October 1963, with Mandela named as Accused Number One and facing the death penalty. The defence case opened the following April. Mandela's speech lasted four hours. He denied he was a Communist and described himself as an African patriot who admired the Magna Carta and the Bill of Rights. His concluding words inspired support throughout the world.

Our fight is against real, and not imaginary hardships, or, to use the language of the State Prosecutor, 'so-called hardships'. We fight against two features which are the hallmarks of African life in South Africa, and which are entrenched by legislation which we seek to have repealed. These features are poverty and lack of human dignity, and we do not need Communists, or so-called 'agitators', to teach us about these things.

The whites enjoy what may well be the highest standard of living in the world, whilst Africans live in poverty and misery. Forty per cent of the Africans live in hopelessly overcrowded and, in some cases, drought-stricken reserves, where soil erosion and the overworking of the soil make it impossible for them to live properly off the land. Thirty per cent are labourers, labour tenants, and squatters on white farms and work and live under conditions similar to those of the serfs of the Middle Ages. The other thirty per cent live in towns where they have developed economic and social habits which bring them closer, in many respects, to white standards. Yet forty-six per cent of all African families in Johannesburg do not earn enough to keep them going.

The complaint of Africans, however, is not only that they are poor and whites are rich, but that the laws which are made by the whites are designed to preserve this situation. There are two ways to break out of poverty. The first is by formal education, and the second is by the worker acquiring a greater skill at his work and thus higher wages. As far as Africans are concerned, both these avenues of advancement are deliberately curtailed by legislation.

The present Government has always sought to hamper Africans in their search for education. There is compulsory education for all white children at virtually no cost to their parents, be they rich or poor. Similar facilities are not provided for African children. In 1960–61, the per capita government spending on African students at state-funded schools was estimated at R12.46. In the same year, the per capita spending on white children in the Cape Province (which are the only figures available to me) was R144.57. The present Prime Minister said during the debate on the Bantu Education Bill in 1953: 'When I have control of Native education, I will reform it so that Natives will be taught from childhood to realize that equality with Europeans is not for them ... People who believe in equality are not desirable teachers for Natives. When my Department controls Native education, it will know for what class of higher education a Native is fitted, and whether he will have a chance in life to use his knowledge.'

The other main obstacle to the economic advancement of the Africans is the industrial colour bar by which all the better jobs of industry are reserved for whites only. Moreover, Africans are not allowed to form trade unions, which have recognition under the Industrial Conciliation Act. The Government often answers its critics by saying that Africans in South Africa are economically better off than the inhabitants of the other countries in Africa. Our complaint is not that we are poor by comparison with people in other countries, but that we are poor by comparison with white people in our own country, and that we are prevented by legislation from altering this imbalance.

Hundreds and thousands of Africans are thrown into gaol each year under pass laws. Even worse than this is the fact that pass laws keep husband and wife apart and lead to the breakdown of family life.

Poverty and the breakdown of family life have secondary effects. Children wander about the streets of the townships because they have no schools to go to, or no money to enable them to go to school, or no parents at home to see that they go to school because both parents, if there be two, have to work to keep the family alive. This leads to a breakdown in moral standards, to an alarming rise in illegitimacy and to growing violence which erupts, not only politically but everywhere. Life in the townships is dangerous; there is not a day that goes by without somebody being stabbed or assaulted. And violence is carried out of the townships into the white living areas. People are afraid to walk alone in the streets after dark. House-breakings and robberies are increasing despite the fact that the death sentence can now be imposed for such offences. Death sentences cannot cure the festering sore. The only cure is to alter the conditions under which the Africans are forced to live, and to meet their legitimate grievances.

We want to be part of the general population, and not confined to living in our ghettos. African men want to have their wives and children to live with them where they work, and not to be forced into an unnatural existence in men's hostels. Our women want to be left with their men folk, and not to be left permanently widowed in the Reserves. We want to be allowed out after 11 p.m. and not to be confined to our rooms like little children. We want to be allowed to travel in our own country, and seek work where we want to, and not where the Labour Bureau tells us to. We want a just share in the whole of South Africa; we want security and a stake in society.

Above all, my lord, we want equal political rights, because without them our disabilities will be permanent. I know this sounds revolutionary to the whites in this country, because the majority of voters will be Africans. This makes the white man fear democracy. But this fear cannot be allowed to stand in the way of the only solution which will guarantee racial harmony and freedom for all. It is not true that the enfranchisement of all will result in racial domination. Political division, based on colour, is entirely artificial, and when it disappears, so will the domination of one colour group by another. The ANC has spent half a century fighting against racialism. When it triumphs, as it certainly must, it will not change that policy.

This then is what the ANC is fighting. Our struggle is a truly national one. It is a struggle of the African people, inspired by our own suffering and our own experience. It is a struggle for the right to live.

During my lifetime I have dedicated my life to this struggle of the African people. I have fought against white domination, and I have fought against black domination. I have cherished the ideal of a democratic and free society in which all persons live together in harmony with equal opportunities. It is an ideal which I hope to live for, and to see realized. But my lord, if needs be, it is an ideal for which I am prepared to die.

On 11 June, Mandela and the seven other defendants were sentenced to life imprisonment. Mandela returned to Robben Island, where he was put in a stone cell measuring two metres by two metres, lit by a forty-watt bulb and set to hard labour in a quarry. He spent twenty-seven years in prison.

•

LYNDON B. JOHNSON
Ann Arbor, Michigan, 22 May 1964

'The Great Society'

At first, as he sought a slogan to encapsulate the mission of his presidency and to follow the idealism of the New Deal, Lyndon Johnson thought of A Better Deal.

It was one of his speech-writers, Richard Goodwin, who had earlier worked with President Kennedy, who dreamt up the phrase The Great Society. When Johnson failed to arouse any strong enthusiasm for A Better Deal, he began to weave the theme of The Great Society into his speeches – and used the phrase on nineteen occasions in March and April, but it was not recognized as his slogan until Goodwin wrote Johnson's speech for the University of Michigan.

For a century we laboured to settle and to subdue a continent. For half a century we called upon unbounded invention and untiring industry to create an order of plenty for all of our people.

The challenge of the next half century is whether we have the wisdom to use that wealth to enrich and elevate our national life, and to advance the quality of our American civilization.

Your imagination, your initiative, and your indignation will determine whether we build a society where progress is the servant of our needs, or a society where old values and new visions are buried under unbridled growth. For in your time we have the opportunity to move not only towards the rich society and the powerful society, but upward to the Great Society.

The Great Society rests on abundance and liberty for all. It demands an end to poverty and racial injustice, to which we are totally committed in our time. But that is just the beginning.

The Great Society is a place where every child can find knowledge to enrich his mind and to enlarge his talents. It is a place where leisure is a welcome chance to build and reflect, not a feared cause of boredom and restlessness. It is a place where the city of man serves not only the needs of the body and the demands of commerce but the desire for beauty and the hunger for community.

It is a place where man can renew contact with nature. It is a place which honours creation for its own sake and for what it adds to the understanding of the race. It is a place where men are more concerned with the quality of their goals than the quantity of their goods.

But most of all, the Great Society is not a safe harbour, a resting place, a final objective, a finished work. It is a challenge constantly renewed, beckoning us towards a destiny where the meaning of our lives matches the marvellous products of our labour . . .

Our society will never be great until our cities are great. Today the frontier of imagination and innovation is inside those cities and not beyond their borders.

New experiments are already going on. It will be the task of your generation to make the American city a place where future generations will come, not only to live but to live the good life . . .

A second place where we begin to build the Great Society is in our countryside. We have always prided ourselves on being not only America the strong and America the free, but America the beautiful. Today that beauty is in danger. The water we drink, the food we eat, the very air that we breathe, are threatened with pollution. Our parks are overcrowded, our seashores overburdened. Green fields and dense forests are disappearing.

A few years ago we were greatly concerned about the 'Ugly American.' Today we must act to prevent an ugly America.

For once the battle is lost, once our natural splendour is destroyed, it can never be recaptured. And once man can no longer walk with beauty or wonder at nature his spirit will wither and his sustenance be wasted.

A third place to build the Great Society is in the classrooms of America. There your children's lives will be shaped. Our society will not be great until every young mind is set free to scan the farthest reaches of thought and imagination. We are still far from that goal.

Today, eight million adult Americans, more than the entire population of Michigan, have not finished five years of school. Nearly twenty million have not finished eight years of school. Nearly fifty-four million – more than one-quarter of all America – have not even finished high school . . .

In many places, classrooms are overcrowded and curricula are outdated. Most of our qualified teachers are underpaid, and many of our paid teachers are unqualified. So we must give every child a place to sit and a teacher to learn from. Poverty must not be a bar to learning, and learning must offer an escape from poverty . . .

There are those timid souls who say this battle cannot be won; that we are condemned to a soulless wealth. I do not agree. We have the power to shape the civilization that we want. But we need your will, your labour, your hearts, if we are to build that kind of society.

Those who came to this land sought to build more than just a new country. They sought a new world. So I have come here today to your campus to say that you can make their vision our reality. So let us from this moment begin our work so that in the future men will look back and say: It was then, after a long and weary way, that man turned the exploits of his genius to the full enrichment of his life.

The Civil Rights bill, which was part of the Kennedy legislative programme, was hurried on to the statute book by Johnson and became law on 2 July 1964. It was the most important measure passed in the aftermath of President Kennedy's assassination and tackled almost all the problems about which Southern blacks had been protesting so strongly.

●

BARRY GOLDWATER
San Francisco, 16 July 1964

'Extremism in defence of liberty is no vice'

By the summer of 1964, Barry Goldwater (1909–), the leading Conservative political spokesman in the United States during the Kennedy administration, had arrived centre stage in American history at a time when intellectual vitality seemed to have run out of the generations-old liberal orthodoxy that had dominated American politics since Roosevelt.

At the Cow Palace, Richard Nixon was about to nominate him as Republican candidate against Lyndon Johnson in the presidential election. His speech-writers had worked on his speech for more than two weeks. Goldwater had gone through it five times. No word was unmeasured. The speech was to proclaim a new morality, an uncompromising challenge to the course American politics had followed for the past thirty years within his own party as well as the Democrats.

After being portrayed as crazy, stupid and bloodthirsty, Goldwater was an embittered man who decided to go it alone and offer no compromise. The speech signalled the tenor of his campaign which became notorious for his advocacy of increased opposition to world communism and hostility to the power of federal government. The last two lines were underlined in his text.

The Good Lord raised this mighty Republican Republic to be a home for the brave and to flourish as the land of the free – not to stagnate in the swampland of collectivism, not to cringe before the bully of Communism.

Now my fellow Americans, the tide has been running against freedom. Our people have followed false prophets. We must, and we shall, return to proven ways – not because they are old, but because they are true.

We must, and we shall, set the tide running again in the cause of freedom. And this party, with its every action, every word, every breath and every heartbeat, has but a single resolve, and that is freedom.

Freedom made orderly for this nation by our constitutional government. Freedom under a government limited by laws of nature and of nature's God. Freedom balanced so that order lacking liberty will not become the slavery of the prison cell; balanced so that liberty lacking order will not become the licence of the mob and of the jungle.

Now, we Americans understand freedom. We have earned it: we have lived for it, and we have died for it. This nation and its people are freedom's models in a searching world. We can be freedom's missionaries in a doubting world . . .

Those who seek to live your lives for you, to take your liberty in return for relieving you of yours; those who elevate the state and downgrade the citizen, must see ultimately a world in which earthly power can be substituted for Divine Will. And this nation was founded upon the rejection of that notion and upon the acceptance of God as the author of freedom.

Now those who seek absolute power, even though they seek it to do what they regard as good, are simply demanding the right to enforce their own version of heaven on earth, and let me remind you they are the very ones who always create the most hellish tyranny.

Absolute power does corrupt, and those who seek it must be suspect and must be opposed. Their mistaken course stems from false notions, ladies and gentlemen, of equality. Equality, rightly understood as our founding fathers understood it, leads to liberty and to the emancipation of creative differences; wrongly understood, as it has been so tragically in our time, it leads first to conformity and then to despotism.

Fellow Republicans, it is the cause of Republicanism to resist concentrations of power, private or public, which enforce such conformity and inflict such despotism.

It is the cause of Republicanism to insure that power remains in the hands of the people – and, so help us God, that is exactly what a Republican President will do with the help of a Republican Congress.

It is further the cause of Republicanism to restore a clear understanding of the tyranny of man over man in the world at large. It is our cause to dispel the foggy thinking which avoids hard decisions in the delusion that a world of conflict will somehow resolve itself into a world of harmony, if we just don't rock the boat or irritate the forces of aggression – and this is hogwash.

It is, further, the cause of Republicanism to remind ourselves, and the world, that only the strong can remain free: that only the strong can keep the peace.

Today – today in our beloved country – we have an Administration which seems eager to deal with Communism in every coin known – from gold to wheat; from consulates to confidence, and even human freedom itself.

Now the Republican cause demands that we brand Communism as the principal disturber of peace in the world. Indeed, we should brand it as the only significant disturber of the peace . . .

And I want to make this abundantly clear – I don't intend to let peace or freedom be torn from our grasp, because of lack of strength, or lack of will – and that I promise you Americans.

I can see a day when all the Americas – North and South – will be linked in a mighty system – a system in which the errors and misunderstandings of the past will be submerged one by one in a rising tide of prosperity and interdependence . . .

Balance, diversity, creative difference – these are the elements of the Republican equation. Republicans agree, Republicans agree heartily, to disagree on many, many of their applications. But we have never disagreed on the basic fundamental issues of why you and I are Republicans.

This is a party – this Republican party is a party – for free men. Not for blunt followers and not for conformists.

Back in 1858 Abraham Lincoln said this of the Republican party, and I quote him because he probably could have said it during the last week or so: It was so composed of strained, discordant, and even hostile elements . . .

Yet all of these elements agreed on one paramount objective: to arrest the programme of slavery, and place it in the course of its ultimate extinction.

Anyone who joins us in all sincerity we welcome. Those, those who do not care for our cause, we don't expect to enter our ranks in any case. And let our Republicanism so focused and so dedicated not be made fuzzy and futile by unthinking and stupid labels.

I would remind you that extremism in the defence of liberty is no vice!

And let me remind you also that moderation in the pursuit of justice is no virtue!

Goldwater's speech ended not only the Eisenhower era in American politics but also the reign of pragmatism in the Republican party. He won only five states in the election which Johnson won with sixty-one per cent of the popular vote, the biggest majority ever achieved by an American president at that time. Goldwater returned to the Senate in 1969 and was later influential in persuading Richard Nixon to step down from the presidency after the Watergate scandal in 1974.

•

RONALD REAGAN
Nationwide television address, 27 October 1964

'*A time for choosing*'

A lifelong Democrat, Ronald Reagan (1911–) switched sides and became co-chairman of Californians for Barry Goldwater in 1964. Reagan got his first real exposure to the airwaves as a salesman for General Electric, travelling the country to boost GE Theater. As he campaigned for Goldwater, his campaign speeches were similar in their tone and message to those he had been giving in his GE presentations.

'One night a few weeks before the election,' Reagan recalled later, 'I addressed a fundraiser at the Coconut Grove in Los Angeles. When the evening was over, a delegation of high-powered Republicans waited for me. They asked whether I would deliver that same speech on nationwide TV if they raised the money to buy the time.'

Goldwater at one stage wanted to cancel the address, since he had been attacked for his views on social security, but relented after he heard a copy of the soundtrack. Reagan's election address, which became known as The Speech, was broadcast on NBC.

Those who would trade our freedom for the soup kitchen of the welfare state have told us that they have a utopian solution of peace without victory. They call their policy 'accommodation.' And they say if we only avoid any direct confrontation with the enemy, he will forget his evil ways and learn to love us. All who oppose them are indicted as warmongers. They say we offer simple answers to complex problems. Well, perhaps there is a simple answer ... not an easy one ... but a simple one, if you and I have the courage to tell our elected officials that we want our *national* policy based upon what we know in our hearts is morally right.

We cannot buy our security, our freedom from the threat of the bomb by committing an immorality so great as saying to a billion human beings now in slavery behind the Iron Curtain, 'Give up your dreams of freedom because to save our own skin, we are willing to make a deal with your slave-masters.' Alexander Hamilton said, 'A nation which can prefer disgrace to danger is prepared for a master, and deserves one!' Let's set the record straight. There is no argument over the choice between peace and war, but there is only one guaranteed way you can have peace . . . and you can have it in the next second . . . surrender!

Admittedly there is a risk in any course we follow other than this, but every lesson in history tells us that the greater risk lies in appeasement, and this is the specter our well-meaning liberal friends refuse to face . . . that their policy of accommodation is appeasement, and it gives no choice between peace and war, only between fight or surrender. If we continue to accommodate, continue to back and retreat, eventually we have to face the final demand – the ultimatum. And what then? When Nikita Khrushchev has told his people he knows what our answer will be? He has told them that we are retreating under the pressure of the cold war, and someday when the time comes to deliver the ultimatum, our surrender will be voluntary because by that time we will have been weakened from within spiritually, morally, and economically. He believes this because from our side he has heard voices pleading for 'peace at any price' or 'better Red than dead', or as one commentator put it, he would rather 'live on his knees than die on his feet'. And therein lies the road to war, because those voices don't speak for the rest of us. You and I know and do not believe that life is so dear and peace so sweet as to be purchased at the price of chains and slavery. If nothing in life is worth dying for, when did this begin – just in the face of this enemy? – or should Moses have told the children of Israel to live in slavery under the pharaohs? Should Christ have refused the cross? Should the patriots at Concord Bridge have thrown down their guns and refused to fire the shot heard round the world? The martyrs of history were not fools, and our honored dead who gave their lives to stop the advance of the Nazis didn't die in vain! Where, then, is the road to peace? Well, it's a simple answer after all.

You and I have the courage to say to our enemies, 'There is a price we will not pay.' There is a point beyond which they must not advance! This is the meaning in the phrase of Barry Goldwater's 'peace through strength!' Winston Churchill said that 'the destiny of man is not measured by material computation. When great forces are on the move in the world, we learn we are spirits – not animals.' And he said, 'There is something going on in time and space, and beyond time and space, which, whether we like it or not, spells duty.' You and I have a rendezvous with destiny. We will preserve for our children this, the last best hope of man on earth, or we will sentence them to take the last step into a thousand years of darkness.

We will keep in mind and remember that Barry Goldwater has faith in us. He has faith that you and I have the ability and the dignity and the right to make our own decisions and determine our own destiny.

Thank you.

Reagan's speech raised $8 million. Whatever its effect on Goldwater's defeat, it soon changed Reagan's entire life and contributed significantly to his emergence as the spokesman of the Republican right.

•

LYNDON B. JOHNSON
Washington, DC, 15 March 1965

'We shall overcome'

Although his achievements were to be overshadowed by Vietnam, Lyndon Johnson's five years in the White House saw the completion of civil-rights legislation, the Federal Education Act of 1965 and the establishment of Medicare in pursuit of his ideal of The Great Society.

As he contemplated the Voting Rights Act of 1965, Johnson was worried about the reaction of Congress but was persuaded that a speech to the

House would not be interpreted as a sign of panic and would also show that he was being bipartisan.

At 8 p.m. and due to deliver his speech at 9 p.m., he was still writing. The speech never made the teleprompter and was read from a rough copy. As he came to the most famous section, Johnson paused for breath. 'In that fleeting moment,' he wrote in his memoirs, 'my thoughts turned to the picket lines in Birmingham, the sit-ins in North Carolina, the marches in Selma. A picture rose before my eyes — a picture of blacks and whites marching together, side by side, chanting and singing the anthem of the civil rights movement. I raised my arms.'

Mr Speaker, Mr President, members of the Congress, I speak tonight for the dignity of man and the destiny of democracy.

I urge every member of both parties, Americans of all religions and of all colors, from every section of this country, to join me in that cause.

At times, history and fate meet at a single time in a single place to shape a turning-point in man's unending search for freedom.

So it was at Lexington and Concord. So it was a century ago at Appomattox. So it was last week in Selma, Alabama.

There, long suffering men and women peacefully protested the denial of their rights as Americans. Many were brutally assaulted. One good man — a man of God — was killed.

There is no cause for pride in what has happened in Selma. There is no cause for self-satisfaction in the long denial of equal rights of millions of Americans. But there is cause for hope and for faith in our democracy in what is happening here tonight.

For the cries of pain and the hymns of oppressed people have summoned into convocation all the majesty of great Government — the Government of the greatest nation on earth.

Our mission is at once the oldest and the most basic of this country — to right wrong, to do justice, to serve man.

In our time we have come to live with the moments of great crisis. Our lives have been marked with debate about great issues, issues of war and peace, issues of prosperity and depression.

But rarely in any time does an issue bare the secret heart of

America itself. Rarely are we met with a challenge, not to our growth or abundance, or our welfare or our security, but rather to the values and the purposes and the meaning of our beloved nation.

The issue of equal rights for American Negroes is such an issue.

And should we defeat every enemy, and should we double our wealth and conquer the stars, and still be unequal to this issue, then we will have failed as a people and as a nation.

For, with a country as with a person, 'What is a man profited if he shall gain the whole world, and lose his own soul?'

There is no Negro problem. There is no Southern problem. There is no Northern problem. There is only an American problem.

And we are met here tonight as Americans – not as Democrats or Republicans; we're met here as Americans to solve that problem.

This was the first nation in the history of the world to be founded with a purpose. The great phrases of that purpose still sound in every American heart, North and South:

'All men are created equal.' 'Government by consent of the governed.' 'Give me liberty or give me death.'

And those are not just clever words, and those are not just empty theories.

In their name Americans have fought and died for two centuries and tonight around the world they stand there as guardians of our liberty risking their lives.

Those words are promised to every citizen that he shall share in the dignity of man. This dignity cannot be found in a man's possessions. It cannot be found in his power or in his position: It really rests on his right to be treated as a man equal in opportunity to all others.

It says that he shall share in freedom. He shall choose his leaders, educate his children, provide for his family according to his ability and his merits as a human being.

To apply any other test, to deny a man his hopes because of his colour or race or his religion or the place of his birth is not only to do injustice, it is to deny America and to dishonour the dead who gave their lives for American freedom.

Our fathers believed that if this noble view of the rights of man was to flourish it must be rooted in democracy. The most basic right of all was the right to choose your own leaders.

The history of this country in large measure is the history of expansion of that right to all of our people. Many of the issues of civil rights are very complex and most difficult. But about this there can and should be no argument: every American citizen must have an equal right to vote.

There is no reason which can excuse the denial of that right. There is no duty which weighs more heavily on us than the duty we have to insure that right. Yet the harsh fact is that in many places in this country men and women are kept from voting simply because they are Negroes.

Every device of which human ingenuity is capable has been used to deny this right. The Negro citizen may go to register only to be told that the day is wrong, or the hour is late, or the official in charge is absent.

And if he persists and if he manages to present himself to the registrar, he may be disqualified because he did not spell out his middle name, or because he abbreviated a word on the application. And if he manages to fill out an application, he is given a test.

The registrar is the sole judge of whether he passes this test. He may be asked to recite the entire Constitution, or explain the most complex provisions of state law.

And even a college degree cannot be used to prove that he can read and write. For the fact is that the only way to pass these barriers is to show a white skin.

Experience has clearly shown that the existing process of law cannot overcome systematic and ingenious discrimination. No law that we now have on the books, and I have helped to put three of them there, can insure the right to vote when local officials are determined to deny it. In such a case, our duty must be clear to all of us.

The Constitution says that no person shall be kept from voting because of his race or his colour. We have all sworn an oath before God to support and to defend that Constitution. We must now act in obedience to that oath.

On Wednesday, I will send to Congress a law designed to eliminate illegal barriers to the right to vote . . .

Outside this chamber is the outraged conscience of a nation, the grave concern of many nations and the harsh judgement of history on our acts.

But even if we pass this bill the battle will not be over.

What happened in Selma is part of a far larger movement which reaches into every section and state of America. It is the effort of American Negroes to secure for themselves the full blessings of American life.

Their cause must be our cause too. Because it's not just Negroes but really it's all of us who must overcome the crippling legacy of bigotry and injustice. And we shall overcome.

As a man whose roots go deeply into Southern soil, I know how agonizing racial feelings are. I know how difficult it is to reshape the attitudes and the structure of our society. But a century has passed – more than one hundred years – since the Negro was freed.

And he is not fully free tonight.

It was more than one hundred years ago that Abraham Lincoln – a great President of another party – signed the Emancipation Proclamation. But emancipation is a proclamation and not a fact.

A century has passed – more than one hundred years – since equality was promised, and yet the Negro is not equal.

A century has passed since the day of promise, and the promise is unkept. The time of justice has now come, and I tell you that I believe sincerely that no force can hold it back. It is right in the eyes of man and God that it should come, and when it does, I think that day will brighten the lives of every American.

For Negroes are not the only victims. How many white children have gone uneducated? How many white families have lived in stark poverty? How many white lives have been scarred by fear, because we wasted energy and our substance to maintain the barriers of hatred and terror?

And so I say to all of you here and to all in the nation tonight that those who appeal to you to hold on to the past do so at the cost of denying you your future. This great rich, restless country can offer opportunity and education and hope to all – all, black and white, all, North and South, sharecropper and city dweller.

These are the enemies: poverty, ignorance, disease. They are our enemies, not our fellow man, not our neighbour. And these enemies too – poverty, disease and ignorance – we shall overcome.

The speech was seen as the zenith of the first three years of Johnson's presidency. Johnson signed the Voting Rights Bill four months later on 6 August.

•

LYNDON B. JOHNSON
Baltimore, Maryland, 7 April 1965

'Our generation has a dream'

From the moment when American planes hit the first military target in North Vietnam early in February 1965, President Johnson was subjected to an increasingly heavy propaganda barrage from Hanoi, Peking and Moscow. He decided he needed to make a major statement on Vietnam to the American people and accepted an invitation to speak at Johns Hopkins University in Baltimore.

Meanwhile seventeen non-aligned nations had issued an appeal for peace talks, delivered to Washington on 1 April. Anxious to get the speech right, Johnson gave private previews of it to leading critics of his Vietnam policy. Then at 9 p.m. on 7 April he stepped on to the podium at Johns Hopkins and into the glare of the television lights and defended his Vietnam policy.

This will be a disorderly planet for a long time. In Asia, as elsewhere, the forces of the modern world are shaking old ways and uprooting ancient civilizations. There will be turbulence and struggle and even violence. Great social change – as we see in our own country now – does not always come without conflict.

We must also expect that nations will on occasion be in dispute with us. It may be because we are rich, or powerful; or because we have made some mistakes; or because they honestly fear our intentions. However, no nation need ever fear that we desire their land, or to impose our will, or to dictate their institutions.

But we will always oppose the effort of one nation to conquer another nation.

We will do this because our own security is at stake.

But there is more to it than that. For our generation has a dream. It is a very old dream. But we have the power and now we have the opportunity to make that dream come true.

For centuries nations have struggled among each other. But we dream of a world where disputes are settled by law and reason. And we will try to make it so.

For most of history men have hated and killed one another in battle. But we dream of an end to war. And we will try to make it so.

For all existence most men have lived in poverty, threatened by hunger. But we dream of a world where all are fed and charged with hope. And we will help to make it so.

The ordinary men and women of North Viet-Nam and South Viet-Nam – of China and India – of Russia and America – are brave people. They are filled with the same proportions of hate and fear, of love and hope. Most of them want the same things for themselves and their families. Most of them do not want their sons to ever die in battle, or see their homes, or the homes of others, destroyed.

Well, this can be their world yet. Man now has the knowledge – always before denied – to make this planet serve the real needs of the people who live on it.

I know this will not be easy. I know how difficult it is for reason to guide passion, and love to master hate. The complexities of this world do not bow easily to pure and consistent answers.

But the simple truths are there just the same. We must all try to follow them as best we can.

We often say how impressive power is. But I do not find it impressive at all. The guns and the bombs, the rockets and the warships, are all symbols of human failure. They are necessary symbols. They protect what we cherish. But they are witness to human folly.

A dam built across a great river is impressive.

In the countryside where I was born, and where I live, I have seen the night illuminated, and the kitchens warmed, and the homes heated, where once the cheerless night and the ceaseless cold held sway. And all this happened because electricity came to our area along the humming wires of the REA. Electrification of the countryside – yes, that, too, is impressive.

A rich harvest in a hungry land is impressive.

The sight of healthy children in a classroom is impressive.

These – not mighty arms – are the achievements which the American Nation believes to be impressive.

And, if we are steadfast, the time may come when all other nations will also find it so.

Every night before I turn out the lights to sleep I ask myself this question: Have I done everything that I can do to unite this country? Have I done everything I can to help unite the world, to try to bring peace and hope to all the peoples of the world? Have I done enough?

Ask yourselves that question in your homes – and in this hall tonight. Have we, each of us, all done all we could? Have we done enough?

We may well be living in the time foretold many years ago when it was said: 'I call heaven and earth to record this day against you, that I have set before you life and death, blessing and cursing: therefore choose life, that both thou and thy seed may live.'

This generation of the world must choose: destroy or build, kill or aid, hate or understand.

We can do all these things on a scale never dreamed of before.

Well, we will choose life. In so doing we will prevail over the enemies within man, and over the natural enemies of all mankind.

Next day, Washington delivered its formal reply, incorporating the main thoughts of the Johns Hopkins speech, to the seventeen non-aligned nations. On 9 April, Radio Peking said Johnson's offer of negotiation without preconditions was full of 'lies and deceptions'. Moscow described the offer as 'noisy propaganda'. 'The door to peace remained closed,' Johnson wrote in his memoirs.

•

ROY JENKINS
London, 23 May 1966

'This is the goal'

Roy Jenkins (1920–) was one of the great reforming Labour home secretaries of twentieth-century British politics as well as one of the best chancellors.

He quickly determined to strike a more upbeat note on race relations and wanted to provide a 'favourable splash' for the launching of Mark Bonham Carter as the first chairman of the new Race Relations Board. The speech was memorable in its definition of racial integration, which became one of the most provocative issues in British politics in the 1960s.

The weekend before the speech Jenkins stayed in the Provost's Lodge at King's College, Cambridge. 'On the Saturday evening,' he wrote in his memoirs, 'we went to the Founder's Obit Service in the chapel, during which, in the obscurity of the provostial stalls, I continued to scribble away . . .' That was when he wrote the passage about the universities and culture, of which he was subsequently 'rather proud'.

Integration is perhaps rather a loose word. I do not regard it as meaning the loss, by immigrants, of their own national characteristics and culture. I do not think that we need in this country a 'melting-pot', which will turn everybody out in a common mould, as one of a series of carbon copies of someone's misplaced vision of the stereotyped Englishman.

It would be bad enough if that were to occur to the relatively few in this country who happen to have pure Anglo-Saxon blood in their veins. If it were to happen to the rest of us, to the Welsh (like myself), to the Scots, to the Irish, to the Jews, to the mid-European, and to still more recent arrivals, it would be little short of a national disaster. It would deprive us of most of the positive advantages of immigration, which, as I shall develop in a moment, I believe to be very great indeed.

I define integration, therefore, not as a flattening process of assimilation but as equal opportunity, accompanied by cultural diversity, in an atmosphere of mutual tolerance. This is the goal. We may fall a little short of its full attainment, as have other communities both in the past and in the present. But if we are to maintain any sort of world reputation for civilized living and social cohesion, we must get far nearer to its achievement than is the case today. In so far as this is something which can be brought about by Government action, this is now a Home Office responsibility. I welcome this. We have traditionally had the responsibility for the control of admission – of aliens for many years past, and more recently of Commonwealth citizens. I regard this as a distasteful but necessary duty. My instincts are all against the restriction of free movement, whether for work or education or pleasure, from one country to another. Distasteful though it may be, however, it remains a duty.

In present circumstances we are bound, as almost everyone now recognizes, to contain the flow of immigrants within the economic and social capacity of the country to absorb them – the social factor being for the moment, I believe, more restrictive than the economic. There are of course differing views about that absorptive capacity, but the Government has a clear responsibility to see that it is not put so high as to create a widespread resistance to effective integration policies. Equally it must not be so unreasonably low as to create an embittered sense of apartness in the immigrant community itself. But this will depend, in my view, not only on the numerical decisions but on the way these decisions are administered; and it is my firm intention to do so as sympathetically as I possibly can, especially when dealing with hard borderline cases.

There are some people, many of them by no means illiberal, who believe that if everybody would only stay at home in their own countries, the world would be a much easier and better place. From this view I firmly dissent. Easier it might conceivably be, but certainly not better or more civilized or innovating.

For centuries past this and every other country which has played a part in the mainstream of world events has benefited immensely from its immigrants. Some of them came in much more aggressive ways than those we are discussing today, but at least from the Norman Conquest, to the wave of German and Austrian and Czechoslovak refugees in the thirties, we have been constantly stimulated and jolted out of our natural island lethargy by a whole series of immigrations. Those who came were always made unwelcome by some people, but they have rarely failed to make a contribution out of proportion to their numbers. If anyone doubts this let them look at British business today, and at the phenomenal extent to which the more successful companies have been founded – or rejuvenated – by men whose origin was outside these islands.

But this is not merely a matter of business. Where in the world is there a university which could preserve its fame, or a cultural centre which would keep its eminence, or a metropolis which could hold its drawing power if it were to turn inwards and serve only its own hinterland and its own racial group? To live apart, for a person, a city, a country, is to lead a life of declining intellectual stimulation.

Nor should we underestimate the special contribution which has been made by the recent immigrants from the West Indies, from India and Pakistan, and from other Commonwealth countries. Some are highly gifted with outstanding talents in a wide variety of human activities. They and many others are making a major contribution to our national welfare and prosperity. They work in our hospitals as doctors and nurses, they build houses and run transport services in our cities. They help to fill the many labour shortages, particularly in urban areas, particularly in vital but undermanned public services which go with a full employment society.

Let there be no suggestion therefore that immigration, in reasonable numbers, is a cross we have to bear, and no pretence that if only those who have come could find jobs back at home, our problems could be at an end. So far from this being the case, our doctor shortage would become still more chronic; many of our hospitals and institutions, particularly those performing tasks (like the care of the aged) which are medically unglamorous but socially essential, would have to close down; and our urban public transport systems would be reduced to skeleton services with mounting public inconvenience and a disastrous effect upon private car road congestion.

There is therefore no overall rational basis for resentment of the coloured immigrant population in our midst. Far from hindering our successful national development, they positively help it. But resentment does not always spring from rational causes, particularly when, as is the case with coloured immigrants, their skin and their cultural differences make them natural targets for those who are looking for scapegoats.

A few people, whether out of political opportunism or personal inadequacy, have deliberately whipped up prejudice, playing on fear and ignorance, and blaming the immigrants for problems which were none of their making -- but which stemmed from previous parsimony in housing, schools and welfare services. Of course there are some who have legitimate individual grievances against an immigrant, just as white men can have against white men, or black men against black men. But this is not the root of the problem. The root is community prejudice, and it is that with which, whether it springs from fear or inadequacy or less reputable motives, we have to deal.

I say *have to deal* because I am perfectly sure, first, that American experience, although it can sometimes be misleading in this field, shows clearly that this is not a problem which solves itself without positive action; and, secondly, because, unless we can solve it this will be a major blot on our record for the rest of this century, a constant source of weakness abroad, a handicap to full economic development . . .

The task which confronts us all is a crucial but not a daunting one. We have a population which is only two per cent coloured, although the proportion is of course appreciably higher in some areas. More important perhaps is the fact that we have as yet no established habit of hostility or bitterness on either side of the colour frontier. Such a habit could grow and grow quickly but it is hardly there yet. The problem is too new for that. We therefore start not indeed with a clean slate – there are already a few ugly marks upon it, but they are still relatively few.

But what we do have in this country is a great absorptive and adaptative tradition. For three centuries we have softened civil conflicts and adjusted our political system to the demands of a constantly changing economic and class structure. The problem we are discussing today makes less demands upon our capacity for tolerance and change than many which we have successfully surmounted in the past. But the way in which we face it, particularly in the next few years, can have a great effect upon our future. If we overcome we shall have a new message to offer the world. If we fail we shall be building up, both inside and outside the country, vast difficulties for future generations of English people.

•

ROBERT KENNEDY
Cape Town, 7 June 1966

'*A tiny ripple of hope*'

The address by Robert Kennedy (1925–68) to the National Union of South African Students' Day of Affirmation, an annual protest affirming the students' commitment to human liberty and academic freedom in the face of government oppression, was his finest speech.

As Attorney-General in his brother's administration, Robert Kennedy had championed civil rights for black Americans. After his election as Senator for New York in 1965, he began campaigning for the Democratic nomination for the presidency in 1968 and won wide support from the blacks and underprivileged.

His visit to South Africa was ignored by the Verwoerd government but there was pandemonium when Kennedy arrived at the University of Cape Town where he was greeted by a crowd of 18,000. An unlit Grecian torch, carried at the head of the procession, symbolized the fate of academic freedom in South Africa.

In a speech that skilfully placed the South African struggle for freedom in the context of the worldwide campaign to break down the barriers of nationality, race and class, Kennedy expressed his fundamental political philosophy. He spoke not only to the students of South Africa but to the youth of the world.

We stand here in the name of freedom.

At the heart of that Western freedom and democracy is the belief that the individual man, the child of God, is the touchstone of value and all society, groups, the state, exist for his benefit. Therefore the enlargement of liberty for individual human beings must be the supreme goal and the abiding practice of any Western society.

The first element of this individual liberty is the freedom of speech.

The right to express and communicate ideas, to set oneself apart from the dumb beasts of field and forest; to recall governments to their duties and obligations; above all, the right to affirm one's membership and allegiance to the body politic – to society – to the men with whom we share our land, our heritage and our children's future.

Hand in hand with freedom of speech goes the power to be heard – to share in the decisions of government which shape men's lives. Everything that makes life worthwhile – family, work, education, a place to rear one's children and a place to rest one's head – all this rests on decisions of government; all can be swept away by a government which does not heed the demands of its people. Therefore, the essential humanity of men can be protected and preserved only where government must answer – not just to those of a particular religion, or a particular race; but to all its people.

And even government by the consent of the governed, as in our own Constitution, must be limited in its power to act against its people: so that there may be no interference with the right to worship, or with the security of the home; no arbitrary imposition of pains or penalties by officials high or low; no restriction on the freedom of men to seek education or work or opportunity of any kind, so that each man may become all he is capable of becoming.

These are the sacred rights of Western society. These are the essential differences between us and Nazi Germany as they were between Athens and Persia.

They are the essence of our difference with Communism today. I am inalterably opposed to Communism because it exalts the state over the individual and the family, and because of the lack of freedom of speech, of protest, of religion and of the press, which is characteristic of totalitarian states.

The way of opposition to Communism is not to imitate its dictatorship, but to enlarge individual human freedom – in our own countries and all over the globe. There are those in every land who would label as 'Communist' every threat to their privilege. But as I have seen on my travels in all sections of the world, reform is not Communism. And the denial of freedom, in whatever name, only strengthens the very Communism it claims to oppose.

For two centuries, my own country has struggled to overcome the self-imposed handicap of prejudice and discrimination based on nationality, social class or race – discrimination profoundly repugnant to the theory and command of our Constitution. Even as my father grew up in Boston, signs told him that 'No Irish need apply.'

Two generations later President Kennedy became the first Catholic to head the nation; but how many men of ability had, before 1961, been denied the opportunity to contribute to the nation's progress because they were Catholic, or of Irish extraction.

In the last five years, the winds of change have blown as fiercely in the United States as anywhere in the world. But they will not — they cannot — abate.

For there are millions of Negroes untrained for the simplest of jobs, and thousands every day denied their full equal rights under the law; and the violence of the disinherited, the insulted and injured, looms over the streets of Harlem and Watts and Southside Chicago.

But a Negro American trains as an astronaut, one of mankind's first explorers into outer space; another is the chief barrister of the United States Government, and dozens sit on the benches of court; and another, Dr Martin Luther King, is the second man of African descent to win the Nobel Peace Prize for his nonviolent efforts for social justice between the races.

We must recognize the full human equality of all our people — before God, before the law, and in the councils of government. We must do this not because it is economically advantageous — although it is; not because the laws of God and man command it — although they do command it; not because people in other lands wish it so. We must do it for the single and fundamental reason that it is the right thing to do.

And this must be our commitment outside our borders as it is within.

It is your job, the task of the young people of this world, to strip the last remnants of that ancient, cruel belief from the civilization of man.

Each nation has different obstacles and different goals, shaped by the vagaries of history and experience. Yet as I talk to young people around the world I am impressed not by diversity but by the closeness of their goals, their desires and concerns and hope for the future. There is discrimination in New York, apartheid in South Africa and serfdom in the mountains of Peru. People starve in the streets in India; intellectuals go to jail in Russia; thousands are slaughtered in Indonesia; wealth is lavished on armaments everywhere. These are differing evils. But they are the common works of man.

And therefore they call upon common qualities of conscience and of indignation, a shared determination to wipe away the unnecessary sufferings of our fellow human beings at home and particularly around the world.

It is these qualities which make of youth today the only true international community. More than this I think that we could agree on what kind of a world we want to build. It would be a world of independent nations, moving towards international community, each of which protected and respected basic human freedoms. It would be a world which demanded of each government that it accept its responsibility to insure social justice.

Just to the north here are lands of challenge and opportunity – rich in natural resources, land and minerals and people. Yet they are also lands confronted by the greatest odds – overwhelming ignorance, internal tensions and strife, and an often destructive and hostile nature. Many of these nations, as colonies, were oppressed and exploited. Yet they have not estranged themselves from the broad traditions of the West; they are hoping and gambling their progress and stability on the chance that we will meet our responsibilities to help them overcome their poverty.

In another world, cleansed of hate and fear and artificial barriers, South Africa could play an outstanding role in that effort. This is without question a pre-eminent repository of the wealth and knowledge and skill of the continent. Here are the greater part of Africa's research scientists and steel production, most of its reservoirs of coal and electric power. In your faculties and councils, here in this very audience, are hundreds and thousands of men who could transform the lives of millions for all time to come.

But that help cannot be accepted if we – within our own countries or in our relations with others – deny individual integrity and the common humanity of man.

Our answer is the world's hope; it is to rely on youth. The cruelties and obstacles of this swiftly changing planet will not yield to obsolete dogmas and outworn slogans. It cannot be moved by those who cling to a present which is already dying, who prefer the illusion of security to the excitement of danger.

It demands the qualities of youth: not a time of life but a state of mind, a temper of the will, a quality of the imagination, a predominance of courage over timidity, of the appetite for adventure over the love of ease.

As I have seen, and as I have said – in Europe, in Asia, in Latin America, and now in South Africa – it is a revolutionary world we live in; and thus, I have said in Latin America, in Asia, in Europe and in the United States, it is young people who must take the lead.

'There is,' said an Italian philosopher, 'nothing more difficult to take in hand, more perilous to conduct, or more uncertain in its success than to take the lead in the introduction of a new order of things.' Yet this is the measure of the task of your generation and the road is strewn with many dangers.

First, is the danger of futility; the belief there is nothing one man or one woman can do against the enormous array of the world's ills – against misery and ignorance, injustice and violence. Yet many of the world's great movements of thought and action have flowed from the world of a single man. A young monk began the Protestant Reformation, a young general extended an empire from Macedonia to the borders of the earth and a young woman reclaimed the territory of France.

Each time a man stands up for an ideal, or acts to improve the lot of others, or strikes out against injustice, he sends forth a tiny ripple of hope, and crossing each other from a million different centres of energy and daring, those ripples build a current that can sweep down the mightiest walls of oppression and resistance.

The second danger is that of practicality; of those who say that hopes and beliefs must bend before immediate necessities. Of course if we would act effectively we must deal with the world as it is. We must get things done.

But if there was one thing President Kennedy stood for that touched the most profound feeling of young people across the world, it was the belief that idealism, high aspirations and deep convictions are not incompatible with the most practical and efficient of programmes – that there is no basic inconsistency between ideals and realistic possibilities – no separation between the deepest desires of heart and mind and the rational application of human effort to human problems.

A third danger is timidity. For every ten men who are willing to face the guns of an enemy there is only one willing to brave the disapproval of his fellow, the censure of his colleagues, the wrath of his society. Moral courage is a rarer commodity than bravery in battle or great intelligence. Yet it is the one essential, vital quality for those who seek to change a world which yields most painfully to change.

For the fortunate among us is comfort; the temptation to follow the easy and familiar paths of personal ambition and financial success so grandly spread before those who have the privilege of education. But that is not the road history has marked out for us.

There is a Chinese curse which says, 'May he live in interesting times.' Like it or not, we live in interesting times. They are times of danger and uncertainty; but they are also more open to the creative energy of men than any other time in history. And everyone here will ultimately be judged – will ultimately judge himself – on the effort he has contributed to building a new world society and the extent to which his ideals and goals have shaped that effort.

So we part, I to my country and you to remain. We are – if a man of forty can claim that privilege – fellow members of the world's largest younger generation. Each of us have our own work to do. I know at times you must feel very alone with your problems and difficulties. But I want to say how impressed I am with what you stand for and the effort you are making.

Like the young people of my own country and of every country I have visited, you are in many ways more closely united to these brothers of your time than to the older generations in your nation; determined to build a better future; that you know, as President Kennedy said to the youth of my country, that 'the energy, the faith, the devotion which we bring to this endeavour will light our country and all who serve it – and the glow from that fire can truly light the world.'

Robert Kennedy won a thundering ovation. Two years later, after winning the California primary election, he was shot and died on 6 June. On the stark white wall over his grave is carved a sentence from his South African speech: 'Each time a man stands up for an ideal, or acts to improve the lot of others, or strikes out against injustice, he sends forth a tiny ripple of hope.'

•

LYNDON B. JOHNSON
Washington, DC, 31 March 1968

'I shall not seek nor will I accept nomination as your president'

As America sank deeper into the quagmire of the Vietnam war in 1968, President Johnson was spiritually and physically exhausted. Television screens were filled with images of horror showing the devastation of Vietnam, the sufferings of its people and the sufferings of American soldiers.

On 20 January, the Vietcong launched the Tet offensive, which involved American troops in desperate battles for control of their bases at Da Nang and Khe Sanh and even the grounds of the US embassy in Saigon. Robert Kennedy and Eugene McCarthy were openly campaigning for the Democratic nomination for the presidential election. Johnson, who said in his memoirs that he had always intended to retire at the end of his first full term, read the signals.

He hoped that by suspending the bombing of North Vietnam he would open the way to peace negotiations and accepted that his candidacy would both split the Democrats further and weaken the United States' negotiating position.

Johnson prepared two perorations for his speech, given from the White House at the end of March. At 9.35 p.m. and well into his speech, his mind was made up. Watched by eighty-five million Americans, his face registering powerful emotions, he glanced at his wife and raised his right arm – the prearranged signal that he was going, after all, to speak the extra words that had been prepared.

Then the president looked into the camera. 'Fifty-two months and ten days ago . . .' he began, and gave up his burden.

Of those to whom much is given, much is asked. I cannot say and no man could say that no more will be asked of us.

Yet, I believe that now, no less than when the decade began, this generation of Americans is willing to 'pay any price, bear any burden, meet any hardship, support any friend, oppose any foe to assure the survival and the success of liberty.'

Since those words were spoken by John F. Kennedy, the people of America have kept that compact with mankind's noblest cause.

And we shall continue to keep it.

Yet, I believe we must always be mindful of this one thing, whatever the trials and the tests ahead. The ultimate strength of our country and our cause will lie not in powerful weapons or infinite resources or boundless wealth, but will lie in the unity of our people.

This I believe very deeply.

Throughout my entire public career I have followed the personal philosophy that I am a free man, an American, a public servant, and a member of my party, in that order always and only.

For thirty-seven years in the service of our Nation, first as a Congressman, as a Senator, and as Vice-President, and now as your President, I have put the unity of the people first. I have put it ahead of any divisive partisanship.

And in these times as in times before, it is true that a house divided against itself by the spirit of faction, of party, of region, of religion, of race, is a house that cannot stand.

There is division in the American house now. There is divisiveness among us all tonight. And holding the trust that is mine, as President of all the people, I cannot disregard the peril to the progress of the American people and the hope and the prospect of peace for all peoples.

So, I would ask all Americans, whatever their personal interests or concern, to guard against divisiveness and all its ugly consequences.

Fifty-two months and ten days ago, in a moment of tragedy and trauma, the duties of this office fell upon me. I asked then for your help and God's, that we might continue America on its course, binding up our wounds, healing our history, moving forward in new unity, to clear the American agenda and to keep the American commitment for all of our people.

United we have kept that commitment. United we have enlarged that commitment.

Through all time to come, I think America will be a stronger nation, a more just society, and a land of greater opportunity and fulfilment because of what we have all done together in these years of unparalleled achievement.

Our reward will come in the life of freedom, peace, and hope that our children will enjoy through ages ahead.

What we won when all of our people united just must not now be lost in suspicion, distrust, selfishness, and politics among any of our people.

Believing this as I do, I have concluded that I should not permit the Presidency to become involved in the partisan divisions that are developing in this political year.

With America's sons in the fields far away, with America's future under challenge right here at home, with our hopes and the world's hopes for peace in the balance every day, I do not believe that I should devote an hour or a day of my time to any personal partisan causes or to any duties other than the awesome duties of this office – the Presidency of your country.

Accordingly, I shall not seek, and I will not accept, the nomination of my party for another term as your President.

But let men everywhere know, however, that a strong, a confident, and a vigilant America stands ready tonight to seek an honourable peace – and stands ready tonight to defend an honoured cause – whatever the price, whatever the burden, whatever the sacrifice that duty may require.

Hubert Humphrey, Johnson's chosen successor, was narrowly defeated in the election by Richard Nixon.

•

ENOCH POWELL
Birmingham, 20 April 1968

'*I seem to see "the River Tiber foaming with much blood"*'

No speech in Britain in the past fifty years had so violent and powerful an impact on public opinion or was more notorious and memorable than the address Enoch Powell gave in Birmingham in 1968. It was one of a series of inflammatory speeches, initially attacking Kenyan Asian immigrants, which Powell's critics considered a particularly potent stimulus to racial antagonism but which nevertheless articulated the fears and prejudices of many Britons, particularly in working-class inner cities.

Once a professor of Greek and a former Conservative minister of health, Powell (1912–) had become a right-wing nationalist who had quarrelled violently with the Tory leader Edward Heath. Powell believed that the British Nationality Act had enabled the arrival of a big immigrant population with consequences so long ignored that when it was no longer possible for the government and parliament to remain blind to them they had become all but irremediable.

In this speech in April, Powell openly raised the spectre of racial conflict and called for the repatriation of black and other Commonwealth immigrants.

The supreme function of statesmanship is to provide against preventable evils. In seeking to do so, it encounters obstacles which are deeply rooted in human nature. One is that by the very order of things such evils are not demonstrable until they have occurred: at each stage in their onset there is room for doubt and for dispute whether they be real or imaginary. By the same token, they attract little attention in comparison with current troubles, which are both indisputable and pressing. Hence the besetting temptation of all politics to concern itself with the immediate present at the expense of the future. Above all, people are disposed to mistake predicting troubles for causing troubles and even for desiring troubles: 'if only', they love to think, 'if only people wouldn't talk about it, it probably wouldn't happen'. Perhaps this habit goes back to the primitive belief that the word and the thing, the name and the object, are identical. At all events, the discussion of future grave but, with effort now, avoidable evils is the most unpopular and at the same time the most necessary occupation for the politician. Those who knowingly shirk it, deserve, and not infrequently receive, the curses of those who come after.

A week or two ago I fell into conversation with a constituent, a middle-aged, quite ordinary working man employed in one of our nationalized industries. After a sentence or two about the weather, he suddenly said: 'If I had the money to go, I wouldn't stay in this country.' I made some deprecatory reply, to the effect that even this government wouldn't last for ever; but he took no notice, and continued: 'I have three children, all of them been through grammar school and two of them married now, with family. I shan't be satisfied till I have seen them all settled overseas. In this country in fifteen or twenty years' time the black man will have the whip hand over the white man.'

I can already hear the chorus of execration. How dare I say such a horrible thing? How dare I stir up trouble and inflame feelings by repeating such a conversation? The answer is that I do not have the right not to do so. Here is a decent, ordinary fellow-Englishman, who in broad daylight in my own town says to me, his Member of Parliament, that this country will not be worth living in for his children. I simply do not have the right to shrug my shoulders and think about something else. What he is saying, thousands and hundreds of thousands are saying and thinking – not throughout Great Britain, perhaps, but in the areas that are already undergoing the total transformation to which there is no parallel in a thousand years of English history.

In fifteen or twenty years, on present trends, there will be in this country three and a half million Commonwealth immigrants and their descendants. That is not my figure. That is the official figure given to Parliament by the spokesman of the Registrar-General's office. There is no comparable official figure for the year 2000; but it must be in the region of five to seven million, approximately one-tenth of the whole population, and approaching that of Greater London. Of course, it will not be evenly distributed from Margate to Aberystwyth and from Penzance to Aberdeen. Whole areas, towns and parts of towns across England will be occupied by different sections of the immigrant and immigrant-descended population.

As time goes on, the proportion of this total who are immigrant descendants, those born in England, who arrived here by exactly the same route as the rest of us, will rapidly increase. Already by 1985 those born here would constitute the majority. It is this fact above all which creates the extreme urgency of action now, of just that kind of action which is hardest for politicians to take, action where the difficulties lie in the present but evils to be prevented or minimized lie several parliaments ahead.

The natural and rational first question for a nation confronted by such a prospect is to ask: 'How can its dimensions be reduced?' Granted it be not wholly preventable, can it be limited, bearing in mind that numbers are of the essence. The significance and consequences of an alien element introduced into a country or population are profoundly different according to whether that element is one per cent or ten per cent. The answers to the simple and rational question are equally simple and rational: by stopping, or virtually stopping, further inflow, and by promoting the maximum outflow. Both answers are part of the official policy of the Conservative Party.

It almost passes belief that at this moment twenty or thirty additional immigrant children are arriving from overseas in Wolverhampton alone every week – and that means fifteen or twenty additional families a decade or two hence. Those whom the gods wish to destroy, they first make mad. We must be mad, literally mad, as a nation to be permitting the annual inflow of some fifty thousand dependants, who are for the most part the material of the future growth of the immigrant-descended population. It is like watching a nation busily engaged in heaping up its own funeral pyre. So insane are we that we actually permit unmarried persons to immigrate for the purpose of founding a family with spouses and fiancés whom they have never seen. Let no one suppose that the flow of dependants will automatically tail off. On the contrary, even at the present admission rate of only five thousand a year by voucher, there is sufficient for a further twenty-five thousand dependants per annum *ad infinitum*, without taking into account the huge reservoir of existing relations in this country – and I am making no allowance at all for fraudulent entry. In these circumstances nothing will suffice but that the total inflow for settlement be reduced at once to negligible proportions, and that the necessary legislative and administrative measures be taken without delay. I stress the words 'for settlement'. This has nothing to do with the entry of Commonwealth citizens, any more than of aliens, into this country, for the purposes of study or of improving their qualifications, like (for instance) the Commonwealth doctors who, to the advantage of their own countries, have enabled our hospital service to be expanded faster than would otherwise have been possible. These are not, and never have been, immigrants.

I turn to re-emigration. If all immigration ended tomorrow, the rate of growth of the immigrant-descended population would be substantially reduced, but the prospective size of this element in the population would still leave the basic character of the national danger unaffected. This can only be tackled while a considerable proportion of the total still comprises persons who entered this country during the last ten years or so. Hence the urgency of implementing now the second element of the Conservative Party's policy: the encouragement of re-emigration. Nobody can make an estimate of the numbers which, with generous grants and assistance would choose either to return to their countries of origin or go to other countries anxious to receive the manpower and the skills they represent. Nobody knows, because no such policy has yet been attempted. I can only say that, even at present, immigrants in my own constituency from time to time come to me, asking if I can find them assistance to return home. If such a policy were adopted and pursued, with the determination which the gravity of the alternative justifies, the resultant outflow could appreciably alter the prospects for the future.

It can be no part of any policy that existing families should be kept divided; but there are two directions in which families can be reunited, and if our former and present immigration laws have brought about the division of families, albeit voluntary or semi-voluntary, we ought to be prepared to arrange for them to be reunited in their countries of origin. In short, suspension of immigration and encouragement of re-emigration belong together, logically and humanly, as two aspects of the same approach.

The third element of the Conservative Party's policy is that all who are in this country as citizens should be equal before the law and that there shall be no discrimination or difference made between them by public authority. As Mr Heath has put it, we will have no 'first-class citizens' and 'second-class citizens'. This does not mean that the immigrant and his descendants should be elevated into a privileged or special class or that the citizen should be denied his right to discriminate in the management of his own affairs between one fellow-citizen and another or that he should be subjected to inquisition as to his reasons and motives for behaving in one lawful manner rather than another.

There could be no grosser misconception of the realities than is entertained by those who vociferously demand legislation as they call it 'against discrimination', whether they be leaderwriters of the same kidney and sometimes on the same newspapers which year after year in the 1930s tried to blind this country to the rising peril which confronted it, or archbishops who live in palaces, faring delicately, with the bedclothes pulled right over their heads. They have got it exactly and diametrically wrong. The discrimination and the deprivation, the sense of alarm and of resentment, lies not with the immigrant population but with those among whom they have come and are still coming. This is why to enact legislation of the kind before Parliament at this moment is to risk throwing a match on to gunpowder. The kindest thing that can be said about those who propose and support it is that they know not what they do.

Nothing is more misleading than comparison between the Commonwealth immigrant in Britain and the American negro. The negro population of the United States, which was already in existence before the United States became a nation, started literally as slaves and were later given the franchise and other rights of citizenship, to the exercise of which they have only gradually and still incompletely come. The Commonwealth immigrant came to Britain as a full citizen, to a country which knew no discrimination between one citizen and another, and he entered instantly into the possession of the rights of every citizen, from the vote to free treatment under the National Health Service. Whatever drawbacks attended the immigrants – and they were drawbacks which did not, and do not, make admission into Britain by hook or by crook appear less than desirable – arose not from the law or from public policy or from administration but from those personal circumstances and accidents which cause, and always will cause, the fortunes and experience of one man to be different from another's.

But while to the immigrant entry to this country was admission to privileges and opportunities eagerly sought, the impact upon the existing population was very different. For reasons which they could not comprehend, and in pursuance of a decision by default, on which they were never consulted, they found themselves made strangers in their own country. They found their wives unable to obtain hospital beds in childbirth, their children unable to obtain school places, their homes and neighbourhoods changed beyond recognition, their plans and prospects for the future defeated; at work they found that employers hesitated to apply to the immigrant worker the standards of discipline and competence required of the native-born worker; they began to hear, as time went by, more and more voices which told them that they were now the unwanted. On top of this, they now learn that a one-way privilege is to be established by Act of Parliament: a law, which cannot, and is not intended, to operate to protect them or redress their grievances, is to be enacted to give the stranger, the disgruntled and the *agent provocateur* the power to pillory them for their private actions.

The other dangerous delusion from which those who are wilfully or otherwise blind to realities suffer, is summed up in the word 'integration'. To be integrated into a population means to become for all practical purposes indistinguishable from its other members. Now, at all times, where there are marked physical differences, especially of colour, integration is difficult, though over a period, not impossible. There are among the Commonwealth immigrants who have come to live here in the last fifteen years or so, many thousands whose wish and purpose is to be integrated and whose every thought and endeavour is bent in that direction. But to imagine that such a thing enters the heads of a great and growing majority of immigrants and their descendants is a ludicrous misconception, and a dangerous one to boot.

We are on the verge of a change. Hitherto it has been force of circumstance and of background which has rendered the very idea of integration inaccessible to the greater part of the immigrant population – that they never conceived or intended such a thing, and that their numbers and physical concentration meant the pressures towards integration which normally bear upon any small minority did not operate. Now we are seeing the growth of positive forces acting against integration, of vested interests in the preservation and sharpening of racial and religious differences, with a view to the exercise of actual domination, first over fellow-immigrants and then over the rest of the population. The cloud no bigger than a man's hand, that can so rapidly overcast the sky, has been visible recently in Wolverhampton and has shown signs of spreading quickly. The words I am about to use, verbatim as they appeared in the local press of 17 February [1968], are not mine, but those of a Labour Member of Parliament who is a Minister in the Government. 'The Sikh community's campaign to maintain customs inappropriate in Britain is much to be regretted. Working in Britain, particularly in the public services, they should be prepared to accept the terms and conditions of their employment. To claim special communal rights (or should one say rites?) leads to a dangerous fragmentation within society. This communalism is a canker; whether practised by one colour or another it is to be strongly condemned.' All credit to John Stonehouse for having had the insight to perceive that, and the courage to say it.

For these dangerous and divisive elements the legislation proposed in the Race Relations Bill is the very pabulum they need to flourish. Here is the means of showing that the immigrant communities can organize to consolidate their members, to agitate and campaign against their fellow-citizens, and to overawe and dominate the rest with legal weapons which the ignorant and the ill-informed have provided. As I look ahead, I am filled with foreboding. Like the Roman, I seem to see 'the River Tiber foaming with much blood'. The tragic and intractable phenomenon which we watch with horror on the other side of the Atlantic but which there is interwoven with the history and existence of the States itself, is coming upon us here by our own volition and our own neglect. Indeed, it has all but come. In numerical terms, it will be of American proportions long before the end of the century. Only resolute and urgent action will avert it even now. Whether there will be the public will to demand and obtain that action, I do not know. All I know is that to see, and not to speak, would be the great betrayal.

After the uproar provoked by the speech, Powell was disowned by Tory leader Edward Heath – but in the East End of London dockers and immigration officers from Heathrow airport marched on behalf of Powell's views. The Race Relations Act, introducing measures against discrimination on grounds of race, colour or ethnic or national origin, became law the following November.

•

RICHARD NIXON
Miami, 8 August 1968

'The time has come for an honest government'

Richard Nixon (1913–) was General Eisenhower's vice-president but lost the presidential battle narrowly to John F. Kennedy in 1960. Two years later he failed to become Governor of California, ascribing his defeat to the hostility of the media. His political career seemed over. Yet the Republican disaster of 1964, when Goldwater lost to Lyndon Johnson, encouraged Nixon's supporters to run him for the presidency in 1968 and he gained the nomination.

Nixon declared that his nomination address was designed to let his audience see the whole man. After his years in the political wilderness, the speech was the most important of Nixon's political life and was made even as news of the violence in the Miami ghetto was starting to filter out. Nixon cribbed an oratorical device from Martin Luther King. I have a dream, said King. I see a day, declared Nixon.

As we look at America, we see cities enveloped in smoke and flame. We hear sirens in the night. We see Americans dying on distant battlefields abroad. We see Americans hating each other; fighting each other; killing each other at home.

And as we see and hear these things, millions of Americans cry out in anguish: Did we come all this way for this? Did American boys die in Normandy and Korea and in Valley Forge for this?

Listen to the answers to those questions.

It is another voice, it is a quiet voice in the tumult of the shouting. It is the voice of the great majority of Americans, the forgotten Americans, the nonshouters, the nondemonstrators. They're not racists or sick; they're not guilty of the crime that plagues the land; they are black, they are white; they're native born and foreign born; they're young and they're old.

They work in American factories, they run American businesses.

They serve in government; they provide most of the soldiers who die to keep it free. They give drive to the spirit of America. They give lift to the American dream. They give steel to the backbone of America.

They're good people. They're decent people; they work and they save and they pay their taxes and they care.

Like Theodore Roosevelt, they know that this country will not be a good place for any of us to live in unless it's a good place for all of us to live in . . .

America's in trouble today not because her people have failed, but because her leaders have failed. And what America needs are leaders to match the greatness of her people.

And this great group of Americans – the forgotten Americans and others – know that the great question Americans must answer by their votes in November is this: Whether we shall continue for four more years the policies of the last five years.

And this is their answer, and this is my answer to that question. When the strongest nation in the world can be tied down for four years in a war in Vietnam with no end in sight, when the richest nation in the world can't manage its own economy, when the nation with the greatest tradition of the rule of law is plagued by unprecedented lawlessness, when a nation that has been known for a century for equality of opportunity is torn by unprecedented racial violence, and when the President of the United States cannot travel abroad or to any major city at home without fear of a hostile demonstration – then it's time for new leadership for the United States of America.

My fellow Americans, tonight I accept the challenge and the commitment to provide that new leadership for America and I ask you to accept it with me.

And let us accept this challenge not as a grim duty but as an exciting adventure in which we are privileged to help a great nation realize its destiny and let us begin by committing ourselves to the truth, to see it like it is and tell it like it is, to find the truth, to speak the truth and to live the truth. That's what we will do.

We've had enough of big promises and little action. The time has come for an honest government in the United States of America.

My fellow Americans, I believe that historians will recall that 1968 marked the beginning of the American generation in world history. Just to be alive in America, just to be alive at this time is an experience unparalleled in history. Here's where the action is.

Think: Thirty-two years from now most of Americans living today will celebrate a New Year that comes once in a thousand years.

Eight years from now, in the second term of the next President, we will celebrate the 200th anniversary of the American Revolution.

And by our decision in this we – all of us here, all of you listening on television and radio – we will determine what kind of nation America will be on its 200th birthday. We will determine what kind of a world America will live in in the year 2000.

This is the kind of day I see for America on that glorious Fourth eight years from now: I see a day when Americans are once again proud of their flag; when once again at home and abroad it is honoured as the world's greatest symbol of liberty and justice.

I see a day when the President of the United States is respected and his office is honoured because it is worthy of respect and worthy of honour. I see a day when every child in this land, regardless of his background, has a chance for the best education that our wisdom and schools can provide, and an equal chance to go just as high as his talents will take him . . .

Government can provide opportunity, but opportunity means nothing unless people are prepared to seize it.

A President can ask for reconciliation in the racial conflict that divides Americans, but reconciliation comes only from the hearts of people.

And tonight, therefore, as we make this commitment, let us look into our hearts, and let us look down into the faces of our children.

Is there anything in the world that should stand in their way?

None of the old hatreds mean anything when you look down into the faces of our children. In their faces is our hope, our love and our courage.

Tonight, I see the face of a child. He lives in a great city, he's black or he's white, he's Mexican, Italian, Polish, none of that matters. What matters: he's an American child.

That child in that great city is more important than any politician's promise. He is America, he is a poet, he is a scientist, he's a great teacher, he's a proud craftsman, he's everything we've ever hoped to be in everything we dare to dream about.

He sleeps the sleep of a child, and he dreams the dreams of a child. And yet when he awakens, he awakens to a living nightmare of poverty, neglect and despair.

He fails in school, he ends up on welfare. For him the American system is one that feeds his stomach and starves his soul. It breaks his heart. And in the end it may take his life on some distant battlefield.

To millions of children in this rich land this is their prospect, but this is only part of what I see in America.

I see another child tonight. He hears a train go by. At night he dreams of faraway places where he'd like to go. It seems like an impossible dream. But he is helped on his journey through life. A father who had to go to work before he finished the sixth grade sacrificed everything he had so that his sons could go to college.

A gentle Quaker mother with a passionate concern for peace quietly wept when he went to war but she understood why he had to go.

A great teacher, a remarkable football coach, an inspirational minister encouraged him on his way. A courageous wife and loyal children stood by him in victory and also in defeat.

And in his chosen profession of politics, first there were scores, then hundreds, then thousands, and finally millions who worked for his success.

And tonight he stands before you, nominated for President of the United States of America.

You can see why I believe so deeply in the American dream.

For most of us the American revolution has been won, the American dream has come true. What I ask of you tonight is to help me make that dream come true for millions to whom it's an impossible dream today.

•

BETTY FRIEDAN
Chicago, 1969

'A woman's civil right'

A forty-two-year-old housewife and mother of three shocked American social structures to the core in 1963 when she published The Feminine Mystique, *the best seller that launched the modern women's movement. Betty Friedan (1921–) contended that deeply entrenched attitudes and social barriers imprisoned women in a 'housewife trap'. She called for expanded career opportunities, equality with men and set out to destroy the myth of the happy housewife. Some women burned their bras; others cast off their aprons – or their husbands.*

'I did not set out consciously to start a revolution when I wrote The Feminine Mystique,' *Friedan wrote later, 'but it changed my life, as a woman and as a writer, and other women tell me it changed theirs.' She went on to become the first president of the National Organization of Women and Founder of the National Women's Political Caucus.*

At the first national conference for repeal of abortion laws, Betty Friedan gave this powerful speech proclaiming abortion as a woman's civil right.

Women, even though they're almost too visible as sex objects in this country, are invisible people. As the Negro was the invisible man, so women are the invisible people in America today: women who have a share in the decisions of the mainstream of government, of politics, of the church – who don't just cook the church supper, but preach the sermon; who don't just look up the ZIP codes and address the envelopes, but make the political decisions; who don't just do the housework of industry, but make some of the executive decisions. Women, above all, who say what their own lives and personalities are going to be, and no longer listen to or even permit male experts to define what 'feminine' is or isn't.

The essence of the denigration of women is our definition as sex object. To confront our inequality, therefore, we must confront both society's denigration of us in these terms and our own self-denigration as people.

Am I saying that women must be liberated from sex? No. I am saying that sex will only be liberated to be a human dialogue, sex will only cease to be a sniggering, dirty joke and an obsession in this society, when women become active self-determining people, liberated to a creativity beyond motherhood, to a full human creativity.

Am I saying that women must be liberated from motherhood? No. I am saying that motherhood will only be a joyous and responsible human act when women are free to make, with full conscious choice and full human responsibility, the decisions to become mothers. Then, and only then, will they be able to embrace motherhood without conflict, when they will be able to define themselves not just as somebody's mother, not just as servants of children, not just as breeding receptacles, but as people for whom motherhood is a freely chosen part of life, freely celebrated while it lasts, but for whom creativity has many more dimensions, as it has for men.

Then, and only then, will motherhood cease to be a curse and a chain for men and for children. For despite all the lip service paid to motherhood today, all the roses sent on Mother's Day, all the commercials and the hypocritical ladies' magazines' celebration of women in their roles as housewives and mothers, the fact is that all television or night-club comics have to do is go before a microphone and say the words 'my wife,' and the whole audience erupts into gales of guilty, vicious and obscene laughter.

The hostility between the sexes has never been worse. The image of women in avant-garde plays, novels and movies, and behind the family situation comedies on television is that mothers are man-devouring, cannibalistic monsters, or else Lolitas, sex objects – and objects not even of heterosexual impulse, but of sadomasochism. That impulse – the punishment of women – is much more of a factor in the abortion question than anybody ever admits.

Motherhood is a bane almost by definition, or at least partly so, as long as women are forced to be mothers – and only mothers – against their will. Like a cancer cell living its life through another cell, women today are forced to live too much through their children and husbands (they are too dependent on them, and therefore are forced to take too much varied resentment, vindictiveness, inexpressible resentment and rage out on their husbands and children).

Perhaps it is the least understood fact of American political life: the enormous buried violence of women in this country today. Like all oppressed people, women have been taking their violence out on their own bodies, in all the maladies with which they plague the MDs and the psychoanalysts. Inadvertently, and in subtle and insidious ways, they have been taking their violence out, too, on their children and on their husbands, and sometimes they're not so subtle.

The battered-child syndrome that we are hearing more and more about from our hospitals is almost always to be found in the instance of unwanted children, and women are doing the battering, as much or more than men. In the case histories of psychologically and physically maimed children, the woman is always the villain, and the reason is our definition of her: not only as passive sex object, but as mother, servant, someone else's mother, someone else's wife.

Am I saying that women have to be liberated from men? That men are the enemy? No. I am saying the *men* will only be truly liberated to love women and to be fully themselves when women are liberated to have a full say in the decisions of their lives and their society.

Until that happens, men are going to bear the guilty burden of the passive destiny they have forced upon women, the suppressed resentment, the sterility of love when it is not between two fully active, joyous people, but has in it the element of exploitation. And men will not be free to be all they can be as long as they must live up to an image of masculinity that disallows all the tenderness and sensitivity in a man, all that might be considered feminine. Men have enormous capacities in them that they have to repress and fear in order to live up to the obsolete, brutal, bear-killing, Ernest Hemingway, crew-cut Prussian, napalm-all-the-children-in-Vietnam, bang-bang-you're-dead image of masculinity. Men are not allowed to admit that they sometimes are afraid. They are not allowed to express their own sensitivity, their own need to be passive sometimes and not always active. Men are not allowed to cry. So they are only half-human, as women are only half-human, until we can go this next step forward. All the burdens and responsibilities that men are supposed to shoulder alone makes them, I think, resent women's pedestal, much as that pedestal may be a burden for women.

This is the real sexual revolution. Not the cheap headlines in the papers about at what age boys and girls go to bed with each other and whether they do it with or without the benefit of marriage. That's the least of it. The real sexual revolution is the emergence of women from passivity, from the point where they are the easiest victims for all the seductions, the waste, the worshiping of false gods in our affluent society, to full self-determination and full dignity. And it is the emergence of men from the stage where they are inadvertent brutes and masters to sensitive, complete humanity.

This revolution cannot happen without radical changes in the family as we know it today; in our concepts of marriage and love, in our architecture, our cities, our theology, our politics, our art. Not that women are special. Not that women are superior. But these expressions of human creativity are bound to be infinitely more various and enriching when women and men are allowed to relate to each other beyond the strict confines of the *Ladies' Home Journal*'s definition of the Mamma and Papa marriage.

If we are finally allowed to become full people, not only will children be born and brought up with more love and responsibility than today, but we will break out of the confines of that sterile little suburban family to relate to each other in terms of all of the possible dimensions of our personalities – male and female, as comrades, as colleagues, as friends, as lovers. And without so much hate and jealousy and buried resentment and hypocrisies, there will be a whole new sense of love that will make what we call love on Valentine's Day look very pallid.

It's crucial, therefore, that we see this question of abortion as more than a quantitative move, more than a politically expedient move. Abortion repeal is not a question of political expediency. It is part of something greater. It is historic that we are addressing ourselves this weekend to perhaps the first national confrontation of women and men. Women's voices are finally being heard aloud, saying it the way it is about the question of abortion both in its most basic sense of morality and in its new political sense as part of the unfinished revolution of sexual equality.

In this confrontation, we are making an important milestone in this marvelous revolution that began long before any of us here were born and which still has a long way to go. As the pioneers from Mary Wollstonecraft to Margaret Sanger gave us the consciousness that brought us from our several directions here, so we here, in changing the very terms of the debate on abortion to assert woman's right to choose, and to define the terms of our lives ourselves, move women further to full human dignity. Today, we moved history forward . . .

•

EDWARD HEATH
London, 28 October 1971

'Millions will rejoice'

Edward Heath (1910–), who became British prime minister in 1970, had always been a strong supporter of British entry into the European Common Market. The

Schuman plan for a European Iron and Steel Commission was the subject of his
maiden speech in 1950. He had been Britain's chief negotiator when Harold
Macmillan tried to join the Common Market in 1961 but was foiled by Charles
de Gaulle, the French president.

Negotiations to join the Common Market began again as soon as Heath became
prime minister. There were crucial talks with de Gaulle's successor, Georges
Pompidou, in May 1971 which removed many of the obstacles to British member-
ship.

When the House of Commons debated the decision of principle of whether to
apply for membership in October 1971, both the Labour and Tory parties were
split. Heath made the concluding speech of the great debate which marked a
decisive turning-point in British history.

I have sometimes felt that among those who have been in this
debate seeking to balance up the advantages and disadvantages
there was a desire for a degree of certainty which is never obtain-
able in human affairs. Hon. Members will not ask for it in their
lives, in their own businesses. As a nation we have never hitherto asked for it in a trading agreement or in international affairs,
either economic or political. Anyone who studies the length of
our trading agreements outside will accept that that is the
case . . .

It is understandable after ten years of negotiation and frustration
that many in debate and many in the country outside have fought
and talked in terms of 'we' and 'they'. Some, I think, have been
overwhelmed by a fear that this country in an organization such as
the Community must always be dominated by 'they'. That is
certainly not how the rest of the Community sees it. But we are
approaching the point where, if this House so decides tonight, it
will become just as much our Community as their Community.
We shall be partners, or shall be cooperating, and we shall be
trying to find common solutions to common problems of all the
members of an enlarged Community.

We have confidence that we can benefit as well as contribute,
that we can further our own interests and the interests of the
Community at one and the same time. After all, the leaders of all

three parties in this House accept the principle of entry into the European Community, as the Right Hon. Gentleman reaffirmed this afternoon. The Community is not governed by any particular party ideology. How can it be, with a Socialist Government in the Federal Republic, with a Right-wing Government in France, with a coalition in Italy containing Socialists? Of course not. What is more, all the opposition parties in the member countries of the Community support membership of the Community just as much as the governing parties . . .

Surely we must consider the consequences of staying out. We cannot delude ourselves that an early chance would be given us to take the decision again. We should be denying ourselves and succeeding generations the opportunities which are available to us in so many spheres; opportunities which we ourselves in this country have to seize. We should be leaving so many aspects of matters affecting our daily lives to be settled outside our own influence. That surely cannot be acceptable to us. We should be denying to Europe, also – let us look outside these shores for a moment – its full potential, its opportunities of developing economically and politically, maintaining its security, and securing for all its people a higher standard of prosperity.

All the consequences of that for many millions of people in Europe must be recognized tonight in the decision the House is taking. In addition, many projects for the future of Europe have been long delayed. There has been great uncertainty, and tonight all that can be removed – (*Hon. Members:* 'No.')

Throughout my political career it is well known that I have had the vision of a Britain in a united Europe; a Britain which would be united economically to Europe and which would be able to influence decisions affecting our own future, and which would enjoy a better standard of life and a fuller life. I have worked for a Europe which will play an increasing part in meeting the needs of those parts of the world which still lie in the shadow of want . . . I want Britain as a member of a Europe which is united politically, and which will enjoy lasting peace and the greater security which would ensue.

Nor do I believe that the vision of Europe – and the Right Hon. Gentleman raised this specific point – is an unworthy vision, or an ignoble vision or an unworthy cause for which to have worked – (*Interruption.*) I have always made it absolutely plain to the British people that consent to this course would be given by Parliament – (*Hon. Members: 'Resign.'*) Parliament is the Parliament of all the people.

When we came to the end of the negotiations in 1963, after the veto had been imposed, the negotiator on behalf of India said:

> When you left India some people wept. And when you leave Europe tonight some will weep. And there is no other people in the world of whom these things could be said.

That was a tribute from the Indian to the British. But tonight when this House endorses this Motion many millions of people right across the world will rejoice that we have taken our rightful place in a truly united Europe.

Sixty-seven Labour MPs defied the party whip and voted with the Tories. Another twenty abstained. Acceptance of applying for entry to Europe was passed by a majority of 112. The European Community Bill passed through the Commons in 1972 by seventeen votes. Britain became a member of the European Economic Community on 1 January 1973.

●

HAROLD EVANS
London, 4 March 1974

'A press which is half free'

Under the editorship of Harold Evans (1928–), the Sunday Times *of London became one of the world's greatest campaigning newspapers, particularly during its long fight for compensation for the children who were born deformed after their mothers took the drug Thalidomide during pregnancy. There is no*

American First Amendment in Britain and Evans constantly sought to extend the frontiers of journalistic investigation, often coming into conflict with the restrictions of the English law. The British constantly proclaim the virtues of their 'free press', but in this lecture, sponsored by Granada Television and given in the historic setting of London's ancient Guildhall, Evans compared the situations of British and American newspapers and concluded that the British press was only half free.

Our philosophy and, in turn, our law and our attitudes have been conditioned to defend free speech rather than free inquiry ... We have a press which is half free, I believe, because its needs and the needs of the society it serves have outgrown a philosophy rooted in the simpler virtues of free expression. Reality today requires ethical justification for free inquiry and for unimpeded publication of fact rather than of opinion. The Americans already have a phrase: The Right to Know. It is almost un-English, for we rely on the liberal defence of free expression so memorably bequeathed to us by Milton, Locke and Mill.

Truth is good for men, and truth will emerge if all discussion is submitted to the powerful test of the reason of the rational man. Free expression is a natural right for human dignity and happiness. You know that. I agree with it too but it is not enough. The ethic is too much centred on the rights of free speech, too much concerned with the individual's opinions. This is understandable, historically. Much of last century's newspaper was a pamphlet of opinions rather than a journal of news. It was invective, not investigation, that got the early newspapers into trouble and needed to be justified. George III clapped John Wilkes in the Tower for his diatribe not for his documents. Even some of the greatest utterances by newspapermen have been powered by a defence of free opinion. 'The first duty of the Press is to obtain the earliest and most correct intelligence of the events of the time, and instantly, by disclosing them to make them the common property of the nation.' Every copy-boy knows of the famous words of *The Times* of 6 February 1852, attributed to Delane, but written in fact by Robert Lowe and Henry Reeve. Often editors get the credit for things they do not really write, and sometimes the blame . . .

But it was not, as might appear from a paraphrase, called for in defence of some right of investigation and disclosure. What had happened was that Lord Derby had attacked *The Times* for its *opinions* on Louis Napoleon. 'It is incumbent on the Press', he said, 'to maintain that tone of moderation and respect even in expressing frankly their opinions on foreign affairs which would be required of every man who pretends to guide public opinion.' Statesmen, it said, deal mainly with rights and interests; the press with opinions and sentiments.

It was just seven years after the *Times* leader that John Stuart Mill said that the government or a popular majority should not be permitted 'to prescribe opinions' to the public or to determine 'what doctrines or what arguments they shall be allowed to hear'.

The peculiar evil which robbed the human race, was 'silencing the expression of an opinion'. It was on this basis that an independent press erected its defences for the next one hundred years. Every word of what Mill said stands today but the modern press cannot survive or achieve full freedom simply by arguing from the classical virtues of free speech. There will not be a murmur of dissent about John Stuart Mill from men and women who daily, in government, law and all centres of power restrict the flow of information or stamp 'confidential' on the documents. They believe in freedom of speech as passionately as any journalist. What they have not perceived or been convinced of is that only with the freest flow of facts is freedom of opinion of much value. The assumption of Mill and the Liberals was that there was a free flow of intelligence just as the classical economists assumed a perfect market and free competition. Nobody wrote about guaranteeing the free flow of information. It was, for one thing, an infinitely smaller problem. Government and security were less complex. In the newspapers the élite simply argued with the élite.

Today the press must be sustained by what it does for society, this very different society, rather than by simply what it does for

the soul of the individual. It certainly remains for the press a virtue
to ventilate opinion. Concentration of control imposes on us today
duties of greater access for the public so that we escape the jibe of
Huey Long about Henry Luce: 'The owner of *Time* Magazine',
said Long, 'is like the owner of a shoe shop who stocks only the
shoes to fit *hisself*.' But it is not by diversity of opinion that the
press can defend its claims. It is by its interpretation and description
of reality, and it is in this area that we in Britain are so bedevilled.
We all of us live in what Walter Lippmann called 'an invisible
environment' – a world where without a great continuing flow of
information we are blind and defenceless. We can see and understand our visible world of home and neighbourhood; but we
cannot without a free press know of the planning decision which
will bring a motorway through the back garden; or the circumstances why our children are not learning to read properly; or why
a quarrel in the Middle East should stop our machinery and
darken our homes. Governments as well as citizens need a free
and inquiring press. With a volatile, pluralistic electorate, and a
complex bureaucracy, a free press provides an indispensable
feedback system from governed to the governing, from consumers
to producers, from the regions to the centre, and not least from
one section of the bureaucracy to another . . .

Governments cannot govern well without reliable reporting
and criticism. They do not have the knowledge. No intelligence
system, no bureaucracy, can offer the information provided by
competitive reporting; the cleverest secret agents of the police
state are inferior to the plodding reporter of the democracy. It is
one of the strengths of society with a competent and plural system
of free communication that feedback happens automatically. Every
political lawyer and bureaucrat understands this about trade, that
the feedback of customers exercising choice is a corrective
mechanism for the manufacturer. Every politician and bureaucrat
professes to believe it about government, but in office persuades
himself that the limitations of information he imposes or accepts
are imperceptible or necessary for national security, relations with
foreign governments, the preservation of the latest coalitions.

As William Haley once said, everybody believes in freedom of information until it runs into his own vested interest, whether he be a Minister or a trade-union leader, or a bishop or the secretary of a professional body. But concealment corrodes the chance of creating confidence between governed and governing, manager and managed. It induces alienation. People come to identify the state or local government not with themselves, but with something remote and incomprehensible. Secrecy creates anxieties and suspicions that outweigh any temporary convenience . . . The suffocation that results from habits of secrecy and suppression is not generally realized by people who do not have to deal with them every day of their lives. I believe it underlies some of the divisions and some of the muddle we experience. The press, of course, is the object of some popular suspicion.

There are certainly exaggerated ideas about our powers. Newspapers have no more rights than the ordinary citizen. We are not detectives with rights of search. We are not civil servants with powers under regulations to know about anybody's property, income or family. We are not Parliamentarians with rights to summon witnesses and to protection for our privileges. We do not seek all these rights. But we would certainly like to be relieved of some of the restraints based on the exercise of an ordinary citizen's rights to know . . .

If I am right about the proper role of the Press today, there is a failing on two sides, for it has to be acknowledged that there is a shortcoming in our press performance in the way we live up to the doctrine of social responsibility I sketched earlier. It was during years of neglect by all the mainland British press that the seeds of violence were sown in Ulster. Part of our weakness has been due to the philosophy of free speech we picked up, part to our slow emergence from, in Walter Lippmann's phrase, a minor craft to an underdeveloped profession. But we have, I think, made strides and are too often blamed for the excesses of a different time. We need now to develop the intellectual and moral disciplines of a profession. If we dig more diligently we must not devalue so-called routine reporting. We cannot claim greater access if we

ignore what is available or diminish its worth because it is not
half-concealed. We must not allow our necessary scepticism to
degenerate into cynicism. We cannot claim our rights simply as
entertainers, though boring we do not want to be. We cannot
claim them if we intrude too many of our own views. We must
always correct error; but at the same time we must resist the ideas
that only the perfect press is entitled to be free. The right to be
free means the right to be free.

Harold Evans became editor of The Times *in 1981 but left a year later after
falling out with Rupert Murdoch, whose News International had bought the paper
from the Canadian Thomson Organization. He became editorial director of US
News and World Report and, later, publisher of Random House in New
York.*

•

RICHARD NIXON
Washington, DC, 9 August 1974

'*Au revoir*'

*The Watergate scandal arose after employees of a Republican Party organization
were caught seeking to remove bugging devices from the Democratic Party campaign
headquarters in the Watergate apartment block in 1972. As the scandal grew,
mainly because of the reporting of the* Washington Post, *it became clear that
Richard Nixon had secretly taped all conversations in his White House office.
Many also became convinced that he was either implicated in illegal activities or so
abnormally suspicious that he was not fit to be president.*

*Steps were taken to secure his removal by impeachment – but Nixon became the
first United States president to resign from office. Gerald Ford, his successor,
gave him a comprehensive pardon.*

As he left the White House, Nixon made this speech to the staff.

You are here to say goodbye to us, and we don't have a good word
for it in English – the best is *au revoir*. We will see you again . . .

Sure, we have done some things wrong in this Administration, and the top man always takes the responsibility, and I have never ducked it. But I want to say one thing: We can be proud of it — five and a half years. No man or no woman came into this Administration and left it with more of this world's goods than when he came in. No man or no woman ever profited at the public expense or the public till. That tells something about you.

Mistakes, yes. But for personal gain, never. You did what you believed in. Sometimes right, sometimes wrong. And I only wish that I were a wealthy man — at the present time, I have got to find a way to pay my taxes — (*laughter*) — and if I were, I would like to recompense you for the sacrifices that all of you have made to serve in government.

But you are getting something in government — and I want you to tell this to your children, and I hope the Nation's children will hear it, too — something in government service that is far more important than money. It is a cause bigger than yourself. It is the cause of making this the greatest nation in the world, the leader of the world, because without our leadership, the world will know nothing but war, possibly starvation or worse, in the years ahead. With our leadership it will know peace, it will know plenty . . .

We think sometimes when things happen that don't go the right way; we think that when you don't pass the bar exam the first time — I happened to, but I was just lucky; I mean, my writing was so poor the bar examiner said, 'We have just got to let the guy through.' We think that when someone dear to us dies, we think that when we lose an election, we think that when we suffer a defeat that all is ended.

Not true. It is only a beginning, always. The young must know it; the old must know it. It must always sustain us, because the greatness comes not when things go always good for you, but the greatness comes and you are really tested, when you take some knocks, some disappointments, when sadness comes, because only if you have been in the deepest valley can you ever know how magnificent it is to be on the highest mountain.

MARGARET THATCHER
Brighton, 10 October 1975

'Let me give you my vision'

Margaret Thatcher (1925–) became the first woman leader of the Conservative Party when she beat Edward Heath in the leadership ballot of February 1975. Her election marked a significant shift within the party towards a more radical version of Toryism and away from the consensual centrism of the Keynesian mixed-economy policies of the previous thirty years. Monetarism, denationalisation, tax cuts and control of the money supply were the policies that were soon to be espoused.

She set out the new Thatcherite political stall in her first speech as leader to the Conservative Party conference and was greeted by rolling breakers of cheers, shouts and foot-stamping. The speech had a difficult birth. Sir Ronald Millar, her principal speechwriter, has described how it was not finished until ten past five on the morning it was to be delivered as Mrs Thatcher sought a peroration that satisfied her. 'Oh no! No, that won't do at all,' she said at one stage. 'Sorry, what's wrong with it?' 'It's just not me, dear.'

Whenever I visit Communist countries their politicians never hesitate to boast about their achievements. They know them all by heart; they reel off the facts and figures, claiming this is the rich harvest of the Communist system. Yet they are not prosperous as we in the West are prosperous, and they are not free as we in the West are free.

Our capitalist system produces a far higher standard of prosperity and happiness because it believes in incentive and opportunity, and because it is founded on human dignity and freedom. Even the Russians have to go to a capitalist country – America – to buy enough wheat to feed their people – and that after more than fifty years of a State-controlled economy. Yet they boast incessantly, while we, who have so much more to boast about, for ever criticize and decry. Is it not time we spoke up for our way of life?

After all, no Western nation has to build a wall round itself to keep its people in.

So let us have no truck with those who say the free-enterprise system has failed. What we face today is not a crisis of capitalism but of Socialism. No country can flourish if its economic and social life is dominated by nationalization and State control.

The cause of our shortcomings does not, therefore, lie in private enterprise. Our problem is not that we have too little Socialism. It is that we have too much. If only the Labour Party in this country would act like Social Democrats in West Germany. If only they would stop trying to prove their Socialist virility by relentlessly nationalizing one industry after another.

Of course, a halt to further State control will not on its own restore our belief in ourselves, because something else is happening to this country. We are witnessing a deliberate attack on our values, a deliberate attack on those who wish to promote merit and excellence, a deliberate attack on our heritage and our great past, and there are those who gnaw away at our national self-respect, rewriting British history as centuries of unrelieved gloom, oppression and failure – as days of hopelessness, not days of hope. And others, under the shelter of our education system, are ruthlessly attacking the minds of the young ... blatant tactics of intimidation designed to undermine the fundamental beliefs and values of every student, tactics pursued by people who are the first to insist on their own civil rights while seeking to deny them to the rest of us.

We must not be bullied or brainwashed out of our beliefs. No wonder so many of our people, some of the best and the brightest, are depressed and talking of emigrating. Even so, I think they are wrong. They are giving up too soon. Many of the things we hold dear are threatened as never before, but none has yet been lost, so stay here, stay and help us defeat Socialism so that the Britain you have known may be the Britain your children will know.

These are the two great challenges of our time – the moral and political challenge, and the economic challenge. They have to be faced together and we have to master them both.

What are our chances of success? It depends on what kind of people we are. What kind of people are we? We are the people that in the past made Great Britain the workshop of the world, the people who persuaded others to buy British, not by begging them to do so but because it was best.

We are a people who have received more Nobel Prizes than any other nation except America, and head for head we have done better than America, twice as well in fact.

We are the people who, among other things, invented the computer, the refrigerator, the electric motor, the stethoscope, rayon, the steam turbine, stainless steel, the tank, television, penicillin, radar, the jet engine, hovercraft, float glass and carbon fibres, et cetera – and the best half of Concorde.

We export more of what we produce than either West Germany, France, Japan or the United States, and well over ninety per cent of these exports come from private enterprise. It is a triumph for the private sector and all who work in it, and let us say so loud and clear.

With achievements like that who can doubt that Britain can have a great future, and what our friends abroad want to know is whether that future is going to happen.

Well, how can we Conservatives make it happen?

Let me give you my vision: a man's right to work as he will, to spend what he earns, to own property, to have the State as servant and not as master – these are the British inheritance. They are the essence of a free country and on that freedom all our other freedoms depend.

But we want a free economy, not only because it guarantees our liberties, but also because it is the best way of creating wealth and prosperity for the whole country, and it is this prosperity alone which can give us the resources for better services for the community, better services for those in need.

By their attack on private enterprise, this Labour Government has made certain that there will be next to nothing available for improvements in our social services over the next few years. We must get private enterprise back on the road to recovery, not merely to give people more of their own money to spend as they choose, but to have more money to help the old and the sick and the handicapped. And the way to recovery is through profits, good profits today leading to high investment, leading to well-paid jobs, leading to a better standard of living tomorrow. No profits mean no investment and that means a dying industry geared to yesterday's world, and that means fewer jobs tomorrow.

Some Socialists seem to believe that people should be numbers in a State computer. We believe they should be individuals. We are all unequal. No one, thank heavens, is quite like anyone else, however much the Socialists may pretend otherwise. We believe that everyone has the right to be unequal. But to us, every human being is equally important. Engineers, miners, manual workers, shop assistants, farmworkers, postmen, housewives – these are the essential foundations of our society, and without them there would be no nation. But there are others with special gifts who should also have their chance, because if the adventurers who strike out in new directions in science, technology, medicine, commerce and industry are hobbled, there can be no advance. The spirit of envy can destroy; it can never build. Everyone must be allowed to develop the abilities he knows he has within him, and she knows she has within her, in the way they choose.

Freedom to choose is something we take for granted until it is in danger of being taken away. Socialist Governments set out perpetually to restrict the area of choice, and Conservative Governments to increase it. We believe that you become a responsible citizen by making decisions for yourself, not by having them made for you. But they are made for you by Labour all right!

•

MICHAEL FOOT
Blackpool, 29 September 1976

'*The red flame of Socialist courage*'

Michael Foot (1913–) is one of the great dissenters and romantics of British politics, a man whose heroes are Swift, Hazlitt and Byron and who

identifies with the Levellers as well as Cromwell and Whigs as well as nonconform-
ists. According to the British historian Kenneth O. Morgan, he embodies a
powerful creative thrust of popular radicalism that has been constant in British
public life for two centuries.

Foot is also a magnificent orator, at his best when defying and denouncing
Tories and defending his beloved Labour Party against the slurs and sneers of
its opponents. After years as a rebel on the left wing of the Party, he became
Secretary of State for Employment in Harold Wilson's third government in
1974.

Trade-unionists were angry with the Labour government in 1976. It was
dealing with an inflation rate of twenty per cent and the unions were opposing
government intervention in collective wage bargaining and wanted utterly to reject
statutory incomes control.

On the first day of the Labour Party conference, Foot, for many years the
idol of the conference as the bitterest critic of official policies but now a cabinet
minister, made a dramatic appeal to the conference to endorse the Wilson govern-
ment's anti-inflation policy. If they failed to support the government's policy, he
said in a passionate speech, they could bring about the end of the Labour govern-
ment.

No one is less surprised than myself that this Conference has been
dominated, and will continue to be dominated in my judgement,
by the rising anxieties and fears and anger of our people about
unemployment up and down this country . . . Unemployment on this
level is totally unacceptable to the Labour Movement. Of course,
our unemployment is part of an affliction affecting the whole
Western world; the Western world is gripped by the most complex
and perilous recession which we have seen since 1945. It is indeed,
in my judgement, a crisis of Capitalism of a most formidable
character, and we have to muster all our energies, all our skill, to
deal with it.

Let me start therefore by telling you what is my deepest instinct
about the whole of this situation; it is of first importance for our
country, and no less for our Labour Movement, that this crisis
should be faced and surmounted by a Labour Government acting
in the closest alliance and good faith with the trade-union move-

ment of this country. (*Applause.*) If we were to fall apart, I shudder to think what would be the consequences for our people, for our young people and old alike, in unemployment and in all the other associated consequences. I shudder to think also what would be the consequence for our democratic institutions themselves. It is only three or four years ago that a Conservative Government used the opportunity which we gave them after 1970 to introduce the most insidious attack on trade unionism in this country which we have seen in this century.

If we were ever fools enough to allow them to get the levers of power again, the whips would be changed to scorpions for our chastisement. Let us not make any mistake about that . . .

People sometimes say: we will agree to some arrangement between the Government and the trade unions about wages, but only when you have the full panoply of Socialist measures actually put into full operation. I understand the argument, but I say it is unworkable. There is not a single Government in the world aspiring to change society that could work upon that system of transition, whether it is Communist, Maoist, Yugoslav, anything. Of course you could not work on that basis, and so I say, for anyone to argue that there shall be no concession to a Labour Government on these measures until all the other measures are in operation, that is not merely a recipe for the destruction of this Labour Government, it is a recipe for the destruction of any Labour Government. That has to be faced, too.

I am very glad that this Conference is going to be dominated also by the demand for new systems of investment, in the National Enterprise Board and the planning agreements and all the other matters that we have discussed and which we have had in our Party programmes. Of course, that is of paramount importance. But do not let anybody imagine that investment is a soft option. Investment is not a soft option. You can learn it from *Das Kapital* as well as from anywhere else, and I hope I will not be convicted for that. You can read it all there. Investment means very often, almost always, forgoing present claims in order to have future benefits. And you can do it by not so many methods. You can do it by the brutal capitalist methods of the nineteenth century, or you can do it by the equally brutal, or maybe even more outrageous, methods of twentieth-century Stalinism, or you can do it by the politics of persuasion, by the Social Contract. You can do it that way. You can do it the democratic way, which is the heart and soul of our Labour Movement, and always has been. And it is that method by which we are going to seek for our success.

We must face the crisis, beat the inflation, start the regeneration of British industry, lift this scourge of unemployment from our people. This is what we must do. It is the greatest summons that has come to our Labour Party in the seventy-five years of its existence.

We face an economic typhoon of unparalleled ferocity, the worst the world has seen since the 1930s. Joseph Conrad wrote a book called *Typhoon*, and at the end he told people how to deal with it. He said, 'Always facing it, Captain McWhirr: that's the way to get through.' Always facing it, that is the way we have got to solve this problem. We do not want a Labour Movement that tries to dodge it; we do not want people in a Labour Cabinet to try to dodge it. We want people who are prepared to show how they are going to face it, and we need the united support of the Labour Movement to achieve it.

I believe that we can make this Conference one of the greatest in our history, not by stifling dissent or criticism or debate, however ferociously the criticisms may be put: of course not. Indeed, there would not be any life left in this Party if it had not been for those prepared to come along and advocate sometimes unpopular opinions and stand up for them, and discover that those unpopular opinions sometimes became accepted. So I am not asking for any dull uniformity or anything of the sort. I am asking this Movement to exert itself as it has never done before, to show the qualities which we have, the Socialist imagination that exists in our Movement, the readiness to re-forge the alliance, stronger than ever, between the Government and the trade unions, and above all to show the supreme quality in politics, the red flame of Socialist courage. That is what we have got to do to save our country, and that is what can come from this Conference. (*Applause. A standing ovation.*)

When Harold Wilson resigned in 1976, James Callaghan defeated Michael Foot for the leadership of the Labour Party and became prime minister. Foot became leader of the House of Commons and succeeded Callaghan in 1980 as leader of the party which had been defeated in the 1979 general election by Margaret Thatcher. Foot was beaten by Margaret Thatcher in the election of 1983. He retired from the House of Commons in 1992.

•

ALEXANDER SOLZHENITSYN
Cambridge, Massachusetts, 8 June 1978

'*What is the joy about?*'

After serving in the Red Army and being decorated for bravery during the Second World War, Alexander Solzhenitsyn (1919–) was sent to a labour camp from 1945 to 1953 after making critical remarks about Stalin in letters to a friend. He was then sent into exile in Siberia until 1956.

One Day in the Life of Ivan Denisovich, *his novel exposing the misery of Stalin's 'gulags', was published in 1962 and approved by Khrushchev. His experience of the gulags also inspired* Cancer Ward, The First Circle *and* The Gulag Archipelago, *all of which were banned.*

Although Solzhenitsyn was awarded the Nobel Prize for Literature in 1970, he was harangued in the Soviet press, charged with treason and sent into exile in 1974 after The Gulag Archipelago *was published in the West.*

As this speech at Harvard University's annual commencement ceremony demonstrated, Solzhenitsyn did not trumpet his gratitude to the West. Instead he denounced a Western way of life that he saw as spoilt, silly and empty of spiritual values.

A decline in courage may be the most striking feature which an outside observer notices in the West today. The Western world has lost its civic courage, both as a whole and separately, in each country, in each government, in each political party and, of course, in the United Nations. Such a decline in courage is particularly noticeable among the ruling and intellectual élites, causing an impression of a loss of courage by the entire society. There remain many courageous individuals, but they have no determining influence on public life. Political and intellectual functionaries exhibit this depression, passivity and perplexity in their actions and in their statements, and even more so in their self-serving rationales as to how realistic, reasonable and intellectually and even morally justified it is to base state policies on weakness and cowardice . . .

Must one point out that from ancient times a decline in courage has been considered the beginning of the end? . . .

When the modern Western states were being formed, it was proclaimed as a principle that governments are meant to serve man and that man lives in order to be free and pursue happiness. (See, for example, the American Declaration of Independence.) Now at last during past decades technical and social progress has permitted the realization of such aspirations: the welfare state. Every citizen has been granted the desired freedom and material goods in such quantity and of such quality as to guarantee in theory the achievement of happiness, in the debased sense of the word which has come into being during those same decades. (In the process, however, one psychological detail has been overlooked: the constant desire to have still more things and a still better life, and the struggle to this end imprints many Western faces with worry and even depression, though it is customary to carefully conceal such feelings. This active and tense competition comes to dominate all human thought and does not in the least open a way to free spiritual development.) The individual's independence from many types of state pressure has been guaranteed; the majority of the people have been granted well-being to an extent their fathers and grandfathers could not even dream about; it has become possible to raise young people according to these ideals, preparing them for and summoning them towards physical bloom, happiness, possession of material goods, money and leisure, towards an almost unlimited freedom in the choice of pleasures. So who should now renounce all this, why and for the sake of what should one risk one's precious life in defence of the common good, and particularly in the nebulous case when the security of one's nation must be defended in an as yet distant land?

Even biology tells us that a high degree of habitual well-being is not advantageous to a living organism. Today, well-being in the life of Western society has begun to reveal its pernicious mask . . .

Should I be asked whether I would propose the West, such as it is today, as a model to my country, I would frankly have to answer negatively. No, I could not recommend your society as an ideal for the transformation of ours. Through deep suffering, people in our country have now achieved a spiritual development of such intensity that the Western system in its present state of spiritual exhaustion does not look attractive. Even those characteristics of your life which I have just enumerated are extremely saddening.

A fact which cannot be disputed is the weakening of human personality in the West, while in the East it has become firmer and stronger. Six decades for our people and three decades for the people of Eastern Europe; during that time we have been through a spiritual training far in advance of Western experience. The complex and deadly crush of life has produced stronger, deeper and more interesting personalities than those generated by standardized Western well-being. Therefore, if our society were to be transformed into yours, it would mean an improvement in certain aspects, but also a change for the worse on some particularly significant points. Of course, a society cannot remain in an abyss of lawlessness as is the case in our country. But it is also demeaning for it to stay on such a soulless and smooth plane of legalism as is the case in yours. After the suffering of decades of violence and oppression, the human soul longs for things higher, warmer and purer than those offered by today's mass living habits, introduced as by a calling card by the revolting invasion of commercial advertising, by TV stupor and by intolerable music.

All this is visible to numerous observers from all the worlds of our planet. The Western way of life is less and less likely to become the leading model.

There are telltale symptoms by which history gives warning to a threatened or perishing society. Such are, for instance, a decline of the arts or a lack of great statesmen. Indeed, sometimes the warnings are quite explicit and concrete. The centre of your democracy and of your culture is left without electric power for a few hours only, and all of a sudden crowds of American citizens start looting and creating havoc. The smooth surface film must be very thin, then, the social system quite unstable and unhealthy.

But the fight for our planet, physical and spiritual, a fight of cosmic proportions, is not a vague matter of the future; it has already started. The forces of Evil have begun their decisive offensive; you can feel their pressure, yet your screens and publications are full of prescribed smiles and raised glasses. What is the joy about?

Solzhenitsyn was pardoned in 1991, after the collapse of the Soviet Union.

•

JAMES CALLAGHAN
Brighton, 5 September 1978

'I have promised nobody'

As Chancellor of the Exchequer, Home Secretary and then Foreign Secretary, James Callaghan (1912–) was a dominating minister in Harold Wilson's three governments. He spoke for the heartland of the Labour movement and was custodian of its traditional values. When Harold Wilson resigned in 1976, he beat Michael Foot for the leadership of the Labour Party and became prime minister of a minority government.

As the autumn of 1978 approached, he was widely expected to announce a general election in October and there was no better platform on which to launch the campaign than the annual meeting of the Trades Union Congress. He gave a manifesto speech, but then started teasing his audience, departing from his prepared text to sing: 'There was I, waiting at the church . . .'

This was his peroration, which still left his decision unknown, but which made a withering denunciation of Margaret Thatcher.

I have promised nobody that I shall be at the altar in October, nobody at all. So all I want to add this afternoon is that I certainly intend to indicate my intentions very shortly on this matter. When I do so I shall do it in the belief that people have come to trust that this Government does not flatter in its actions now to deceive later. We do not cut corners when the national interest is at stake. We are ready to argue out honest differences with our friends openly and without bitterness. The Government will fight for what we believe to be in the best interests of the country and our people, even if it is not instantly popular. Let others stoop if they must to scapegoat politics. So the unions are a convenient whipping boy. So are the coloured immigrants. So is expenditure on welfare. In Scotland last week the leader of the Conservative Party even turned the word 'entitlement' into a matter for scorn. Well, I am the first to insist that our responsibilities and our obligations to one another are as important as our rights, but I never expected, even from this hard, uncaring, abrasive Conservative leadership that we have today, that the word 'entitlement' could be twisted to beat the poorest and the neediest in our society.

So here and now I serve notice that we shall match tolerance against prejudice, policies against slogans, cooperation against conflict, unity against racialism and sectarian divisions: that we will not tolerate policies that would require the sick to pay if they go to visit their doctor or spend time in hospital; or policies that would endanger people's jobs by simple-minded theories.

Two days later Callaghan startled the nation by announcing in a party political broadcast that he had decided against an election. It was a fateful decision. There was a winter of discontent, symbolized by undug graves, closed schools and overflowing dustbins, as the unions fought against pay restraint. When

Callaghan was forced to call an election in 1979 after losing a confidence vote in the House of Commons, he was defeated by Margaret Thatcher, who went on to win the next two elections.

•

ROY JENKINS
London, 22 November 1979

'Home Thoughts from Abroad'

The 1979 Dimbleby Lecture, broadcast annually by the BBC in memory of the great broadcaster Richard Dimbleby, helped to change the course of British politics.

Roy Jenkins had resigned as the Labour government's Home Secretary in 1976 to prepare for his appointment as president of the European Economic Community commission and had left the Labour Party. He used the opportunity of the Dimbleby Lecture to voice his disenchantment with the warring ideologies of the two main British political parties and offered the hope of a new party of the centre based on European models.

Jenkins offers in his memoirs a fascinating insight into the hard work of writing such a speech. His first attempt at composition occurred on 14 August and by 15 October he had a text, nearly sufficient to fill the forty-eight minutes required. But it was not right. 'It was far too long and leisurely on historical analysis and not nearly strong enough on prescription.' On 1 November he wrote from 9.15 a.m. to 1.00 and then from 3.15 to 8.15 p.m. and had a comprehensive text, about fifteen hundred words too long.

Six days later he read a tautened and typed version through during a train journey and did a run-through of the full text at a BBC studio on 12 November. He then continued to titivate the lecture in Brussels until he had to seal it up for the release of copies to the press.

On the day of the lecture, he also made three speeches in Brussels before departing for London.

A few decades ago there were quite a lot of people who believed that a single election victory could be the beginning of the millennium. It was a view perhaps more prevalent, because of greater optimism or utopianism, on the Left than on the Right. It was certainly held by many Labour supporters in 1945. More recently, however, I have the impression that it applies equally or more strongly on the Right.

A governing party must have the self-confidence to want power and to believe that its exercise of it can tilt the country in the right direction. But it should also have the humility to recognize on any likely projection of the past, its power will come to an end, probably in about six years, maybe less, only exceptionally more. The test of its statesmanship in the context of history will not therefore be how many trees it pulls up by the roots but how it fits into a continuous process of adaptation in which leadership is combined with sensitivity to national mood . . .

This is not a recipe for inaction or for the avoidance of controversy. Some of the most bitterly contested measures of the past 150 years – the electoral reform bills, the repeal of the Corn Laws, the curbing of the powers of the House of Lords, the initiation of social security, or, to take an example from the Right, the setting up of independent television – have been inviolate once they were on the statute book because they quickly became part of the social fabric and could only have been undone at the cost of unacceptable electoral damage to the opposing party.

All this implies a certain respect by politicians for the opinions of their opponents. But that is surely both possible and desirable. In their memoirs, written with the benignity of old age, it generally comes through. Indeed, where bitterness remains, it is more often directed against previous colleagues than against previous opponents.

Yet when they are seeking or exercising power there is only too often a shrill and unconvincing attempt to portray almost everyone on the other side as either a fool or a knave. Each successive Tory government is the most reactionary since that of Lord Liverpool, or some other hobgoblin figure shrouded in the past. Each successive Labour government has been the most rapacious, doctrinaire and unpatriotic conspiracy to be seen this side of the Iron Curtain. Either might, I suppose, be true in the future, but it cannot all have been true in the past, and I do not believe that it either convinces or pleases the electorate.

One major disadvantage of excessive political partisanship is that it fosters precisely the sort of industrial mood which is rapidly turning Britain into a manufacturing desert. If, on the House of Commons floor, it is always the fault of the other side, how can politicians preach convincingly against the prevalence of such a mood on the shop-floor?

This, some people will say with horror, is an unashamed plea for the strengthening of the political centre. Why not? The vocation of politicians ought to be to represent, to channel, to lead the aspirations of the electorate. These aspirations, not on every issue, but in essential direction, pull far more towards the centre than towards the extremes. The general mood is not that of reaction or of putting the clock back. But nor is it one of support for class selfishness or for revolution, whether it be utopian or malevolent.

Our great failure, now for decades past, has been lack of adaptability. Sometimes this rigidity is a source of strength. It was very good not to be too adaptable in 1940. But overall it is a source of weakness. Some societies – France in the second half of the Third Republic, pre-revolutionary Russia, the Austro-Hungarian Empire – have been still less adaptable than our own. But they hardly provide grounds for comfort. Compared with post-war Germany, post-war Japan, Fifth Republican France (industrially at least), the United States for virtually the whole of its history, compared for that matter with early Victorian Britain – modern Britain has been sluggish, uninventive and resistant to voluntary change, not merely economically but socially and politically as well. We cannot successfully survive unless we can make our society more adaptable; and an unadaptable political system works heavily against this. Politicians cannot cling defensively to their present somewhat ossified party and political system while convincingly advocating the acceptance of change everywhere else in industry and society. 'Everybody change but us' is never a good slogan.

The paradox is that we need more change accompanied by more stability of direction. It is a paradox but not a contradiction. Too often we have superficial and quickly reversed political change without much purpose or underlying effect. This is not the only paradox. We need the innovating stimulus of the free-market economy without either the unacceptable brutality of its untrammelled distribution of rewards or its indifference to unemployment. This is by no means an impossible combination. It works well in a number of countries. It means that you accept the broad line of division between the public and the private sectors and do not constantly threaten those in the private sector with nationalization or expropriation.

You encourage them without too much interference to create as much wealth as possible, but use the wealth so created both to give a return for enterprise and to spread the benefits throughout society in a way that avoids the disfigurement of poverty, gives a full priority to public education and health services, and encourages cooperation and not conflict in industry and throughout society. You use taxation for this purpose, but not just to lop off rewards. The state must know its place, which should be an important but far from an omnipotent one. You recognize that there are certain major economic objectives, well beyond merely regulatory ones like the control of the money supply, which can only be achieved by public action, often on an international scale. Two clear contemporary examples are first the breaking of the link, now fairly long-standing, but by no means inevitable, between economic growth and the consumption of oil; and second, by coordinated government purchasing policy, ensuring that this country and Europe as a whole is a major producer and not merely a passive purchaser of the products of the electronic/telecommunications revolution. Success or failure on these two points will largely determine whether we with our partners are a leading or second-rate industrial group in the world of the 1990s. You use market forces to help achieve such objectives but do not for a moment pretend that they, unguided and unaided, can do the whole job.

You also make sure that the state knows its place, not only in relation to the economy, but in relation to the citizen. You are in favour of the right of dissent and the liberty of private conduct. You are against unnecessary centralization and bureaucracy. You want to devolve decision-making wherever you sensibly can. You want parents in the school system, patients in the health service, residents in the neighbourhood, customers in both nationalized and private industry, to have as much say as possible. You want the nation to be self-confident and outward-looking, rather than insular, xenophobic and suspicious. You want the class system to fade without being replaced either by an aggressive and intolerant proletarianism or by the dominance of the brash and selfish values of a 'get rich quick' society. You want the nation, without eschewing necessary controversy, to achieve a renewed sense of cohesion and common purpose.

These are some of the objectives which I believe could be assisted by a strengthening of the radical centre. I believe that such a development could bring into political commitment the energies of many people of talent and goodwill who, although perhaps active in many other voluntary ways, are at present alienated from the business of government, whether national or local, by the sterility and formalism of much of the political game. I am sure this would improve our politics. I think the results might also help to improve our national performance. But of that I cannot be certain. I am against too much dogmatism here. We have had more than enough of it. But at least we could escape from the pessimism of Yeats's 'Second Coming', where

> The best lack all conviction, while the worst
> Are full of passionate intensity

and

> Things fall apart; the centre cannot hold.

Two Saturdays later both Shirley Williams and Bill Rodgers, who with

*Jenkins were to be three of the Gang of Four who founded the Social
Democratic Party in 1981, visited Jenkins. Neither had been frightened off by
the lecture and both were prepared in certain circumstances to break with the
Labour Party.*

*Jenkins's lecture proved to be the single most important event in placing
on the agenda for serious discussion the idea of a new party in the middle
ground of British politics; it was a seminal text of what a new party could stand
for.*

*After the SDP was formed, initially with Jenkins as leader, it subsequently
entered an alliance with the Liberal Party – and the alliance briefly threatened
to overtake the Labour Party and become the dominant party of opposition to
the Tories. After the 1987 general election, the SDP faded away and many
members joined a new Liberal Democrat Party. But the threat from the alliance
transformed the Labour Party, whose policies became similar to those that
Jenkins espoused in his Dimbleby Lecture.*

•

EDWARD KENNEDY
New York, 12 August 1980

'The dream shall never die'

*Senator Edward Kennedy's campaign for president in 1980 ended when he was
decisively beaten by President Jimmy Carter at the Democrat convention. Yet
although Carter won the nomination, it was Kennedy (1932–) who made the best
speech and who got the loudest cheers when he and Carter appeared together on the
platform.*

*On the day after his defeat, Kennedy brought the convention alive with
a brilliant defence of the Democrats' traditional policies, a scathing attack
on Ronald Reagan, and a moving and defiant statement of the Kennedys'
faith.*

There were hard hours on our journey, and often we sailed
against the wind. But always we kept our rudder true, and there
were so many of you who stayed the course and shared our

hope. You gave your help; but even more, you gave your hearts.

Because of you, this has been a happy campaign. You welcomed Joan, me and our family into your homes and neighbourhoods, your churches, your campuses, your union halls. When I think back of all the miles and all the months and all the memories, I think of you. I recall the poet's words, and I say: What golden friends I have.

Among you, my golden friends across this land, I have listened and learned.

I have listened to Kenny Dubois, a glassblower in Charleston, West Virginia, who has ten children to support but has lost his job after thirty-five years, just three years short of qualifying for his pension . . .

I have listened to the grandmother in East Oakland who no longer has a phone to call her grandchildren because she gave it up to pay the rent on her small apartment.

I have listened to young workers out of work, to students without the tuition for college, and to families without the chance to own a home. I have seen the closed factories and the stalled assembly lines of Anderson, Indiana and South Gate, California, and I have seen too many, far too many idle men and women desperate to work. I have seen too many, far too many working families desperate to protect the value of their wages from the ravages of inflation.

Yet I have also sensed a yearning for new hope among the people in every state where I have been. And I have felt it in their handshakes, I saw it in their faces, and I shall never forget the mothers who carried children to our rallies. I shall always remember the elderly who have lived in an America of high purpose and who believe that it can all happen again.

Tonight, in their name, I have come here to speak for them. And for their sake, I ask you to stand with them. On their behalf I ask you to restate and reaffirm the timeless truth of our party.

I congratulate President Carter on his victory here. (*Applause*.)

I am confident that the Democratic Party will reunite on the basis of Democratic principles, and that together we will march towards a Democratic victory in 1980. (*Applause.*)

And someday, long after this convention, long after the signs come down, and the crowds stop cheering, and the bands stop playing, may it be said of our campaign that we kept the faith. May it be said of our party in 1980 that we found our faith again.

And may it be said of us, both in dark passages and in bright days, in the words of Tennyson that my brothers quoted and loved, and that have special meaning for me now: 'I am a part of all that I have met/Tho' much is taken, much abides/That which we are, we are –/One equal temper of heroic hearts/strong in will/ To strive, to seek, to find, and not to yield.'

For me, a few hours ago, this campaign came to an end. For all those whose cares have been our concern, the work goes on, the cause endures, the hope still lives, and the dream shall never die.

•

MICHAEL HESELTINE
Blackpool, 15 October 1981

'We are reaping the whirlwind of all our yesterdays'

As Secretary of State for the Environment in Margaret Thatcher's first government, Michael Heseltine (1933–), one of the outstanding orators of the contemporary British Tory Party, was charged with studying the problems of Merseyside, the region around the declining seaport of Liverpool, after the summer riots of 1980. Heseltine always sat uncomfortably in Thatcher governments: he still believed in what had become the unfashionable view that state intervention could help to reverse decades of decline in Britain's inner cities.

Speaking to the Conservative conference a year later, he made an impassioned call that Conservative politics must deny rioters and wreckers any fertile ground to sow the seeds of discontent. He appealed to the one-nation doctrines of

Disraeli and Iain Macleod that had kept the Tory Party in the forefront of British politics. Self-help (the Thatcherite creed) had a limited meaning in an inner-city community where forty per cent of young kids were without work, he declared.

Then he moved into the main thrust of his speech.

I come from South Wales. This nation is still suffering from the legacies, from the folklore and from the memories of those bitter inter-war years. They have fuelled a venom in the Labour Party and in the trade unions that has set back our industrial society almost beyond redemption.

This is the great challenge for our party, for we alone believe in politics as a process of healing, of drawing together and of building together on common strengths. There is not a person here who has not cheered to the echo the great names, the great phrases that secured for·our party a well-nigh incredible record of governing Britain over so long a period.

It required great courage when Disraeli first talked of one nation. It did not represent a conventional view of the time. It flew in the teeth of much that was contemporary experience. But he led the Tory Party through the great traumas of his day because he, in advance of his time, had the vision to lead in his time. Today we cheer the memory of that man. When I joined this party Iain Macleod was a deeply controversial politician, fighting against bitter criticism to keep us close to those same traditions of compassion and tolerance. Those traditions are not ours to squander or abuse. For a brief time they are entrusted to us to make relevant in today's world. They are the traditions that have kept our party in the forefront of British politics in the centre of power.

In our generation we must show the same courage and vision as the leaders whose memories we so frequently applaud. What talk of equality of opportunity? What do those words actually mean in the inner cities today? What do they mean to the black communities? We now have large immigrant communities in British cities. Let this party's position be absolutely clear. They are British. They live here. They vote here. However tight the immigration legislation – and in everyone's interests it should be tight – there will be a large black community in this country tomorrow, just as there is today. There are no schemes of significant repatriation that have any moral, social or political credibility.

I will and I do condemn the handful of blacks who rioted. But I condemn just as strongly the whites who rioted alongside them. I totally support the police in their brave and unenviable task of restoring stability in our society.

But the rioters were a tiny section of the black and white populations, the overwhelming majority of whom deplore the riots as vehemently as we do. But the fact remains that of those black communities, who stand for the same values that I have described, far too many – our people – know that the education they obtain, the jobs they are offered and the careers that are opened to them do not match up to the finest traditions upon which we pride ourselves.

There is a challenge here in the conditions that we took on from the Labour Party – because it totally failed to match the scale of the challenge to be found in the inner cities . . .

Few of us can remember such testing times for this nation . . . we are reaping the whirlwind of all our yesterdays. Decade after decade we have denied our industry the climate for sufficient innovation and investment. Too often we have slaughtered the capital programmes to pay for the over-burgeoning consumption of the public sector. We have extracted as wages today what we should have left as investment for tomorrow. We have, too often, squandered our inheritance, and our inner cities are just a signpost of a journey of despair.

There will be no recovery without more resources. Preferably those resources will be in the form of investment from the private sector or from the better use of existing public programmes. But if the case can be made it may also be from extra public expenditure. From wherever it comes it will require an effort of will by a community of people for a common purpose.

You will say to me, 'What of the wreckers? What of those who will not work, those who strike without cause, those who thump

the elderly, smash in the windows and thrive on a life of crime?'
Every generation has its wreckers. There have been riots in other
times, but our faith has always told us that one cannot sow the
seeds of discontent on a stable society. They can flourish only if
they find fertile ground. Our politics and policies must deny that
fertile ground. Yes, of course, our political opponents will fight us
– as soon as they stop fighting each other. But we have the mettle
for that fight.

*Heseltine won a standing ovation. He resigned from Margaret Thatcher's govern-
ment in 1986 and challenged her for the leadership of the Tory Party in 1990. On
the first ballot he won more votes than Mrs Thatcher and precipitated her
downfall, but lost to John Major, whose Cabinet he subsequently joined.*

•

MARGARET THATCHER
Cheltenham, 3 July 1982

'The Falklands Factor'

*When Margaret Thatcher decided to send a task force of 10,000 men to
recapture the Falkland Islands after they had been invaded by Argentina, she
played for the highest stakes and won triumphantly. The British success was
attributed to Mrs Thatcher's nerve and determination. The 'Iron Lady' of
Soviet propaganda proved iron indeed. From being the least popular British
prime minister of modern times, Mrs Thatcher became the new Boadicea, the
embodiment of toughness and resolve.*

*The 'Falklands Factor', noted in this nationalistic speech to a rally of
Conservative women, ensured that she won the general election of 1983, her
second election victory.*

Today we meet in the aftermath of the Falklands Battle. Our
country has won a great victory and we are entitled to be proud.
This nation had the resolution to do what it knew had to be done
– to do what it knew was right.

We fought to show that aggression does not pay, and that the robber cannot be allowed to get away with his swag. We fought with the support of so many throughout the world: the Security Council, the Commonwealth, the European Community, and the United States. Yet we also fought alone – for we fought for our own people and for our own sovereign territory.

Now that it is all over, things cannot be the same again, for we have learnt something about ourselves – a lesson which we desperately needed to learn. When we started out, there were the waverers and the faint-hearts: the people who thought that Britain could no longer seize the initiative for herself; the people who thought we could no longer do the great things which we once did; and those who believed that our decline was irreversible – that we could never again be what we were. There were those who would not admit it – even perhaps some here today – people who would have strenuously denied the suggestion but – in their heart of hearts – they too had their secret fears that it was true: that Britain was no longer the nation that had built an Empire and ruled a quarter of the world.

Well, they were wrong. The lesson of the Falklands is that Britain has not changed and that this nation still has those sterling qualities which shine through our history. This generation can match their fathers and grandfathers in ability, in courage, and in resolution. We have not changed. When the demands of war and the dangers to our own people call us to arms – then we British are as we have always been – competent, courageous and resolute.

When called to arms – ah, that's the problem. It took the battle in the South Atlantic for the shipyards to adapt ships way ahead of time; for dockyards to refit merchantmen and cruise liners, to fix helicopter platforms, to convert hospital ships – all faster than was thought possible; it took the demands of war for every stop to be pulled out and every man and woman to do their best.

British people had to be threatened by foreign soldiers and British territory invaded and then – why then – the response was incomparable. Yet why does it need a war to bring out our qualities and reassert our pride? Why do we have to be invaded before we throw aside our selfish aims and begin to work together as only we can work, and achieve as only we can achieve?

That really is the challenge we as a nation face today. We have to see that the spirit of the South Atlantic – the real spirit of Britain – is kindled not only by war but can now be fired by peace.

We have the first prerequisite. We know we can do it – we haven't lost the ability. That is the Falklands Factor. We have proved ourselves to ourselves. It is a lesson we must not now forget. Indeed, it is a lesson which we must apply to peace just as we have learnt it in war. The faltering and the self-doubt has given way to achievement and pride. We have the confidence and we must use it.

Just look at the Task Force as an object lesson. Every man had his own task to do and did it superbly. Officers and men, senior NCO and newest recruit – every one realized that his contribution was essential for the success of the whole. All were equally valuable – each was differently qualified. By working together, each was able to do more than his best. As a team they raised the average to the level of the best and by each doing his utmost together they achieved the impossible. That's an accurate picture of Britain at war – not yet of Britain at peace. But the spirit has stirred and the nation has begun to assert itself. Things are not going to be the same again.

●

ROBERT RUNCIE
London, 26 July 1982

'*Our neighbours are indeed like us*'

Although it continued to lose members during the 1970s and 1980s, the Church of England remained a powerful source of social criticism and often upset Conservative ministers.

Dr Robert Runcie (1921–), who won the Military Cross during the Second

*World War, was appointed Archbishop of Canterbury by Margaret Thatcher
but their relationship was uneasy. After her own triumphalism over victory
in the Falklands war, she was said to be particularly upset by this muted
and moderate sermon from Dr Runcie at a service of thanksgiving in St
Paul's Cathedral, although she never commented publicly on her views of the
sermon. Runcie dared to suggest that people were mourning Argentina as
well as Britain – and that they should also be remembered in the nation's
prayers.*

Our hope as Christians is not fundamentally in man's naked
goodwill and rationality. We believe that he can overcome the
deadly selfishness of class or sect or race by discovering himself as
a child of the universal God of love. When a man realizes that he
is a beloved child of the Creator of all, then he is ready to see his
neighbours in the world as brothers and sisters. That is one reason
why those who dare to interpret God's will must never claim him
as an asset for one nation or group rather than another. War
springs from the love and loyalty which should be offered to God
being applied to some God-substitute, one of the most dangerous
being nationalism.

This is a dangerous world where evil is at work nourishing the
mindless brutality which killed and maimed so many in this city
last week. Sometimes, with the greatest reluctance, force is necessary to hold back the chaos which injustice and the irrational
element in man threaten to make of the world. But having said
that, all is not lost and there is hope. Even in the failure of war
there are springs of hope. In that great war play by Shakespeare,
Henry V says: 'There is some soul of goodness in things evil,
would men observingly distil it out.' People are mourning on
both sides of this conflict. In our prayers we shall quite rightly
remember those who are bereaved in our own country and the
relations of the young Argentinian soldiers who were killed.
Common sorrow could do something to reunite those who were
engaged in this struggle. A shared anguish can be a bridge of
reconciliation. Our neighbours are indeed like us.

I have had an avalanche of letters and advice about this service.

Some correspondents have asked 'why drag God in?' as if the intention was to wheel up God to endorse some particular policy or attitude rather than another. The purpose of prayer and of services like this is very different and there is hope for the world in the difference. In our prayers we come into the presence of the living God. We come with our very human emotions, pride in achievement and courage, grief at loss and waste. We come as we are and not just mouthing opinions and thanksgiving which the fashion of the moment judges acceptable. As we pour into our prayer our mourning, our pride, our shame and our convictions, which will inevitably differ from person to person, if we are really present and really reaching out to God and not just demanding his endorsement, then God is able to work upon us. He is able to deepen and enlarge our compassion and to purify our thanksgiving. The parent who comes mourning the loss of a son may find here consolation, but also a spirit which enlarges our compassion to include all those Argentinian parents who have lost sons.

Man without God finds it difficult to achieve this revolution inside himself. But talk of peace and reconciliation is just fanciful and theoretical unless we are prepared to undergo such a revolution. Many of the reports I have heard about the troops engaged in this war refer to moments when soldiers have been brought face to face with what is fundamental in life and have found new sources of strength and compassion even in the midst of conflict. Ironically, it has sometimes been those spectators who remained at home, whether supporters or opponents of the conflict, who continue to be most violent in their attitudes and untouched in their deepest selves.

Man without God is less than man. In meeting God, a man is shown his failures and his lack of integrity, but he is also given strength to turn more and more of his life and actions into love and compassion for other men like himself. It is necessary to the continuance of life on this planet that more and more people make this discovery. We have been given the choice. Man possesses the power to obliterate himself, sacrificing the whole race on the altar of some God-substitute. Or he can choose life in partnership with

God the Father of all. I believe that there is evidence that more
and more people are waking up to the realization that this crucial
decision peers us in the face here and now.

Cathedrals and churches are always places into which we bring
human experiences – birth, marriage, death, our flickering communion with God, our fragile relationships with each other, so
that they may be deepened and directed by the spirit of Christ.
Today we bring our mixture of thanksgiving, sorrows and aspirations for a better ordering of this world. Pray God that he may
purify, enlarge and redirect these in the ways of his kingdom of
love and peace. Amen.

Dr Runcie retired in 1991.

•

NEIL KINNOCK
Bridgend, 7 June 1983

'I warn you'

*The Labour Party, led by Michael Foot, was in deep disarray during the
British general election of 1983 and its manifesto was described as the longest
suicide note in history. One of Foot's most devoted lieutenants was Neil
Kinnock, a Welsh Labour MP on the left wing of the party and a rising
star.*

*Kinnock showed in this speech, delivered on the eve of the election, that he is a
natural orator. It was clear, he declared, that a new Thatcher government would
cut spending on health, education, and pensions and increase unemployment, taxes
and interest rates. 'I warn you,' he went on . . .*

If Margaret Thatcher is re-elected as Prime Minister, *I warn you*

I warn you that you will have pain –
When healing and relief depend upon payment.

I warn you that you will have ignorance –
When talents are untended and wits are wasted, when learning is a privilege and not a right.

I warn you that you will have poverty –
When pensions slip and benefits are whittled away by a Government that won't pay in an economy that can't pay.

I warn you that you will be cold –
When fuel charges are used as a tax system that the rich don't notice and the poor can't afford.

I warn you that you must not expect work –
When many cannot spend, more will not be able to earn. When they don't earn, they don't spend. When they don't spend, work dies.

I warn you not to go into the streets alone after dark or into the streets in large crowds of protest in the light.

I warn you that you will be quiet –
When the curfew of fear and the gibbet of unemployment make you obedient.

I warn you that you will have defence of a sort –
With a risk and at a price that passes all understanding.

I warn you that you will be home-bound –
When fares and transport bills kill leisure and lock you up.

I warn you that you will borrow less –
When credit, loans, mortgages and easy payments are refused to people on your melting income.

If Margaret Thatcher wins, she will be more a Leader than a Prime Minister. That power produces arrogance and when it is toughened by Tebbitry and flattered and fawned upon by spineless sycophants, the boot-licking tabloid Knights of Fleet Street and placemen in the Quangos, the arrogance corrupts absolutely.

If Margaret Thatcher wins –

I warn you not to be ordinary.

I warn you not to be young.

I warn you not to fall ill.

I warn you not to get old.

The successful resolution of the Falklands conflict was still vivid in the British memory and Margaret Thatcher won an easy election victory.

Four months later Neil Kinnock was elected leader of the Labour Party.

•

POPE JOHN PAUL II
Częstochowa, Poland, 18 June 1983

'We do not want a Poland which costs us nothing'

John Paul II, the Polish pope, made three visits to his native land. The third of these, in 1983, when Solidarity, the Polish workers' union, had been banned, was the most significant. On this visit, John Paul II said he had come to cry out before Europe and the world for the forgotten people of Eastern Europe.

On Saturday, 18 June, the Pope's helicopter took him to Częstochowa where he spoke, often in code, to what the London Times *described as 'a ragamuffin army of a million young pilgrims' from the weather-worn battlement of the Jasna Góra monastery.*

Dozens of Solidarity banners sprouted in the crowd as the Pope uttered certain trigger words – 'workers', or 'solidarity' (with a small 's') – or made any reference to truth or oppression or human rights.

He was greeted by huge applause, applause that was almost frightening, according to The Times, *when voiced by so many people in such a confined space.*

Our Lady of Jasna Góra is the teacher of true love for all. And this is particularly important for you, dear young people. In you, in fact, is decided that form of love which all of your life will have and, through you, human life on Polish soil: the matrimonial, family, social and national form – but also the priestly, religious and missionary one. Every life is determined and evaluated by the interior form of love. Tell me what you love, and I will tell you who you are.

I watch! How beautiful it is that this word is found in the call of Jasna Góra. It possesses a profound evangelical ancestry: Christ says many times: 'Watch' (Matt. 26: 41). Perhaps also from the Gospel it passed into the tradition of scouting. In the call of Jasna Góra it is the essential element of the reply that we wish to give to the love by which we are surrounded in the sign of the Sacred Icon.

The response to this love must be precisely the fact that I watch!

What does it mean, 'I watch'?

It means that I make an effort to be a person with a conscience. I do not stifle this conscience and I do not deform it; I call good and evil by name, and I do not blur them; I develop in myself what is good, and I seek to correct what is evil, by overcoming it in myself. This is a fundamental problem which can never be minimized or put on a secondary level. No! It is everywhere and always a matter of the first importance. Its importance is all the greater in proportion to the increase of circumstances which seem to favour our tolerance of evil and the fact that we easily excuse ourselves from this, especially if adults do so.

My dear friends! It is up to you to put up a firm barrier against immorality, a barrier – I say – to those social vices which I will not here call by name but which you yourselves are perfectly aware of. You must demand this of yourselves, even if others do not demand it of you. Historical experiences tell us how much the immorality of certain periods cost the whole nation. Today when we are fighting for the future form of our social life, remember that this form depends on what people will be like. Therefore: watch!

Christ said to the apostles, during his prayer in Gethsemane: 'Watch and pray that you may not enter into temptation' (Matt. 26: 41).

'I watch' also means: I see another. I do not close in on myself, in a narrow search for my own interests, my own judgements. 'I watch' means: love of neighbour; it means: fundamental interhuman solidarity.

Before the Mother of Jasna Góra I wish to give thanks for all the proofs of this solidarity which have been given by my compatriots, including Polish youth, in the difficult period of not many months ago. It would be difficult for me to enumerate here all the forms of this solicitude which surrounded those who were interned, imprisoned, dismissed from work, and also their families. You know this better than I. I received only sporadic news about it.

May this good thing, which appeared in so many places and so many ways, never cease on Polish soil. May there be a constant confirmation of that 'I watch' of the call of Jasna Góra, which is a response to the presence of the Mother of Christ in the great family of the Poles.

'I watch' also means: I feel responsible for this great common inheritance whose name is Poland. This name defines us all. This name obliges us all. This name costs us all.

Perhaps at times we envy the French, the Germans or the Americans because their name is not tied to such a historical price and because they are so easily free: while our Polish freedom costs so much.

My dear ones, I will not make a comparative analysis. I will only say that it is what costs that constitutes value. It is not, in fact, possible to be truly free without an honest and profound relationship with values. We do not want a Poland which costs us nothing. We watch, instead, beside all that makes up the authentic inheritance of the generations, seeking to enrich it. A nation, then, is first of all rich in its people. Rich in man. Rich in youth. Rich in every individual who watches in the name of truth: it is truth, in fact, that gives form to love.

My dear young friends! Before our common Mother and the Queen of our hearts, I desire finally to say to you that she knows your sufferings, your difficult youth, your sense of injustice and humiliation, the lack of prospects for the future that is so often felt, perhaps the temptations to flee to some other world.

Even if I am not among you every day, as was the case for many years in the past, nevertheless I carry in my heart a great solicitude. A great, enormous solicitude. A solicitude for you. Precisely because 'on you depends tomorrow'.

I pray for you every day.

It is good that we are here together at the hour of the call of Jasna Góra. In the midst of the trials of the present time, in the midst of the trial through which your generation is passing, this call of the millennium continues to be a programme.

In it is contained a fundamental way out. Because the way out in whatever dimension – economic, social, political – must happen first in man. Man cannot remain with no way out.

Mother of Jasna Góra, you who have been given to us by Providence for the defence of the Polish nation, accept this evening this call of the Polish youth together with the Polish Pope, and help us to persevere in hope! Amen.

When freedom came to Eastern Europe in 1989, the Pope's speeches in Poland in 1983 were considered as one of the main contributions in bolstering the defiant human spirit that brought the walls of oppression tumbling down.

•

DENIS HEALEY
London, 27 February 1984

'The great she-elephant, she who must be obeyed'

One of the earliest and most memorable attacks on the prime ministerial style of Margaret Thatcher was made by Denis Healey (1917–), one of the most combative and bruising speakers in the House of Commons. Healey, a former Labour

Defence Secretary and Chancellor of the Exchequer, was speaking during a debate on a proposal by the Thatcher government to abolish the right of workers at GCHQ, the British intelligence eavesdropping station at Cheltenham, to belong to a union.

Every trade unionist in Britain feels threatened by what the Government have done. The anger felt by trade unionists was felt deeply by everyone, not least Mr Murray [Lionel 'Len' Murray, leader of the Trades Union Congress], who attended the meeting with the Prime Minister last week, because she was felt to be accusing trade unions of lack of patriotism, of being prepared to risk people's lives and to break their promises. The Foreign Secretary made it crystal clear in his speech that that, in his view, is what trade union membership at GCHQ must imply. I ask the Government to recognize that they really cannot talk in those terms to people such as Terry Duffy and Kate Losinska, who are now leading the campaign against the Government. What a miracle the Government have achieved in the trade union movement.

I have not wasted time on the Foreign Secretary this afternoon, although I am bound to say that I feel that some of his colleagues must be a bit tired by now of his hobbling around from one of the doorsteps to another, with a bleeding hole in his foot and a smoking gun in his hand, telling them that he did not know it was loaded.

The Foreign Secretary, however, is not the real villain in this case; he is the fall guy. Those of us with long memories will feel that he is rather like poor van der Lubbe in the Reichstag fire trial. We are asking ourselves the question that was asked at the trial: who is the Mephistopheles behind this shabby Faust? The answer to that is clear. The handling of this decision by – I quote her own Back Benchers – the great she-elephant, she who must be obeyed, the Catherine the Great of Finchley, the Prime Minister herself, has drawn sympathetic trade unionists, such as Len Murray, into open revolt. Her pig-headed bigotry has prevented her closest colleagues and Sir Robert Armstrong from offering and accepting a compromise.

The Right Hon. Lady, for whom I have a great personal affection, has formidable qualities, a powerful intelligence and immense courage, but those qualities can turn into horrendous vices, unless they are moderated by colleagues who have more experience, understanding and sensitivity. As she has got rid of all those colleagues, no one is left in the Cabinet with both the courage and the ability to argue with her.

I put it to all Conservative Members, but mainly to the Government Front Bench, that to allow the Right Hon. Lady to commit Britain to another four years of capricious autocracy would be to do fearful damage not just to the Conservative Party but to the state. She has faced them with the most damaging of all conflicts of loyalty. They must choose between the interests of their country, our nation's security and our cohesion as a people and the obstinacy of an individual. I hope that they resolve this conflict in the interests of the nation. If not, they will carry a heavy responsibility for the tragedies that are bound to follow.

∙

PRINCE CHARLES
London, 30 May 1984

'A monstrous carbuncle'

It was the 150th anniversary of the Royal Institute of British Architects and the anniversary dinner was being held in the historic setting of Hampton Court, a few miles from central London. The hall was lit by candles, the evening was graced by the first masque commissioned since the eighteenth century – and the annual gold medal was being presented by Britain's future King, Charles, Prince of Wales.

The 700 architects were in for a shock if they were expecting princely platitudes from their honoured guest. Instead the prince launched into a forthright attack on architects who designed houses for the approval of fellow architects instead of the tenants. Ever since, however, the speech has been remembered for his damning indictment of a proposed extension to the National Gallery in London's Trafalgar Square as a 'monstrous carbuncle'.

At last people are beginning to see that it is possible, and important in human terms, to respect old buildings, street plans and traditional scales and at the same time not to feel guilty about a preference for façades, ornaments and soft materials. At last, after witnessing the wholesale destruction of Georgian and Victorian housing in most of our cities, people have begun to realize that it *is* possible to restore old buildings and, what is more, that there are architects willing to undertake such projects.

For far too long, it seems to me, some planners and architects have consistently ignored the feelings and wishes of the mass of ordinary people in this country. Perhaps, when you think about it, it is hardly surprising as architects tend to have been trained to design buildings from scratch – to tear down and rebuild . . . A large number of us have developed a feeling that architects tend to design houses for the approval of fellow architects and critics, not for the tenants.

To be concerned about the way people live, about the environment they inhabit and the kind of community that is created by that environment should surely be one of the prime requirements of a really good architect. It has been most encouraging to see the development of community architecture as a natural reaction to the policy of decanting people to new towns and overspill estates where the extended family patterns of support were destroyed and the community life was lost. Now, moreover, we are seeing the gradual expansion of housing cooperatives, particularly in the inner-city areas of Liverpool, where the tenants are able to work with an architect of their own who listens to their comments and their ideas and tries to design the kind of environment they want, rather than the kind which tends to be imposed upon them without any degree of choice . . .

What I believe is important about community architecture is that it has shown ordinary people that their views are worth having; that architects and planners do not necessarily have the monopoly of knowing best about taste, style and planning; that they need not be made to feel guilty or ignorant if their natural preference is for the more traditional designs – for a small garden, for courtyards, arches and porches – and that there is a growing number of architects prepared to listen and to offer imaginative ideas . . .

It would be a tragedy if the character and skyline of our capital city were to be further ruined and St Paul's dwarfed by yet another giant glass stump, better suited to downtown Chicago than the City of London. It is hard to imagine that London before the last war must have had one of the most beautiful skylines of any great city, if those who recall it are to be believed. Those who do, say that the affinity between buildings and the earth, in spite of the city's immense size, was so close and organic that the houses looked almost as though they had grown out of the earth and had not been imposed upon it – grown, moreover, in such a way that as few trees as possible were thrust out of the way. Those who knew it then and loved it, as so many British love Venice without concrete stumps and glass towers, and those who can imagine what it was like, must associate with the sentiments in one of Aldous Huxley's earliest and most successful novels, *Antic Hay*, where the main character, an unsuccessful architect, reveals a model of London as Christopher Wren wanted to rebuild it after the Great Fire and describes how Wren was so obsessed with the opportunity the fire gave the city to rebuild itself into a greater and more glorious vision. What, then, are we doing to our capital city now? What have we done to it since the bombing during the war? What are we shortly going to do to one of its most famous areas – Trafalgar Square? Instead of designing an extension to the elegant façade of the National Gallery which complements it and continues the concept of columns and domes, it looks as if we may be presented with a kind of vast municipal fire station, complete with the sort of tower that contains the siren.

I would understand better this type of High Tech approach if you demolished the whole of Trafalgar Square and started again with a single architect responsible for the entire layout, but what is proposed is like a monstrous carbuncle on the face of a much loved and elegant friend. Apart from anything else, it defeats me why anyone wishing to display the early Renaissance pictures belonging to the gallery should do so in a new gallery so manifestly at odds with the whole spirit of that age of astonishing proportion. Why can't we have those curves and arches that express feeling in design? What is wrong with them? Why has everything got to be vertical, straight, unbending, only at right angles – and functional?

The 'monstrous carbuncle' was never built. The plan by Peter Ahrends was scrapped and Robert Venturi, an American architect, won a competition to design the gallery's new Sainsbury wing. In 1988 Prince Charles wrote and produced A Vision of Britain, *a television documentary about his views on architecture which was later published as a book.*

•

RONALD REAGAN
Pointe du Hoc, Normandy, 6 June 1984

'Let us make a vow to the dead'

According to his speech-writer Peggy Noonan, Ronald Reagan would and did read out anything she put in front of him. Even so, there was a quality to Reagan's speeches, whatever their cosy folksiness or the showbiz schmaltz that so infuriated his detractors, that touched hearts and made people weep genuine tears – as they did on this occasion commemorating the Normandy invasion of the Second World War.

It was an emotional day which became a celebration of heroism and sacrifice, Reagan wrote in his retirement. 'I stood there on that windswept point with the ocean behind me. Before me were the boys who forty years before had fought their way up from the ocean. Some rested under the white crosses and Stars of David that stretched out across the landscape. Others sat right in front of me. They looked like elderly businessmen, yet these were the kids who climbed the cliffs.'

We're here to mark that day in history when the Allied peoples joined in battle to reclaim this continent to liberty. For four long years, much of Europe had been under a terrible shadow. Free nations had fallen, Jews cried out in the camps, millions cried out for liberation. Europe was enslaved, and the world prayed for its rescue. Here in Normandy the rescue began. Here the Allies stood and fought against tyranny in a giant undertaking unparalleled in human history.

We stand on a lonely, windswept point on the northern shore of France. The air is soft, but forty years ago at this moment, the air was dense with smoke and the cries of men, and the air was filled with the crack of rifle fire and the roar of cannon. At dawn, on the morning of the 6th of June 1944, 225 Rangers jumped off the British landing craft and ran to the bottom of these cliffs. Their mission was one of the most difficult and daring of the invasion: to climb these sheer and desolate cliffs and take out the enemy guns. The Allies had been told that some of the mightiest of these guns were here and they would be trained on the beaches to stop the Allied advance.

The Rangers looked up and saw the enemy soldiers – at the edge of the cliffs shooting down at them with machine-guns and throwing grenades. And the American Rangers began to climb. They shot rope ladders over the face of these cliffs and began to pull themselves up. When one Ranger fell, another would take his place. When one rope was cut, a Ranger would grab another and begin his climb again. They climbed, shot back, and held their footing. Soon, one by one, the Rangers pulled themselves over the top, and in seizing the firm land at the top of these cliffs, they began to seize back the continent of Europe. Two hundred and twenty-five came here. After two days of fighting only ninety could still bear arms.

Behind me is a memorial that symbolizes the Ranger daggers that were thrust into the top of these cliffs. And before me are the men who put them there.

These are the boys of Pointe du Hoc. These are the men who took the cliffs. These are the champions who helped free a continent. These are the heroes who helped end a war.

Gentlemen, I look at you and I think of the words of Stephen Spender's poem. You are men who in your 'lives fought for life . . . and left the vivid air signed with your honor' . . .

Forty summers have passed since the battle that you fought here. You were young the day you took these cliffs; some of you were hardly more than boys, with the deepest joys of life before you. Yet you risked everything here. Why? Why did you do it? What impelled you to put aside the instinct for self-preservation and risk your lives to take these cliffs? What inspired all the men of the armies that met here? We look at you, and somehow we know the answer. It was faith, and belief; it was loyalty and love.

The men of Normandy had faith that what they were doing was right, faith that they fought for all humanity, faith that a just God would grant them mercy on this beachhead or on the next. It was the deep knowledge – and pray God we have not lost it – that there is a profound moral difference between the use of force for liberation and the use of force for conquest. You were here to liberate, not to conquer, and so you and those others did not doubt your cause. And you were right not to doubt.

You all knew that some things are worth dying for. One's country is worth dying for, and democracy is worth dying for, because it's the most deeply honorable form of government ever devised by man. All of you loved liberty. All of you were willing to fight tyranny, and you knew the people of your countries were behind you.

•

MARIO CUOMO
San Francisco, 16 July 1984

'Make this nation remember how futures are built'

Mario Cuomo (1932–), whose father arrived in the United States from Italy speaking not a word of English, has been governor of New York since 1982. He is probably the best-read man prominent in American politics – an introspective intellectual who loves the Bible and John Donne, prefers his mass in Latin and reveres Sir Thomas More. That love of English shows in his speeches, which he insists on writing himself, giving them an eloquence which few contemporaries, apart from Edward Kennedy, can match.

As the Democrats met in San Francisco in 1984 to elect a candidate to fight Ronald Reagan as he stood for a second term, Cuomo was selected to give the keynote address. His scintillating speech, with its soaring rhetoric, was one of the most rousing heard at a Democrat convention for years and stamped Cuomo as the Democrats' greatest stump orator.

Ten days ago, President Reagan admitted that although some people in this country seemed to be doing well nowadays, others were unhappy, and even worried, about themselves, their families and their futures.

The President said he didn't understand that fear. He said 'Why, this country is a shining city on a hill.'

The President is right. In many ways we *are* 'a shining city on a hill'.

But the hard truth is that not everyone is sharing in this city's splendor and glory.

A shining city is perhaps all the President sees from the portico of the White House and the veranda of his ranch, where everyone seems to be doing well.

But there's another part of the city, the part where some people can't pay their mortgages and most young people can't afford one, where students can't afford the education they need and middle-class parents watch the dreams they hold for their children, evaporate.

In this part of the city there are more poor than ever, more families in trouble, more and more people who need help but can't find it.

Even worse: there are elderly people who tremble in the basements of the houses there.

There are people who sleep in the city's streets, in the gutter, where the glitter doesn't show.

There are ghettos where thousands of young people, without an education or a job, give their lives away to drug dealers every day.

There is despair, Mr President, in faces you never see, in the places you never visit in your shining city.

In fact, Mr President, this nation is more a 'tale of two cities' than it is a 'shining city on a hill'.

Maybe if you visited more places, Mr President, you'd understand.

Maybe if you went to Appalachia where some people still live in sheds, and to Lackawanna where thousands of unemployed steel workers wonder why we subsidized foreign steel while we surrender their dignity to unemployment and to welfare checks, maybe if you stepped into a shelter in Chicago and talked with some of the homeless there: maybe Mr President, if you asked a woman who'd been denied the help she needs to feed her children because you say we need the money to give a tax break to a millionaire or to build a missile we can't even afford to use – maybe then you'd understand.

Maybe, Mr President.

But I'm afraid not.

Because, the truth is, this is how we were warned it would be.

President Reagan told us from the beginning that he believed in a kind of social Darwinism, survival of the fittest. 'Government can't do everything,' we were told, 'so it should settle for taking care of the strong and hope that economic ambition and charity will do the rest. Make the rich richer and what falls from their table will be enough for the middle class and those trying to make it into the middle class.'

The Republicans called it trickle-down when Hoover tried it. Now they call it supply side. It is the same shining city for those relative few who are lucky enough to live in its good neighborhoods.

But for the people who are excluded – locked out – all they can do is to stare from a distance at that city's glimmering towers.

It's an old story. As old as our history.

The difference between Democrats and the Republicans has always been measured in courage and confidence.

The Republicans believe the wagon train will not make it to the frontier unless some of our old, some of our young, and some of our weak are left behind by the side of the trail.

The strong will inherit the land!

We Democrats believe that we can make it all the way with the whole family intact.

We have. More than once.

Ever since Franklin Roosevelt lifted himself from his wheelchair to lift this nation from its knees, wagon train after wagon train. To new frontiers of education, housing, peace. The whole family aboard, constantly reaching out to extend and enlarge that family. Lifting them up into the wagon on the way. Blacks and Hispanics, people of every ethnic group, and native Americans – all those struggling to build their families and claim some small share of America.

For nearly fifty years we carried them to new levels of comfort, security, dignity, even affluence.

Some of us are in this room today only because this nation had that confidence.

It would be wrong to forget that.

So, we are here at this convention to remind ourselves where we come from and to claim the future for ourselves and for our children.

Today our great Democratic Party, which has saved this nation from depression, from Fascism, from racism, from corruption, is called upon to do it again ... This time to save the nation from confusion and division, from the threat of eventual fiscal disaster and most of all from a fear of a nuclear holocaust ...

We must win this case on the merits.

We must get the American public to look past the glitter, beyond the showmanship ... to reality, to the hard substance of things. And we will do that not so much with speeches that sound good as with speeches that are good and sound ...

We must make the American people hear our 'tale of two cities.'

We must convince them that we don't have to settle for two

cities, that we can have one city, indivisible, shining for *all* its people . . .

To succeed we will have to surrender small parts of our individual interests, to build a platform we can *all* stand on, at once, comfortably – proudly singing out the truth for the nation to hear, in chorus, its logic so clear and commanding that no slick commercial, no amount of geniality, no martial music will be able to muffle it.

We Democrats must unite so that the entire nation can. Surely the Republicans won't bring the convention together, their policies divide the nation . . . into the lucky and the left-out, the royalty and the rabble.

The Republicans are willing to treat that division as victory. They would cut this nation in half, into those temporarily better off and those worse off than before, and call it recovery.

We should not be embarrassed or dismayed if the process of unifying is difficult, even at times wrenching.

Unlike any other party, we embrace men and women of every colour, every creed, every orientation, every economic class. In our family are gathered everyone from the abject poor of Essex County in New York, to the enlightened affluent of the gold coasts of both ends of our nation. And in between is the heart of our constituency, the middle class . . . The people not rich enough to be worry free but not poor enough to be on welfare. Those who work for a living because they have to. White collar and blue collar. Young professionals, men and women in small business desperate for the capital and contracts they need to prove their worth.

We speak for the minorities who have not yet entered the mainstream.

For ethnics who want to add their culture to the mosaic that is America.

For women indignant that we refuse to etch into our governmental commandments the simple rule 'Thou shalt not sin against equality,' a commandment so obvious it can be spelled in three letters . . . ERA!

For young people demanding an education and a future.

For senior citizens terrorized by the idea that their only security . . . their *social* security . . . is being threatened.

For millions of reasoning people fighting to preserve our environment from greed and stupidity and fighting to preserve our very existence from a macho intransigence that refuses to make intelligent attempts to discuss the possibility of nuclear holocaust with our enemy. Refusing because they believe we can pile missiles so high that they will pierce the clouds and the sight of them will frighten our enemies into submission . . .

That struggle to live with dignity is the real story of the shining city. It's a story I didn't read in a book, or learn in a classroom. I saw it, and lived it, like many of you.

I watched a small man with thick calluses on both hands work fifteen and sixteen hours a day. I saw him once literally bleed from the bottoms of his feet, a man who came here uneducated, alone, unable to speak the language, who taught me all I needed to know about faith and hard work by the simple eloquence of his example. I learned about our kind of democracy from my father. I learned about our obligation to each other from him and from my mother. They asked only for a chance to work and to make the world better for their children and to be protected in those moments when they would not be able to protect themselves. This nation and its government did that for them.

And that they were able to build a family and live in dignity and see one of their children go from behind their little grocery store on the other side of the tracks in South Jamaica where he was born, to occupy the highest seat in the greatest state of the greatest nation in the only world we know, is an ineffably beautiful tribute to the Democratic process.

We Democrats *still* have a dream. We *still* believe in this nation's future.

And this is our answer – *our* credo.

We believe in *only* the government we need but we insist on all the government we need.

We believe in a government characterized by fairness and

reasonableness, a reasonableness that goes beyond labels, that doesn't distort or promise to do what it knows it can't do.

A government strong enough to use the words 'love' and 'compassion' and smart enough to convert our noblest aspirations into practical realities.

We believe in encouraging the talented, but we believe that while survival of the fittest may be a good working description of the process of evolution, a government of humans should elevate itself to a higher order, one which fills the gaps left by chance or a wisdom we don't understand.

We would rather have laws written by the patron of this great city, the man called the 'world's most sincere democrat' – St Francis of Assisi – than laws written by Darwin.

We believe, as Democrats, that a society as blessed as ours, the most affluent democracy in the world's history, that can spend trillions on instruments of destruction, ought to be able to help the middle class in its struggle, ought to be able to find work for all who can do it, room at the table, shelter for the homeless, care for the elderly and infirm, hope for the destitute.

We proclaim as loudly as we can the utter insanity of nuclear proliferation and the need for a nuclear freeze, if only to affirm the simple truth that peace is better than war because life is better than death.

We believe in firm but fair law and order, in the union movement, in privacy for people, openness by government, civil rights, and human rights.

We believe in a single fundamental idea that describes better than most textbooks and any speech what a proper government should be. The idea of family, mutuality, the sharing of benefits and burdens for the good of all. Feeling one another's pain. Sharing one another's blessings. Reasonably, honestly, fairly – without respect to race, or sex, or geography or political affiliation.

We believe we must be the family of America, recognizing that at the heart of the matter we are bound one to another, that the problems of a retired schoolteacher in Duluth are *our* problems. That the future of the child in Buffalo is *our* future. The struggle of a disabled man in Boston to survive, to live decently is *our* struggle. The hunger of a woman in Little Rock, *our* hunger. The failure anywhere to provide what reasonably we might, to avoid pain, is *our* failure.

For fifty years we Democrats created a better future for our children, using traditional Democratic principles as a fixed beacon, giving us direction and purpose, but constantly innovating, adapting to new realities: Roosevelt's Alphabet programmes; Truman's Nato and the GI Bill of Rights; Kennedy's intelligent tax incentives and the Alliance for Progress; Johnson's Civil Rights; Carter's Human Rights and the nearly miraculous Camp David Peace Accord.

We will have America's first woman Vice-President: the child of immigrants, a New Yorker, opening with one magnificent stroke a whole new frontier for the United States.

It will happen – *if we make it happen.*

I ask you – ladies and gentlemen, brothers and sisters – for the good of all of us – for the love of this great nation, for the family of America – for the love of God, please, make this nation remember how futures are built.

There was an ecstatic, roared and prolonged ovation for Cuomo. 'A florid rendition of fine-sounding rhetoric,' said Republican critics but the speech enhanced Cuomo's reputation as a rising Democrat star and restored morale in a year when Reagan won another overwhelming victory.

•

RONALD REAGAN
Oval Office of the White House, 28 January 1986

'The future doesn't belong to the fainthearted'

A few hours after the spectacular Challenger *space shuttle disaster, President Reagan delivered this address to the nation. It was a characteristic example of the Reagan style – homely, almost conversational but achieving exactly the right emotion. The speech was memorable for its closing lines, which were from the poem 'High Flight', a sonnet written by John Gillespie Magee, a Canadian pilot who flew Spitfires from Britain during the Second World War and who was killed at the age of nineteen in December 1941.*

This was a classic case of a speech-writer – Peggy Noonan, who learned the poem at school – remembering the appropriate quotation at the right moment. Reagan was present when the actor Tyrone Power returned from the war and recited 'High Flight' from memory at a homecoming party. The poem was used for years as the close-down reading of a Washington television station.

Nineteen years ago, almost to the day, we lost three astronauts in a terrible accident on the ground. But we've never lost an astronaut in flight; we've never had a tragedy like this. And perhaps we've forgotten the courage it took for the crew of the shuttle; but they, the *Challenger* Seven, were aware of the dangers, but overcame them and did their jobs brilliantly. We mourn seven heroes: Michael Smith, Dick Scobee, Judith Resnik, Ronald McNair, El-lison Onizuka, Gregory Jarvis, and Christa McAuliffe. We mourn their loss as a nation together.

For the families of the seven, we cannot bear, as you do, the full impact of this tragedy. But we feel the loss, and we're thinking about you so very much. Your loved ones were daring and brave, and they had that special grace, that special spirit that says, 'Give me a challenge and I'll meet it with joy.' They had a hunger to explore the universe and discover its truths. They wished to serve, and they did. They served all of us.

We've grown used to wonders in this century. It's hard to dazzle us. But for twenty-five years the United States space programme has been doing just that. We've grown used to the idea of space, and perhaps we forget that we've only just begun. We're still pioneers. They, the members of the *Challenger* crew, were pioneers.

And I want to say something to the schoolchildren of America who were watching the live coverage of the shuttle's takeoff. I know it is hard to understand, but sometimes painful things like this happen. It's all part of the process of exploration and discovery. It's all part of taking a chance and expanding man's horizons. The future doesn't belong to the fainthearted; it belongs to the brave. The *Challenger* crew was pulling us into the future, and we'll continue to follow them . . .

There's a coincidence today. On this day 390 years ago, the great explorer Sir Francis Drake died aboard ship off the coast of Panama. In his lifetime the great frontiers were the oceans, and a historian later said, 'He lived by the sea, died on it, and was buried in it.' Well, today we can say of the *Challenger* crew: Their dedication was, like Drake's, complete.

The crew of the space shuttle *Challenger* honoured us by the manner in which they lived their lives. We will never forget them, nor the last time we saw them, this morning, as they prepared for the journey and waved goodbye and 'slipped the surly bonds of earth' to 'touch the face of God.'

•

NEIL KINNOCK
Llandudno, 15 May 1987

'Why am I the first Kinnock in a thousand generations to be able to get to university?'

Even his rivals acknowledged that Neil Kinnock, in his first election as leader of the Labour Party in 1987, fought an energetic and effective campaign. That was particularly true on television where his party political broadcasts were made by Hugh Hudson, the celebrated director of the Oscar-winning Chariots of Fire.

The most memorable of the television broadcasts showed Kinnock and Glenys, his wife, strolling in the hills above Llandudno on the North Wales coast, and included extracts from this speech to the Welsh Labour Party.

The rousing passion of his speech and the emotional atmosphere in the packed conference hall became a hallmark of Kinnock's election rallies and demonstrated that, when he speaks from the soul rather than a sanitized script prepared so as not to frighten away potential voters with the bogy of a socialist government, he is the greatest British orator of his generation.

We are democratic socialists. We care all the time. We don't think it's a soft sentiment, we don't think it's 'wet'.

We think that care is the essence of strength.

And we believe that because we know that strength without care is savage and brutal and selfish.

Strength with care is compassion — the practical action that is needed to help people lift themselves to their full stature.

That's real care — It is not soft or weak. It is tough and strong.

But where do we get that strength to provide that care?

Do we wait for some stroke of good fortune, some benign giant, some socially conscious Samson to come along and pick up the wretched of the earth?

Of course we don't.

We cooperate, we collect together, we coordinate so that everyone can contribute and everyone can benefit, everyone has responsibilities, everyone has rights. That is how we put care into action. That is how we make the weak strong, that is how we lift the needy, that is how we make the sick whole, that is how we give talent the chance to flourish, that is how we turn the unemployed claimant into the working contributor.

We do it together. It is called collective strength, collective care. And its whole purpose is individual freedom.

When we speak of collective strength and collective freedom, collectively achieved, we are not fulfilling that nightmare that Mrs Thatcher tries to paint, and all her predecessors have tried to saddle us with.

We're not talking about uniformity; we're not talking about regimentation; we're not talking about *conformity* — that's their creed. The uniformity of the dole queue; the regimentation of the unemployed young and their compulsory work schemes. The *conformity* of people who will work in conditions, and take orders, and accept pay *because of* mass unemployment that they would laugh at in a free society with full employment.

That kind of freedom for the individual, that kind of liberty can't be secured by most of the people for most of the time if they're just left to themselves, isolated, stranded, with their whole life chances dependent upon luck!

Why am I the first Kinnock in a thousand generations to be able to get to university? Why is Glenys the first woman in her family in a thousand generations to be able to get to university?

Was it because *all* our predecessors were 'thick'? Did they lack talent – those people who could sing, and play, and recite and write poetry; those people who could make wonderful, beautiful things with their hands; those people who could dream dreams, see visions; those people who had such a sense of perception as to know in times so brutal, so oppressive, that they could win their way out of that by coming together?

Were those people not university material? Couldn't they have knocked off all their A-levels in an afternoon?

But why didn't they get it?

Was it because they were weak? – those people who could work eight hours underground and then come up and play football?

Weak? Those women who could survive eleven childbearings, were they weak? Those people who could stand with their backs and their legs straight and face the people who had control over their lives, the ones who owned their workplaces and tried to own them, and tell them, 'No. I won't take your orders.' Were they weak?

Does anybody really think that they didn't get what we had because they didn't have the talent, or the strength, or the endurance, or the commitment?

Of course not. It was because there was no platform upon which they could stand; no arrangement for their neighbours to subscribe to their welfare; no method by which the communities could translate their desires for those individuals into provision for those individuals.

And now, Mrs Thatcher, by dint of privatization, and means test, and deprivation, and division, wants to nudge us back into the situation where everybody can either stand on their own feet, or live on their knees.

That's what this election is about as she parades her visions and values, and we choose to contest them as people with roots in this country, with a future only in this country, with pride in this country. People who know that if we are to have and sustain real individual liberty in this country it requires the collective effort of the whole community.

Of course you hear the Tories talking about freedom. We'll be hearing a great deal of that over the next month from the same people who have spent the last eight years crushing individual freedoms under the weight of unemployment and poverty, squeezing individual rights with cuts and means tests and charges.

I think of the youngsters I meet. Three, four, five years out of school. Never had a job. And they say to me, 'Do you think we'll ever work?'

They live in a free country, but they do not feel free.

I think of the fifty-five-year-old woman I meet who is waiting to go into hospital, her whole existence clouded by pain.

She lives in a free country, but she does not feel free.

I think of the young couple, two years married, living in Mam and Dad's front room because they can't get a home. They ask, 'Will we *ever* get a home of our own?'

They live in a free country, but they do not feel free.

And I think of the old couple who spend months of the winter afraid to turn up the heating, who stay at home because they are afraid to go out after dark, whose lives are turned into a crisis by the need to buy a new pair of shoes.

They live in a free country – indeed, they're of the generation that *fought* for a free country – but they do not feel free.

How can they – and millions like them – have their individual freedom if there is no collective provision?

How can they have strength if they do not have care?

Now they cannot have either because they are locked out of

being able to discharge responsibilities just as surely as they are locked out of being able to exercise rights.

They want to be able to use both.
They do not want feather-bedding, they want a foothold.
They do not want cotton-woolling, they want a chance to contribute.
That is the freedom they want.
That is the freedom we want them to have.

The 1987 British general election marked the high noon of Margaret Thatcher's three governments and she won her third victory – but Kinnock destroyed the Alliance of the Liberals and the Social Democrats as the main alternative to the Tories. The American politician, Joe Biden, was later to pinch a theme from Kinnock's speech and ask: 'Why am I the fourteenth Joe Biden . . .?' Kinnock lost his second general election in 1992 and subsequently resigned as leader of the Labour Party.

•

ARTHUR SCARGILL
Merthyr Tydfil, South Wales, 30 October 1987

'We are fighting for the survival of our culture'

Arthur Scargill (1938–), who became president of the National Union of Mineworkers at the early age of forty-four, is one of the great demagogic orators of British trades-unionism. He is a Marxist who has been described as a Communist of the hard, Stalinist breed, absorbed in the industrial struggle against capitalism.

His career as a union leader was linked from the start with industrial conflict, often with violence, especially when he led the miners on strike against the National Coal Board. He was pitting himself against the iron will of Margaret Thatcher and was crushingly defeated.

Every year, the Merthyr Tydfil Trades Union Council invites a guest speaker to present a lecture in memory of S. O. Davies, a South Wales miners' leader and Labour MP. That lecture was given in 1987 by Arthur Scargill and was a characteristic denunciation of the 'defeatism' of the Labour movement confronted by a government, as he saw it, that was dedicated to destroying the spirit of trades-unionism.

Today our nation, after eight years under the Tories, is on the brink of utter chaos, facing both social and economic collapse. Our basic industries have been butchered. Our manufacturing base has been eroded with hundreds of businesses, large and small, gone to the wall while the nation has become increasingly dependent on imported goods.

The human consequences of this industrial and economic devastation are terrible. Over eight million people struggle for survival on or below the poverty line and four and a half million people are unemployed.

Thousands of families are homeless: the number of homeless families in Britain has doubled since 1978, while the enforced repossession of homes is at an all-time record because so many can no longer manage to maintain mortgage payments. Even more people, meanwhile, try to cope as best they can in derelict, often dangerous dwellings – one and a quarter million homes are unfit to live in, while house-building investment throughout Britain has been slashed by sixty per cent since 1979.

Sickness and ill health of all kinds are rampant, and they are made even more terrible by the crisis in the National Health Service and throughout the welfare system.

The Tories have been utterly ruthless in their butchery of health and welfare provisions. The NHS, once the pride of our nation, has been reduced to a critical condition through hospital closures, medical staff cutbacks, the lack and withdrawal of resources and vital equipment, and the privitization of key services. Approximately 700,000 people wait today for hospital treatment and an increasing number will not receive that treatment before it is too late. Thousands of people who are suffering from serious, often fatal diseases are being turned away through lack of hospital beds and staff.

Our social services are faced with ever-increasing family and community problems as Tory attacks take their toll, with children and old people among those most vulnerable.

Our education system is also in chaos, as students and teachers struggle against yet more cutbacks, fewer resources – and for our youngsters it must seem often a pointless exercise, with jobs, training and access to higher education becoming more and more difficult to attain. Their teachers meanwhile, like many other trade unionists, have had their negotiating rights removed by the Government, and their commitment to teaching the nation's children treated with contempt.

This has become a grim and desperate society – fuelled by unemployment and its social consequences, frustration, rage and despair are rampant all around us. More and more people, I believe, are coming to see themselves as *under attack* – and they are correct.

We are indeed facing a deliberate political attack by Britain's ruling class. A war of attrition is being waged as capitalism, in a condition of acute crisis, lashes out with increasing ferocity to protect itself. The existence of this crisis is now clear for all to see. It has been exposed by the recent collapse of stock markets throughout the capitalist world, triggered off by the slide on Wall Street (which according to experts is the worst slump since 1929).

This collapse will in my view lead inevitably to more hardship for the British people, with a massive increase in unemployment and reduced living standards as capitalism seeks once again to make working people pay for its pursuit of profit and power.

The Tories have based their savage policies on an ideology called monetarism – it is this philosophy which has led to the virtual destruction of our manufacturing industries and in particular to the devastation of our coal, rail and steel industries. The steel industry has lost over 150,000 jobs, and the coal and rail industries have lost approximately 100,000 each within a period of eight years. Parts of our nation such as South Wales have been reduced to a lunar landscape as the Tories have systematically butchered our manufacturing and industrial infrastructure . . .

In seeking to win that absolute control which it must have for even limited survival, the State through the Tory Government has introduced twin measures to destroy or render ineffective all those who oppose it. On the one hand, it has deliberately increased unemployment from just over one million to four and a half million in eight years creating as in the 1930s a situation where thirty to forty people pursue each job vacancy, driven by this emotional blackmail to increasing fear.

At the same time it has introduced vicious legal measures designed to render the British trade-union movement completely ineffective. Indeed Margaret Thatcher has made it absolutely clear that she wants to wipe socialism off the agenda of British politics; to achieve this aim the Tories are determined also to wipe effective trade unionism off the industrial agenda.

Since 1979, we have seen a whole range of anti-trade-union legislation – all of it designed to dismantle the gains achieved by trade unionists in more than a century of struggle. Today, the extent of this legislation is such that Britain's trade-union movement must now be regarded as one of the most oppressed in the world!

Tory legislation has removed trade-union immunity, made secondary action including secondary picketing and mass picketing illegal, and rendered all trade unions vulnerable to legal actions which could result in their bankruptcy. Britain's trade unions have found themselves no longer free to determine their own policies in relation to industrial solidarity action.

Not satisfied however with the most vicious anti-union legislation in the world, the Tories are currently introducing new measures which are so draconian they have staggered and brought forth opposition even from some traditional enemies of the trade-union movement.

The steps taken against British trade unionism can probably only be compared with those taken against our German comrades by Hitler in the 1930s. If this new Tory legislation is left unchallenged, then civil liberties and human rights in Britain are in danger of being wiped out . . .

As life in Britain becomes harder, as frustrations and tensions rise, the State must bring into play all the elements of its machinery in order to suppress any attempts to throw off its power.

The police are used increasingly in paramilitary fashion. The judiciary use greater ruthlessness against any trade union that attempts to stand by its rules and constitution as the experience of the National Union of Mineworkers over the past four years proves. The courts have dealt just as savagely with the Lambeth and Liverpool councillors who refused to betray the commitments made to their communities.

Meanwhile the media, now quite openly under the control of international capitalists such as Murdoch and Maxwell, become even more blatantly the mouthpiece of Tory philosophy. The British capitalist press can make no claim to either objectivity or integrity, whether through the gutter journalism of the tabloids, or the more restrained style of the so-called 'quality' papers; they both play a key role in the daily dissemination of lies and misinformation to the public.

This is but an outline of the situation which today faces the British Labour and trade-union movement. The terrible irony about it is that whilst throughout our movement there is general agreement on the ravages of the Tory attack – and agreement that it should be stopped – we have not united in an effective force to combat those ravages and challenge the system which has forced them on to our class.

On the contrary! Rather than uniting to fight our common enemy, our movement has been diverted time and time again by internal attacks: attacks aimed, disgracefully, at the very sections which have fought so bravely to carry out Labour Party and TUC policies by battling to save jobs, industries, communities and services.

Margaret Thatcher has been absolutely clear in recognizing *her* enemy – it is socialism and she has openly declared her intention of wiping it off the British agenda.

•

EDWARD KENNEDY
Atlanta, 19 July 1988

'Now is the time'

At the Democrat convention in Atlanta in 1988, Senator Edward Kennedy (1932–), introduced by his nephew John Fitzgerald Kennedy Jr, spoke in support of Michael Dukakis, who had been chosen to fight George Bush.

  As his speech ended, he pledged 'every resource' of his mind and spirit to the Democrat cause – and then movingly recalled the dream, and the dreamers, who had inspired Democrats since the 1960s.

You and I have stood together many times, but no time has been more important than this.

The campaign that stretches before us now is a struggle for the souls and the future of America. For we are more than a political coalition, more than a collection of programmes, more than the sum of our prospects and our strategy. Most of all, we are the trustees of a dream.

Twenty years ago, in 1968, we lost two of the most powerful voices of that dream. But they left us their vision, their values, and the hopes they awakened.

In the countless millions of people whose hearts they touched, we remember them now to remind ourselves that the American journey is unfinished, that we stand for change in order to march again towards enduring ideals, that we do not have to settle for things as they are.

Martin Luther King Jr told us something we need to hear anew. He said, 'We are now faced with the fact that tomorrow is today. We are confronted with the fierce urgency of now, in the unfolding life and history. There is such a thing as being too late.' (*Applause.*)

And Dr King also said, 'We must work unceasingly to lift this Nation to a higher destiny, to a new plateau of compassion.'

And in that time there was another voice, only briefly heard, but whose words too have outlasted all the loss in years. Robert Kennedy said, 'Each time a man stands up for an ideal, or acts to improve the lot of others, or strikes out against injustice, he sends forth a tiny ripple of hope. And crossing each other from a million different centres of energy and daring, those ripples build a current that can sweep down the mightiest walls of oppression and resistance.' (*Applause.*)

He was my brother. But he and Dr King were also in the deepest sense brothers to us all. These two, these valiant two, lived for the same dream and were gone only months apart.

And if they were here with us, two decades later, I think I know what they would say: 'Now is the time. Some men see things as they are and say, why? We dream things that never were and say, why not? Now is the time.' (*Spontaneous demonstration.*)

•

MARGARET THATCHER
Bruges, 20 September 1988

'The frontiers of the State'

Margaret Thatcher's attitude to the European Community, which constantly made Britain appear the odd nation out, split her Cabinet, led to the resignation of both Nigel Lawson, Chancellor of the Exchequer, and Sir Geoffrey Howe, Foreign Secretary, and was one of the main reasons for her downfall in 1990. Thatcher was suspicious that the European Community was a recipe for the creeping state socialism and trade-union power that she had seen off in Britain.

No speech by Mrs Thatcher provoked more controversy during her eleven years as prime minister of Britain than her address – drafted by Sir Charles Powell, her adviser on foreign affairs – to the College of Europe in Bruges. The Bruges speech set out in the sharpest focus her opposition to any form of European federalism that would undermine the sovereignty of the nation state – the F-word issue that has since been a dominant theme of principle in British politics.

Europe is not the creation of the Treaty of Rome. Nor is the European idea the property of any group or institution. We British are as much heirs to the legacy of European culture as any other nation. Our links to the rest of Europe, the continent of Europe, have been the *dominant* factor in our history. For 300 years we were part of the Roman Empire and our maps still trace the straight lines of the roads the Romans built. Our ancestors – Celts, Saxons and Danes – came from the continent.

Our nation was – in that favourite Community word – 'restructured' under Norman and Angevin rule in the eleventh and twelfth centuries.

This year we celebrate the three-hundredth anniversary of the Glorious Revolution in which the British crown passed to Prince William of Orange and Queen Mary.

Visit the great churches and cathedrals of Britain, read our literature and listen to our language: all bear witness to the cultural riches which we have drawn from Europe – and other Europeans from us.

We in Britain are rightly proud of the way in which, since Magna Carta in 1215, we have pioneered and developed representative institutions to stand as bastions of freedom. And proud too of the way in which for centuries Britain was a home for people from the rest of Europe who sought sanctuary from tyranny.

But we know that without the European legacy of political ideas we could not have achieved as much as we did. From classical and medieval thought we have borrowed that concept of the rule of law which marks out a civilized society from barbarism. And on that idea of Christendom – for long synonymous with Europe – with its recognition of the unique and spiritual nature of the individual, we still base our belief in personal liberty and other human rights.

Too often the history of Europe is described as a series of interminable wars and quarrels. Yet from our perspective today surely what strikes us most is our common experience. For instance, the story of how Europeans explored and colonized and – yes, without apology – civilized much of the world is an extraordinary tale of talent, skill and courage.

We British have in a special way contributed to Europe. Over the centuries we have fought to prevent Europe from falling under the dominance of a single power. We have fought and we have died for her freedom. Only miles from here in Belgium lie the bodies of 120,000 British soldiers who died in the First World War. Had it not been for that willingness to fight and to die, Europe *would* have been united long before now – but not in liberty, not in justice. It was British support to resistance movements throughout the last war that helped to keep alive the flame of liberty in so many countries until the day of liberation.

All these things alone are proof of our commitment to Europe's future.

The European Community is *one* manifestation of that European identity. But it is not the only one. We must never forget that east of the Iron Curtain peoples who once enjoyed a full share of European culture, freedom and identity have been cut off from their roots. We shall always look on Warsaw, Prague and Budapest as great European cities.

Nor should we forget that European values have helped to make the United States of America into the valiant defender of freedom which she has become.

This is no arid chronicle of obscure facts from the dust-filled libraries of history. It is the record of nearly two thousand years of British involvement *in* Europe, cooperation *with* Europe and contribution *to* Europe, a contribution which today is as valid and as strong as ever. Yes, we have looked also to wider horizons – as have others – and thank goodness for that, because Europe never would have prospered and never will prosper as a narrow-minded, inward-looking club.

The European Community belongs to *all* its members. It must reflect the traditions and aspirations of *all* its members.

And let me be quite clear. Britain does not dream of some cosy, isolated existence on the fringes of the European Community. Our destiny is in Europe, as part of the Community. That is not to say that our future lies *only* in Europe. But nor does that of France or Spain, or indeed any other member.

The Community is not an end in itself. Nor is it an institutional device to be constantly modified according to the dictates of some abstract intellectual concept. Nor must it be ossified by endless regulation.

The European Community is the practical means by which Europe can ensure the future prosperity and security of its people in a world in which there are many other powerful nations and groups of nations . . .

To try to suppress nationhood and concentrate power at the centre of a European conglomerate would be highly damaging and would jeopardize the objectives we seek to achieve.

Europe will be stronger precisely because it has France as France, Spain as Spain, Britain as Britain, each with its own customs, traditions and identity. It would be folly to try to fit them into some sort of identikit European personality.

Some of the founding fathers of the Community thought that the United States of America might be its model.

But the whole history of America is quite different from Europe. People went there to get away from the intolerance and constraints of life in Europe. They sought liberty and opportunity; and their strong sense of purpose has, over two centuries, helped create a new unity and pride in being American – just as our pride lies in being British or Belgian or Dutch or German.

I am the first to say that on many great issues the countries of Europe should try to speak with a single voice. I want to see us work more closely on the things we can do better together than alone. Europe is stronger when we do so, whether it be in trade, in defence, or in our relations with the rest of the world.

But working more closely together does *not* require power to be centralized in Brussels or decisions to be taken by an appointed bureaucracy.

Indeed, it is ironic that just when those countries such as the Soviet Union, which have tried to run everything from the centre, are learning that success depends on dispersing power and decisions away from the centre, some in the Community seem to want to move in the opposite direction.

We have not successfully rolled back the frontiers of the State in Britain only to see them reimposed at a European level, with a European super-State exercising a new dominance from Brussels.

Certainly we want to see Europe more united and with a greater sense of common purpose. But it must be in a way which preserves the different traditions, parliamentary powers and sense of national pride in one's own country; for these have been the source of Europe's vitality through the centuries.

•

VACLAV HAVEL
Prague, 1 January 1990

'A contaminated moral environment'

Communism is Eastern Europe died in 1989 as one by one the Communist regimes in Poland, Czechoslovakia, Hungary, Romania and Bulgaria collapsed. The year ended with the crumbling of the Berlin Wall. It was the springtime of nations, the most exciting year in European history since 1848.

The motto of the year was 'Truth shall prevail' and it was a year of truth for Communism. As Timothy Garton Ash, an eyewitness to the events, puts it: 'There is a real sense in which these regimes lived by the word and perished by the word. For what, after all, happened? A few thousands, then tens of thousands, then hundreds of thousands went on to the streets. They spoke a few words. "Resign," they said. "No more shall we be slaves!" "Free elections." "Freedom!" And the walls of Jericho fell. And with the walls, the communist parties simply crumbled.'

That sense that truth will prevail is what made the first speech by Vaclav Havel, the playwright who was elected Czech president on 29 December 1989, so moving and uplifting in its expression of the defiant human spirit that conquered Communism during that memorable year.

One theme of Havel's work was that under Communism almost everybody lived a double life, saying one thing in public and another in private. It was a theme to which he returned in this speech on New Year's Day, broadcast on radio and television, with his comments on the 'contaminated moral environment' under the Communist regime.

My dear fellow citizens, for forty years you heard from my predecessors on this day different variations of the same theme: how our country flourished, how many million tons of steel we produced, how happy we all were, how we trusted our government, and what bright perspectives were unfolding in front of us.

I assume you did not propose me for this office so that I, too, would lie to you.

Our country is not flourishing. The enormous creative and spiritual potential of our nation is not being used sensibly. Entire branches of industry are producing goods which are of no interest to anyone, while we are lacking the things we need. A state which calls itself a workers' state humiliates and exploits workers. Our obsolete economy is wasting the little energy we have available. A country that once could be proud of the educational level of its citizens spends so little on education that it ranks today as seventy-second in the world. We have polluted our soil, our rivers and forests, bequeathed to us by our ancestors, and we have today the most contaminated environment in Europe. Adult people in our country die earlier than in most other European countries . . .

But all this is still not the main problem. The worst thing is that we live in a contaminated moral environment. We fell morally ill because we became used to saying something different from what we thought. We learned not to believe in anything, to ignore each other, to care only about ourselves. Concepts such as love, friendship, compassion, humility, or forgiveness lost their depth and dimensions, and for many of us they represented only psychological peculiarities, or they resembled gone-astray greetings from ancient times, a little ridiculous in the era of computers and spaceships. Only a few of us were able to cry out loud that the powers that be should not be all-powerful, and that special farms, which produce ecologically pure and top-quality food just for them, should send their produce to schools, children's homes, and hospitals if our agriculture was unable to offer them to all. The previous regime – armed with its arrogant and intolerant ideology – reduced man to a force of production and nature to a tool of production. In this it attacked both their very substance and their mutual relationship. It reduced gifted and autonomous people, skillfully working in their own country, to nuts and bolts of some monstrously huge, noisy, and stinking machine, whose real meaning is not clear to anyone. It cannot do more than slowly but inexorably wear down itself and all its nuts and bolts.

When I talk about contaminated moral atmosphere, I am not talking just about the gentlemen who eat organic vegetables and do not look out of the plane windows. I am talking about all of us. We had all become used to the totalitarian system and accepted it as an unchangeable fact and thus helped to perpetuate it. In other words, we are all – though naturally to differing extents – responsible for the operation of the totalitarian machinery; none of us is just its victim: we are all also its co-creators.

Why do I say this? It would be very unreasonable to understand the sad legacy of the last forty years as something alien, which some distant relative bequeathed us. On the contrary, we have to accept this legacy as a sin we committed against ourselves. If we accept it as such, we will understand that it is up to us all, and up to us only, to do something about it. We cannot blame the previous rulers for everything, not only because it would be untrue but also because it could blunt the duty that each of us faces today, namely, the obligation to act independently, freely, reasonably, and quickly. Let us not be mistaken: the best government in the world, the best parliament and the best president, cannot achieve much on their own. And it would also be wrong to expect a general remedy from them only. Freedom and democracy include participation and therefore responsibility from us all.

If we realize this, then all the horrors that the new Czechoslovak democracy inherited will cease to appear so terrible. If we realize this, hope will return to our hearts.

In the effort to rectify matters of common concern, we have something to lean on. The recent period – and in particular, the last six weeks of our peaceful revolution – has shown the enormous human, moral, and spiritual potential and civic culture that slumbered in our society under the enforced mask of apathy. Whenever someone categorically claimed that we were this or that, I always objected that society is a very mysterious creature and that it is not wise to trust only the face it presents to you. I am happy that I was not mistaken. Everywhere in the world people wonder where those meek, humiliated, skeptical, and seemingly cynical citizens of Czechoslovakia found the marvelous strength to shake from their shoulders in several weeks and in a decent and peaceful way the totalitarian yoke. And let us ask: from where did the young people who never knew another system take their desire for truth, their love of free thought, their political ideas, their civic courage and civic prudence? How did it happen that their parents – the very generation that had been considered as lost – joined them? How is it possible that so many people immediately knew what to do and none of them needed any advice or instruction? . . .

Masaryk* based his politics on morality. Let us try in a new time and in a new way to restore this concept of politics. Let us teach ourselves and others that politics should be an expression of a desire to contribute to the happiness of the community rather than of a need to cheat or rape the community. Let us teach ourselves and others that politics can be not only the art of the possible, especially if this means the art of speculation, calculation, intrigue, secret deals, and pragmatic maneuvering, but that it can even be the art of the impossible, namely, the art of improving ourselves and the world . . .

There are free elections and an election campaign ahead of us. Let us not allow this struggle to dirty the so far clean face of our gentle revolution. Let us not allow the sympathies of the world which we have won so fast to be equally rapidly lost through our becoming entangled in the jungle of skirmishes for power. Let us

---

* Thomas Masaryk (1850–1937) was the first president of Czechoslovakia after it won independence in 1918. The name was anathema to the Communist regime.

not allow the desire to serve oneself to bloom once again under the fair mask of the desire to serve the common good. It is not really important now which party, club, or group will prevail in the elections. The important thing is that the winners will be the best of us, in the moral, civic, political, and professional sense, regardless of their political affiliations. The future policies and prestige of our state will depend on the personalities we select and later elect to our representative bodies . . .

In conclusion, I would like to say that I want to be a president who will speak less and work more. To be a president who will not only look out of the windows of his airplane but who, first and foremost, will always be present among his fellow citizens and listen to them well.

You may ask what kind of republic I dream of. Let me reply: I dream of a republic independent, free, and democratic, of a republic economically prosperous and yet socially just, in short, of a humane republic which serves the individual and which therefore holds the hope that the individual will serve it in turn. Of a republic of well-rounded people, because without such it is impossible to solve any of our problems, human, economic, ecological, social, or political.

The most distinguished of my predecessors opened his first speech with a quotation from the great Czech educator Comenius. Allow me to round off my first speech with my own paraphrase of the same statement:

People, your government has returned to you!

•

NELSON MANDELA
Cape Town, 11 February 1990

'Our march to freedom is irreversible'

Twenty-seven years after he was first imprisoned, Nelson Mandela, a worldwide symbol of resistance to apartheid, now seventy-one and white-haired, walked out of prison with a smile on his face, raised his hand in the clenched-fist salute of the

African National Congress, and made his first speech since he stood in the dock accused of treason. Speaking to a crowd of 50,000 under the majestic shadow of Table Mountain, and watched by a global audience of millions on television, he placed the remaining years of his life in the hands of his people and ended his speech with the words he had uttered from the dock in 1964.

Friends, Comrades and fellow South Africans. I greet you all in the name of peace, democracy and freedom for all. I stand here before you not as a prophet but as a humble servant of you, the people. Your tireless and heroic sacrifices have made it possible for me to be here today. I therefore place the remaining years of my life in your hands . . .

Today the majority of South Africans, black and white, recognize that apartheid has no future. It has to be ended by our own decisive mass action in order to build peace and security. The mass campaign of defiance and other actions of our organization and people can only culminate in the establishment of democracy.

The apartheid destruction on our subcontinent is incalculable. The fabric of family life of millions of my people has been shattered. Millions are homeless and unemployed. Our economy lies in ruins and our people are embroiled in political strife.

Our resort to the armed struggle in 1960 with the formation of the military wing of the ANC, Umkhonto we Sizwe (Spear of the Nation), was a purely defensive action against the violence of apartheid. The factor which necessitated the armed struggle still exists today. We have no option but to continue . . .

Negotiations on the dismantling of apartheid will have to address the overwhelming demand of our people for a democratic, non-racial and unitary South Africa.

There must be an end to white monopoly on political power, and a fundamental restructuring of our political and economic systems to ensure that the inequalities of apartheid are addressed and our society thoroughly democratized.

It must be added that Mr de Klerk himself is a man of integrity, who is acutely aware of the dangers of a public figure not honouring his undertakings. But as an organization, we base our policy and strategy on the harsh reality we are faced with. And this reality is that we are still suffering under the policies of the Nationalist government.

Our struggle has reached a decisive moment. We call on our people to seize this moment, so that the process towards democracy is rapid and uninterrupted.

We have waited too long for our freedom! We can no longer wait. Now is the time to intensify the struggle on all fronts. To relax our efforts now would be a mistake which generations to come will not be able to forgive. The sight of freedom looming on the horizon should encourage us to redouble our efforts. It is only through disciplined mass action that our victory can be assured.

We call on our white compatriots to join us in the shaping of a new South Africa. The freedom movement is a political home for you, too. We call on the international community to continue the campaign to isolate the apartheid regime. To lift sanctions now would be to run the risk of aborting the process towards the complete eradication of apartheid.

Our march to freedom is irreversible. We must not allow fear to stand in our way. Universal suffrage on a common voters' roll in a united, democratic and non-racial South Africa is the only way to peace and racial harmony.

In conclusion I wish to go to my own words during my trial in 1964. They are as true today as they were then. I quote:

'I have fought against white domination and I have fought against black domination. I have cherished the ideal of a democratic and free society in which all persons live together in harmony and with equal opportunity. It is an ideal which I hope to live for and to achieve. But if needs be, it is an ideal for which I am prepared to die. *Amandla* (power)!'

A year later President de Klerk of South Africa announced proposals to dismantle the structure of apartheid.

•

SIR GEOFFREY HOWE
London, 13 November 1990

'*A conflict of loyalty*'

Sir Geoffrey Howe (1927–) served throughout the eleven years of Margaret Thatcher's three administrations, first as Chancellor of the Exchequer, then as Foreign Secretary and finally as Leader of the Commons. By 1990 he was the sole survivor from her first Cabinet. Yet their relationship, which had never been founded on mutual admiration, had sharply deteriorated, mainly because of Mrs Thatcher's distrust of the instincts of the Foreign Office, and her frequent humiliations of Howe, who was also her deputy. The apparently faithful and imperturbable Howe finally snapped and he resigned on 1 November, saying he could no longer serve her with honour.

Howe's pedestrian style was once memorably summed up. Being attacked by him was like being savaged by a dead sheep, said his opponent Denis Healey. Yet in his resignation speech the dead sheep became a lion, drawing audible gasps of surprise from fellow Conservatives (who included Mrs Thatcher). It was 'an act of brilliantly executed matricide', says Sir Ronald Millar, Mrs Thatcher's principal speechwriter, 'each word honed with Aesculapian skill for maximum effect'.

It has been suggested – even, indeed, by some of my right hon. and hon. Friends – that I decided to resign solely because of questions of style and not on matters of substance at all. Indeed, if some of my former colleagues are to be believed, I must be the first Minister in history who has resigned because he was in full agreement with Government policy. The truth is that, in many aspects of politics, style and substance complement each other. Very often, they are two sides of the same coin. . . .

It was a great honour to serve for six years as Foreign and Commonwealth Secretary and to share with my right hon. Friend (*Margaret Thatcher*) in some notable achievements in the European Community. But it was as we moved on to consider the crucial monetary issues in the European context that I came to feel increasing concern. Some of the reasons for that anxiety were made very clear by my right hon. Friend the Member for Blaby (*Nigel Lawson*) in his resignation speech just over twelve months ago. Like him, I concluded at least five years ago that the conduct of our policy against inflation could no longer rest solely on attempts to measure and control the domestic money supply. We had no doubt that we should be helped in that battle, and, indeed, in other respects, by joining the exchange rate mechanism of the European monetary system.

There was, or should have been, nothing novel about joining the ERM; it has been a long-standing commitment. For a quarter of a century after the Second World War, we found that the very similar Bretton Woods regime did serve as a useful discipline. Now, as my right hon. Friend the Prime Minister acknowledged two weeks ago, our entry into the ERM can be seen as an 'extra discipline for keeping down inflation'. However, it must be said that the practical conclusion has been achieved only at the cost of substantial damage to her Administration and, more serious still, to its inflation achievements.

It was the late Lord Stockton, formerly Harold MacMillan, who first put the central point clearly. As long ago as 1962, he argued that we had to place and keep ourselves within the Community. He saw it as essential then as it is today not to cut ourselves off from the realities of power, not to retreat into a ghetto of sentimentality about our past and so diminish our control over our own destiny in the future.

The pity is that the Macmillan view had not been perceived more clearly a decade before in the fifties. It would have spared so many of the struggles of the past twenty years had we been in the Community from the outset, had we been ready, in the much too simple phrase, to 'surrender some sovereignty' at a much earlier stage.

Had we been in from the start we should have had more not less influence over the Europe in which we live today. We should never forget the lesson of that isolation, of being on the outside looking in, for the conduct of today's affairs.

We have done best when we have seen the Community not as a static entity to be resisted and contained, but as an active process which we can shape often decisively provided we allow ourselves to be fully engaged in it with confidence and enthusiasm and in good faith.

We must at all costs avoid presenting ourselves yet again with an over-simplified choice, a false antithesis, a bogus dilemma, between one alternative starkly labelled 'cooperation between independent sovereign states' and a second equally crudely labelled alternative 'a centralized federal super-state' as if there were no middle way in between.

We commit a serious error if we think always in terms of 'surrendering' sovereignty and seek to stand pat for all time on a given deal by proclaiming, as the prime minister did two weeks ago, that we have 'surrendered enough'. The European enterprise is not and should not be seen like that, as some kind of zero sum gain.

Sir Winston Churchill put it much more positively forty years ago when he said: 'It is also possible and not less agreeable to regard [this sacrifice or merger of national sovereignty] as the gradual assumption by all the nations concerned of that larger sovereignty which can alone protect their diverse and distinctive customs and characteristics and their national traditions?'

I find Winston Churchill's perception a good deal more convincing and encouraging for the interests of our nation than the nightmare image sometimes conjured up by the prime minister who sometimes seems to look out on a Continent that is positively teeming with ill-intentioned people scheming, in her words, to 'extinguish democracy', to 'dissolve our national identities', to lead us 'through the back door into a federal Europe'.

What kind of vision is that for our business people who trade there each day, for our financiers who seek to make London the money capital of Europe, or for all the young people of today? These concerns are especially important as we approach the crucially important topic of EMU. We must be positively and centrally involved in this debate and not fearfully and negatively detached. The cost of disengagement here could be very serious indeed . . .

The tragedy is – and it is for me personally, for my party, for our whole people, for the prime minister herself a very real tragedy – that the prime minister's perceived attitude towards Europe is running increasingly serious risks for the future of our nation. It risks minimizing our influence and maximizing our chances of being once again shut out.

We have paid heavily in the past for late starts and squandered opportunities in Europe. We dare not let that happen again. If we detach ourselves completely as a party or as a nation from the middle ground of Europe, the effects will be incalculable and very hard ever to correct.

In my letter of resignation, which I tendered with the utmost sadness and dismay, I said: 'Cabinet government is about trying to persuade one another from within.' That was my commitment to government by persuasion, persuading colleagues and the nation.

I have tried to do that as foreign secretary and since, but I realize now that the task has become futile, of trying to stretch the meaning of words beyond what was credible, and trying to pretend there was a common policy when every step forward risked being subverted by some casual comment or impulsive answer.

The conflict of loyalty, of loyalty to my right hon. Friend the prime minister – and, after all, in two decades together that instinct of loyalty is still very real – and of loyalty to what I perceive to be the true interests of the nation, has become all too great. I no longer believe it possible to resolve that conflict from within this Government. That is why I have resigned. In doing so, I have done what I believe to be right for my party and my country. The time has come for others to consider their own response to the tragic conflict of loyalties with which I have myself wrestled for perhaps too long.

Howe's speech led to the downfall of Margaret Thatcher. Shortly afterwards, Michael Heseltine announced that he would stand against her in the annual leadership election. Mrs Thatcher failed to muster enough votes to win on the first count, subsequently withdrew, and John Major won on the second ballot.

●

TONY BENN
London, 20 November 1991

'I cannot hand away powers lent to me'

Although he is one of the most controversial politicians in Britain, described by one historian as a populist guru of the left, a dissident, an individualist, almost an anarchist, even his most dedicated political opponents acknowledge the power and persuasiveness of Tony Benn's oratory.

That is particularly true of his speeches on Europe. Benn (1925–) campaigned against joining the European Community from the outset of the British debate and has consistently warned against what he sees as the perils of federalism.

As the debate in Britain over a federal Europe intensified towards the end of 1991, with the signing of the Maastricht treaty imminent, Benn, Labour MP for Chesterfield, made this speech to the House of Commons. It was admired by many Conservatives, some his fiercest critics, who believed that on this occasion he spoke for England. Norman Tebbit, a staunch ally of Margaret Thatcher, said it was the best speech he had ever heard in the House.

Some people genuinely believe that we shall never get social justice from the British Government, but we shall get it from Jacques Delors. They believe that a good king is better than a bad Parliament. I have never taken that view. Others believe that the change is inevitable, and that the common currency will protect us from inflation and will provide a wage policy. They believe that it will control speculation and that Britain cannot survive alone. None of those arguments persuade me because the argument has never been about sovereignty.

I do not know what a sovereign is, apart from the one that used to be in gold and the Pope who is a sovereign in the Vatican. We are talking about democracy. No nation – not even the great United States which could, for all I know, be destroyed by a nuclear weapon from a third-world country – has the power to impose its will on other countries. We are discussing whether the British people are to be allowed to elect those who make the laws under which they are governed. The argument is nothing to do with whether we should get more maternity leave from Madame Papandreou than from Madame Thatcher. That is not the issue.

I recognize that when the members of the three Front Benches agree, I am in a minority. My next job therefore is to explain to the people of Chesterfield what we have decided. I will say first, 'My dear constituents, in future you will be governed by people whom you do not elect and cannot remove. I am sorry about it. They may give you better crèches and shorter working hours but you cannot remove them.'

I know that it sounds negative but I have always thought it positive to say that the important thing about democracy is that we can remove without bloodshed the people who govern us. We can get rid of a Callaghan, a Wilson or even a Right Hon. Lady by internal processes. We can get rid of the Right Hon. Member for Huntingdon (*Mr Major*). But that cannot be done in the structure that is proposed. Even if one likes the policies of the people in Europe one cannot get rid of them.

Secondly, we say to my favourite friends, the Chartists and suffragettes, 'All your struggles to get control of the ballot box were a waste of time. We shall be run in future by a few white persons, as in 1832.' The instrument, I might add, is the Royal Prerogative of treaty making. For the first time since 1649 the Crown makes the laws – advised, I admit, by the Prime Minister.

We must ask what will happen when people realize what we have done. We have had a marvellous debate about Europe, but none of us has discussed our relationship with the people who sent us here . . .

If people lose the power to sack their Government one of several things happens. First, people may just slope off. Apathy could destroy democracy. When the turnout drops below 50 per cent, we are in danger . . .

The second thing that people can do is to riot. Riot is an old-fashioned method for drawing the attention of the Government to what is wrong. It is difficult for an elected person to admit it, but the riot at Strangeways produced some prison reforms. Riot has historically played a much larger part in British politics than we are ever allowed to know.

Thirdly, nationalism can arise. Instead of blaming the Treaty of Rome, people say, 'It is those Germans' or 'It is the French'. Nationalism is built out of frustration that people feel when they cannot get their way through the ballot box. With nationalism comes repression. I hope that it is not pessimistic – in my view it is not – to say that democracy hangs by a thread in every country of the world. Unless we can offer people a peaceful route to the resolution of injustices through the ballot box they will not listen to a House that has blocked off that route.

There are many alternatives open to us. One Hon. Member said that he was young and had not fought in the war. He looked at a new Europe. But there have been five Europes this century. There was one run by the King, the Kaiser and the Tsar – they were all cousins so that was very comfortable. They were all Queen Victoria's grandsons. And there was no nonsense about human rights when Queen Victoria's grandsons repressed people. Then there was the Russian revolution. Then there was the inter-war period. Then there was the Anglo-Soviet alliance. Then there was the cold war. Now we have a Boris Yeltsin who has joined the Monday Club. There have been many Europes. This is not the only Europe on offer . . .

Another way would be to have a looser, wider Europe. I have an idea for a Commonwealth of Europe. I am introducing a bill on the subject. Europe would be rather like the British Commonwealth. We would work by consent with people. Or we could accept this ghastly proposal, which is clumsy, secretive, centralized, bureaucratic and divisive. That is how I regard the Treaty of Rome. I was born a European and I will die one. But I have never put my alliance behind the Treaty of Rome. I object to it. I hate being called an anti-European. How can one be anti-European when one is born in Europe? It is like saying that one is anti-British if one does not agree with the Chancellor of the Exchequer. What a lot of nonsense it is.

I ask myself why the House is ready to contemplate abandoning its duties, as I fear that it is. I was elected forty-one years ago this month. This Chamber has lost confidence in democracy. It believes that it must be governed by someone else. It is afraid to use the powers entrusted to it by its constituents. It has traded power for status. One gets asked to go on the telly if one is a Member of Parliament. The Chamber does not want to use its power. It has accepted the role of a spectator and joined what Bagehot called the dignified part of the constitution, leaving the Crown, under the control of the Prime Minister, to be the Executive part.

If democracy is destroyed in Britain it will be not the communists, Trotskyists or subversives but this House which threw it away. The rights that are entrusted to us are not for us to give away. Even if I agree with everything that is proposed, I cannot hand away powers lent to me for five years by the people of Chesterfield. I just could not do it. It would be theft of public rights.

Therefore, there is only one answer. If people are determined to submit themselves to Jacques Delors, Madame Papandreou and the Council of Ministers, we must tell the people what is planned. If people vote for that, they will all have capitulated. Julius Caesar said, 'We are just merging our sovereignty.' So did William the Conqueror.

It is not possible to support the Government's motion. I have told the Chief Whip that I cannot support the Labour motion. I invite the House to vote against the Government's motion and not to support a motion which purports to take us faster into a Community which cannot reflect the aspirations of those who put us here. That is not a nationalist argument nor is it about sovereignty. It is a democratic argument and it should be decisive in a democratic Chamber.

•

SALMAN RUSHDIE
New York, December 1991

'What is my single life worth?'

After publication of his novel The Satanic Verses *Salman Rushdie became the first Western writer to become the victim of a* fatwa, *a death sentence issued by Ayatollah Khomeini of Iran, who decreed that his book was a blasphemy on the Muslim faith. Since 1989 he has lived in hiding under 24-hour-a-day protection by British Special Branch bodyguards.*

Rushdie spent the day of this speech, honouring the 200th anniversary of the First Amendment, in a fourteenth-floor suite with twenty armed bodyguards. The windows were blocked by bullet-proof mattresses. At the Columbia Graduate School of Journalism the audience were frisked before entry and the bomb squad was outside the hall. At the end three plain-clothed policemen escorted Rushdie back into hiding.

A hot-air balloon drifts slowly over a bottomless chasm, carrying several passengers. A leak develops; the balloon starts losing height. The pit, a dark yawn, comes closer. Good grief! The wounded balloon can bear just one passenger to safety; the many must be sacrificed to save the one! But who should live, who should die? And who could make such a choice?

In point of fact, debating societies everywhere regularly make such choices without qualms, for of course what I've described is the given situation of that evergreen favourite, the Balloon Debate, in which, as the speakers argue over the relative merits and demerits of the well-known figures they have placed in disaster's mouth, the assembled company blithely accepts the faintly unpleasant idea that a human being's right to life is increased or diminished by his or her virtues or vices – that we may be born equal but thereafter our lives weigh differently in the scales.

It's only make-believe, after all. And while it may not be very nice, it does reflect how people actually think.

I have now spent over a thousand days in just such a balloon; but, alas, this isn't a game. For most of these thousand days, my fellow-travellers included the Western hostages in the Lebanon, and the British businessmen imprisoned in Iran and Iraq, Roger Cooper and Ian Richter. And I had to accept, and did accept, that for most of my countrymen and countrywomen, my plight counted for less than the others'. In any choice between us, I'd have been the first to be pitched out of the basket and into the abyss. 'Our lives teach us who we are,' I wrote at the end of my essay 'In Good Faith'. Some of the lessons have been harsh, and difficult to learn.

Trapped inside a metaphor, I've often felt the need to redescribe it, to change the terms. This isn't so much a balloon, I've wanted to say, as a bubble, within which I'm simultaneously exposed and sealed off. The bubble floats above and through the world, depriving me of reality, reducing me to an abstraction. For many people, I've ceased to be a human being. I've become an issue, a bother, an 'affair'. Bullet-proofed bubbles, like this one, are reality-proof, too. Those who travel in them, like those who wear Tolkien's rings of invisibility, become wraith-like if they're not careful. They get lost. In this phantom space a man may become the bubble that encases him, and then one day – pop! – he's gone forever.

It's ridiculous – isn't it? – to have to say, but I *am* a human being, unjustly accused, unjustly embubbled. Or is it I who am being ridiculous, as I call out from my bubble, *I'm still trapped in here, folks; somebody, please, get me out?*

Out there where you are, in the rich and powerful and lucky west, has it really been so long since religions persecuted people, burning them as heretics, drowning them as witches, that you can't recognize religious persecution when you see it? . . . The original metaphor has reasserted itself. I'm back in the balloon, asking for the right to live.

What is my single life worth? Despair whispers in my ear: 'Not a lot.' But I refuse to give in to despair.

I refuse to give in to despair because I've been shown love as well as hatred. I know that many people do care, and are appalled by the crazy, upside-down logic of the post-*fatwa* world, in which a single novelist can be accused of having savaged or 'mugged' a whole community, becoming its tormentor (instead of its tarred and feathered victim) and the scapegoat for all its discontents. Many people do ask, for example: When a white pop-star-turned-Islamic-fanatic speaks approvingly about killing an Indian immigrant, how does the Indian immigrant end up being called the racist?

Or, again: What minority is smaller and weaker than a minority of one?

I refuse to give in to despair even though, for a thousand days and more, I've been put through a degree course in worthlessness, my own personal and specific worthlessness. My first teachers were the mobs marching down distant boulevards, baying for my blood, and finding, soon enough, their echoes on English streets. I could not understand the force that makes parents hang murderous slogans around their children's necks. I have learned to understand it. It burns books and effigies and thinks itself holy. But at first, as I watched the marchers, I felt them trampling on my heart.

Once again, however, I have been saved by instances of fair-mindedness, of goodness. Every time I learn that a reader somewhere has been touched by *The Satanic Verses*, moved and entertained and stimulated by it, it arouses deep feelings in me. And there are more and more such readers nowadays, my postbag tells me, readers (including Muslims) who are willing to give my burned, spurned child a fair hearing at long last.

Sometimes I think that, one day, Muslims will be ashamed of what Muslims did in these times, will find the 'Rushdie affair' as improbable as the west now finds martyr-burning. One day they may agree that – as the European Enlightenment demonstrated – freedom of thought is precisely freedom from religious control, freedom from accusations of blasphemy.

Maybe they'll agree, too, that the row over *The Satanic Verses* was at bottom an argument about who should have power over the grand narrative, the Story of Islam, and that that power must belong equally to everyone. That even if my novel were incompetent, its attempt to retell the story would still be important. That if I've failed, others must succeed, because those who do not have power over the story that dominates their lives, power to retell it, rethink it, deconstruct it, joke about it, and change it as times change, truly are powerless, because they cannot think new thoughts.

One day. Maybe. But not today.

Today, my education in worthlessness continues, and what Saul Bellow would call my 'reality instructors' include: the media pundit who suggests that a manly death would be better for me than hiding like a rat; the letter-writer who points out that of course the trouble is that I *look* like the Devil, and wonders if I have hairy shanks and cloven hooves; the 'moderate' Muslim who writes to say that Muslims find it 'revolting' when I speak about the Iranian death threats (it's not the *fatwa* that's revolting, you understand, but my mention of it); the rather more immoderate Muslim who tells me to 'shut up', explaining that if a fly is caught in a spider's web, it should not attract the attention of the spider. I ask the reader to imagine how it might feel to be intellectually and emotionally bludgeoned, from a thousand different directions, every day for a thousand days and more.

Back in the balloon, something longed-for and heartening has happened. On this occasion, *mirabile dictu*, the many have not been sacrificed, but saved. That is to say, my companions, the western hostages and the gaoled businessmen, have by good fortune and the efforts of others managed to descend safely to earth, and have been reunited with their families and friends, with their own, free lives. I rejoice for them, and admire their courage, their resilience. And now I'm alone in the balloon.

Surely I'll be safe now? Surely, now, the balloon will drop safely towards some nearby haven, and I, too, will be reunited with my life? Surely it's my turn now?

But the balloon is over the chasm again; and it's still sinking. I realize that it's carrying a great deal of valuable freight. Trading

relations, armaments deals, the balance of power in the Gulf –
these and other matters of great moment are weighing down
the balloon. I hear voices suggesting that if I stay aboard, this
precious cargo will be endangered. The national interest is being
redefined; am I being redefined out of it? Am I to be jettisoned,
after all?

When Britain renewed relations with Iran at the United Nations
in 1990, the senior British official in charge of the negotiations
assured me in unambiguous language that something very
substantial had been achieved on my behalf. The Iranians, laughing
merrily, had secretly agreed to forget the *fatwa*. (The diplomat put
great stress on this cheery Iranian laughter.) They would 'neither
encourage nor allow' their citizens, surrogates or proxies to act
against me.

Oh, how I wanted to believe that. But in the year-and-a-bit that
followed, we saw the *fatwa* restated in Iran, the bounty money
doubled, the book's Italian translator severely wounded, its
Japanese translator stabbed to death; there was news of an attempt
to find and kill me by contract killers working directly for the
Iranian government through its European embassies. Another such
contract was successfully carried out in Paris, the victim being the
harmless and aged ex-Prime Minister of Iran, Shapour Bakhtiar.

It seems reasonable to deduce that the secret deal made at the
United Nations hasn't worked. Dismayingly, however, the talk as
I write is all of improving relations with Iran still further, while
the 'Rushdie case' is described as a side-issue.

Is this a balloon I'm in, or the dustbin of history?

At the end of 1990, dispirited and demoralized, feeling
abandoned, even then, in consequence of the British government's
decision to patch things up with Iran, and with my marriage at an
end, I faced my deepest grief, my unquenchable sorrow at having
been torn away from, cast out of, the cultures and societies from
which I'd always drawn my strength and inspiration – that is, the
broad community of British Asians, and the broader community
of Indian Muslims. I determined to make my peace with Islam,
even at the cost of my pride. Those who were surprised and

displeased by what I did perhaps failed to see that I was not some deracinated Uncle Tom Wog.

To these people it was apparently incomprehensible that I should seek to make peace between the warring halves of the world, which were also the warring halves of my soul – and that I should seek to do so in a spirit of humility, instead of the arrogance so often attributed to me.

In 'In Good Faith' I wrote: 'Perhaps a way forward might be found through the mutual recognition of [our] mutual pain', but even moderate Muslims had trouble with this notion: what pain, they asked, could I possibly have suffered? *What was I talking about?* As a result, the really important conversations I had in this period were with myself.

I said: Salman, you must send a message loud enough to be heard all over the world. You must make ordinary Muslims see that you aren't their enemy, and make the west understand a little more of the complexity of Muslim culture. It was my hope that westerners might say, well, if he's the one in danger, and yet he's willing to acknowledge the importance of his Muslim roots, then perhaps we ought to start thinking a little less stereotypically ourselves. (No such luck, though. The message you send isn't always the one that's received.)

I reminded myself that I had always argued that it was necessary to develop the nascent concept of the 'secular Muslim', who, like the secular Jews, affirmed his membership of the culture while being separate from the theology. I had recently read the contemporary Muslim philosopher Fouad Zakariya's *Laïcité ou Islamisme*, and been encouraged by Zakariya's attempt to modernize Islamic thought. But, Salman, I told myself, you can't argue from outside the debating chamber. You've got to cross the threshold, go inside the room, and *then* fight for your humanized, historicized, secularized way of being a Muslim.

I recalled my near-namesake, the twelfth-century philosopher Ibn Rushd (Averroës), who argued that (to quote the great Arab historian Albert Hourani), 'not all the words of the Qu'ran should be taken literally. When the literal meaning of Qu'ranic verses appeared to contradict the truths to which philosophers arrived by the exercise of reason, those verses needed to be interpreted metaphorically.'

But Ibn Rushd was a snob. Having propounded an idea far in advance of its time, he qualified it by saying that such sophistication was only suitable for the élite; literalism would do for the masses. Salman, I asked myself, is it time to pick up Ibn Rushd's banner and carry it forward; to say, nowadays such ideas are fit for everybody, for the beggar as well as the prince?

It was with such things in mind – and with my thoughts in a state of some confusion and torment – that I spoke the Muslim creed before witnesses. But my fantasy of joining the fight for the modernization of Muslim thought, for freedom from the shackles of the Thought Police, was stillborn. It never really had a chance. Too many people had spent too long demonizing or totemizing me to listen seriously to what I had to say. In the west, some 'friends' turned against me, called me by yet another set of insulting names. Now I was spineless, pathetic, debased; I had betrayed myself, my Cause; above all, I had betrayed *them*.

I also found myself up against the granite, heartless certainties of Actually Existing Islam, by which I mean the political and priestly power structure that presently dominates and stifles Muslim societies. Actually Existing Islam has failed to create a free society anywhere on earth, and it wasn't about to let me, of all people, argue in favour of one.

Suddenly I was (metaphorically) among people whose social attitudes I'd fought all my life – for example, their attitudes about women (one Islamicist boasted to me that his wife would cut his toenails while he made telephone calls, and suggested I found such a spouse) or about gays (one of the Imams I met in December 1990 was on TV soon afterwards, denouncing Muslim gays as sick creatures who brought shame on their families and who ought to seek medical and psychiatric help). Had I truly fallen in among such people? *That was not what I meant at all*.

Facing the intransigence, the philistine scorn of so much of Actually Existing Islam, I reluctantly concluded that there was no way for me to help bring into the Muslim culture I'd dreamed of, the progressive, irreverent, sceptical, argumentative, playful and *unafraid* culture which is what I've always understood as *freedom*. Not me, not in this lifetime, no chance. Actually Existing Islam, which has all but deified its Prophet, a man who always fought passionately against such deification; which has supplanted a priest-free religion by a priest-ridden one; which makes literalism a weapon and redescriptions a crime, will never let the likes of me in.

Ibn Rushd's ideas were silenced in their time. And throughout the Muslim world today, progressive ideas are in retreat. Actually Existing Islam reigns supreme, and just as the recently destroyed 'Actually Existing Socialism' of the Soviet terror-state was horrifically unlike the utopia of peace and equality of which democratic socialists have dreamed, so also is Actually Existing Islam a force to which I have never given in, to which I cannot submit.

There is a point beyond which conciliation looks like capitulation. I do not believe I passed the point, but others have thought otherwise.

I have never disowned my book, nor regretted writing it. I said I was sorry to have offended people, because I had not set out to do so, and so I am. I explained that writers do not agree with every word spoken by every character they create – a truism in the world of books, but a continuing mystery to *The Satanic Verses* opponents. I have always said that this novel has been traduced.

It has now been more than three years since *The Satanic Verses* was published; that's a long, long 'space for reconciliation'. Long enough. I accept that I was wrong to have given way on this point. *The Satanic Verses* must be freely available and easily affordable, if only because if it is not read and studied, then these years will have no meaning. Those who forget the past are condemned to repeat it.

'Our lives teach us who we are.' I have learned the hard way that when you permit anyone else's description of reality to supplant your own – and such descriptions have been raining down on me, from security advisers, governments, journalists, archbishops, friends, enemies, mullahs – then you might as well be dead. Obviously, a rigid, blinkered, absolutist world-view is the easiest to keep hold of; whereas the fluid, uncertain, metamorphic picture I've always carried about is rather more vulnerable.

Yet I must cling with all my might to that chameleon, that chimera, that shape-shifter, my own soul; must hold on to its mischievous, iconoclastic, out-of-step clown-instincts, no matter how great the storm. And if that plunges me into contradiction and paradox, so be it; I've lived in that messy ocean all my life. I've fished in it for my art. This turbulent sea was the sea outside my bedroom window in Bombay. It is the sea by which I was born, and which I carry within me wherever I go.

'Free speech is a non-starter,' says one of my Islamic extremist opponents. No, sir, it is not. Free speech is the whole thing, the whole ball game. Free speech is life itself.

That's the end of my speech from this ailing balloon. Now it's time to answer the question. What is my single life worth?

Is it worth more or less than the fat contracts and political treaties that are in here with me? Is it worth more or less than good relations with a country which, in April 1991, gave 800 women seventy-four lashes each for not wearing a veil; in which the eighty-year-old writer Mariam Pirouz is still in gaol, and has been tortured; and whose Foreign Minister says, in response to criticism of his country's lamentable human-rights record, 'International monitoring of the human rights situation in Iran should not continue indefinitely . . . Iran could not tolerate such monitoring for long'?

You must decide what you think a friend is worth to his friends, what you think a son is worth to his mother, or a father to his son.

You must decide what a man's conscience and heart and soul are worth. You must decide what you think a writer is worth, what value you place on a maker of stories, and an arguer with the world.

Ladies and gentlemen, the balloon is sinking into the abyss.

●

QUEEN ELIZABETH II
London, 24 November 1992

'*Annus Horribilis*'

As Queen Elizabeth II celebrated her fortieth year on the throne in 1992, the British monarchy was in unprecedented disarray and under unprecedented attack. The Princess Royal had divorced, the Duke and Duchess of York had separated, and the marriage of the Prince and Princess of Wales had been exposed as a sham. Meanwhile, critics of the monarchy accused the Queen of being aloof and out of touch. The bill for the monarchy was too high, they said. The Queen should pay tax.

On 20 November Windsor Castle, one of the Queen's main homes, caught fire. Photographs of the blazing castle had a ring of the apocalypse. Sympathy for the Queen was dissipated, however, when the government said that she would not have to foot any of the bill to restore the castle.

Four days later the Lord Mayor of London, clad in brilliant ermine, was the Queen's host at a City of London lunch to celebrate the Queen's anniversary. The Queen was dressed in darkest navy, as if in mourning, and was suffering from a cold. She was almost croaking as she delivered the first unforgettable speech of her reign in which she accepted criticism but urged that it should be tempered with gentleness, good humour and understanding.

Nineteen ninety-two is not a year I shall look back on with undiluted pleasure. In the words of one of my more sympathetic correspondents, it has turned out to be an 'Annus Horribilis'.

I suspect that I am not alone in thinking it so. Indeed, I suspect that there are very few people or institutions unaffected by these last months of worldwide turmoil and uncertainty. This generosity and wholehearted kindness of the Corporation of the City to Prince Philip and me would be welcome at any time, but at this particular moment, in the aftermath of Friday's tragic fire at Windsor, it is especially so. And, after this last weekend, we appreciate all the more what has been set before us today. Years of experience, however, have made us a bit more canny than the lady, less well versed than us in the splendours of City hospitality, who, when she was offered a balloon glass for her brandy, asked for 'only half a glass, please'. It is possible to have too much of a good thing. A well-meaning Bishop was obviously doing his best when he told Queen Victoria, 'Ma'am, we cannot pray too often, nor too fervently, for the Royal Family.' The Queen's reply was, 'Too fervently, no; too often, yes.'

I, like Queen Victoria, have always been a believer in that old maxim 'moderation in all things'. I sometimes wonder how future generations will judge the events of this tumultuous year. I dare say that history will take a slightly more moderate view than that of some contemporary commentators. Distance is well known to lend enchantment, even to the less attractive views. After all, it has the inestimable advantage of hindsight. But it can also lend an extra dimension to judgement, giving it a leavening of moderation and compassion – even of wisdom – that is sometimes lacking in the reactions of those whose task it is in life to offer instant opinions on all things great and small.

No section of the community has all the virtues, neither does any have all the vices. I am quite sure that most people try to do their jobs as best they can, even if the result is not always entirely successful. He who has never failed to reach perfection has a right to be the harshest critic. There can be no doubt, of course, that criticism is good for people and institutions that are part of public life. No institution – City, Monarchy, whatever – should expect to be free from the scrutiny of those who give it their loyalty and support, not to mention those who don't. But we are all part of the same fabric of our national society and that scrutiny, by one part of another, can be just as effective if it is made with a touch of gentleness, good humour and understanding. This sort of questioning can also act, and it should do so, as an effective engine for change. The City is a good example of the way the process of change can be incorporated into the stability and continuity of a great institution. I particularly admire, my Lord Mayor, the way in which the City has adapted so nimbly to what the Prayer Book calls 'the changes and chances of this mortal life'. You have set an example of how it is possible to remain effective and dynamic without losing those indefinable qualities, style and character. We only have to look around this great hall to see the truth of that.

Forty years is quite a long time. I am glad to have had the chance to witness, and to take part in, many dramatic changes in life in this country. But I am glad to say that the magnificent standard of hospitality given on so many occasions to the Sovereign by the Lord Mayor of London has not changed at all. It is an outward symbol of one other unchanging factor which I value above all – the loyalty given to me and my family by so many people in this country, and the Commonwealth, throughout my reign. You, my Lord Mayor, and all those whose prayers – fervent, I hope, but not too frequent – have sustained me through all these years, are friends indeed. Prince Philip and I give you all, wherever you may be, our most humble thanks.

It was as if the Queen was begging for sympathy and baring her soul in public about the most horrible year of her reign, said the commentators. Annus horribilis, a phrase probably suggested by Sir Robert Fellowes, her private secretary, entered the language and was a gift to headline writers, even though the sceptical headline writers of the Sun, *Britain's biggest-selling daily newspaper, rendered her message as 'One's Bum Year'. Within weeks it was announced that the Queen would pay tax and that the Prince of Wales, heir to the throne, and the Princess of Wales were to separate.*

READ MORE IN PENGUIN

In every corner of the world, on every subject under the sun, Penguin represents quality and variety – the very best in publishing today.

For complete information about books available from Penguin – including Puffins, Penguin Classics and Arkana – and how to order them, write to us at the appropriate address below. Please note that for copyright reasons the selection of books varies from country to country.

In the United Kingdom: Please write to *Dept. EP, Penguin Books Ltd, Bath Road, Harmondsworth, West Drayton, Middlesex UB7 ODA*

In the United States: Please write to *Consumer Sales, Penguin Putnam Inc., P.O. Box 999, Dept. 17109, Bergenfield, New Jersey 07621-0120.* VISA and MasterCard holders call 1-800-253-6476 to order Penguin titles

In Canada: Please write to *Penguin Books Canada Ltd, 10 Alcorn Avenue, Suite 300, Toronto, Ontario M4V 3B2*

In Australia: Please write to *Penguin Books Australia Ltd, P.O. Box 257, Ringwood, Victoria 3134*

In New Zealand: Please write to *Penguin Books (NZ) Ltd, Private Bag 102902, North Shore Mail Centre, Auckland 10*

In India: Please write to *Penguin Books India Pvt Ltd, 210 Chiranjiv Tower, 43 Nehru Place, New Delhi 110 019*

In the Netherlands: Please write to *Penguin Books Netherlands bv, Postbus 3507, NL-1001 AH Amsterdam*

In Germany: Please write to *Penguin Books Deutschland GmbH, Metzlerstrasse 26, 60594 Frankfurt am Main*

In Spain: Please write to *Penguin Books S. A., Bravo Murillo 19, 1° B, 28015 Madrid*

In Italy: Please write to *Penguin Italia s.r.l., Via Benedetto Croce 2, 20094 Corsico, Milano*

In France: Please write to *Penguin France, Le Carré Wilson, 62 rue Benjamin Baillaud, 31500 Toulouse*

In Japan: Please write to *Penguin Books Japan Ltd, Kaneko Building, 2-3-25 Koraku, Bunkyo-Ku, Tokyo 112*

In South Africa: Please write to *Penguin Books South Africa (Pty) Ltd, Private Bag X14, Parkview, 2122 Johannesburg*

READ MORE IN PENGUIN

A CHOICE OF NON-FICTION

African Nights Kuki Gallmann

Through a tapestry of interwoven true episodes, Kuki Gallmann here evokes the magic that touches all African life. The adventure of a moonlit picnic on a vanishing island; her son's entrancement with chameleons and the mystical visit of a king cobra to his grave; the mysterious compassion of an elephant herd – each event conveys her delight and wonder at the whole fabric of creation.

Far Flung Floyd Keith Floyd

Keith Floyd's culinary odyssey takes him to the far-flung East and the exotic flavours of Malaysia, Hong Kong, Vietnam and Thailand. The irrepressible Floyd as usual spices his recipes with witty stories, wry observation and a generous pinch of gastronomic wisdom.

The Reading Solution Paul Kropp with Wendy Cooling

The Reading Solution makes excellent suggestions for books – both fiction and non-fiction – for readers of all ages that will stimulate a love of reading. Listing hugely enjoyable books from history and humour to thrillers and poetry selections, *The Reading Solution* provides all the help you need to ensure that your child becomes – and stays – a willing, enthusiastic reader.

Lucie Duff Gordon Katherine Frank
A Passage to Egypt

'Lucie Duff Gordon's life is a rich field for a biographer, and Katherine Frank does her justice ... what stays in the mind is a portrait of an exceptional woman, funny, wry, occasionally flamboyant, always generous-spirited, and firmly rooted in the social history of her day' – *The Times Literary Supplement*

The Missing of the Somme Geoff Dyer

'A gentle, patient, loving book. It is about mourning and memory, about how the Great War has been represented – and our sense of it shaped and defined – by different artistic media ... its textures are the very rhythms of memory and consciousness' – *Guardian*

READ MORE IN PENGUIN

A CHOICE OF NON-FICTION

The Pillars of Hercules   Paul Theroux

At the gateway to the Mediterranean lie the two Pillars of Hercules. Beginning his journey in Gibraltar, Paul Theroux travels the long way round – through the ravaged developments of the Costa del Sol, into Corsica and Sicily and beyond – to Morocco's southern pillar. 'A terrific book, full of fun as well as anxiety, of vivid characters and curious experiences' – *The Times*

Where the Girls Are   Susan J. Douglas

In this brilliantly researched and hugely entertaining examination of women and popular culture, Susan J. Douglas demonstrates the ways in which music, TV, books, advertising, news and film have affected women of her generation. Essential reading for cultural critics, feminists and everyone else who has ever ironed their hair or worn a miniskirt.

Journals: 1954–1958   Allen Ginsberg

These pages open with Ginsberg at the age of twenty-eight, penniless, travelling alone and unknown in California. Yet, by July 1958 he was returning from Paris to New York as the poet who, with Jack Kerouac, led and inspired the Beats . . .

The New Spaniards   John Hooper

Spain has become a land of extraordinary paradoxes in which traditional attitudes and contemporary preoccupations exist side by side. The country attracts millions of visitors – yet few see beyond the hotels and resorts of its coastline. John Hooper's fascinating study brings to life the many faces of Spain in the 1990s.

A Tuscan Childhood   Kinta Beevor

Kinta Beevor was five when she fell in love with her parents' castle facing the Carrara mountains. 'The descriptions of the harvesting and preparation of food and wine by the locals could not be bettered . . . alive with vivid characters' – *Observer*

READ MORE IN PENGUIN

A CHOICE OF NON-FICTION

The Rise and Fall of Popular Music   Donald Clarke

'He attaches a thumbnail biography to everyone he names, he keeps a beady eye on the commercial angles and his capacity to make connections across decades, and sometimes centuries, is consistently invigorating' – *Sunday Times*

Accountable to None   Simon Jenkins
The Tory Nationalization of Britain

'Brings together, with an insider's authority and anecdotage, both a narrative of domestic Thatcherism and a polemic against its pretensions ... an indispensable guide to the corruptions of power and language which have sustained the illusion that Thatcherism was an attack on "government"' – *Guardian*

James Baldwin: A Biography   David Leeming

A unique and outspoken voice in American culture, James Baldwin rose from the Harlem ghetto to international fame with his beautifully crafted novels, short stories and essays. 'Leeming takes us beyond the surface image of the public figure to reveal aspects of the private self that Baldwin masked in even his most personal essays and autobiographical fiction' – *The New York Times Book Review*

From Sea to Shining Sea   Gavin Young
A Present-day Journey into America's Past

'He catches the mind's eye of the reader very deftly ... and, without losing his sense of irony, gives us a genuine account of the tragedy and the pathos, as well as the optimism and bravery, that created American civilization' – *Mail on Sunday*

In Harm's Way   Martin Bell

'A coruscating account of the dangerous work of a war correspondent, replete with tales of Bell dodging, and in one case not dodging, bullets across the globe in order to bring us our nightly news' – *Independent*

READ MORE IN PENGUIN

A CHOICE OF NON-FICTION

Fisher's Face Jan Morris

Admiral of the Fleet Lord 'Jacky' Fisher (1841–1920) was one of the greatest naval reformers in history. 'An intimate recreation of the man in all his extraordinary complexity, his mercurial humours, his ferocious energy and bloodthirstiness, his childlike innocence, his Machiavellian charm' – *Daily Mail*

Mrs Jordan's Profession Claire Tomalin

The story of Dora Jordan and her relationship with the Duke of Clarence, later King William IV. 'Meticulous biography at its creative best' – *Observer*. 'A fascinating and affecting story, one in which the mutually attractive, mutually suspicious, equally glittering worlds of court and theatre meet, and one which vividly illustrates the social codes of pre-Victorian Britain' – *Sunday Times*

John Major: From Brixton to Downing Street Penny Junor

Within a year of a record-breaking general election victory, John Major became the most unpopular Prime Minister ever. With his party deeply divided and his government lurching from crisis to crisis, few thought he could survive. This absorbing biography uses interviews with family, friends, foes, Cabinet colleagues and the Prime Minister himself to uncover the real John Major.

The Bondage of Fear Fergal Keane

'An important source for anyone trying to understand how South Africa achieved its transfer of power' – *Independent*. 'A first-class journalistic account ... likely to be the most memorable account of this terrible, uplifting time' – *Literary Review*

The Oxbridge Conspiracy Walter Ellis

'A brave book that needed to be written ... Oxbridge imparts to our élite values which, in their anti-commerce, anti-technology, anti-market snobbery, make them unfit to run a modern economy. It is the Oxbridge élite which has presided over the decline of this nation' – *Financial Times*

READ MORE IN PENGUIN

A CHOICE OF NON-FICTION

Citizens Simon Schama

'The most marvellous book I have read about the French Revolution in the last fifty years' – *The Times*. 'He has chronicled the vicissitudes of that world with matchless understanding, wisdom, pity and truth, in the pages of this huge and marvellous book' – *Sunday Times*

1945: The World We Fought For Robert Kee

Robert Kee brings to life the events of this historic year as they unfolded, using references to contemporary newspapers, reports and broadcasts, and presenting the reader with the most vivid, immediate account of the year that changed the world. 'Enthralling ... an entirely realistic revelation about the relationship between war and peace' – *Sunday Times*

Cleared for Take-Off Dirk Bogarde

'It begins with his experiences in the Second World War as an interpreter of reconnaissance photographs ... he witnessed the liberation of Belsen – though about this he says he cannot write. But his awareness of the horrors as well as the dottiness of war is essential to the tone of this affecting and strangely beautiful book' – *Daily Telegraph*

Nine Parts of Desire Geraldine Brooks
The Hidden World of Islamic Women

'She takes us behind the veils and into the homes of women in every corner of the Middle East ... It is in her description of her meetings – like that with Khomeini's widow Khadija, who paints him as a New Man (and one for whom she dyed her hair vamp-red) – that the book excels' – *Observer*. 'Frank, engaging and captivating' – *New Yorker*

Insanely Great Steven Levy

The Apple Macintosh revolutionized the world of personal computing – yet the machinations behind its conception were nothing short of insane. 'One of the great stories of the computing industry ... a cast of astonishing characters' – *Observer*. 'Fascinating edge-of-your-seat story' – *Sunday Times*

READ MORE IN PENGUIN

A CHOICE OF NON-FICTION

Time Out Film Guide   Edited by John Pym

The definitive, up-to-the-minute directory of every aspect of world cinema from classics and silent epics to reissues and the latest releases.

Flames in the Field   Rita Kramer

During July 1944, four women agents met their deaths at Struthof-Natzweiler concentration camp at the hands of the SS. They were members of the Special Operations Executive, sent to Nazi-occupied France in 1943. *Flames in the Field* reveals that the odds against their survival were weighted even more heavily than they could possibly have contemplated, for their network was penetrated by double agents and security was dangerously lax.

Colored People   Henry Louis Gates Jr.

'A wittily drawn portrait of a semi-rural American community, in the years when racial segregation was first coming under legal challenge ... In the most beautiful English ... he recreates a past to which, in every imaginable sense, there is no going back' – *Mail on Sunday*

Naturalist   Edward O. Wilson

'His extraordinary drive, encyclopaedic knowledge and insatiable curiosity shine through on virtually every page' – *Sunday Telegraph*. 'There are wonderful accounts of his adventures with snakes, a gigantic ray, butterflies, flies and, of course, ants ... a fascinating insight into a great mind' – *Guardian*

Roots Schmoots   Howard Jacobson

'This is no exercise in sentimental journeys. Jacobson writes with a rare wit and the book sparkles with his gritty humour ... he displays a deliciously caustic edge in his analysis of what is wrong, and right, with modern Jewry' – *Mail on Sunday*

READ MORE IN PENGUIN

A CHOICE OF NON-FICTION

Mornings in the Dark Edited by David Parkinson
The Graham Greene Film Reader

Prompted by 'a sense of fun' and 'that dangerous third Martini' at a party in June 1935, Graham Greene volunteered himself as the *Spectator* film critic. 'His film reviews are among the most trenchant, witty and memorable one is ever likely to read' – *Sunday Times*

Real Lives, Half Lives Jeremy Hall

The world has been 'radioactive' for a hundred years – providing countless benefits to medicine and science – but there is a downside to the human mastery of nuclear physics. *Real Lives, Half Lives* uncovers the bizarre and secret stories of people who have been exposed, in one way or another, to radioactivity across the world.

Hidden Lives Margaret Forster

'A memoir of Forster's grandmother and mother which reflects on the changes in women's lives – about sex, family, work – across three generations. It is a moving, evocative account, passionate in its belief in progress, punchy as a detective novel in its story of Forster's search for her grandmother's illegitimate daughter. It also shows how biography can challenge our basic assumptions about which lives have been significant and why' – *Financial Times*

Eating Children Jill Tweedie

'Jill Tweedie re-creates in fascinating detail the scenes and conditions that shaped her, scarred her, broke her up or put her back together ... a remarkable story' – *Vogue*. 'A beautiful and courageous book' – Maya Angelou

The Lost Heart of Asia Colin Thubron

'Thubron's journey takes him through a spectacular, talismanic geography of desert and mountain ... a whole glittering, terrible and romantic history lies abandoned along with thoughts of more prosperous times' – *The Times*